S U P E … A N D O R

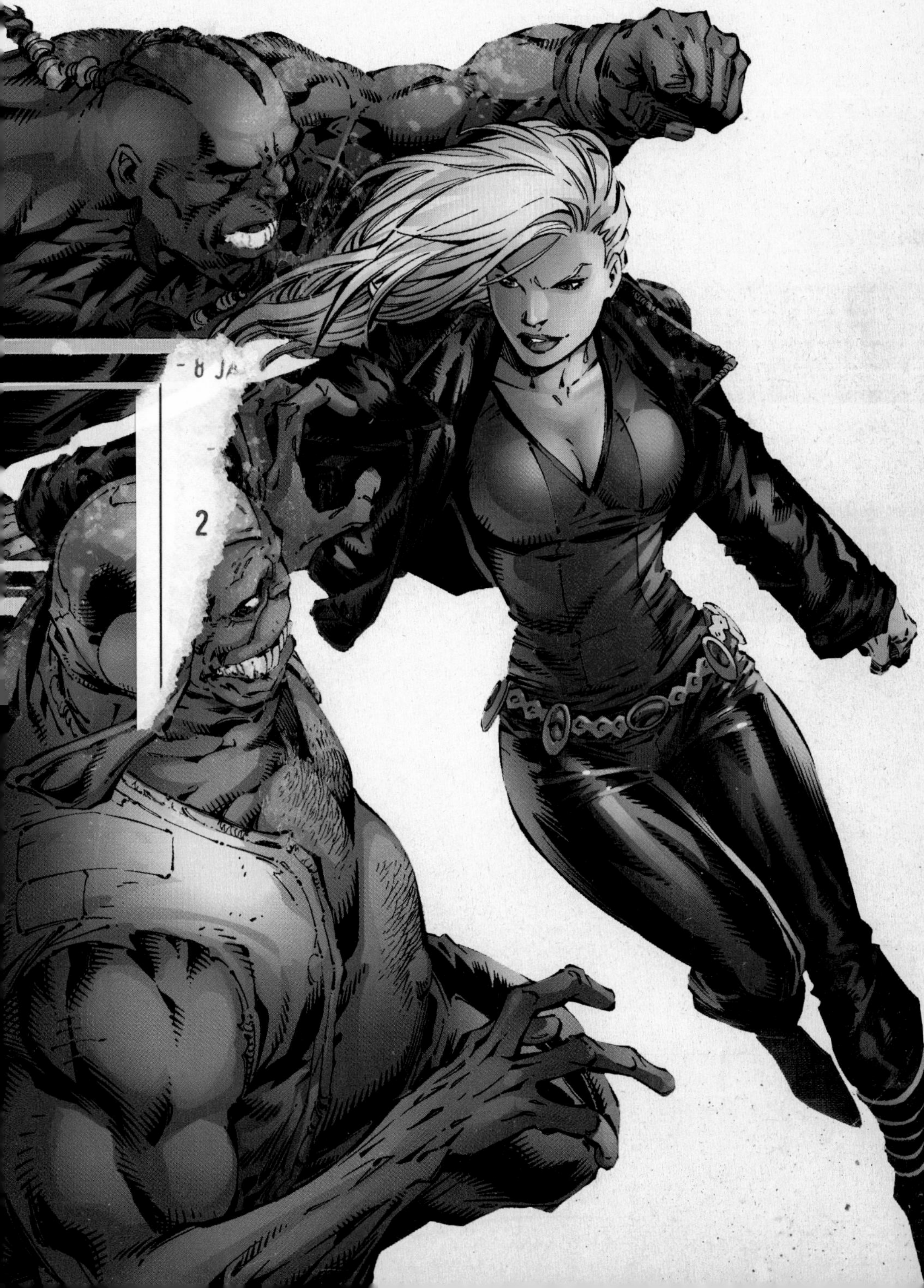

SUPERGIRL

CAN

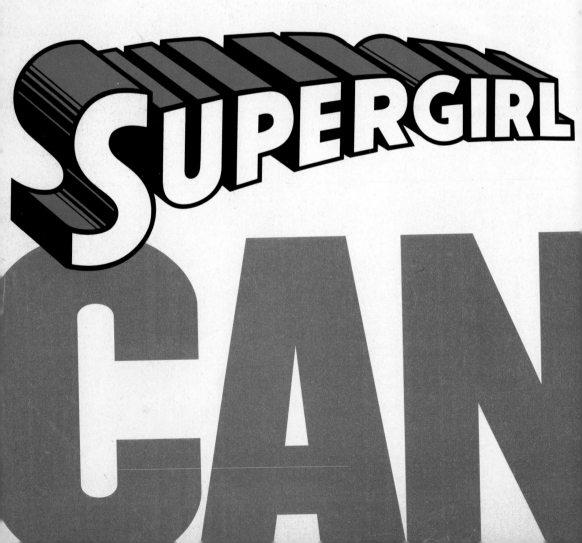

Cover art by Ian Churchill with Peter Steigerwald.

Dan DiDio Senior VP-Executive Editor
Eddie Berganza Mike Carlin Steve Wacker Editors-original series
Jeanine Schaefer Harvey Richards Assistant Editors-original series
Michael Siglain Associate Editor-original series
Bob Joy Editor-collected edition
Robbin Brosterman Senior Art Director
Paul Levitz President & Publisher
Georg Brewer VP-Design & DC Direct Creative
Richard Bruning Senior VP-Creative Director
Patrick Caldon Executive VP-Finance & Operations
Chris Caramalis VP-Finance
John Cunningham VP-Marketing
Terri Cunningham VP-Managing Editor
Stephanie Fierman Senior VP-Sales & Marketing
Alison Gill VP-Manufacturing
Hank Kanalz VP-General Manager, WildStorm
Jim Lee Editorial Director-WildStorm
Paula Lowitt Senior VP-Business & Legal Affairs
MaryEllen McLaughlin VP-Advertising & Custom Publishing
John Nee VP-Business Development
Gregory Noveck Senior VP-Creative Affairs
Cheryl Rubin Senior VP-Brand Management
Jeff Trojan VP-Business Development, DC Direct
Bob Wayne VP-Sales

SUPERGIRL: CANDOR
Published by DC Comics.
Cover, text, and compilation copyright © 2007 DC Comics.
All Rights Reserved. Originally published in single magazine form in
JSA CLASSIFIED 2; JLA 122-123; SUPERMAN 223;
SUPERMAN/BATMAN 27; SUPERGIRL 6-9 Copyright © 2005-2006
DC Comics. All Rights Reserved. All characters, their distinctive
likenesses and related elements featured in this publication are
trademarks of DC Comics. The stories, characters and incidents
featured in this publication are entirely fictional.
DC Comics does not read or accept unsolicited submissions of
ideas, stories or artwork.
DC Comics, 1700 Broadway, New York, NY 10019. A Warner Bros.
Entertainment Company. Printed in Canada. First Printing.

ISBN: 1-4012-1226-3 ISBN 13: 978-1-4012-1206-1

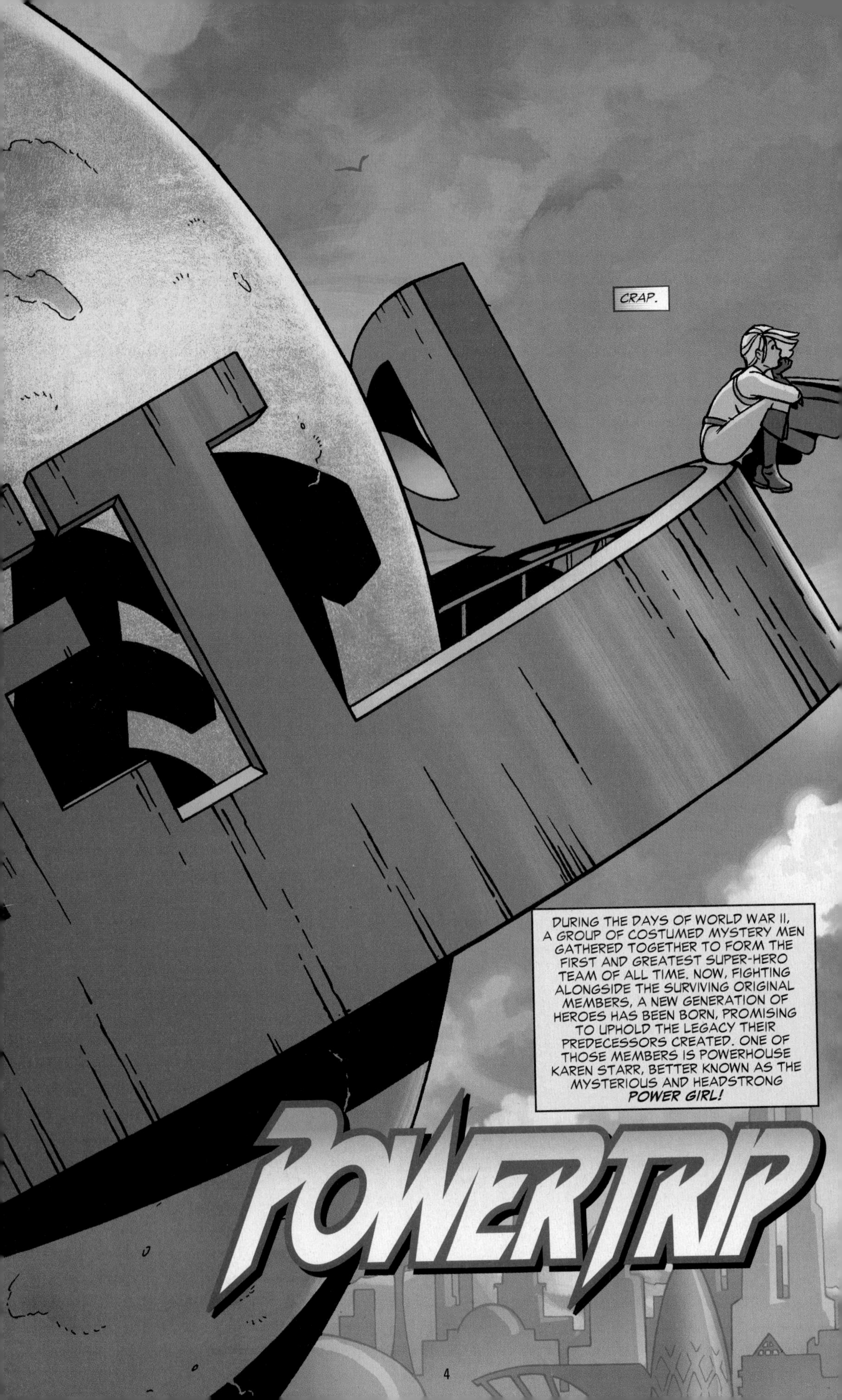
CRAP.
DURING THE DAYS OF WORLD WAR II, A GROUP OF COSTUMED MYSTERY MEN GATHERED TOGETHER TO FORM THE FIRST AND GREATEST SUPER-HERO TEAM OF ALL TIME. NOW, FIGHTING ALONGSIDE THE SURVIVING ORIGINAL MEMBERS, A NEW GENERATION OF HEROES HAS BEEN BORN, PROMISING TO UPHOLD THE LEGACY THEIR PREDECESSORS CREATED. ONE OF THOSE MEMBERS IS POWERHOUSE KAREN STARR, BETTER KNOWN AS THE MYSTERIOUS AND HEADSTRONG POWER GIRL!
POWER TRIP

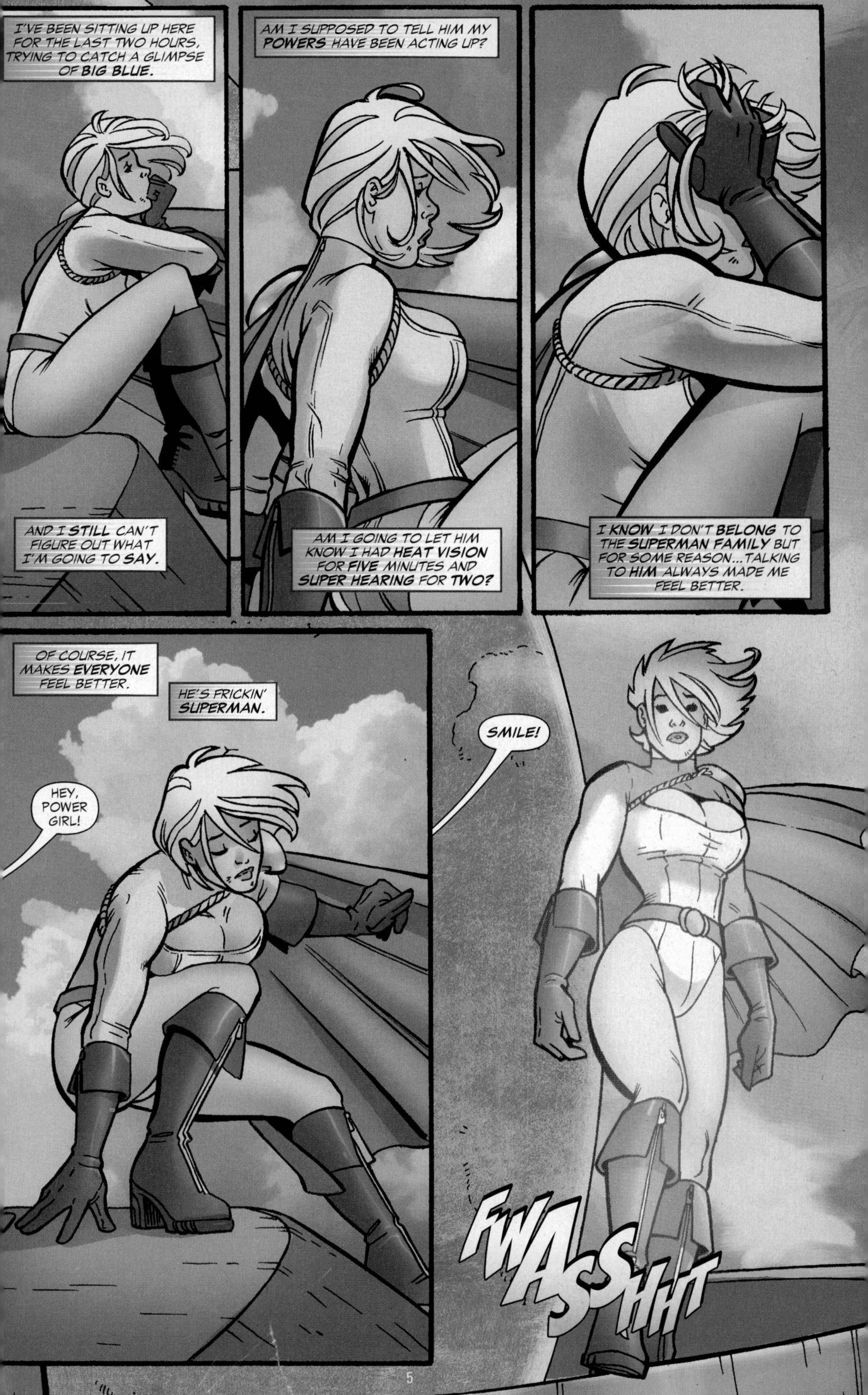
I'VE BEEN SITTING UP HERE FOR THE LAST TWO HOURS, TRYING TO CATCH A GLIMPSE OF BIG BLUE.
AND I STILL CAN'T FIGURE OUT WHAT I'M GOING TO SAY.
AM I SUPPOSED TO TELL HIM MY POWERS HAVE BEEN ACTING UP?
AM I GOING TO LET HIM KNOW I HAD HEAT VISION FOR FIVE MINUTES AND SUPER HEARING FOR TWO?
I KNOW I DON'T BELONG TO THE SUPERMAN FAMILY BUT FOR SOME REASON...TALKING TO HIM ALWAYS MADE ME FEEL BETTER.
OF COURSE, IT MAKES EVERYONE FEEL BETTER.
HE'S FRICKIN' SUPERMAN.
HEY, POWER GIRL!
SMILE!
FWASSHHT

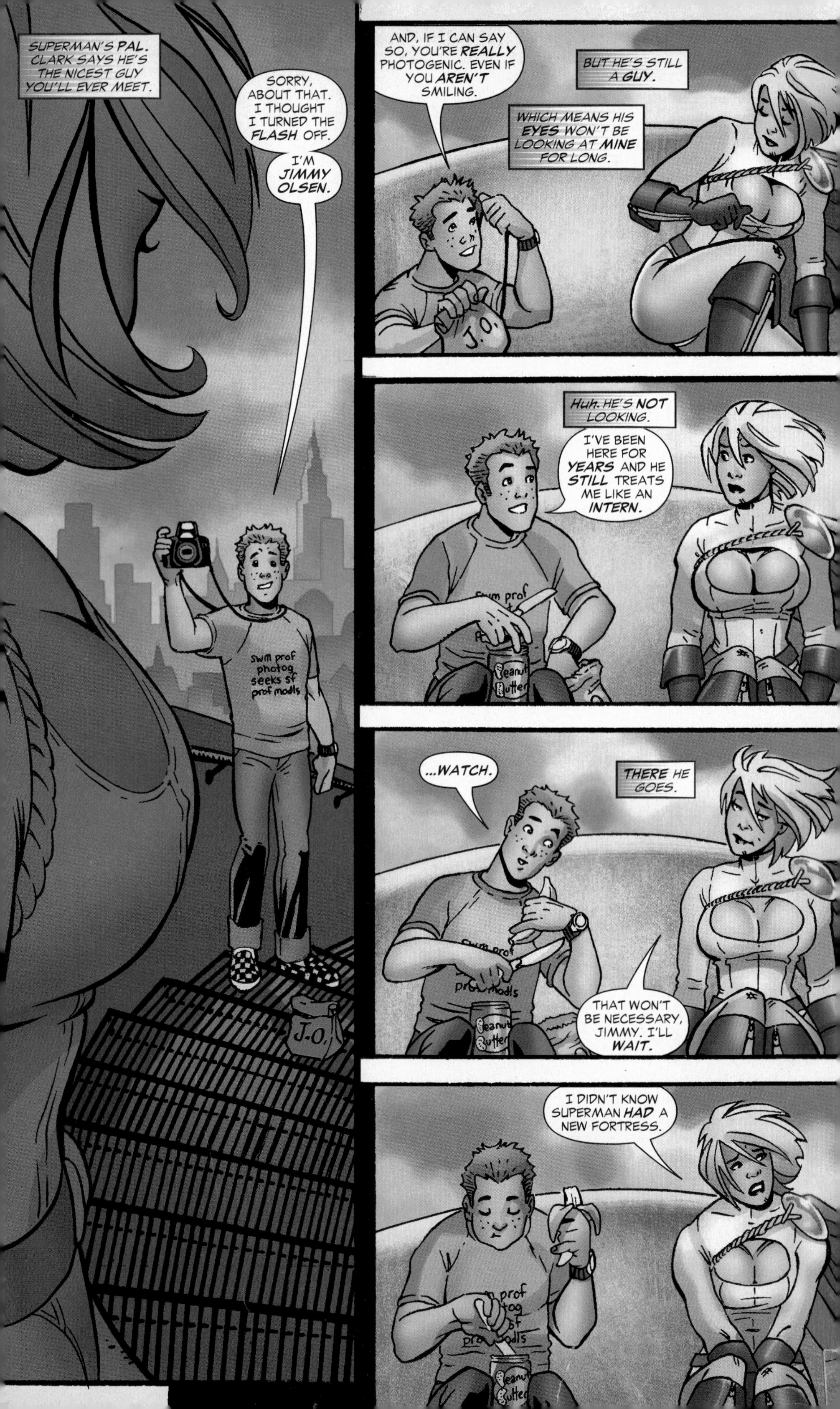
SUPERMAN'S PAL. CLARK SAYS HE'S THE NICEST GUY YOU'LL EVER MEET.
SORRY, ABOUT THAT. I THOUGHT I TURNED THE FLASH OFF.
I'M JIMMY OLSEN.
swm prof photog seeks sf prof modls
J.O.
AND, IF I CAN SAY SO, YOU'RE REALLY PHOTOGENIC. EVEN IF YOU AREN'T SMILING.
BUT HE'S STILL A GUY.
WHICH MEANS HIS EYES WON'T BE LOOKING AT MINE FOR LONG.
Huh. HE'S NOT LOOKING.
I'VE BEEN HERE FOR YEARS AND HE STILL TREATS ME LIKE AN INTERN.
...WATCH.
THERE HE GOES.
THAT WON'T BE NECESSARY, JIMMY. I'LL WAIT.
I DIDN'T KNOW SUPERMAN HAD A NEW FORTRESS.

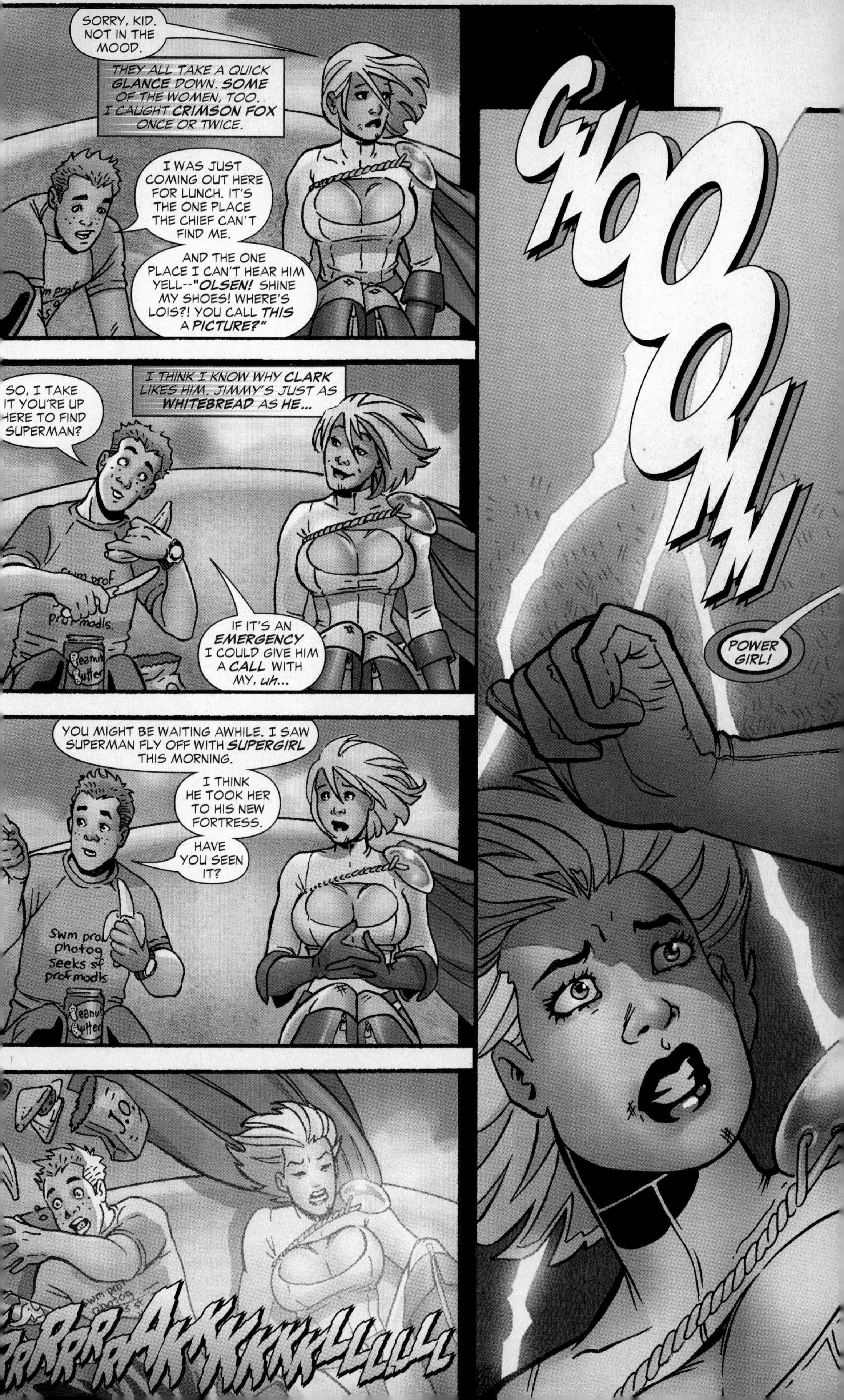
SORRY, KID. NOT IN THE MOOD.
THEY ALL TAKE A QUICK GLANCE DOWN. SOME OF THE WOMEN, TOO. I CAUGHT CRIMSON FOX ONCE OR TWICE.
I WAS JUST COMING OUT HERE FOR LUNCH. IT'S THE ONE PLACE THE CHIEF CAN'T FIND ME.
AND THE ONE PLACE I CAN'T HEAR HIM YELL--"OLSEN! SHINE MY SHOES! WHERE'S LOIS?! YOU CALL THIS A PICTURE?"
I THINK I KNOW WHY CLARK LIKES HIM. JIMMY'S JUST AS WHITEBREAD AS HE...
SO, I TAKE IT YOU'RE UP HERE TO FIND SUPERMAN?
IF IT'S AN EMERGENCY I COULD GIVE HIM A CALL WITH MY, uh...
YOU MIGHT BE WAITING AWHILE. I SAW SUPERMAN FLY OFF WITH SUPERGIRL THIS MORNING.
I THINK HE TOOK HER TO HIS NEW FORTRESS.
HAVE YOU SEEN IT?
RRRRRAKKKKKLLLLLL
GHOOOOM
POWER GIRL!

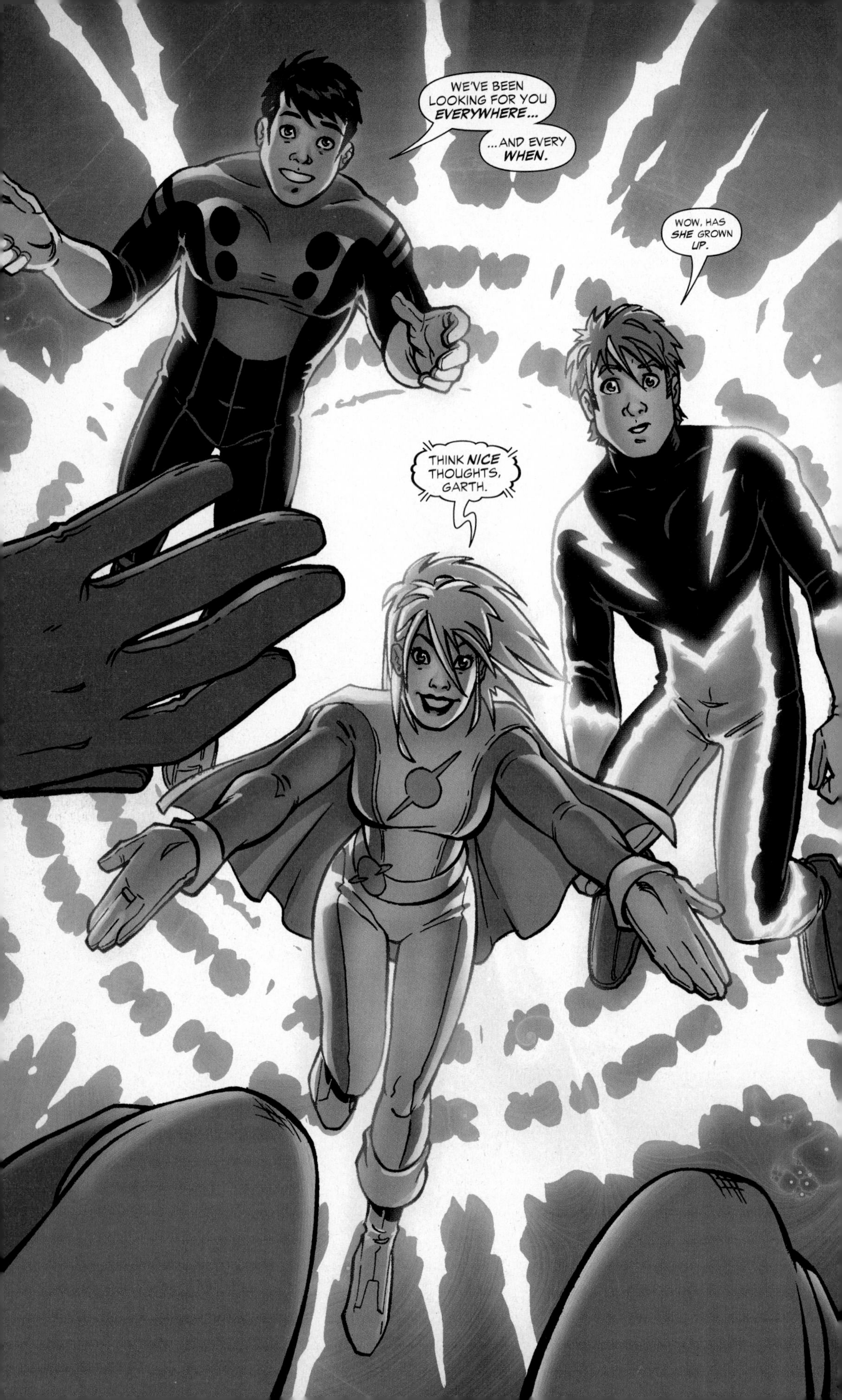
WE'VE BEEN LOOKING FOR YOU EVERYWHERE...
...AND EVERY WHEN.
WOW, HAS SHE GROWN UP.
THINK NICE THOUGHTS, GARTH.

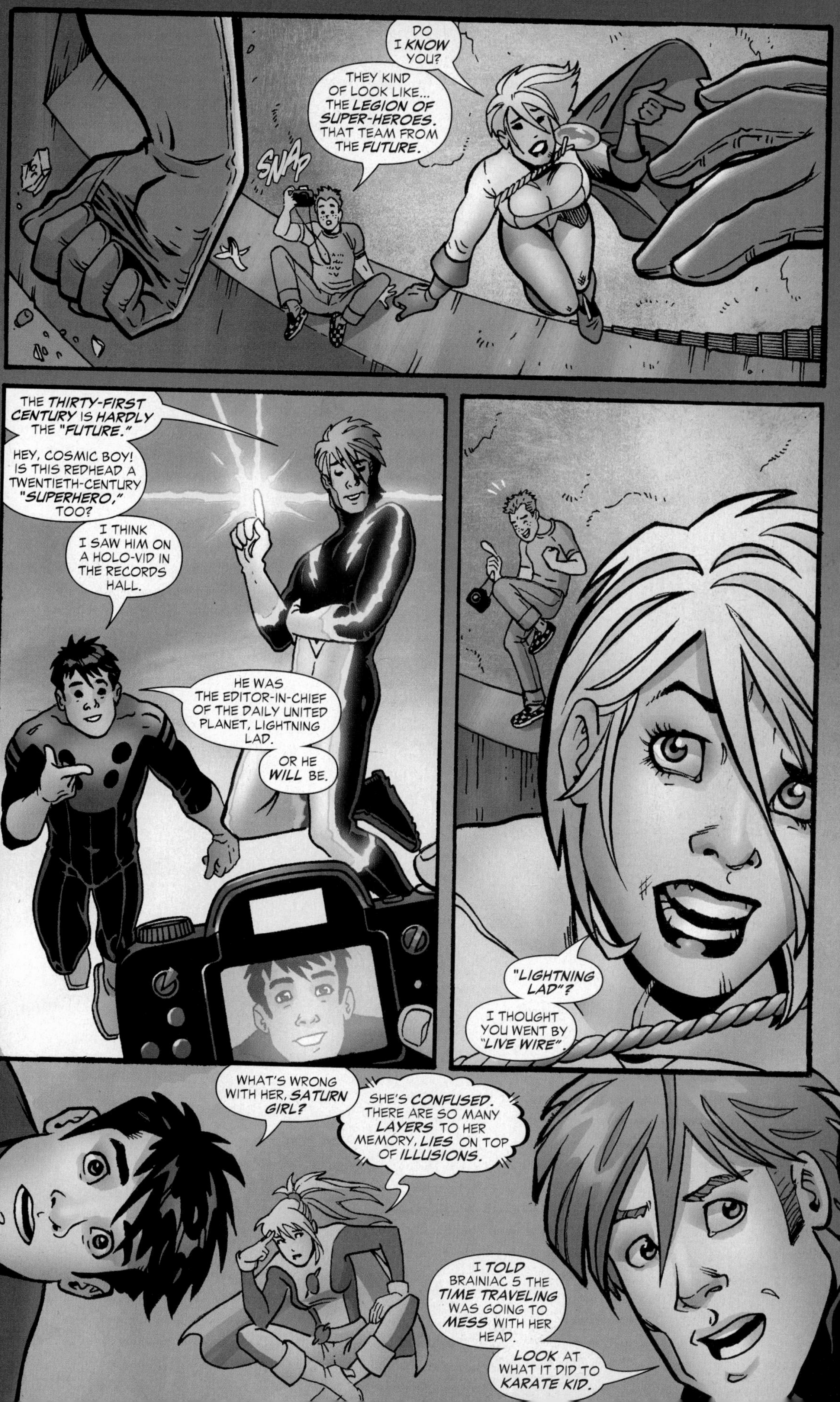
DO I KNOW YOU?
THEY KIND OF LOOK LIKE... THE LEGION OF SUPER-HEROES. THAT TEAM FROM THE FUTURE.
SNAP
THE THIRTY-FIRST CENTURY IS HARDLY THE "FUTURE."
HEY, COSMIC BOY! IS THIS REDHEAD A TWENTIETH-CENTURY "SUPERHERO," TOO?
I THINK I SAW HIM ON A HOLO-VID IN THE RECORDS HALL.
HE WAS THE EDITOR-IN-CHIEF OF THE DAILY UNITED PLANET, LIGHTNING LAD.
OR HE WILL BE.
"LIGHTNING LAD"?
I THOUGHT YOU WENT BY "LIVE WIRE".
WHAT'S WRONG WITH HER, SATURN GIRL?
SHE'S CONFUSED. THERE ARE SO MANY LAYERS TO HER MEMORY, LIES ON TOP OF ILLUSIONS.
I TOLD BRAINIAC 5 THE TIME TRAVELING WAS GOING TO MESS WITH HER HEAD.
LOOK AT WHAT IT DID TO KARATE KID.

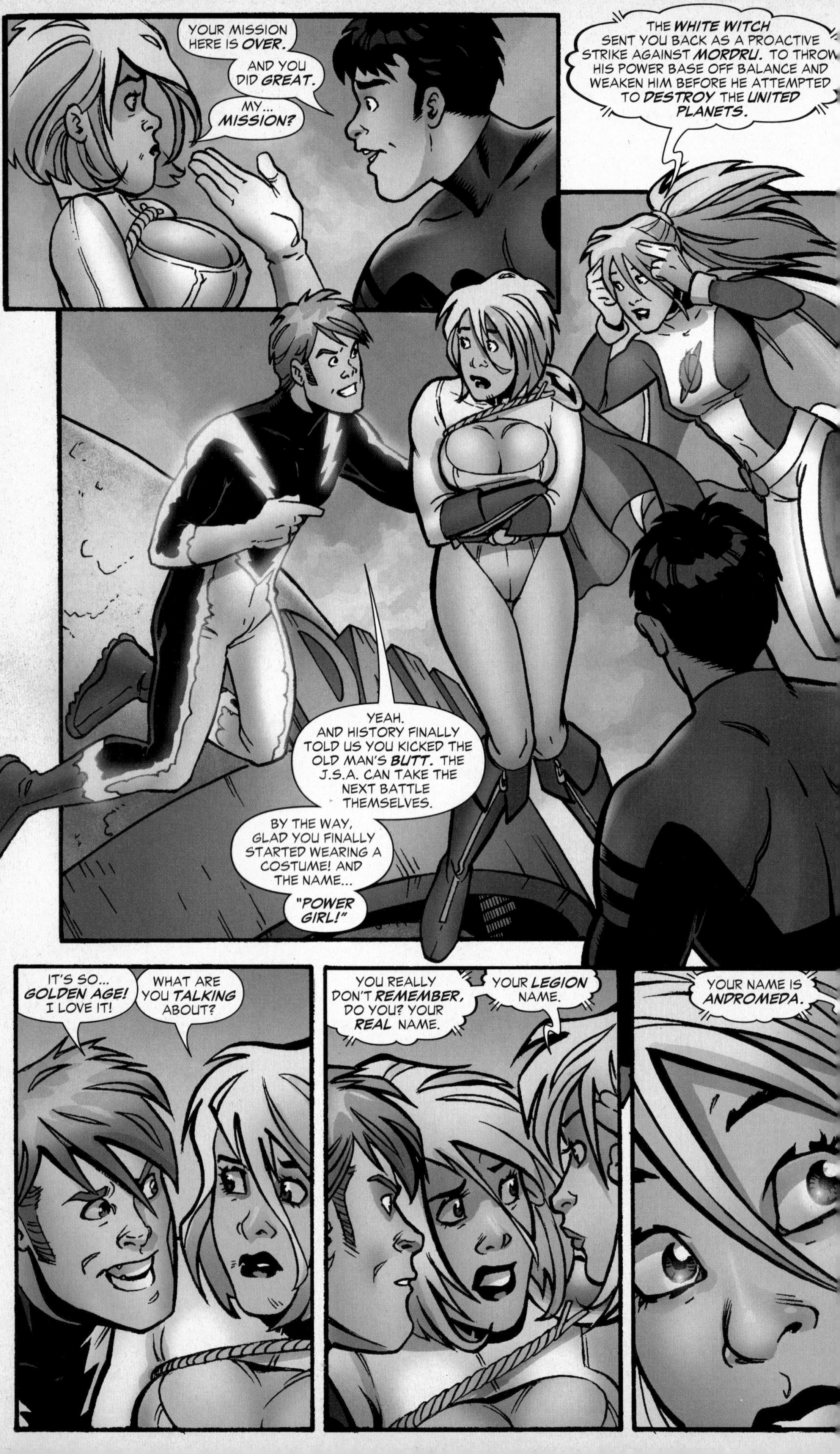
YOUR MISSION HERE IS OVER.
AND YOU DID GREAT.
MY... MISSION?
THE WHITE WITCH SENT YOU BACK AS A PROACTIVE STRIKE AGAINST MORDRU. TO THROW HIS POWER BASE OFF BALANCE AND WEAKEN HIM BEFORE HE ATTEMPTED TO DESTROY THE UNITED PLANETS.
YEAH. AND HISTORY FINALLY TOLD US YOU KICKED THE OLD MAN'S BUTT. THE J.S.A. CAN TAKE THE NEXT BATTLE THEMSELVES.
BY THE WAY, GLAD YOU FINALLY STARTED WEARING A COSTUME! AND THE NAME...
"POWER GIRL!"
IT'S SO... GOLDEN AGE! I LOVE IT!
WHAT ARE YOU TALKING ABOUT?
YOU REALLY DON'T REMEMBER, DO YOU? YOUR REAL NAME.
YOUR LEGION NAME.
YOUR NAME IS ANDROMEDA.

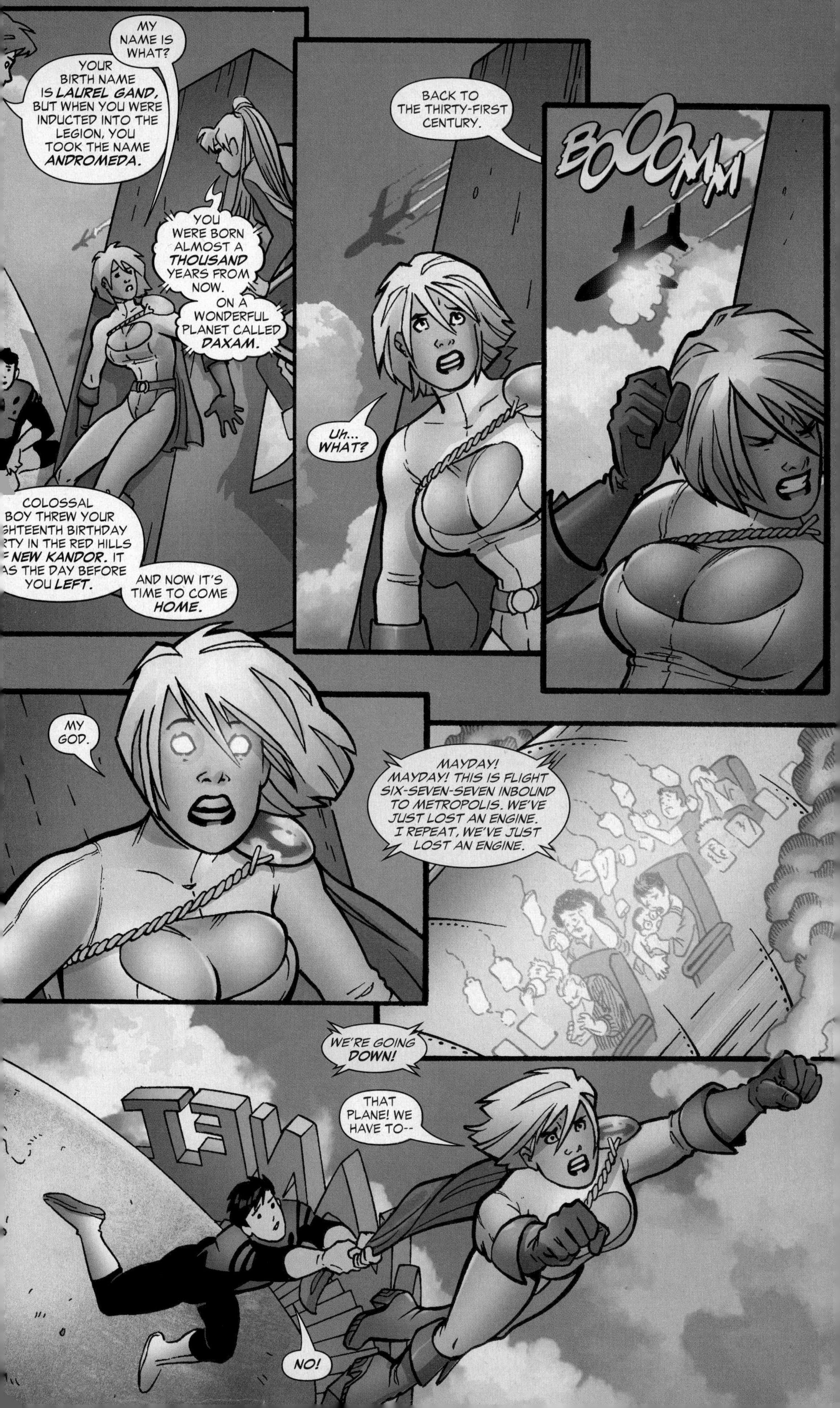

MY NAME IS WHAT?
YOUR BIRTH NAME IS LAUREL GAND, BUT WHEN YOU WERE INDUCTED INTO THE LEGION, YOU TOOK THE NAME ANDROMEDA.
YOU WERE BORN ALMOST A THOUSAND YEARS FROM NOW.
ON A WONDERFUL PLANET CALLED DAXAM.
COLOSSAL BOY THREW YOUR GHTEENTH BIRTHDAY RTY IN THE RED HILLS F NEW KANDOR. IT AS THE DAY BEFORE YOU LEFT.
AND NOW IT'S TIME TO COME HOME.
BACK TO THE THIRTY-FIRST CENTURY.
Uh... WHAT?
BOOOMM
MY GOD.
MAYDAY! MAYDAY! THIS IS FLIGHT SIX-SEVEN-SEVEN INBOUND TO METROPOLIS. WE'VE JUST LOST AN ENGINE. I REPEAT, WE'VE JUST LOST AN ENGINE.
WE'RE GOING DOWN!
THAT PLANE! WE HAVE TO--
NO!

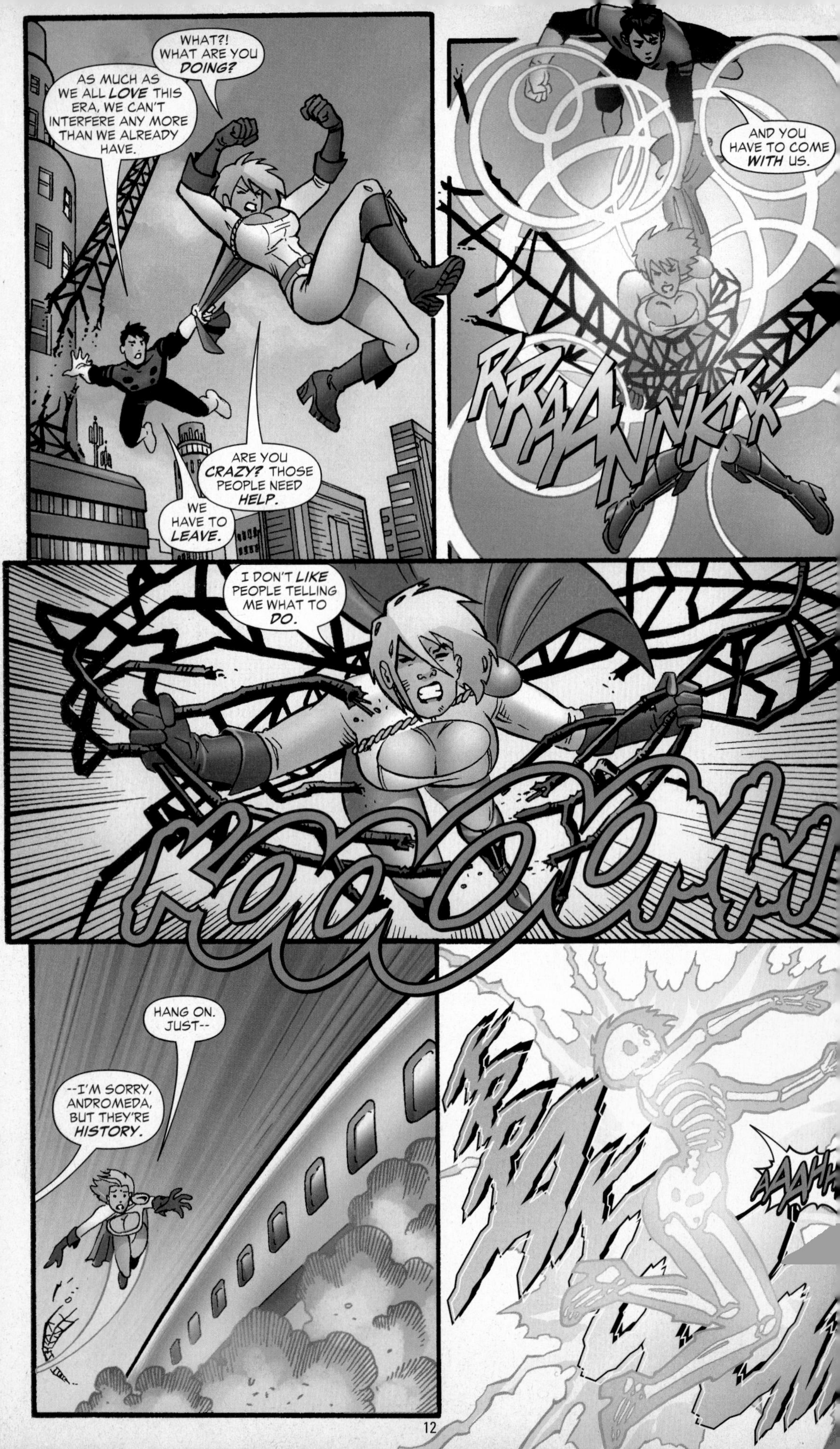

WHAT?! WHAT ARE YOU DOING?
AS MUCH AS WE ALL LOVE THIS ERA, WE CAN'T INTERFERE ANY MORE THAN WE ALREADY HAVE.
ARE YOU CRAZY? THOSE PEOPLE NEED HELP.
WE HAVE TO LEAVE.
AND YOU HAVE TO COME WITH US.
RRAANNKK
I DON'T LIKE PEOPLE TELLING ME WHAT TO DO.
HANG ON. JUST--
--I'M SORRY, ANDROMEDA, BUT THEY'RE HISTORY.
AAAHH

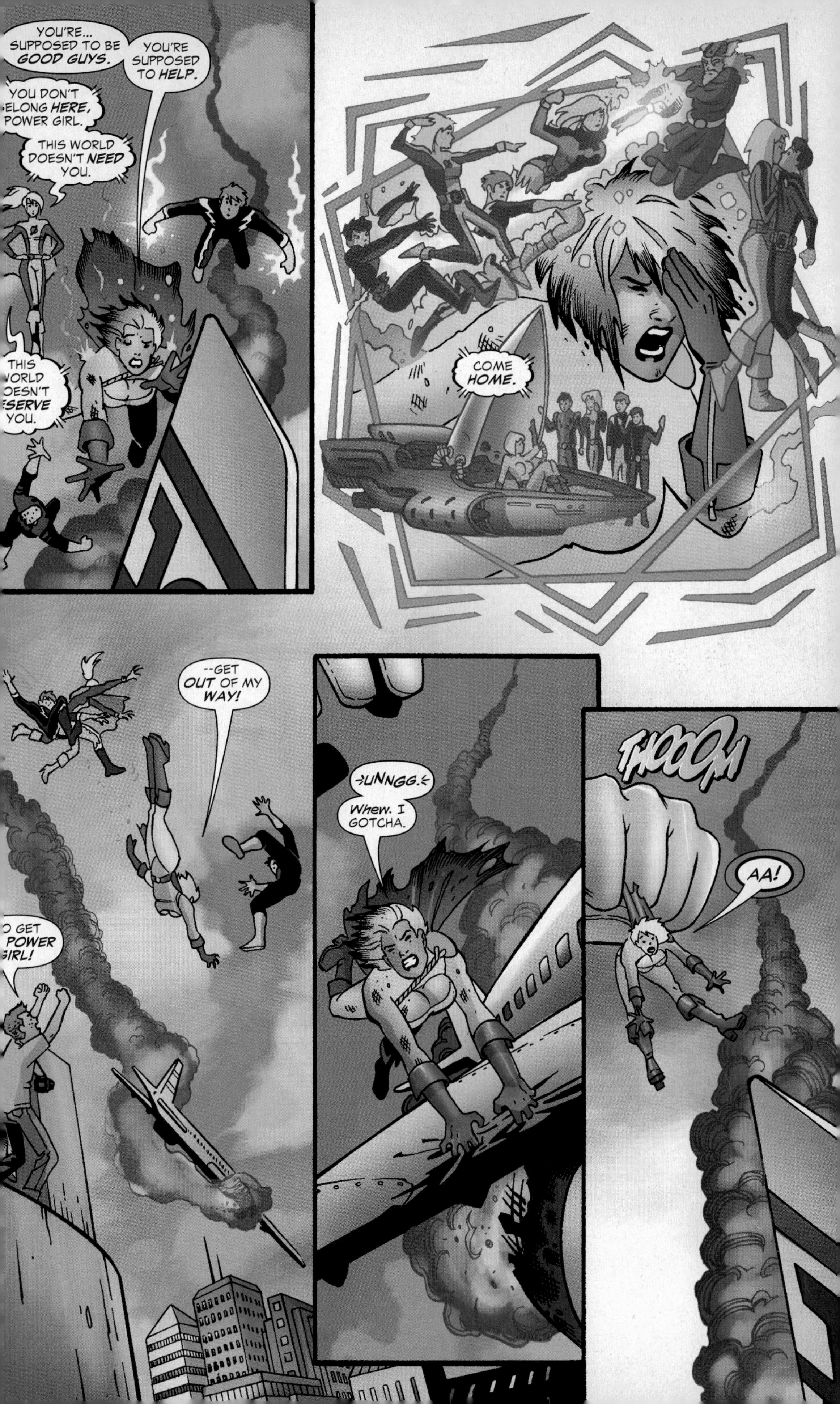

YOU'RE... SUPPOSED TO BE GOOD GUYS.
YOU'RE SUPPOSED TO HELP.
YOU DON'T BELONG HERE, POWER GIRL.
THIS WORLD DOESN'T NEED YOU.
THIS WORLD DOESN'T DESERVE YOU.
COME HOME.
--GET OUT OF MY WAY!
GET POWER GIRL!
UNNGG.
Whew. I GOTCHA.
THOOOM
AA!

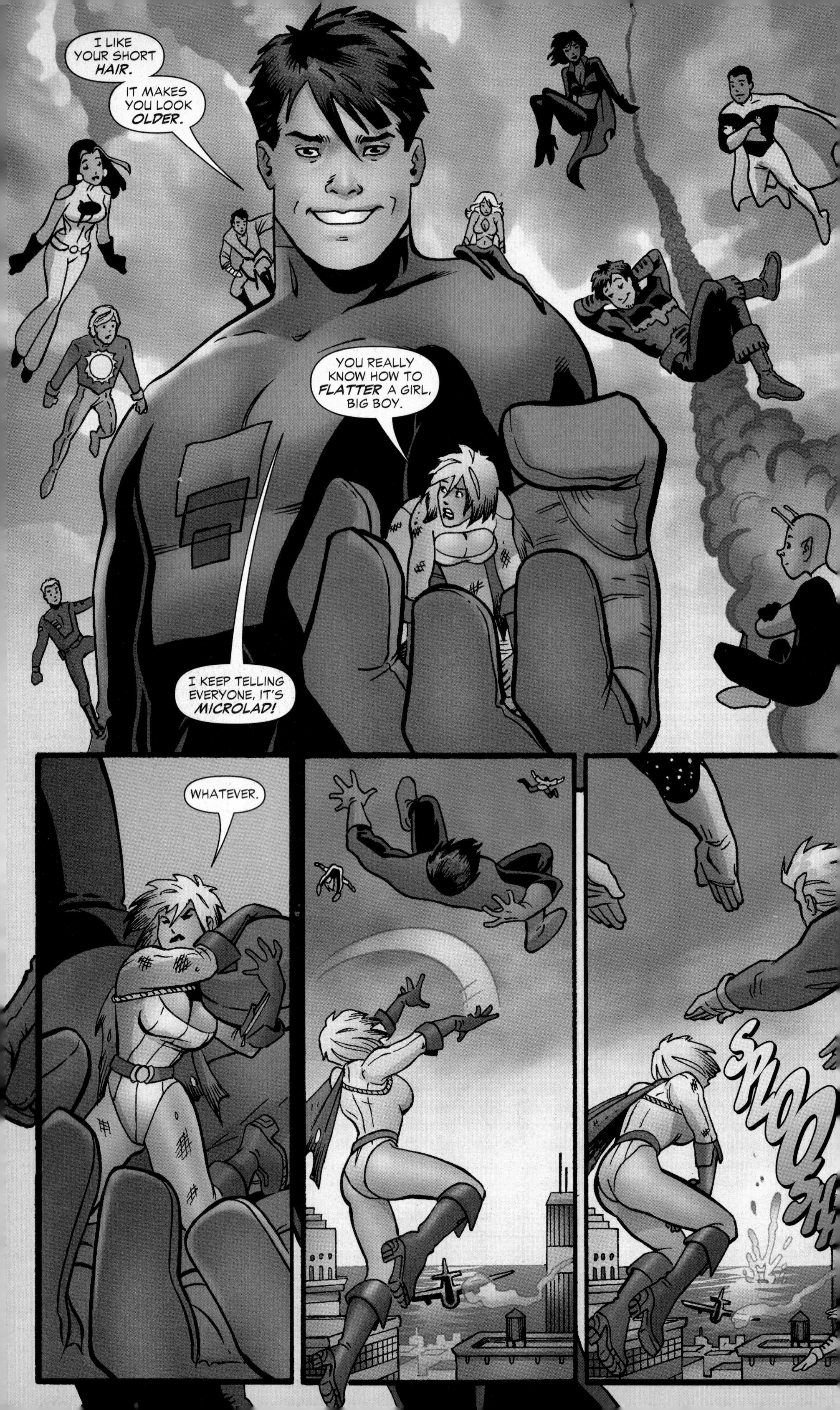
I LIKE YOUR SHORT HAIR.
IT MAKES YOU LOOK OLDER.
YOU REALLY KNOW HOW TO FLATTER A GIRL, BIG BOY.
I KEEP TELLING EVERYONE, IT'S MICROLAD!
WHATEVER.
SNOOSH

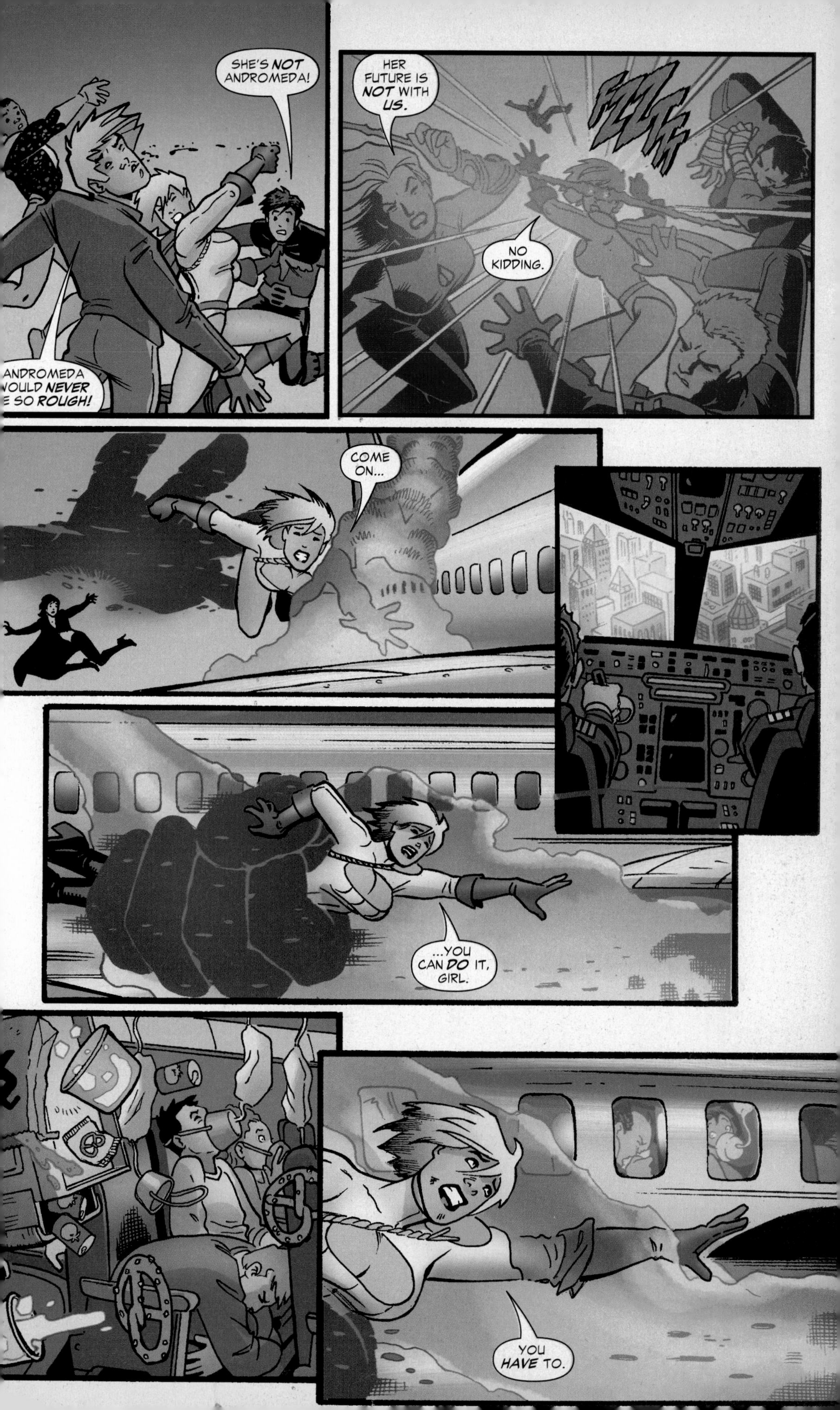
SHE'S NOT ANDROMEDA!
ANDROMEDA WOULD NEVER BE SO ROUGH!
HER FUTURE IS NOT WITH US.
FZZZT
NO KIDDING.
COME ON...
...YOU CAN DO IT, GIRL.
YOU HAVE TO.

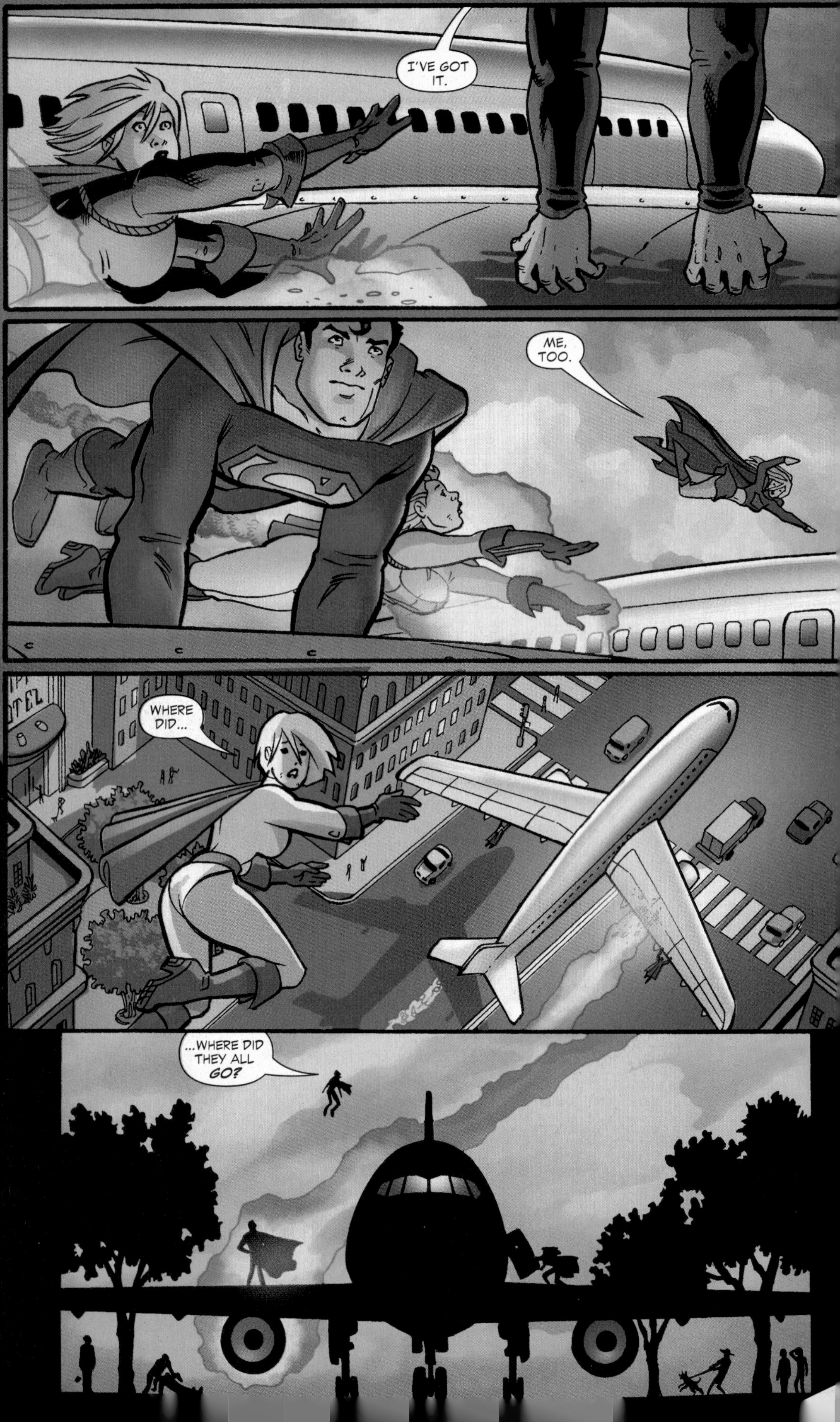
I'VE GOT IT.
ME, TOO.
WHERE DID...
...WHERE DID THEY ALL GO?

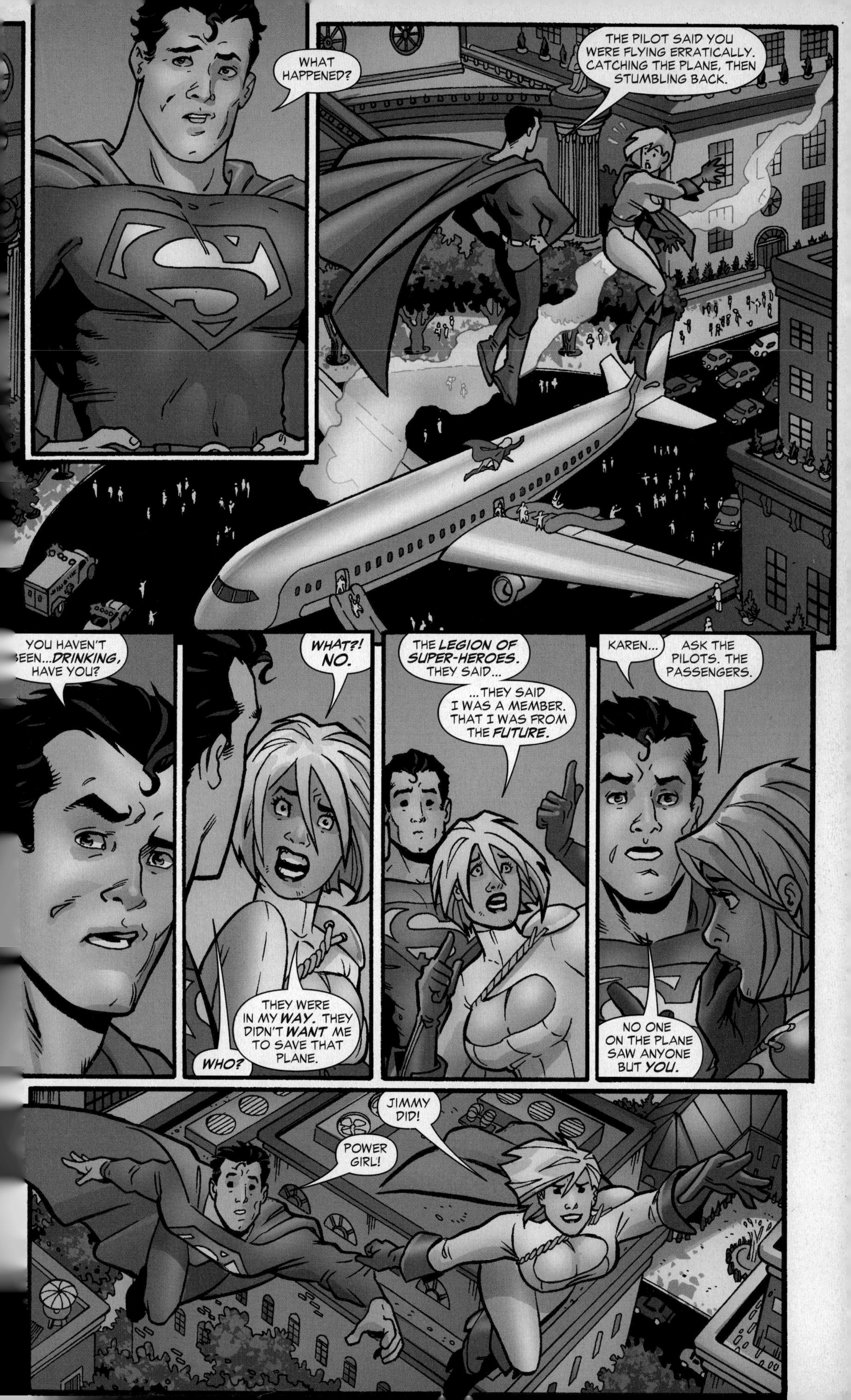
WHAT HAPPENED?
THE PILOT SAID YOU WERE FLYING ERRATICALLY. CATCHING THE PLANE, THEN STUMBLING BACK.
YOU HAVEN'T BEEN...DRINKING, HAVE YOU?
WHAT?! NO.
THEY WERE IN MY WAY. THEY DIDN'T WANT ME TO SAVE THAT PLANE.
WHO?
THE LEGION OF SUPER-HEROES. THEY SAID...
...THEY SAID I WAS A MEMBER. THAT I WAS FROM THE FUTURE.
KAREN...
ASK THE PILOTS. THE PASSENGERS.
NO ONE ON THE PLANE SAW ANYONE BUT YOU.
JIMMY DID!
POWER GIRL!

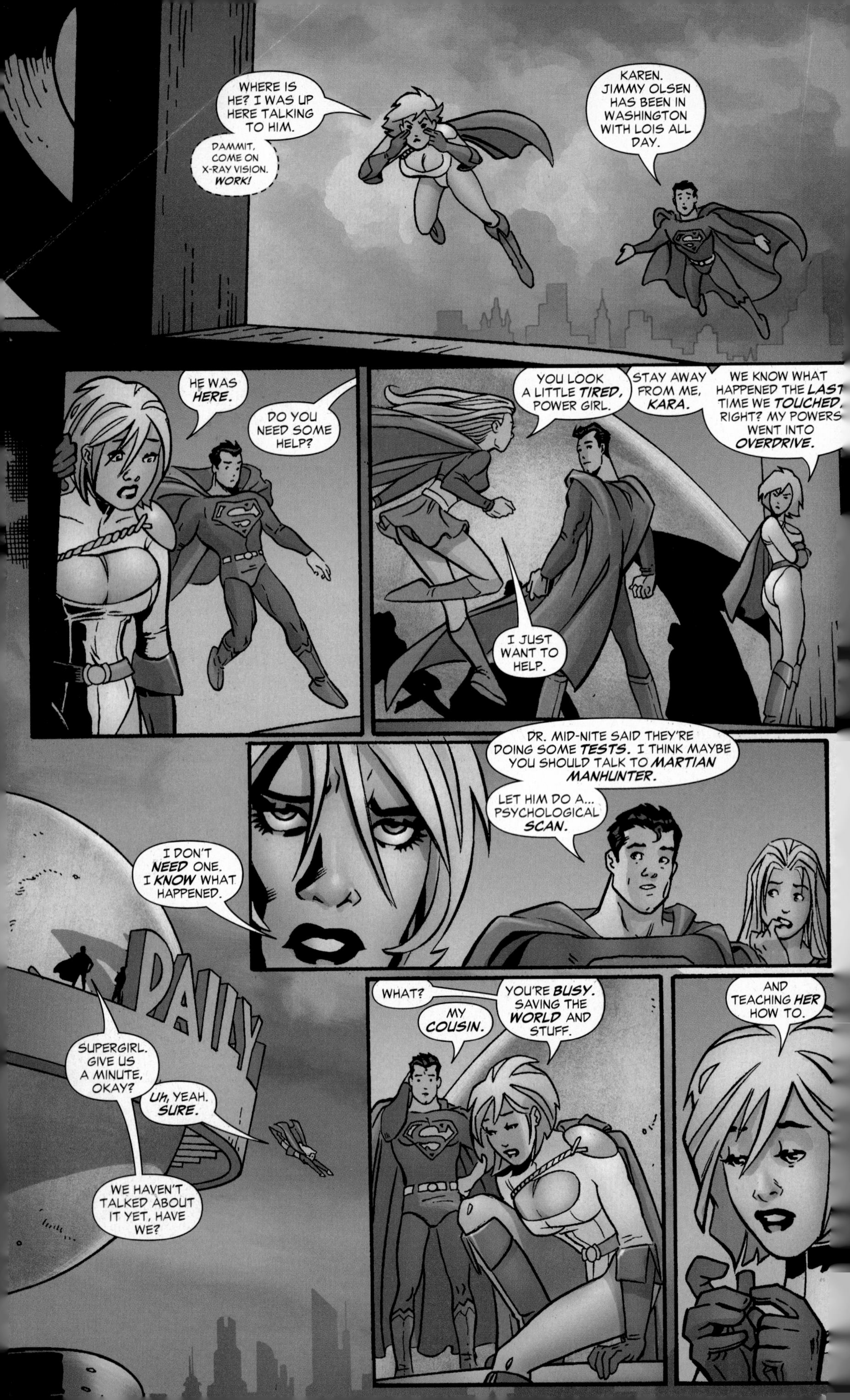
WHERE IS HE? I WAS UP HERE TALKING TO HIM.
DAMMIT, COME ON X-RAY VISION. WORK!
KAREN. JIMMY OLSEN HAS BEEN IN WASHINGTON WITH LOIS ALL DAY.
HE WAS HERE.
DO YOU NEED SOME HELP?
YOU LOOK A LITTLE TIRED, POWER GIRL.
STAY AWAY FROM ME, KARA.
WE KNOW WHAT HAPPENED THE LAST TIME WE TOUCHED, RIGHT? MY POWERS WENT INTO OVERDRIVE.
I JUST WANT TO HELP.
DR. MID-NITE SAID THEY'RE DOING SOME TESTS. I THINK MAYBE YOU SHOULD TALK TO MARTIAN MANHUNTER.
LET HIM DO A... PSYCHOLOGICAL SCAN.
I DON'T NEED ONE. I KNOW WHAT HAPPENED.
DAILY
SUPERGIRL. GIVE US A MINUTE, OKAY?
Uh, YEAH. SURE.
WE HAVEN'T TALKED ABOUT IT YET, HAVE WE?
WHAT?
MY COUSIN.
YOU'RE BUSY. SAVING THE WORLD AND STUFF.
AND TEACHING HER HOW TO.

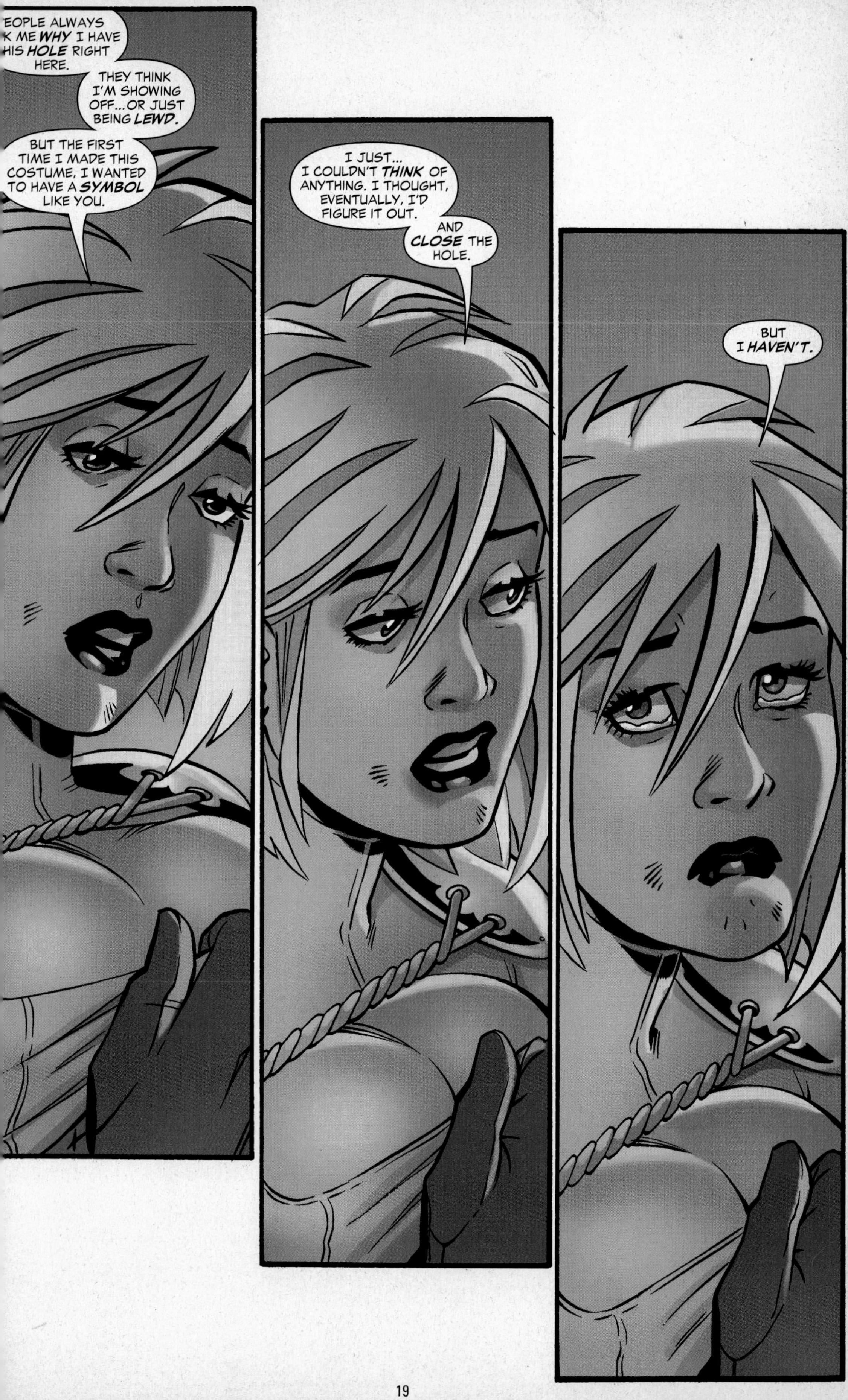
EOPLE ALWAYS K ME WHY I HAVE HIS HOLE RIGHT HERE.
THEY THINK I'M SHOWING OFF...OR JUST BEING LEWD.
BUT THE FIRST TIME I MADE THIS COSTUME, I WANTED TO HAVE A SYMBOL LIKE YOU.
I JUST... I COULDN'T THINK OF ANYTHING. I THOUGHT, EVENTUALLY, I'D FIGURE IT OUT.
AND CLOSE THE HOLE.
BUT I HAVEN'T.

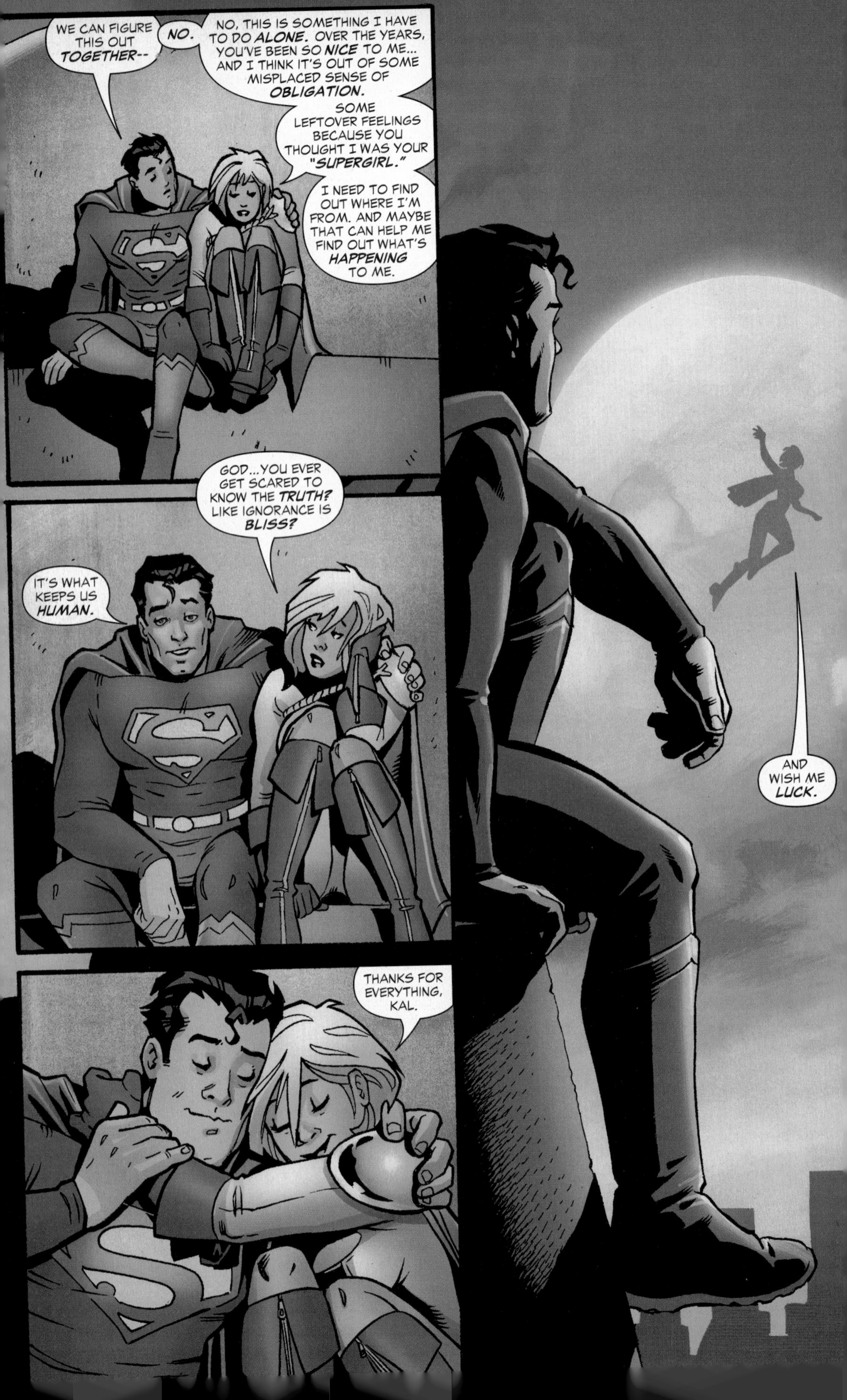
WE CAN FIGURE THIS OUT TOGETHER--
NO.
NO, THIS IS SOMETHING I HAVE TO DO ALONE. OVER THE YEARS, YOU'VE BEEN SO NICE TO ME... AND I THINK IT'S OUT OF SOME MISPLACED SENSE OF OBLIGATION.
SOME LEFTOVER FEELINGS BECAUSE YOU THOUGHT I WAS YOUR "SUPERGIRL."
I NEED TO FIND OUT WHERE I'M FROM. AND MAYBE THAT CAN HELP ME FIND OUT WHAT'S HAPPENING TO ME.
GOD...YOU EVER GET SCARED TO KNOW THE TRUTH? LIKE IGNORANCE IS BLISS?
IT'S WHAT KEEPS US HUMAN.
THANKS FOR EVERYTHING, KAL.
AND WISH ME LUCK.

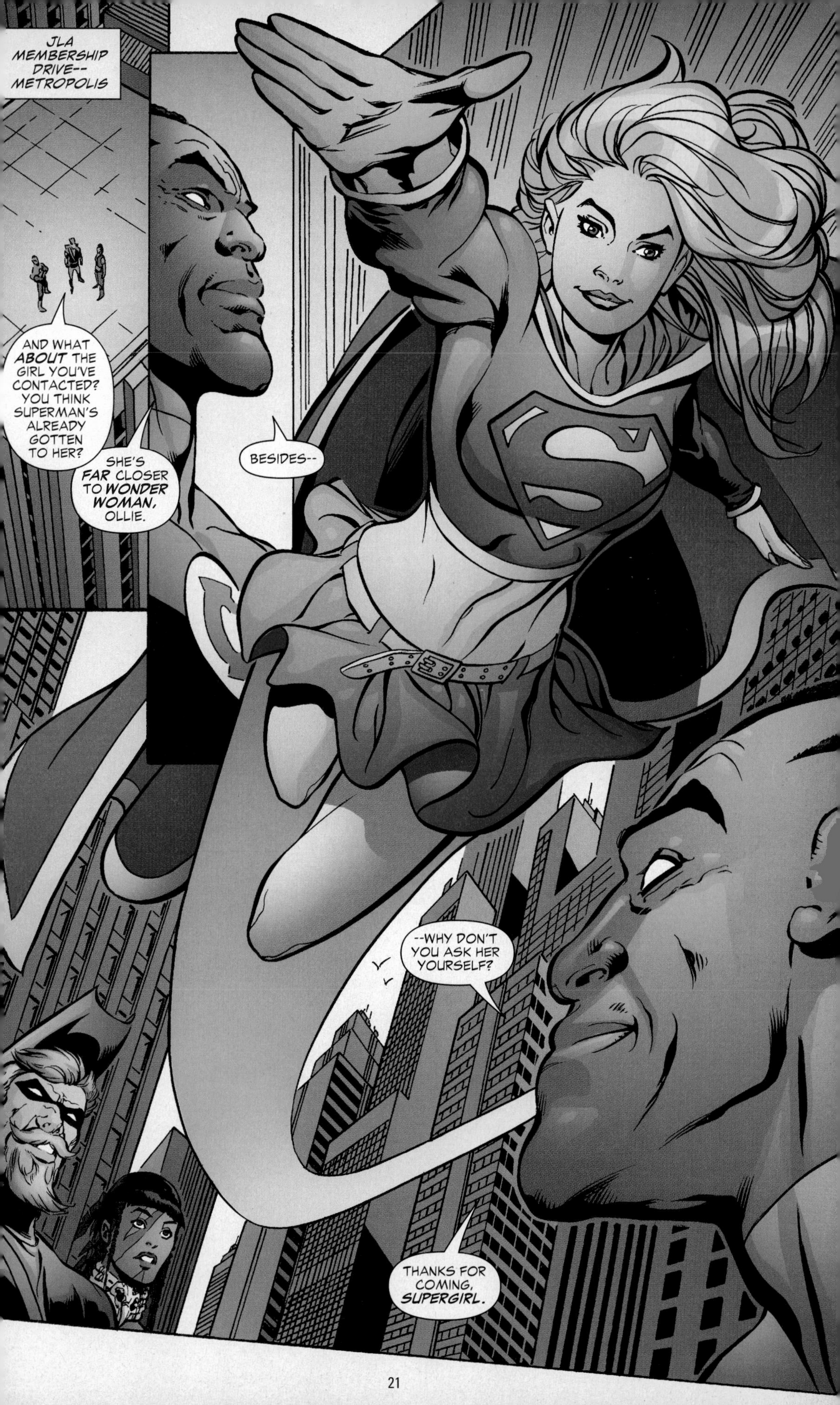
JLA MEMBERSHIP DRIVE-- METROPOLIS
AND WHAT ABOUT THE GIRL YOU'VE CONTACTED? YOU THINK SUPERMAN'S ALREADY GOTTEN TO HER?
SHE'S FAR CLOSER TO WONDER WOMAN, OLLIE.
BESIDES--
--WHY DON'T YOU ASK HER YOURSELF?
THANKS FOR COMING, SUPERGIRL.

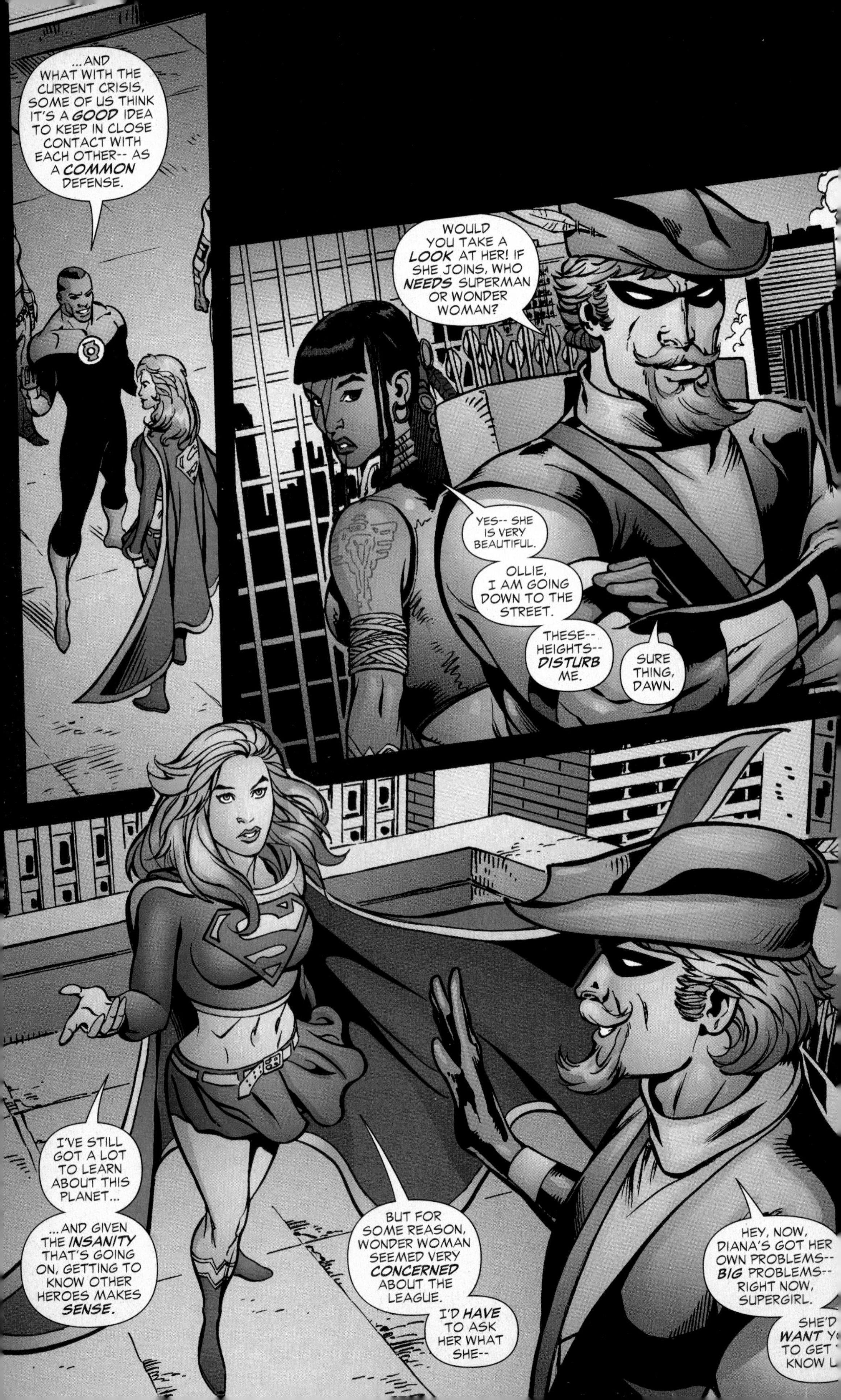

...AND WHAT WITH THE CURRENT CRISIS, SOME OF US THINK IT'S A *GOOD* IDEA TO KEEP IN CLOSE CONTACT WITH EACH OTHER-- AS A *COMMON* DEFENSE.
WOULD YOU TAKE A *LOOK* AT HER! IF SHE JOINS, WHO *NEEDS* SUPERMAN OR WONDER WOMAN?
YES-- SHE IS VERY BEAUTIFUL.
OLLIE, I AM GOING DOWN TO THE STREET.
THESE-- HEIGHTS-- *DISTURB* ME.
SURE THING, DAWN.
I'VE STILL GOT A LOT TO LEARN ABOUT THIS PLANET...
...AND GIVEN THE *INSANITY* THAT'S GOING ON, GETTING TO KNOW OTHER HEROES MAKES *SENSE.*
BUT FOR SOME REASON, WONDER WOMAN SEEMED VERY *CONCERNED* ABOUT THE LEAGUE.
I'D *HAVE* TO ASK HER WHAT SHE--
HEY, NOW, DIANA'S GOT HER OWN PROBLEMS-- *BIG* PROBLEMS-- RIGHT NOW, SUPERGIRL.

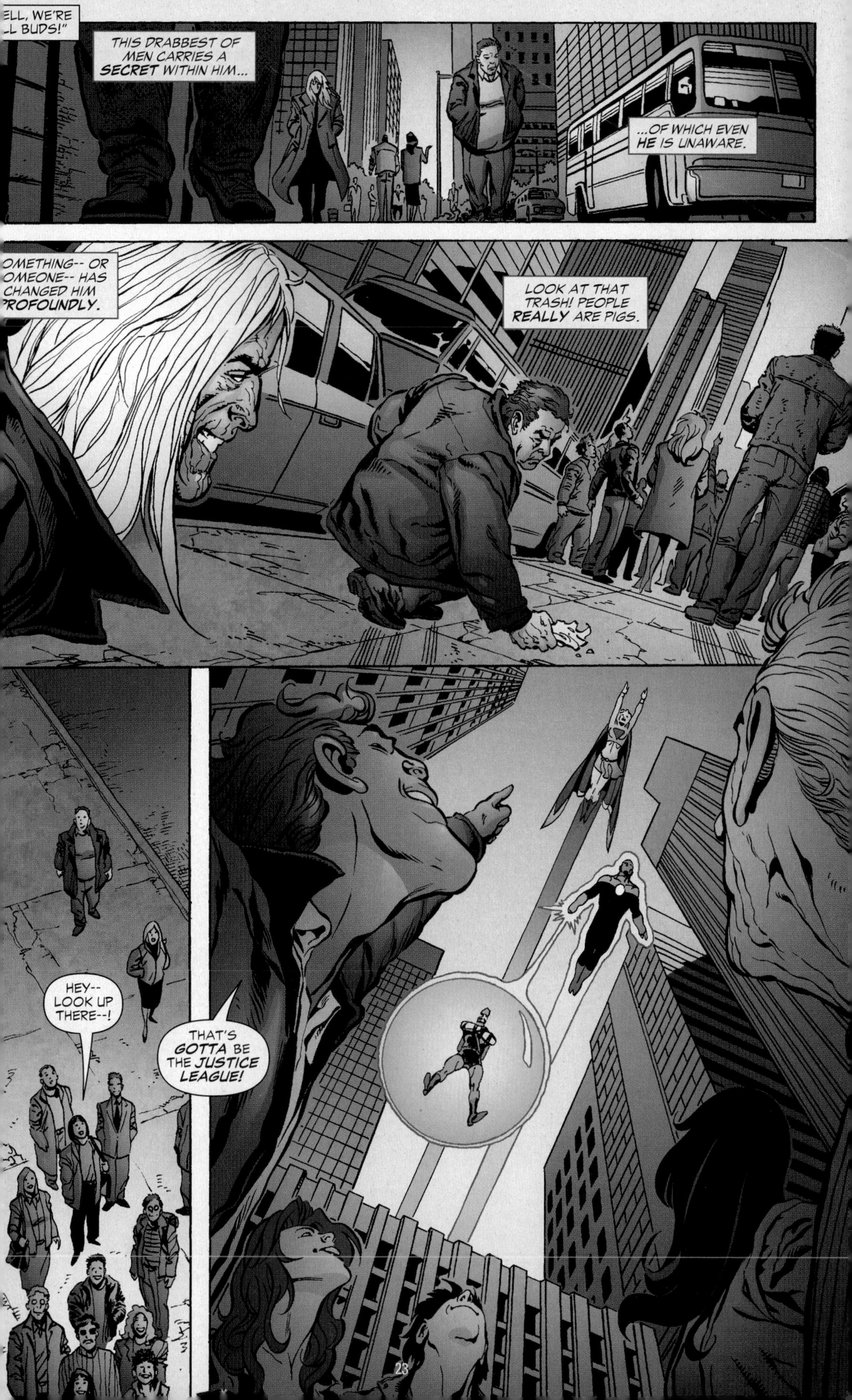

ELL, WE'RE
L BUDS!"
THIS DRABBEST OF MEN CARRIES A SECRET WITHIN HIM...
...OF WHICH EVEN HE IS UNAWARE.
OMETHING-- OR OMEONE-- HAS CHANGED HIM ROFOUNDLY.
LOOK AT THAT TRASH! PEOPLE REALLY ARE PIGS.
HEY-- LOOK UP THERE--!
THAT'S GOTTA BE THE JUSTICE LEAGUE!

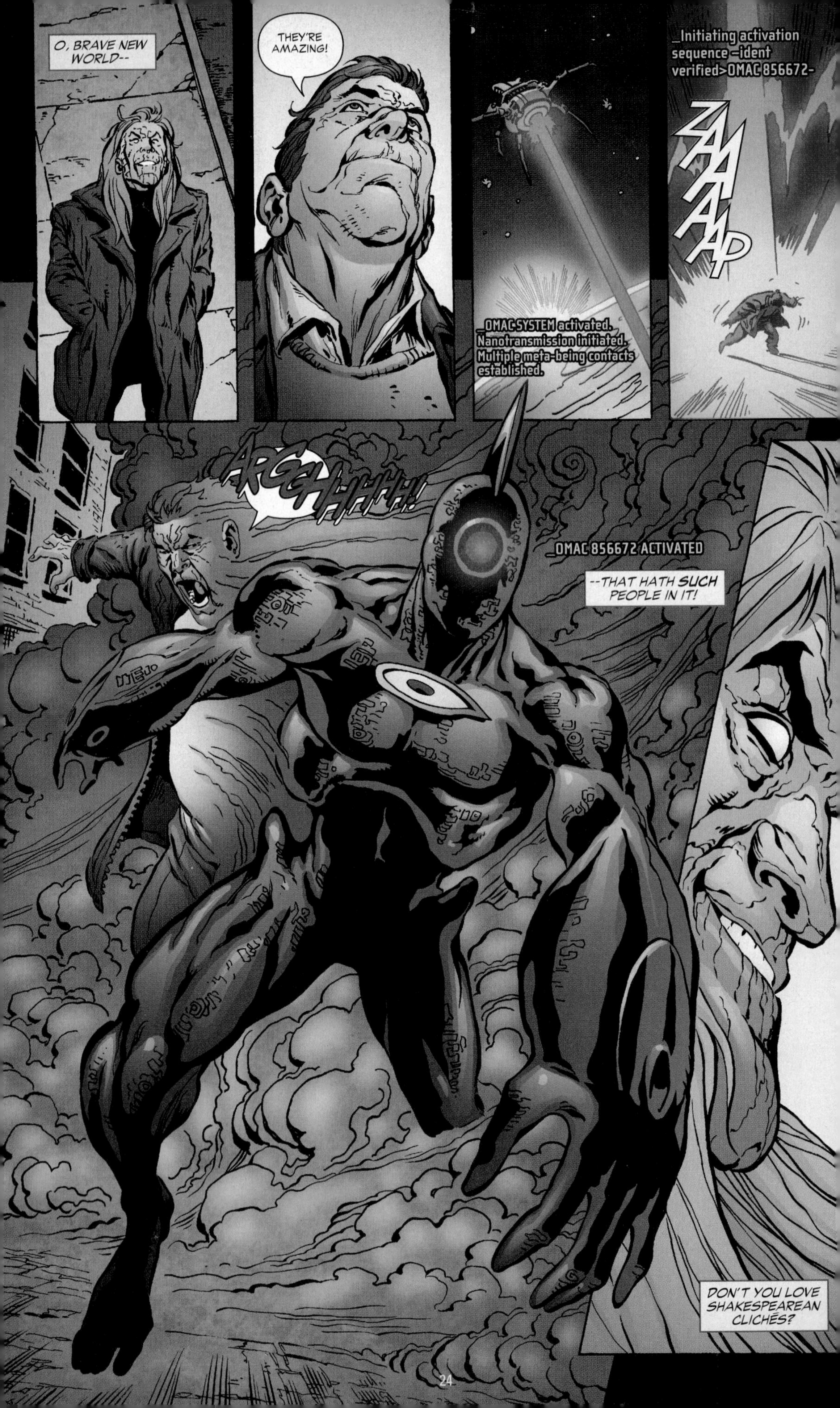

O, BRAVE NEW WORLD--
THEY'RE AMAZING!
_OMAC SYSTEM activated. Nanotransmission initiated. Multiple meta-being contacts established.
_Initiating activation sequence —ident verified>OMAC 856672-
ZAAAAAP
ARGGHHHH!
_OMAC 856672 ACTIVATED
--THAT HATH SUCH PEOPLE IN IT!
DON'T YOU LOVE SHAKESPEAREAN CLICHÉS?

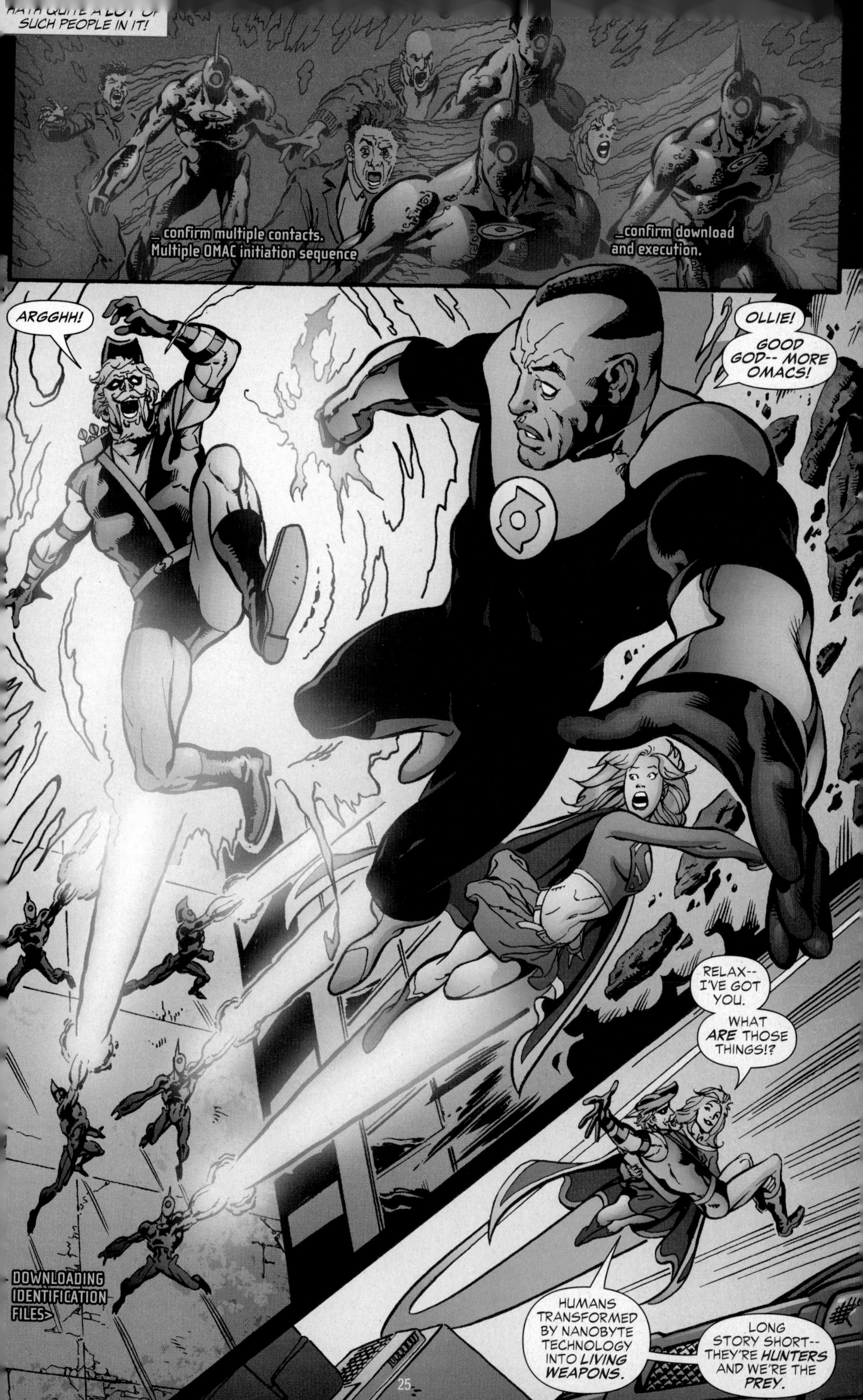
HATH QUITE A LOT OF SUCH PEOPLE IN IT!
_confirm multiple contacts. Multiple OMAC initiation sequence
_confirm download and execution.
ARGGHH!
OLLIE! GOOD GOD-- MORE OMACS!
RELAX-- I'VE GOT YOU.
WHAT ARE THOSE THINGS!?
DOWNLOADING IDENTIFICATION FILES>
HUMANS TRANSFORMED BY NANOBYTE TECHNOLOGY INTO LIVING WEAPONS.
LONG STORY SHORT-- THEY'RE HUNTERS AND WE'RE THE PREY.

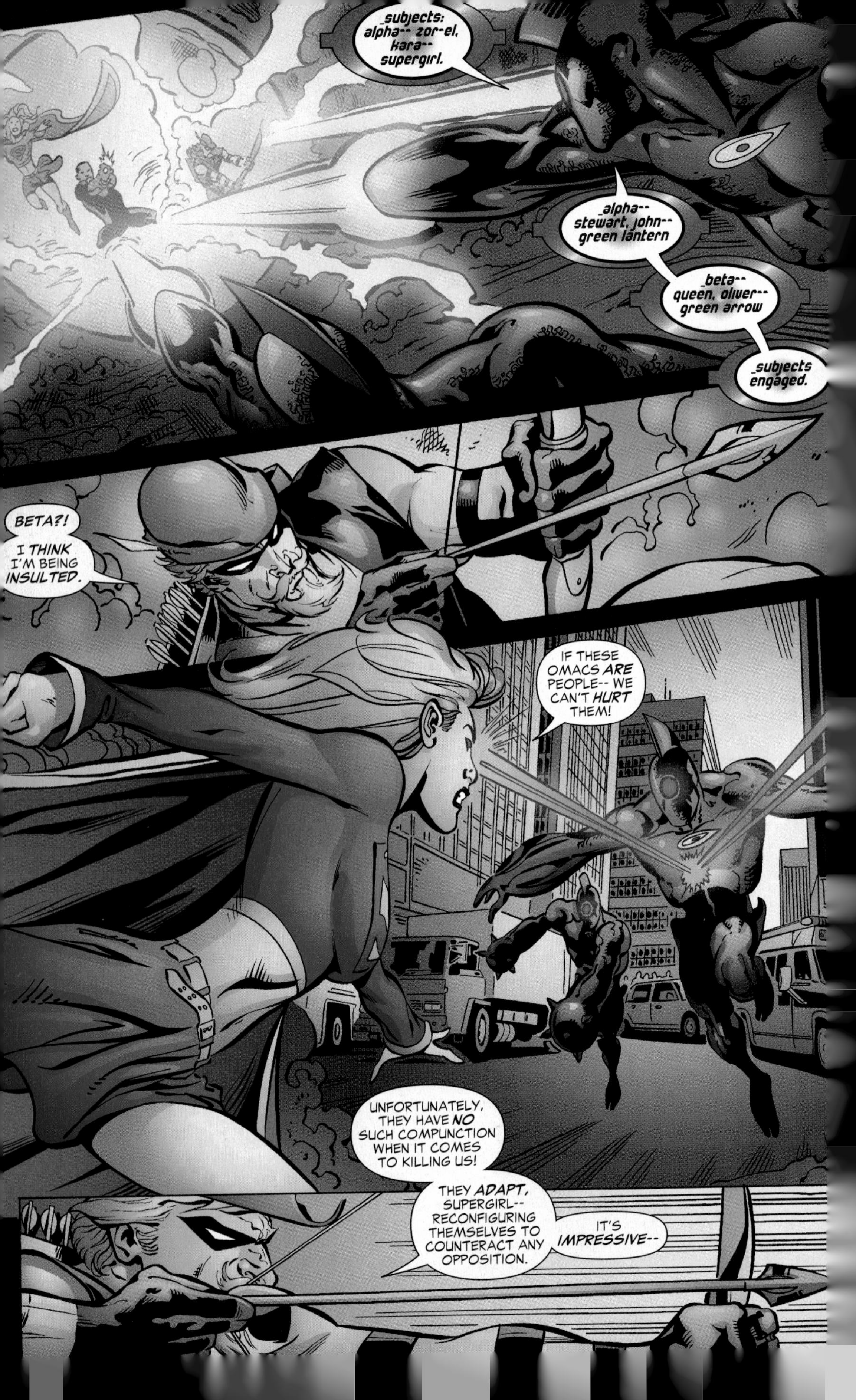
_subjects: alpha-- zor-el, kara-- supergirl.
_alpha-- stewart, john-- green lantern
_beta-- queen, oliver-- green arrow
_subjects engaged.
BETA?!
I THINK I'M BEING INSULTED.
IF THESE OMACS ARE PEOPLE-- WE CAN'T HURT THEM!
UNFORTUNATELY, THEY HAVE NO SUCH COMPUNCTION WHEN IT COMES TO KILLING US!
THEY ADAPT, SUPERGIRL-- RECONFIGURING THEMSELVES TO COUNTERACT ANY OPPOSITION.
IT'S IMPRESSIVE--

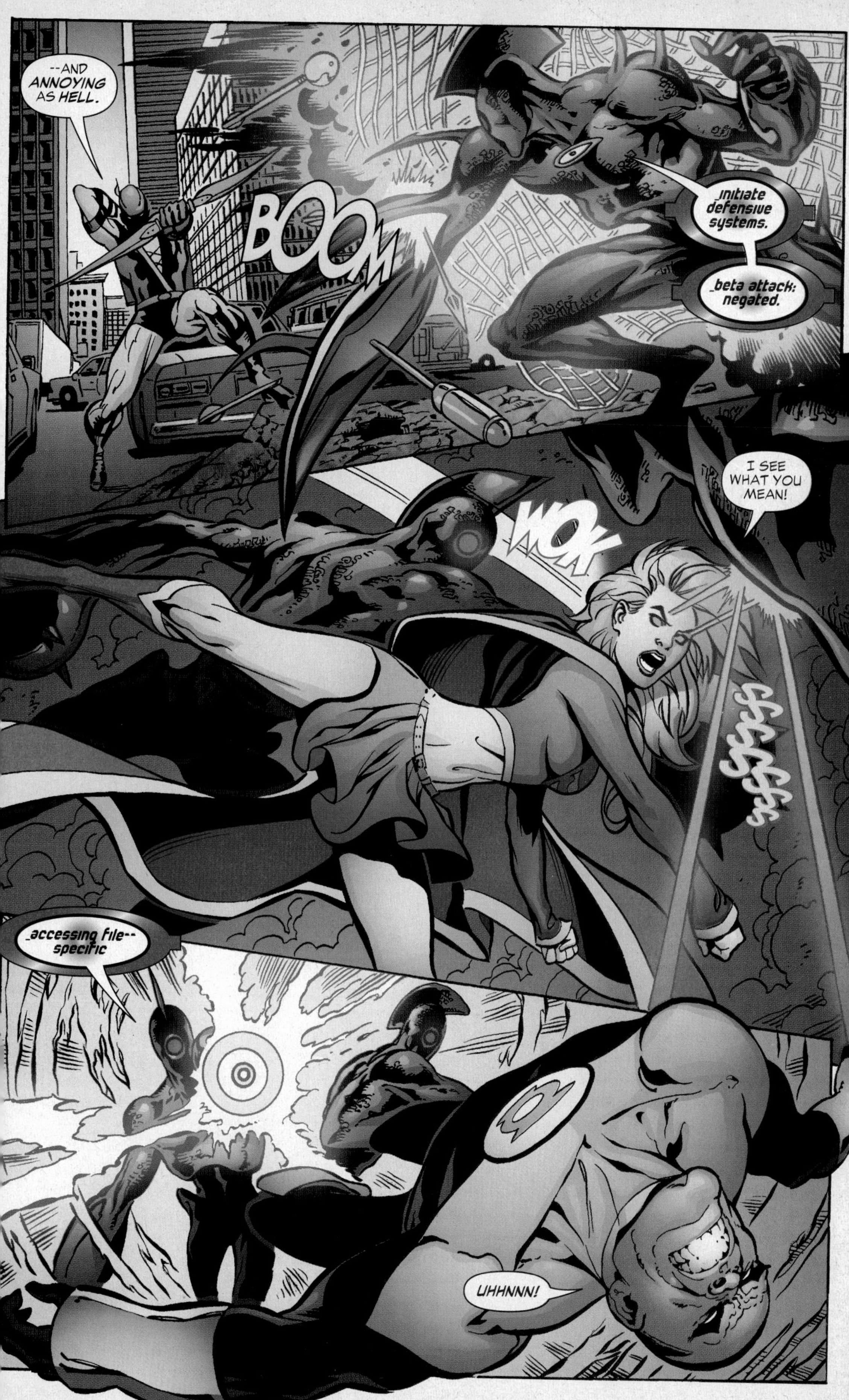
--AND ANNOYING AS HELL.
BOOM
_initiate defensive systems.
_beta attack: negated.
I SEE WHAT YOU MEAN!
WOK
_accessing file-- specific
UHHNNN!

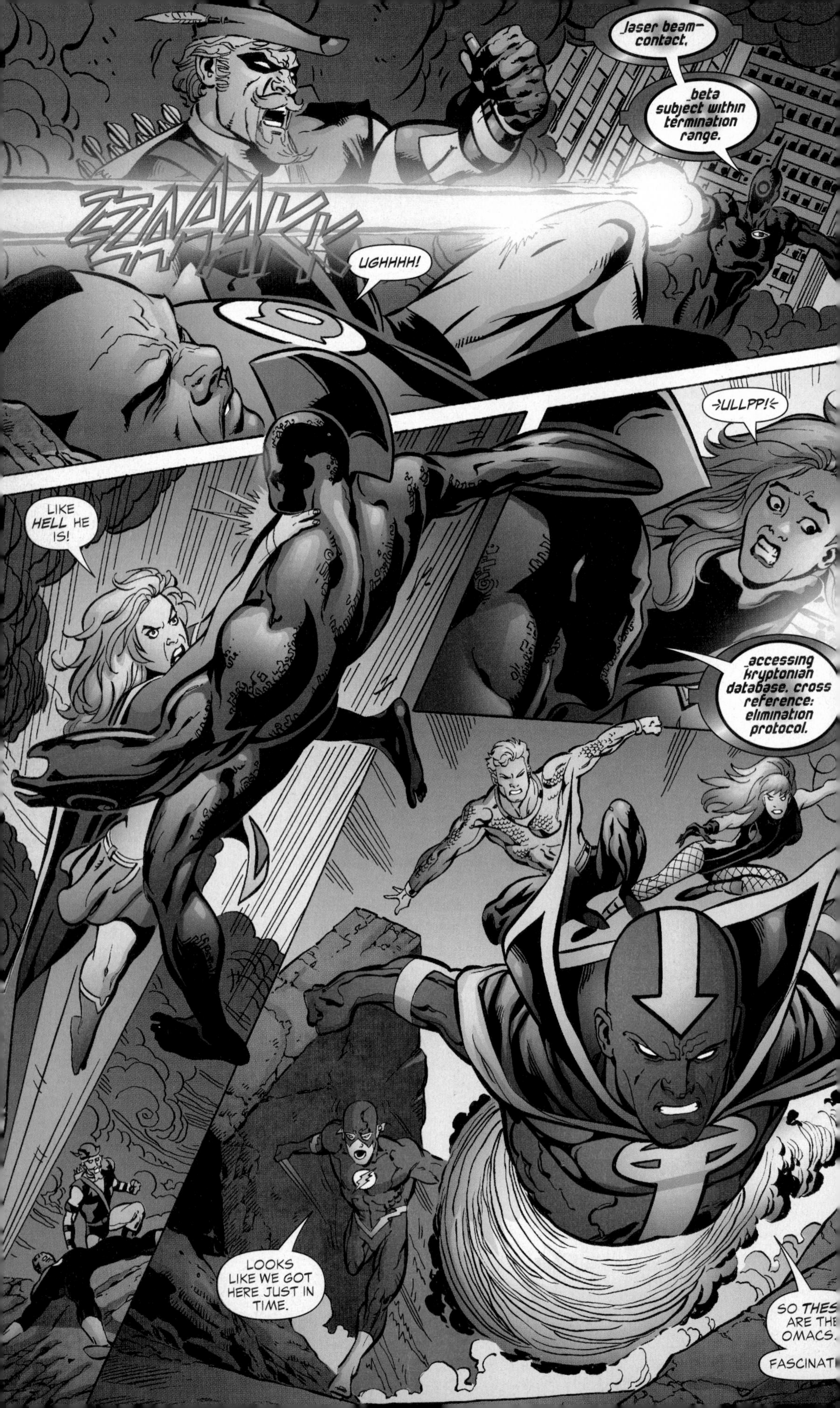
_laser beam-contact.
_beta subject within termination range.
ZZAAKK
UGHHHH!
ULLPP!
LIKE HELL HE IS!
_accessing kryptonian database. cross reference: elimination protocol.
LOOKS LIKE WE GOT HERE JUST IN TIME.

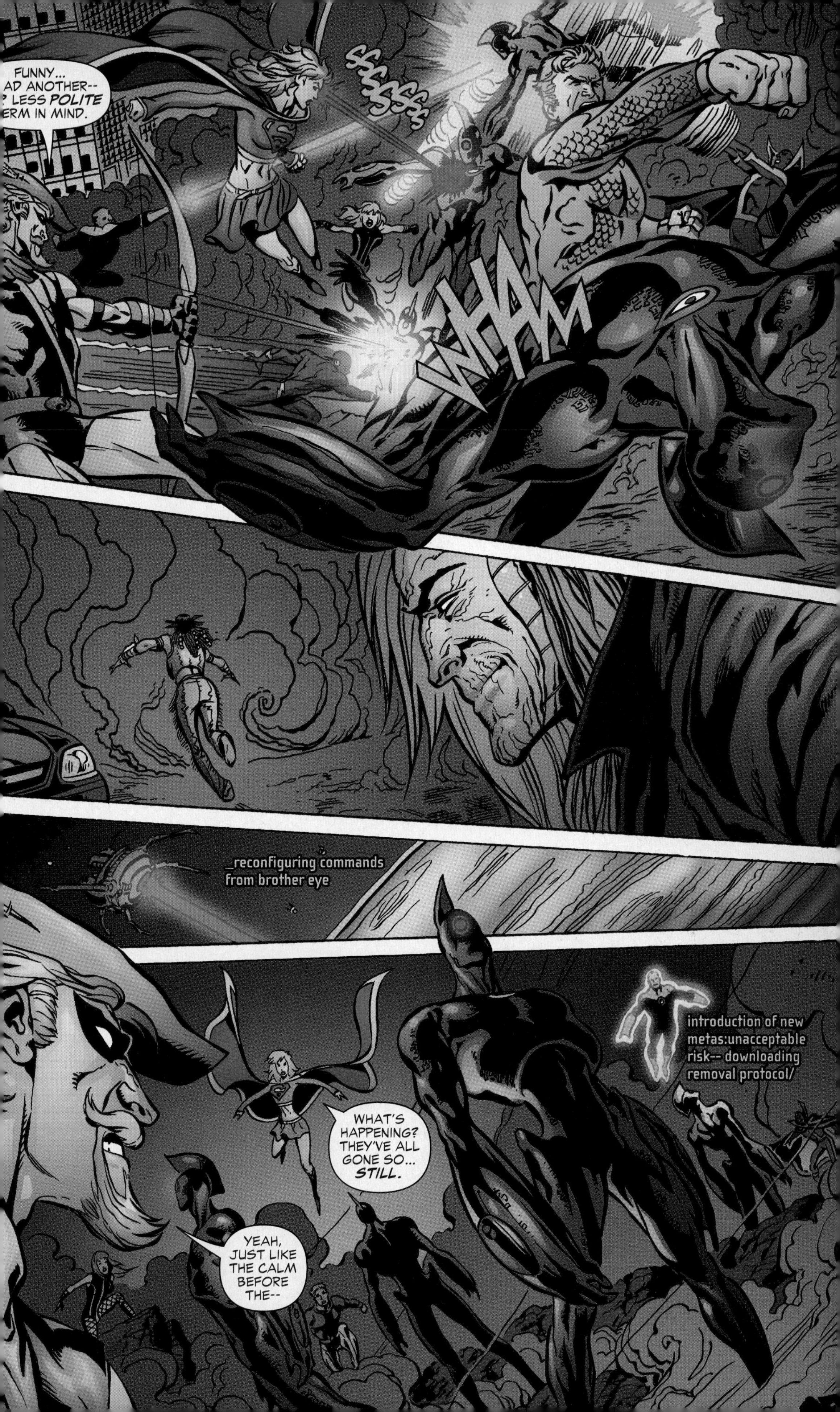
FUNNY... AD ANOTHER-- LESS POLITE ERM IN MIND.
SSSSSSS
WHAM
_reconfiguring commands from brother eye
introduction of new metas:unacceptable risk-- downloading removal protocol/
WHAT'S HAPPENING? THEY'VE ALL GONE SO... STILL.
YEAH, JUST LIKE THE CALM BEFORE THE--

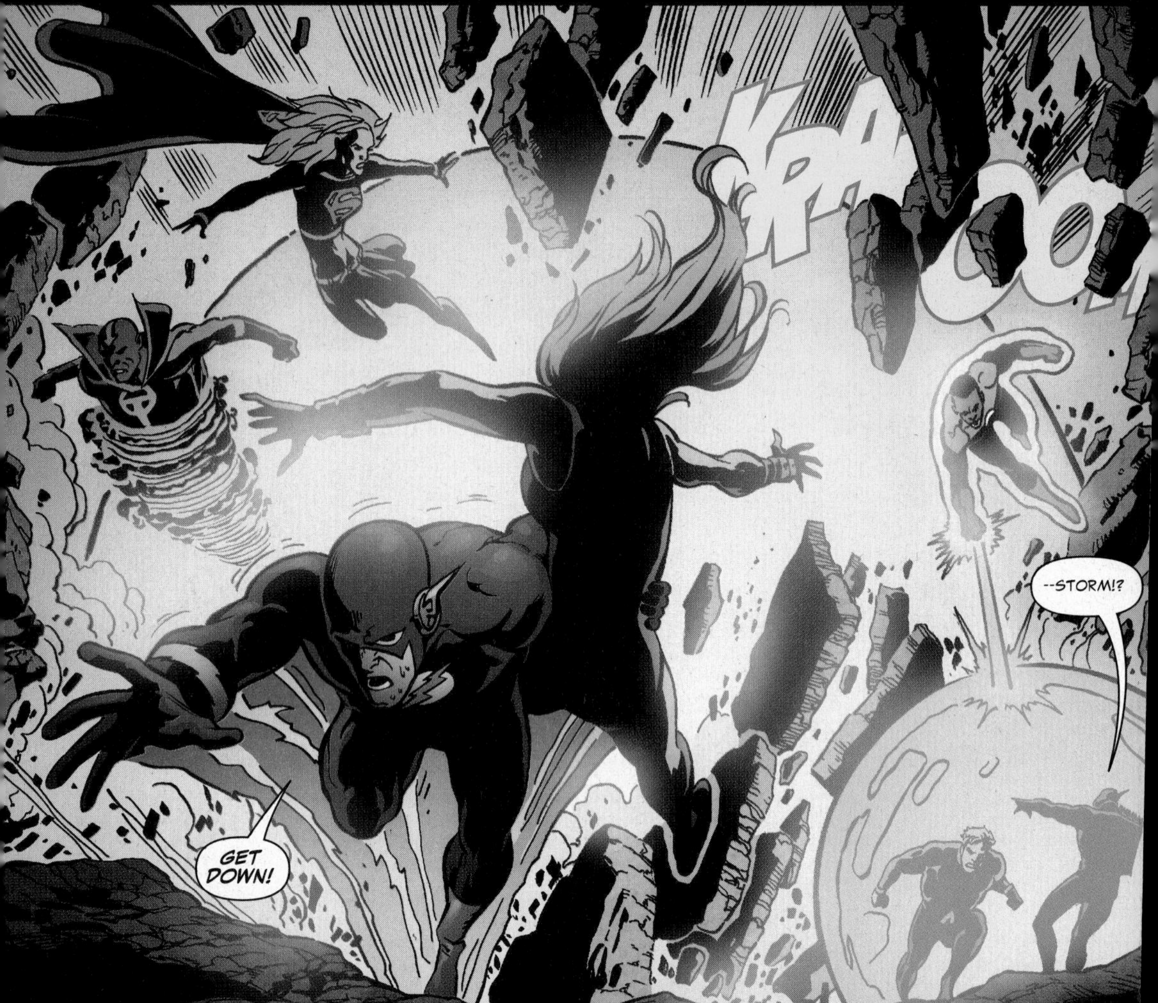
GET DOWN!
--STORM!?

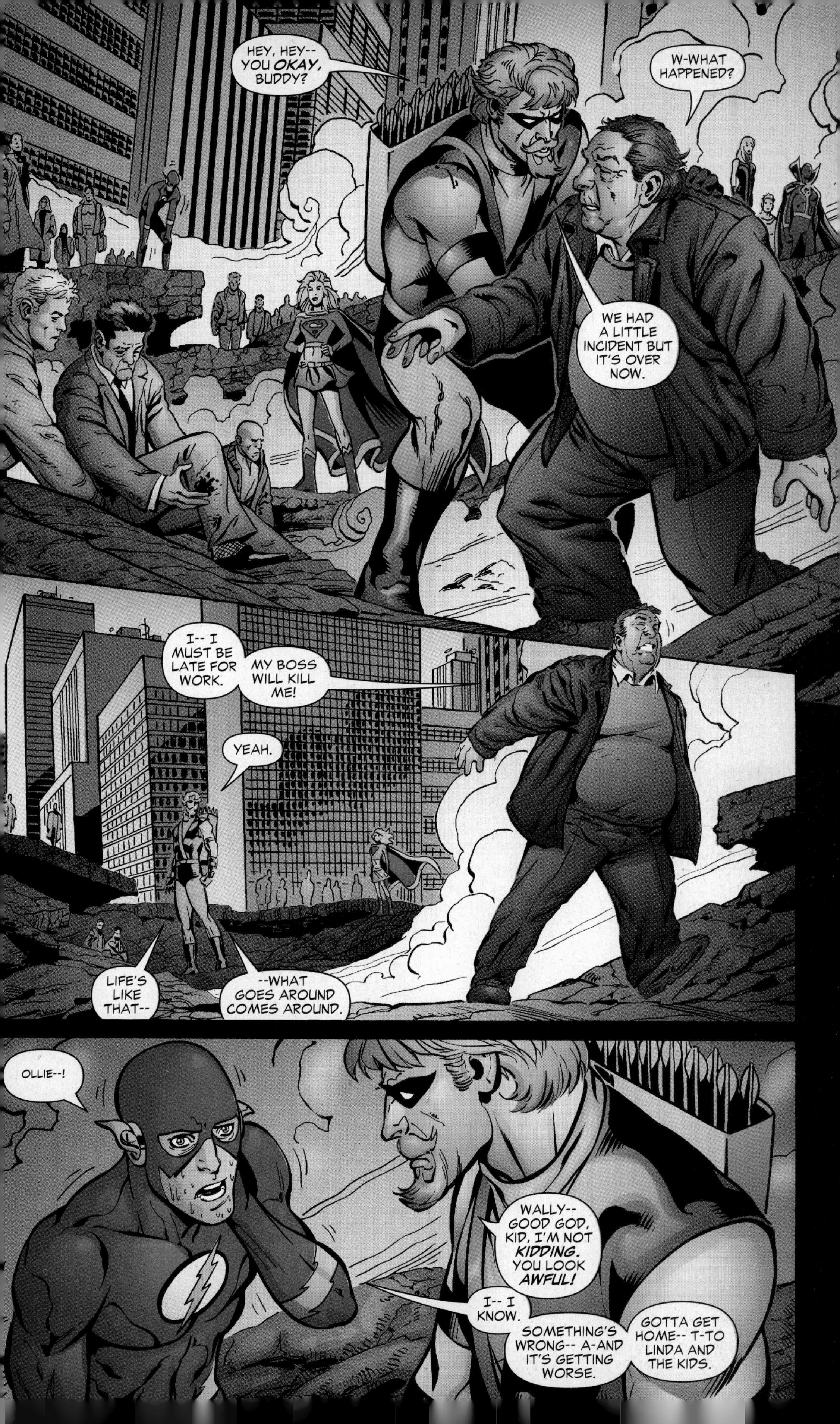
HEY, HEY-- YOU OKAY, BUDDY?
W-WHAT HAPPENED?
WE HAD A LITTLE INCIDENT BUT IT'S OVER NOW.
I-- I MUST BE LATE FOR WORK.
MY BOSS WILL KILL ME!
YEAH.
LIFE'S LIKE THAT--
--WHAT GOES AROUND COMES AROUND.
OLLIE--!
WALLY-- GOOD GOD, KID, I'M NOT KIDDING. YOU LOOK AWFUL!
I-- I KNOW.
SOMETHING'S WRONG-- A-AND IT'S GETTING WORSE.
GOTTA GET HOME-- T-TO LINDA AND THE KIDS.

GO, KID-- GO FAST.

GO NOW.

GOD FORGIVE ME, BUT HE LOOKED LIKE BARRY JUST BEFORE--

WALLY GONE

THAT TOO B I WANT TO SA HELLO

!?

YOU--?!

YOU'RE-- YOU'RE DEAD!?

COME ON, GREEN ARROW-- YOU SHOULD KNOW BETTER THAN MOST--

--DEAD'S NOT WHAT IT USED TO BE.

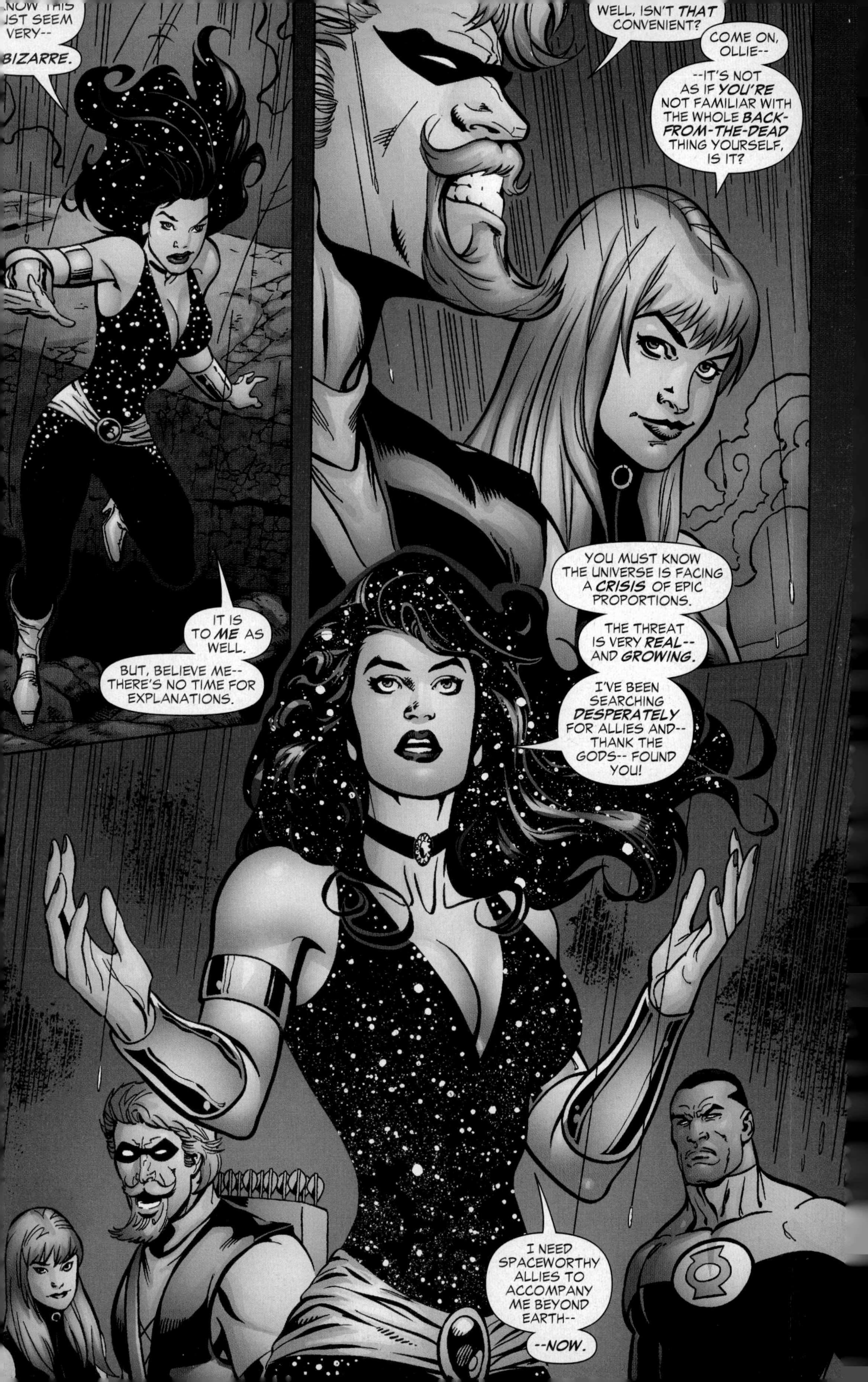

...NOW THIS ...IST SEEM VERY--
BIZARRE.
WELL, ISN'T THAT CONVENIENT?
COME ON, OLLIE--
--IT'S NOT AS IF YOU'RE NOT FAMILIAR WITH THE WHOLE BACK-FROM-THE-DEAD THING YOURSELF, IS IT?
IT IS TO ME AS WELL.
BUT, BELIEVE ME-- THERE'S NO TIME FOR EXPLANATIONS.
YOU MUST KNOW THE UNIVERSE IS FACING A CRISIS OF EPIC PROPORTIONS.
THE THREAT IS VERY REAL-- AND GROWING.
I'VE BEEN SEARCHING DESPERATELY FOR ALLIES AND-- THANK THE GODS-- FOUND YOU!
I NEED SPACEWORTHY ALLIES TO ACCOMPANY ME BEYOND EARTH--
--NOW.

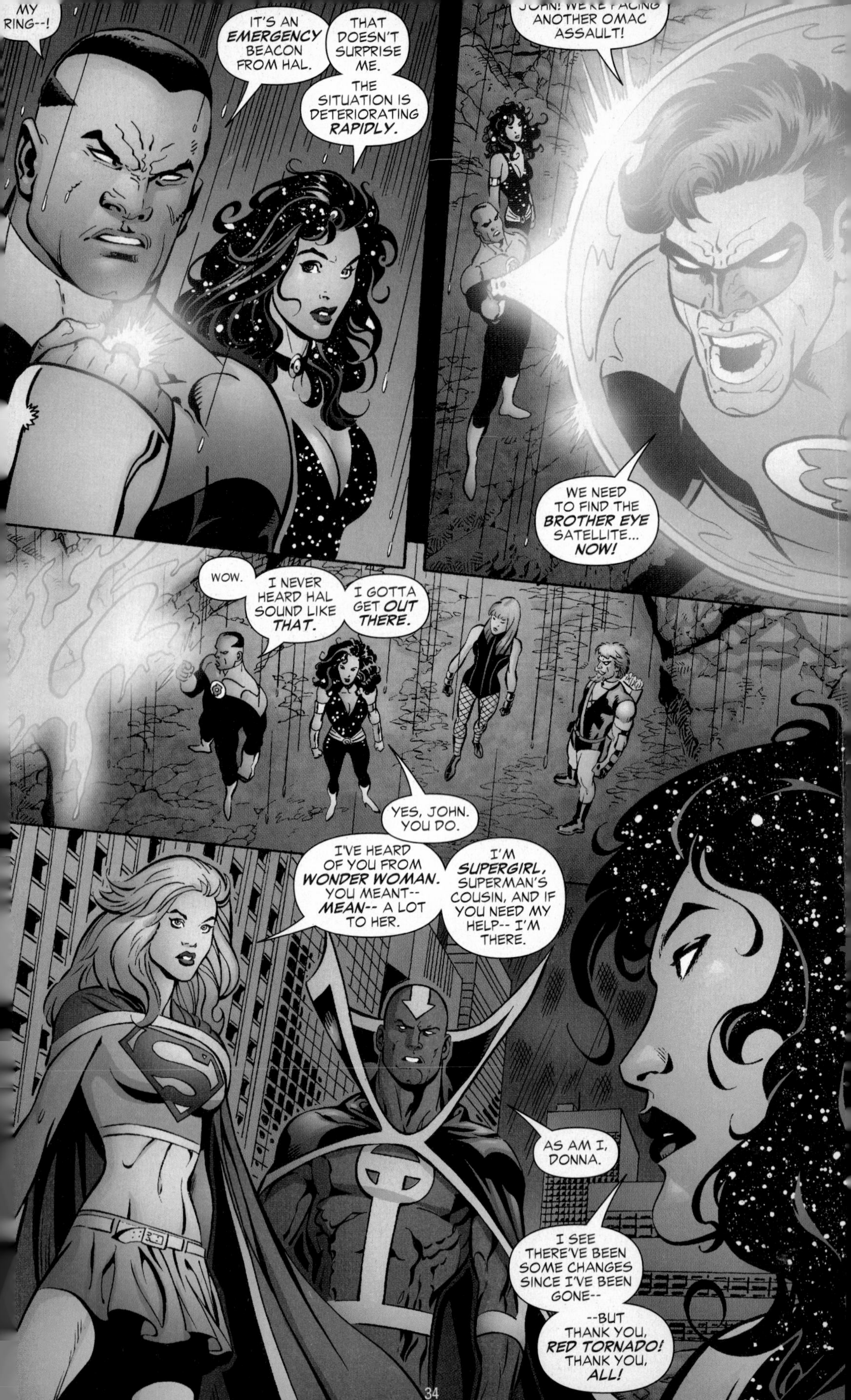
MY RING--!
IT'S AN EMERGENCY BEACON FROM HAL.
THAT DOESN'T SURPRISE ME.
THE SITUATION IS DETERIORATING RAPIDLY.
ANOTHER OMAC ASSAULT!
WE NEED TO FIND THE BROTHER EYE SATELLITE... NOW!
WOW.
I NEVER HEARD HAL SOUND LIKE THAT.
I GOTTA GET OUT THERE.
YES, JOHN. YOU DO.
I'VE HEARD OF YOU FROM WONDER WOMAN. YOU MEANT-- MEAN-- A LOT TO HER.
I'M SUPERGIRL, SUPERMAN'S COUSIN, AND IF YOU NEED MY HELP-- I'M THERE.
AS AM I, DONNA.
I SEE THERE'VE BEEN SOME CHANGES SINCE I'VE BEEN GONE--
--BUT THANK YOU, RED TORNADO! THANK YOU, ALL!

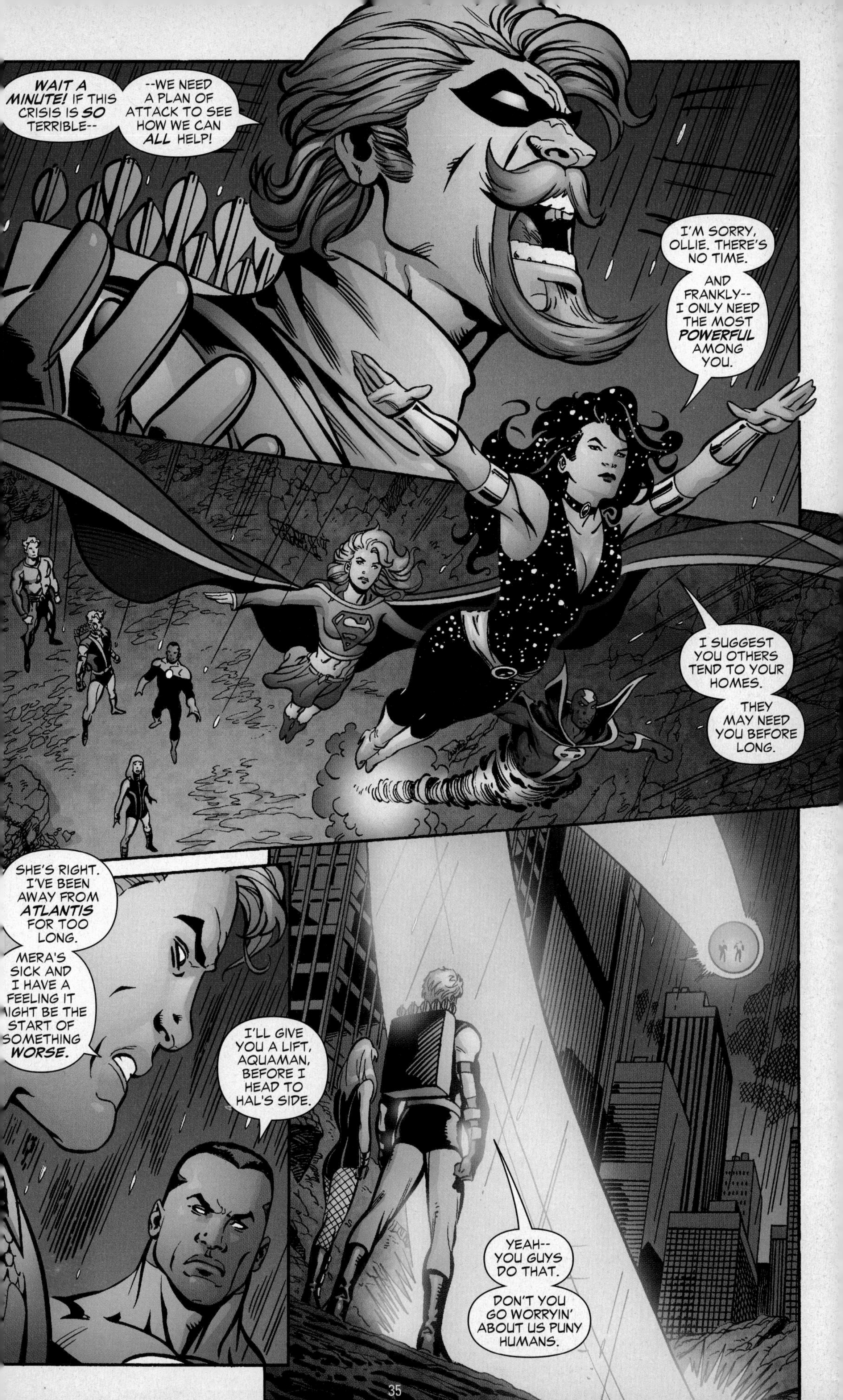
WAIT A MINUTE! IF THIS CRISIS IS SO TERRIBLE--
--WE NEED A PLAN OF ATTACK TO SEE HOW WE CAN ALL HELP!
I'M SORRY, OLLIE. THERE'S NO TIME.
AND FRANKLY-- I ONLY NEED THE MOST POWERFUL AMONG YOU.
I SUGGEST YOU OTHERS TEND TO YOUR HOMES.
THEY MAY NEED YOU BEFORE LONG.
SHE'S RIGHT. I'VE BEEN AWAY FROM ATLANTIS FOR TOO LONG.
MERA'S SICK AND I HAVE A FEELING IT MIGHT BE THE START OF SOMETHING WORSE.
I'LL GIVE YOU A LIFT, AQUAMAN, BEFORE I HEAD TO HAL'S SIDE.
YEAH-- YOU GUYS DO THAT.
DON'T YOU GO WORRYIN' ABOUT US PUNY HUMANS.

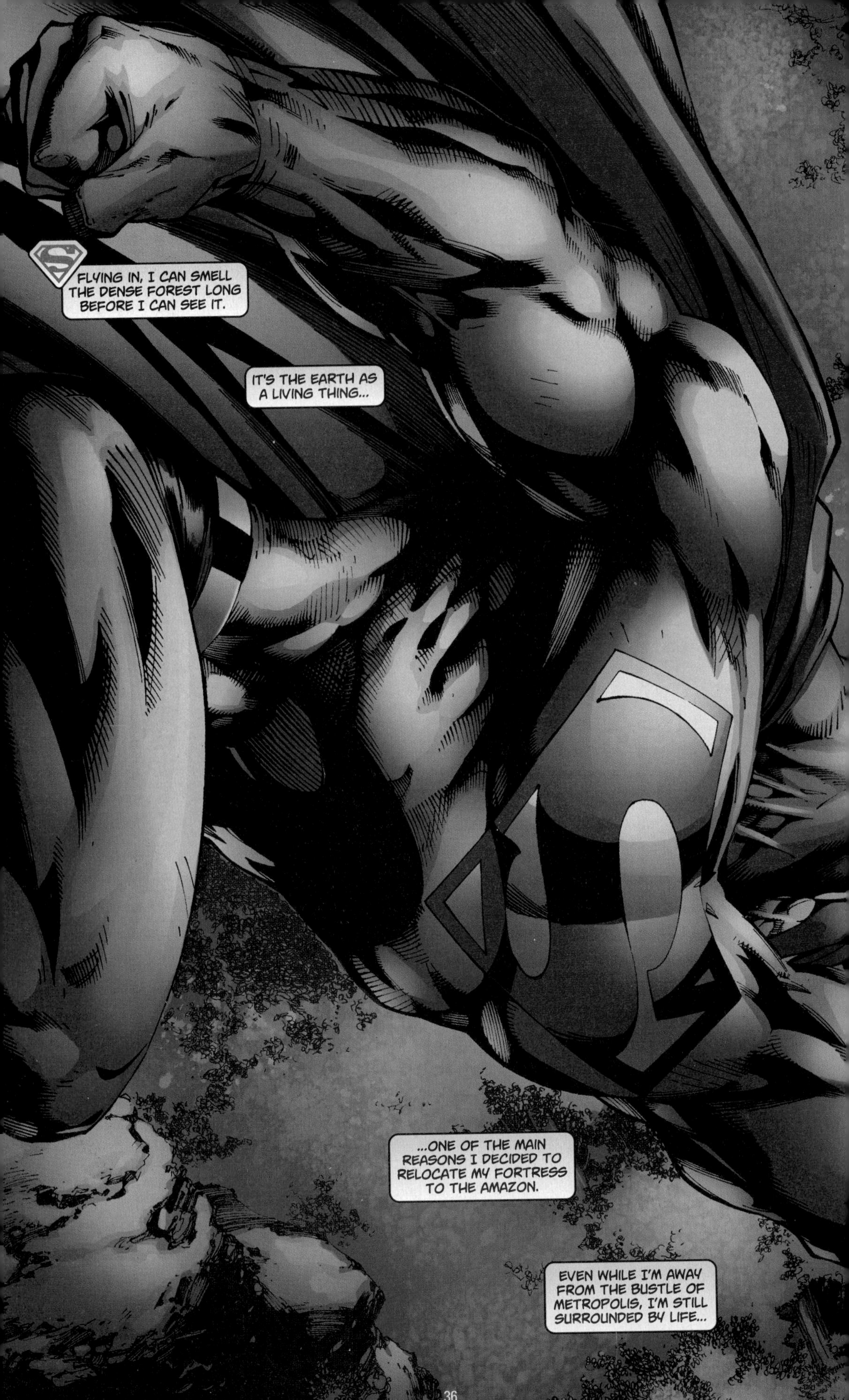

FLYING IN, I CAN SMELL THE DENSE FOREST LONG BEFORE I CAN SEE IT.
IT'S THE EARTH AS A LIVING THING...
...ONE OF THE MAIN REASONS I DECIDED TO RELOCATE MY FORTRESS TO THE AMAZON.
EVEN WHILE I'M AWAY FROM THE BUSTLE OF METROPOLIS, I'M STILL SURROUNDED BY LIFE...

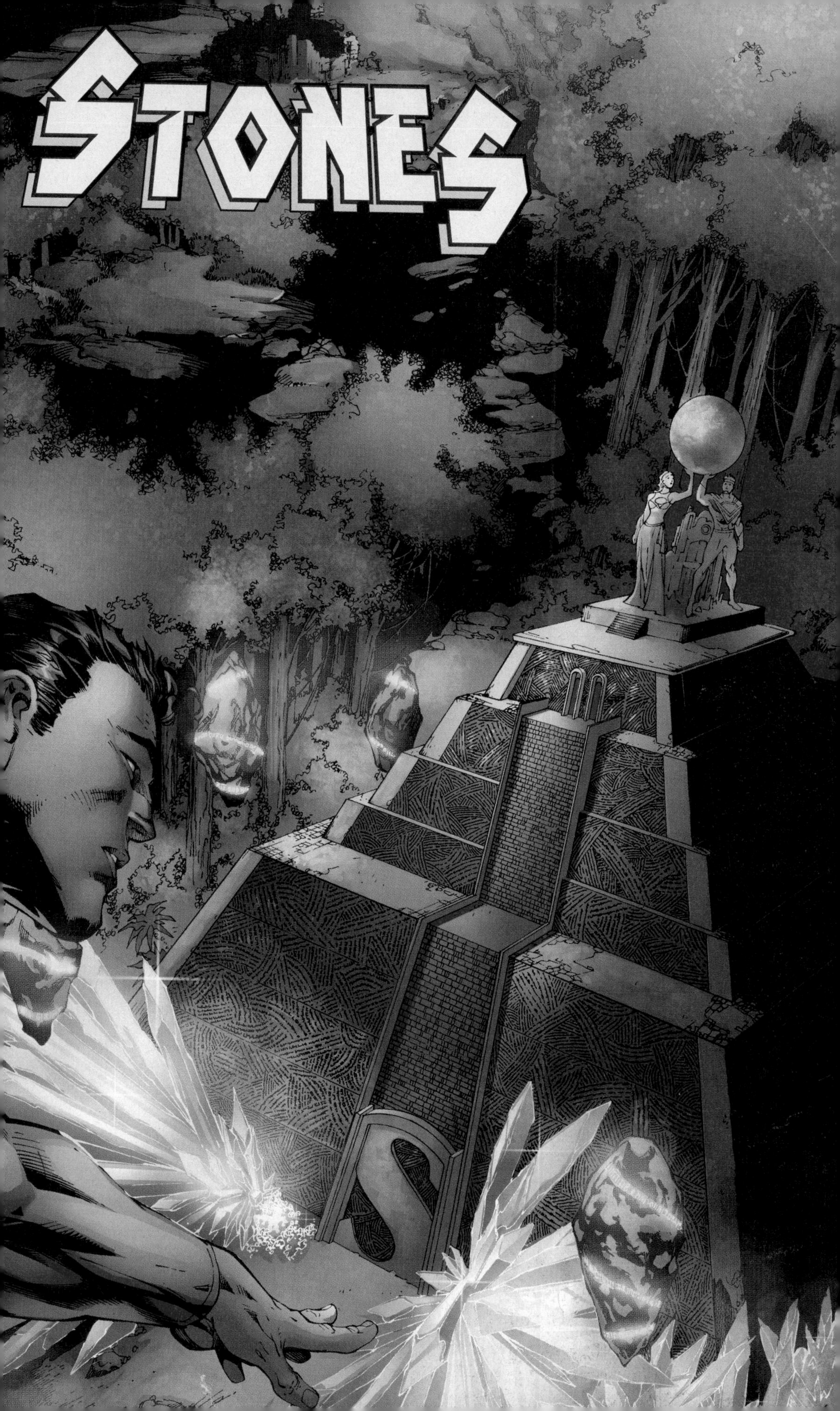
STONES

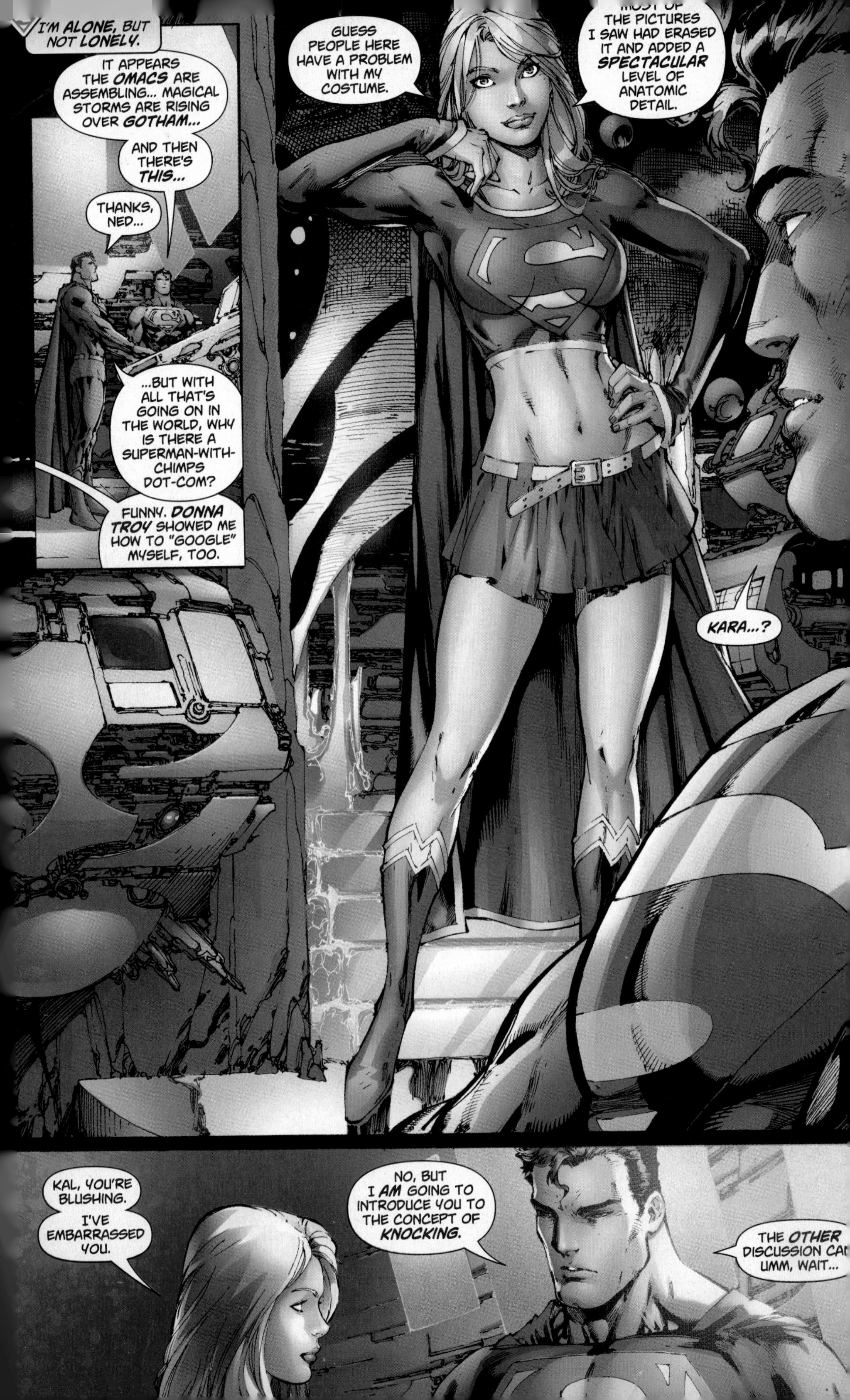
I'M ALONE, BUT NOT LONELY.
IT APPEARS THE OMACS ARE ASSEMBLING... MAGICAL STORMS ARE RISING OVER GOTHAM...
AND THEN THERE'S THIS...
THANKS, NED...
...BUT WITH ALL THAT'S GOING ON IN THE WORLD, WHY IS THERE A SUPERMAN-WITH-CHIMPS DOT-COM?
FUNNY. DONNA TROY SHOWED ME HOW TO "GOOGLE" MYSELF, TOO.
GUESS PEOPLE HERE HAVE A PROBLEM WITH MY COSTUME.
THE PICTURES I SAW HAD ERASED IT AND ADDED A SPECTACULAR LEVEL OF ANATOMIC DETAIL.
KARA...?
KAL, YOU'RE BLUSHING.
I'VE EMBARRASSED YOU.
NO, BUT I AM GOING TO INTRODUCE YOU TO THE CONCEPT OF KNOCKING.
THE OTHER DISCUSSION CA
UMM, WAIT...

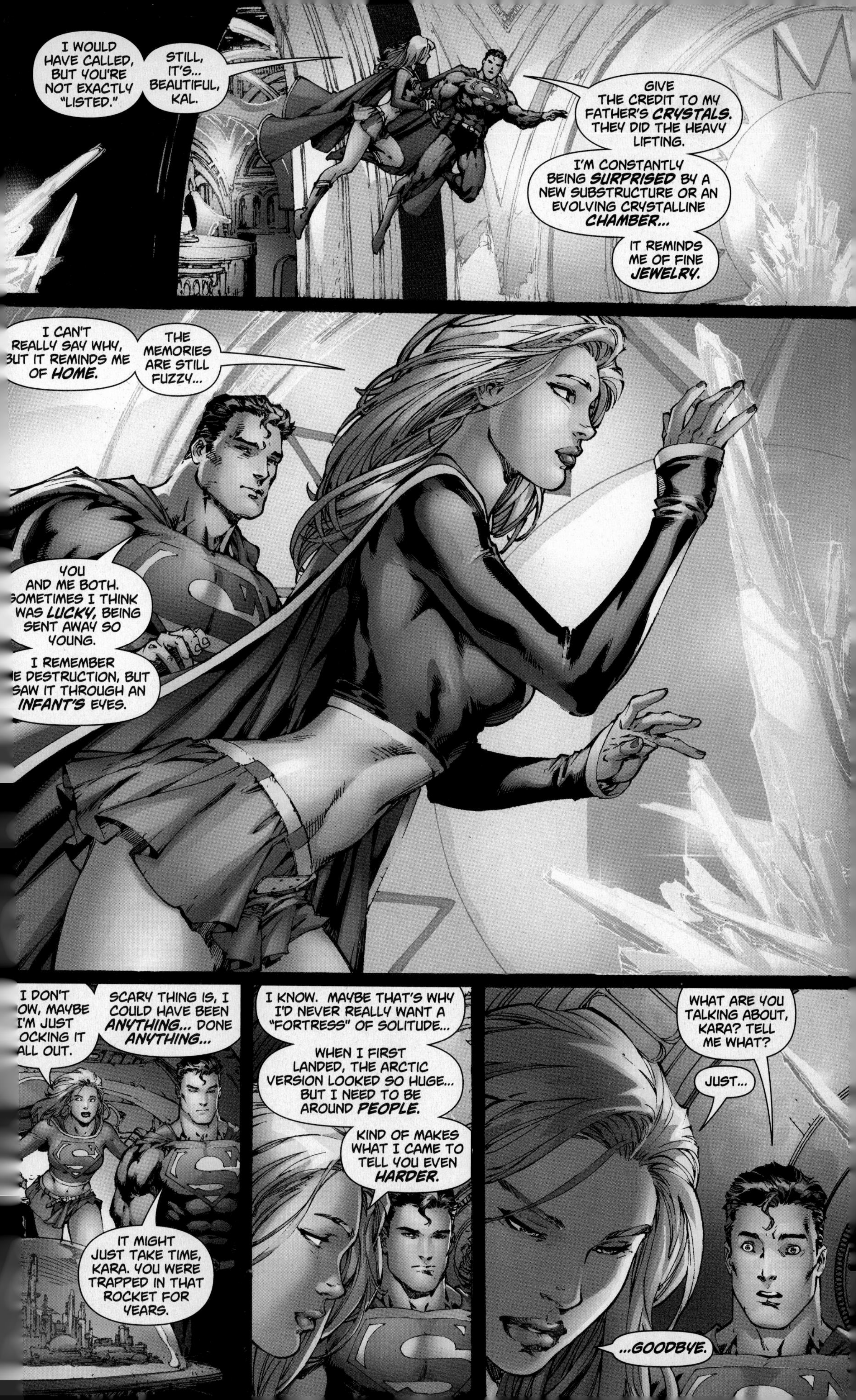

I WOULD HAVE CALLED, BUT YOU'RE NOT EXACTLY "LISTED."
STILL, IT'S... BEAUTIFUL, KAL.
GIVE THE CREDIT TO MY FATHER'S **CRYSTALS.** THEY DID THE HEAVY LIFTING.
I'M CONSTANTLY BEING **SURPRISED** BY A NEW SUBSTRUCTURE OR AN EVOLVING CRYSTALLINE **CHAMBER...**
IT REMINDS ME OF FINE **JEWELRY.**
I CAN'T REALLY SAY WHY, BUT IT REMINDS ME OF **HOME.**
THE MEMORIES ARE STILL FUZZY...
YOU AND ME BOTH. OMETIMES I THINK WAS **LUCKY,** BEING SENT AWAY SO YOUNG.
I REMEMBER E DESTRUCTION, BUT SAW IT THROUGH AN **INFANT'S** EYES.
I DON'T OW, MAYBE I'M JUST OCKING IT ALL OUT.
SCARY THING IS, I COULD HAVE BEEN **ANYTHING...** DONE **ANYTHING...**
IT MIGHT JUST TAKE TIME, KARA. YOU WERE TRAPPED IN THAT ROCKET FOR YEARS.
I KNOW. MAYBE THAT'S WHY I'D NEVER REALLY WANT A "FORTRESS" OF SOLITUDE...
WHEN I FIRST LANDED, THE ARCTIC VERSION LOOKED SO HUGE... BUT I NEED TO BE AROUND **PEOPLE.**
KIND OF MAKES WHAT I CAME TO TELL YOU EVEN **HARDER.**
WHAT ARE YOU TALKING ABOUT, KARA? TELL ME WHAT?
JUST...
...GOODBYE.

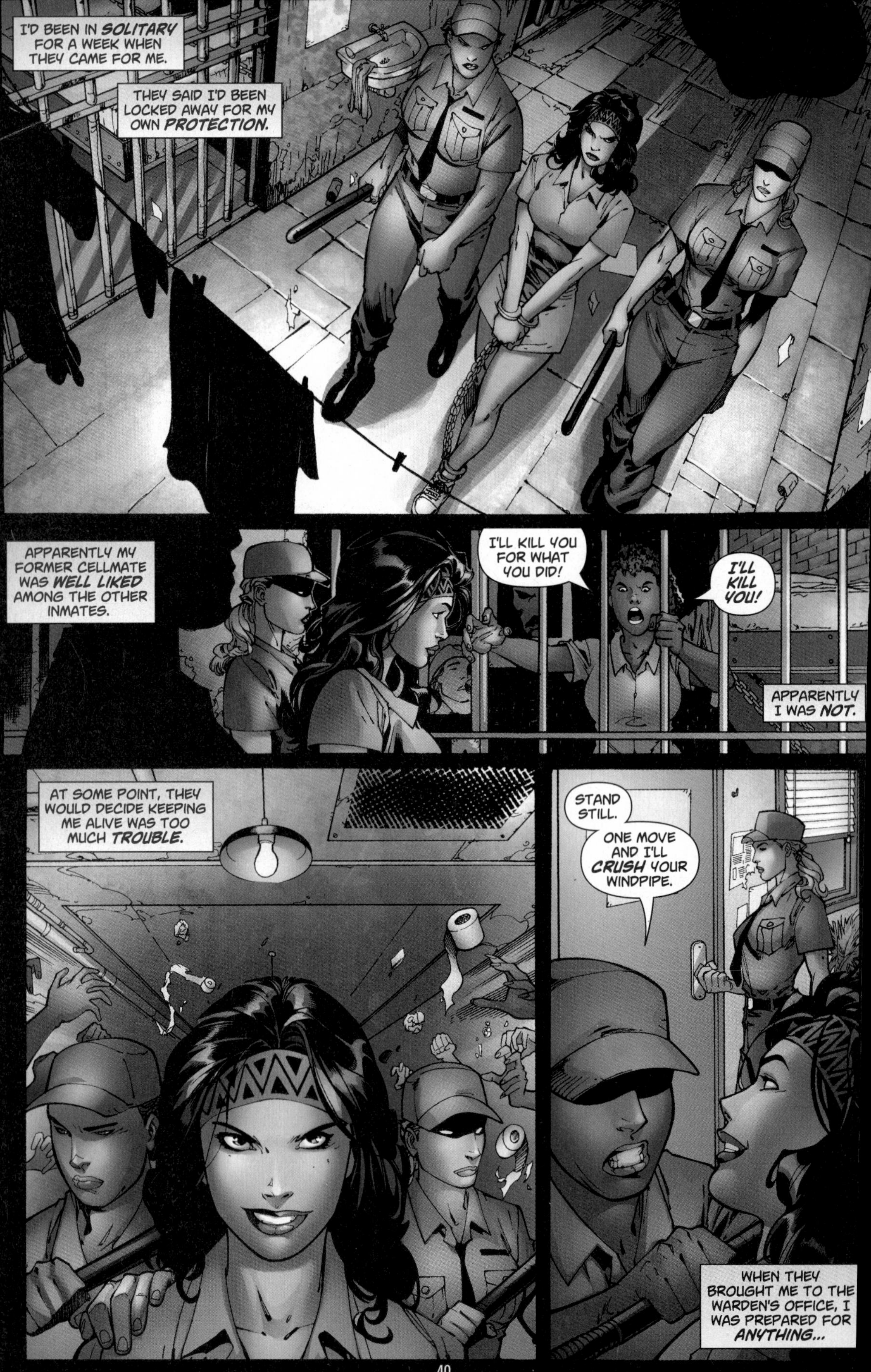
I'D BEEN IN SOLITARY FOR A WEEK WHEN THEY CAME FOR ME.
THEY SAID I'D BEEN LOCKED AWAY FOR MY OWN PROTECTION.
APPARENTLY MY FORMER CELLMATE WAS WELL LIKED AMONG THE OTHER INMATES.
I'LL KILL YOU FOR WHAT YOU DID!
I'LL KILL YOU!
APPARENTLY I WAS NOT.
AT SOME POINT, THEY WOULD DECIDE KEEPING ME ALIVE WAS TOO MUCH TROUBLE.
STAND STILL.
ONE MOVE AND I'LL CRUSH YOUR WINDPIPE.
WHEN THEY BROUGHT ME TO THE WARDEN'S OFFICE, I WAS PREPARED FOR ANYTHING...

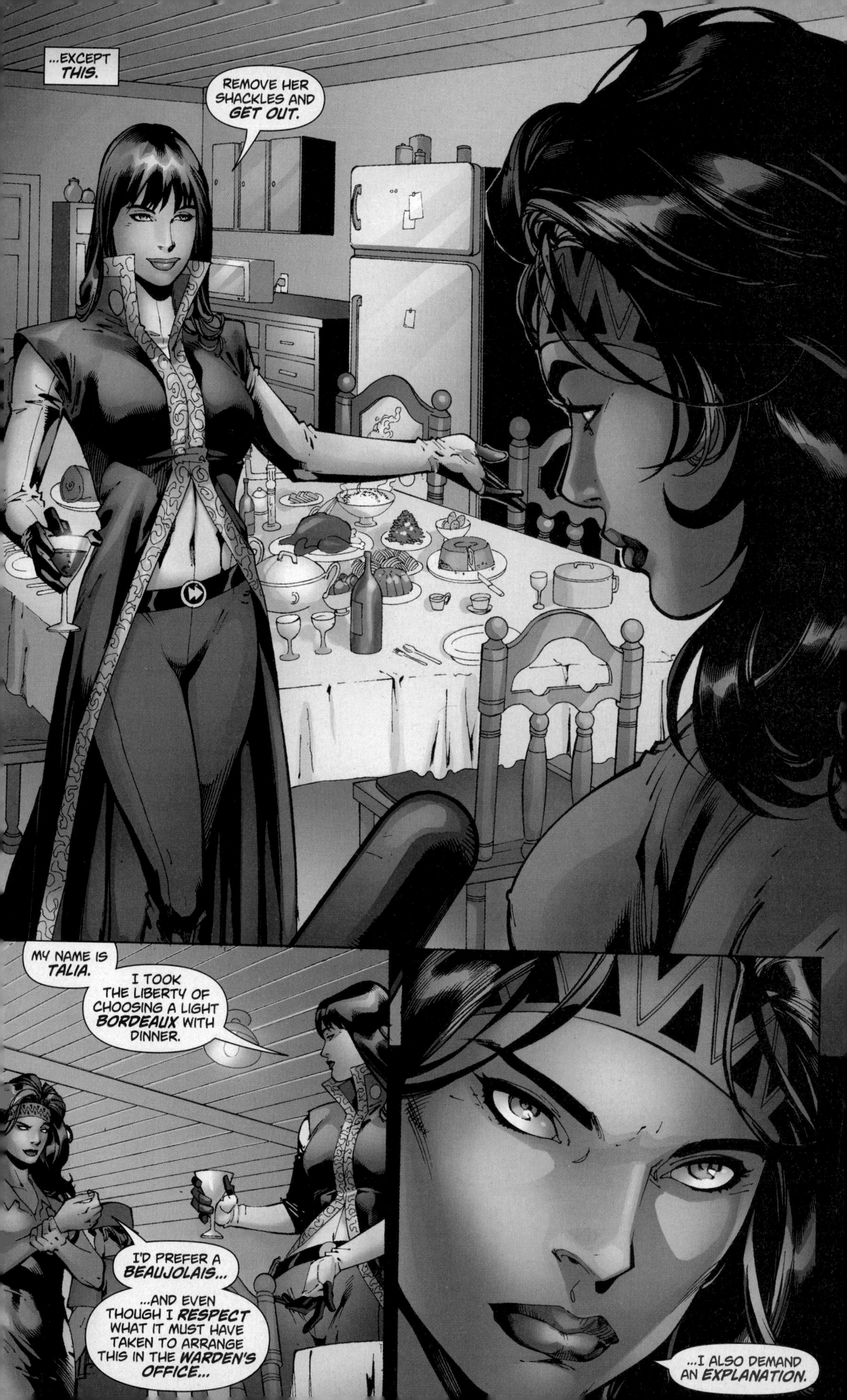
...EXCEPT THIS.
REMOVE HER SHACKLES AND GET OUT.
MY NAME IS TALIA.
I TOOK THE LIBERTY OF CHOOSING A LIGHT BORDEAUX WITH DINNER.
I'D PREFER A BEAUJOLAIS...
...AND EVEN THOUGH I RESPECT WHAT IT MUST HAVE TAKEN TO ARRANGE THIS IN THE WARDEN'S OFFICE...
...I ALSO DEMAND AN EXPLANATION.

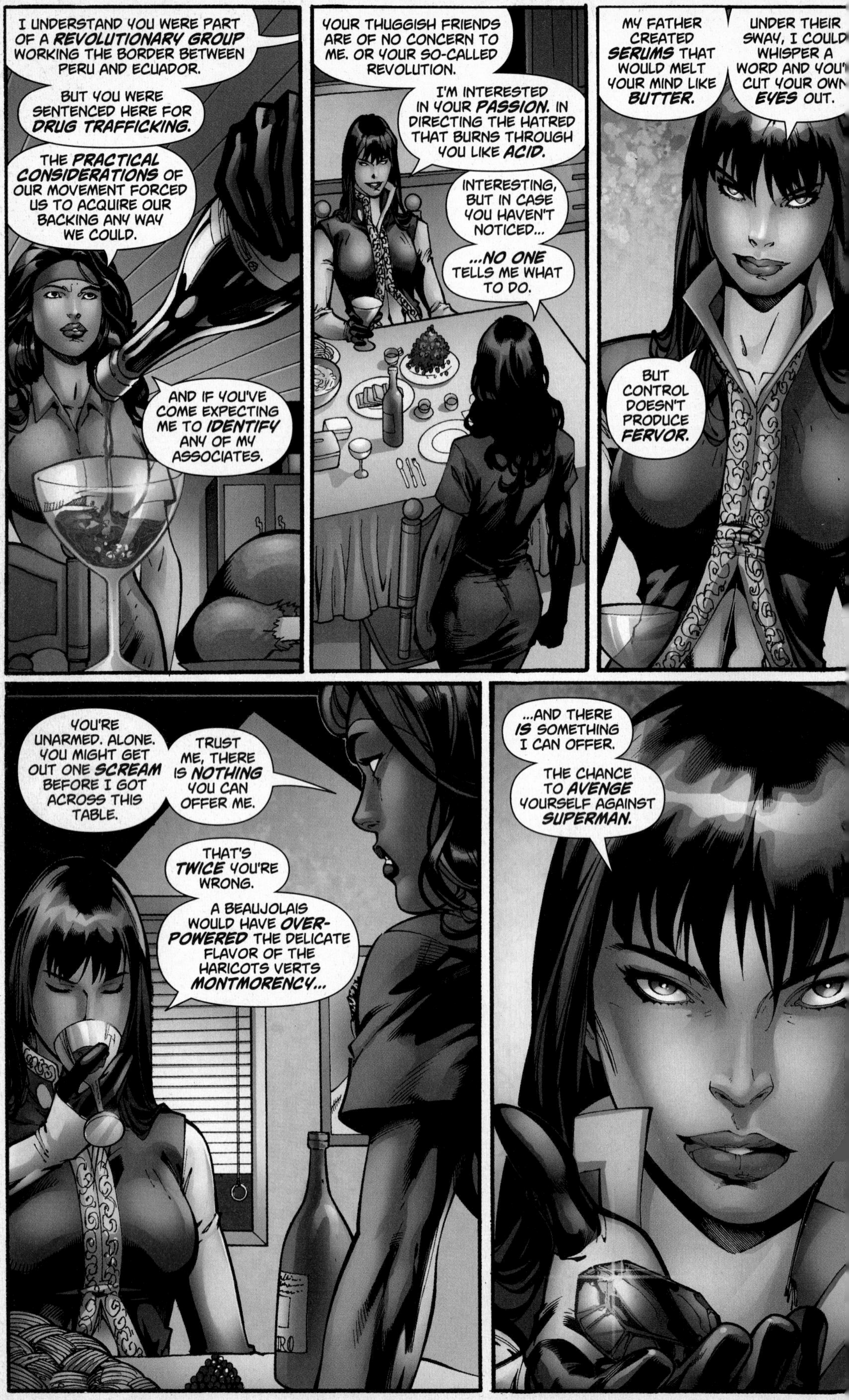
I UNDERSTAND YOU WERE PART OF A REVOLUTIONARY GROUP WORKING THE BORDER BETWEEN PERU AND ECUADOR.
BUT YOU WERE SENTENCED HERE FOR DRUG TRAFFICKING.
THE PRACTICAL CONSIDERATIONS OF OUR MOVEMENT FORCED US TO ACQUIRE OUR BACKING ANY WAY WE COULD.
AND IF YOU'VE COME EXPECTING ME TO IDENTIFY ANY OF MY ASSOCIATES.
YOUR THUGGISH FRIENDS ARE OF NO CONCERN TO ME. OR YOUR SO-CALLED REVOLUTION.
I'M INTERESTED IN YOUR PASSION. IN DIRECTING THE HATRED THAT BURNS THROUGH YOU LIKE ACID.
INTERESTING, BUT IN CASE YOU HAVEN'T NOTICED...
...NO ONE TELLS ME WHAT TO DO.
MY FATHER CREATED SERUMS THAT WOULD MELT YOUR MIND LIKE BUTTER.
UNDER THEIR SWAY, I COULD WHISPER A WORD AND YOU'D CUT YOUR OWN EYES OUT.
BUT CONTROL DOESN'T PRODUCE FERVOR.
YOU'RE UNARMED. ALONE. YOU MIGHT GET OUT ONE SCREAM BEFORE I GOT ACROSS THIS TABLE.
TRUST ME, THERE IS NOTHING YOU CAN OFFER ME.
THAT'S TWICE YOU'RE WRONG.
A BEAUJOLAIS WOULD HAVE OVER-POWERED THE DELICATE FLAVOR OF THE HARICOTS VERTS MONTMORENCY...
...AND THERE IS SOMETHING I CAN OFFER.
THE CHANCE TO AVENGE YOURSELF AGAINST SUPERMAN.

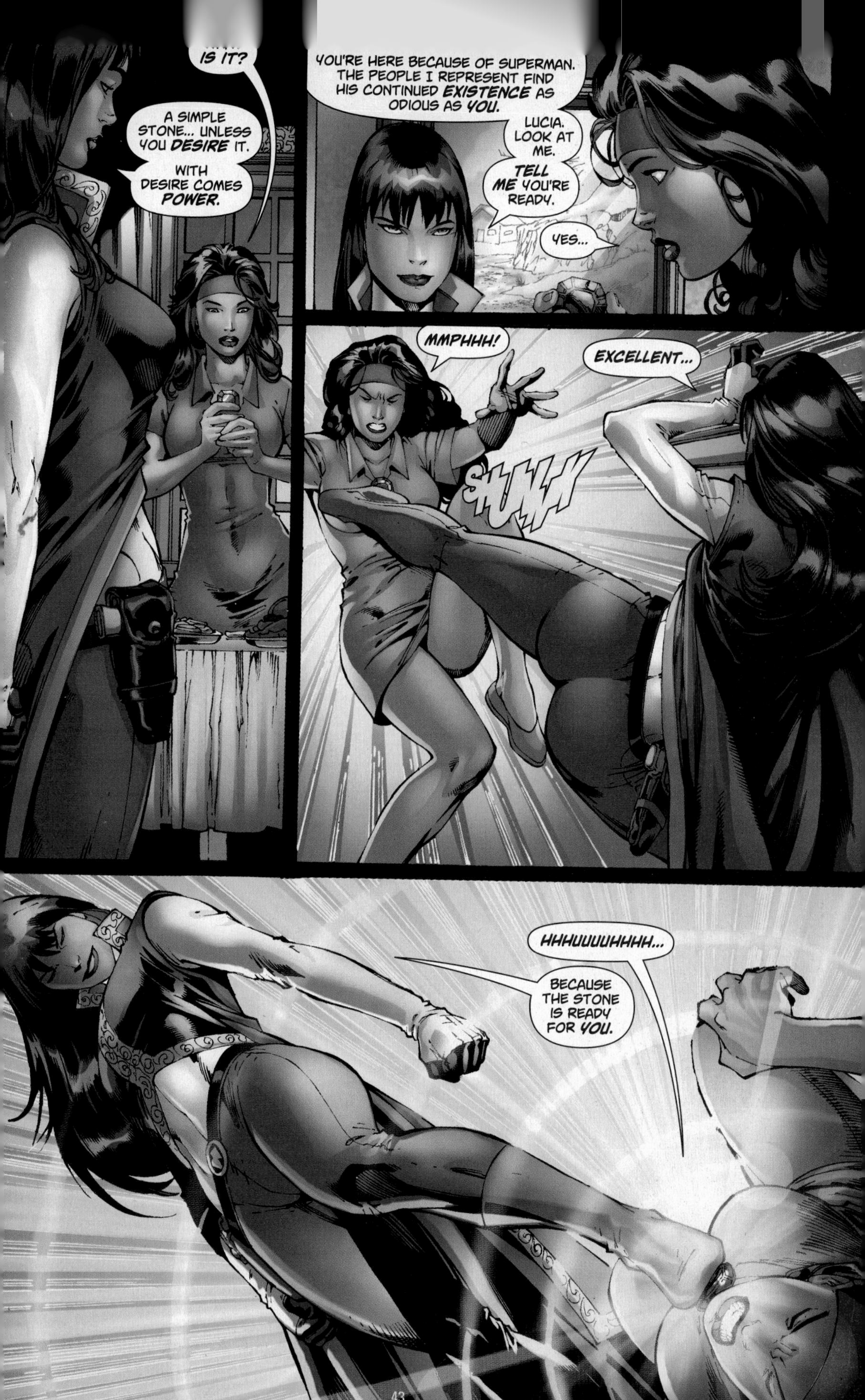
IS IT?
A SIMPLE STONE... UNLESS YOU DESIRE IT.
WITH DESIRE COMES POWER.
YOU'RE HERE BECAUSE OF SUPERMAN. THE PEOPLE I REPRESENT FIND HIS CONTINUED EXISTENCE AS ODIOUS AS YOU.
LUCIA. LOOK AT ME.
TELL ME YOU'RE READY.
YES...
MMPHHH!
EXCELLENT...
SHUNK
HHHUUUUHHHH...
BECAUSE THE STONE IS READY FOR YOU.

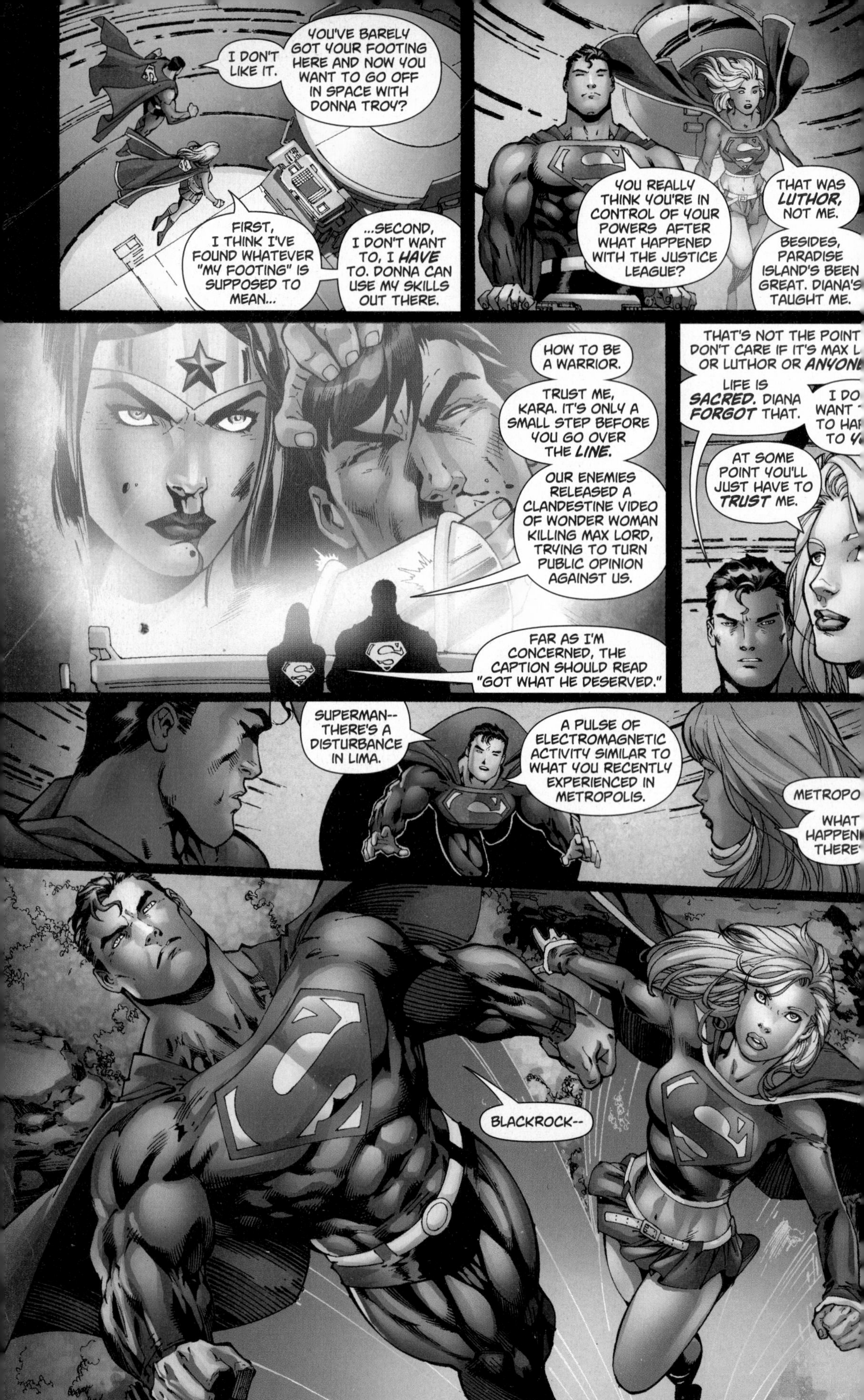

YOU'VE BARELY GOT YOUR FOOTING HERE AND NOW YOU WANT TO GO OFF IN SPACE WITH DONNA TROY?
I DON'T LIKE IT.
FIRST, I THINK I'VE FOUND WHATEVER "MY FOOTING" IS SUPPOSED TO MEAN...
...SECOND, I DON'T WANT TO, I HAVE TO. DONNA CAN USE MY SKILLS OUT THERE.
YOU REALLY THINK YOU'RE IN CONTROL OF YOUR POWERS AFTER WHAT HAPPENED WITH THE JUSTICE LEAGUE?
THAT WAS LUTHOR, NOT ME.
BESIDES, PARADISE ISLAND'S BEEN GREAT. DIANA'S TAUGHT ME.
HOW TO BE A WARRIOR.
TRUST ME, KARA. IT'S ONLY A SMALL STEP BEFORE YOU GO OVER THE LINE.
OUR ENEMIES RELEASED A CLANDESTINE VIDEO OF WONDER WOMAN KILLING MAX LORD, TRYING TO TURN PUBLIC OPINION AGAINST US.
FAR AS I'M CONCERNED, THE CAPTION SHOULD READ "GOT WHAT HE DESERVED."
THAT'S NOT THE POINT
DON'T CARE IF IT'S MAX L
OR LUTHOR OR ANYON
LIFE IS SACRED. DIANA FORGOT THAT.
I DO
WANT
TO HAP
TO Y
AT SOME POINT YOU'LL JUST HAVE TO TRUST ME.
SUPERMAN-- THERE'S A DISTURBANCE IN LIMA.
A PULSE OF ELECTROMAGNETIC ACTIVITY SIMILAR TO WHAT YOU RECENTLY EXPERIENCED IN METROPOLIS.
METROPO
WHAT HAPPEN THERE
BLACKROCK--

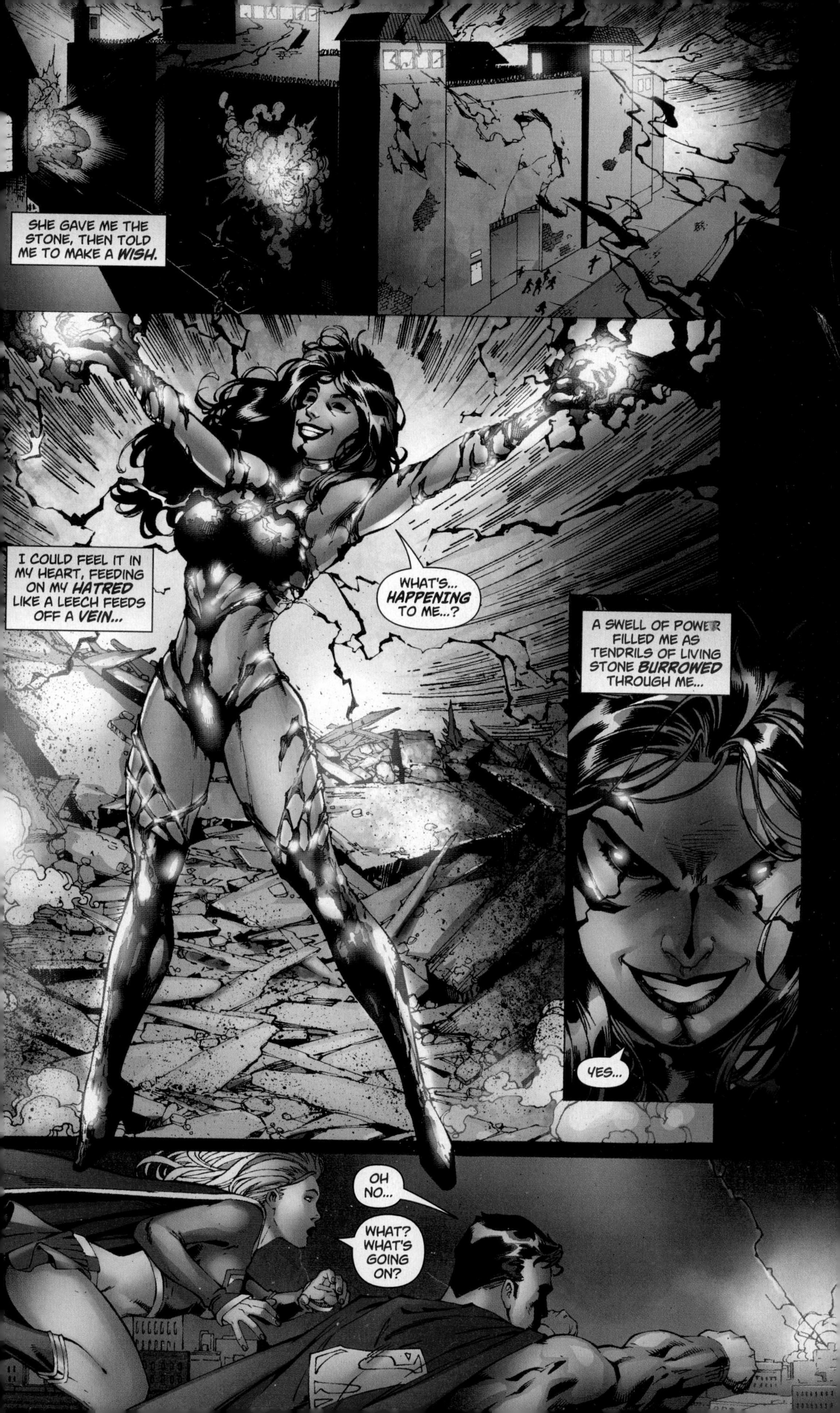
SHE GAVE ME THE STONE, THEN TOLD ME TO MAKE A WISH.
I COULD FEEL IT IN MY HEART, FEEDING ON MY HATRED LIKE A LEECH FEEDS OFF A VEIN...
WHAT'S... HAPPENING TO ME...?
A SWELL OF POWER FILLED ME AS TENDRILS OF LIVING STONE BURROWED THROUGH ME...
YES...
OH NO...
WHAT? WHAT'S GOING ON?

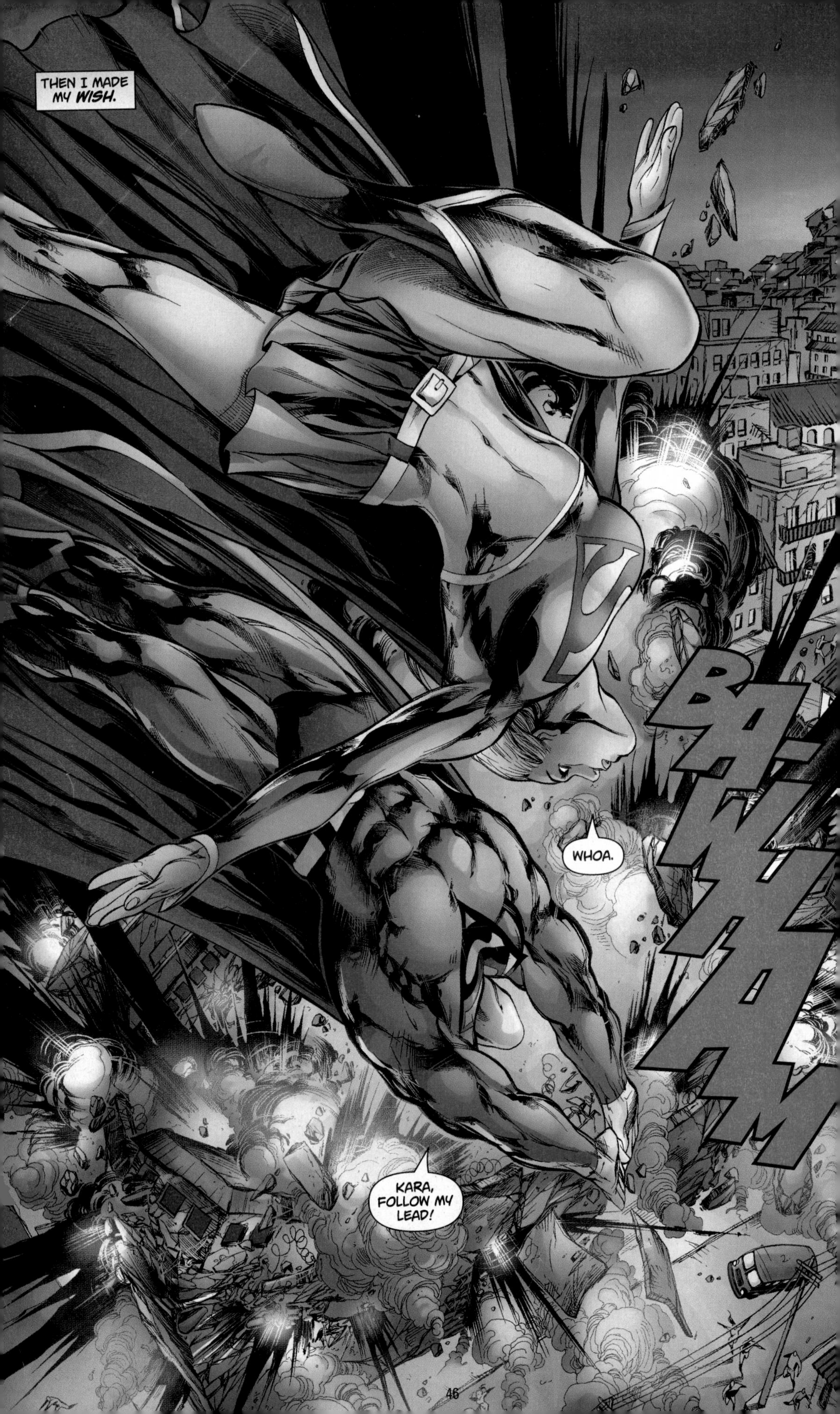
THEN I MADE MY WISH.
WHOA.
KARA, FOLLOW MY LEAD!
BA-WHAM

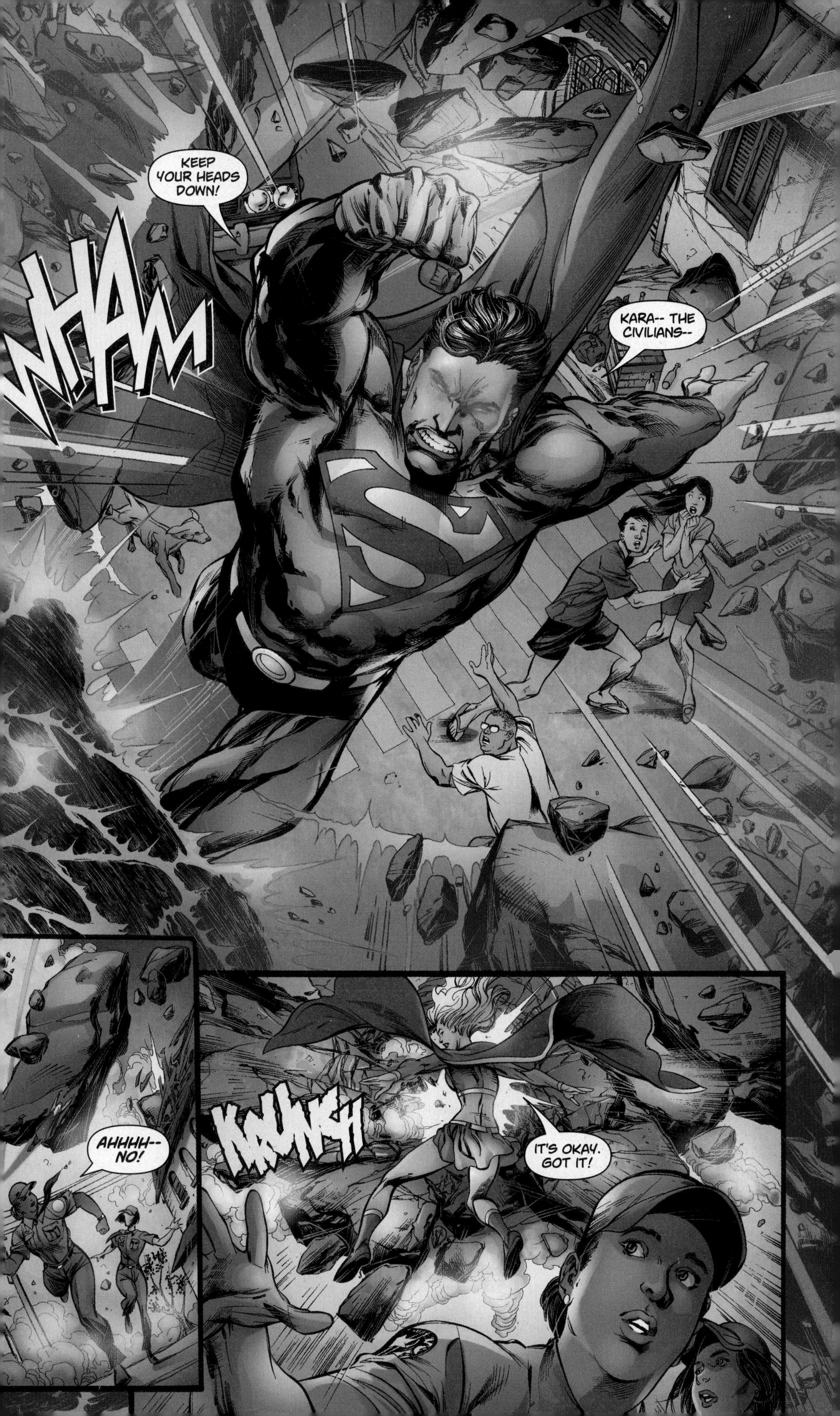
KEEP YOUR HEADS DOWN!
WHAM
KARA-- THE CIVILIANS--
AHHHH-- NO!
KRUNCH
IT'S OKAY. GOT IT!

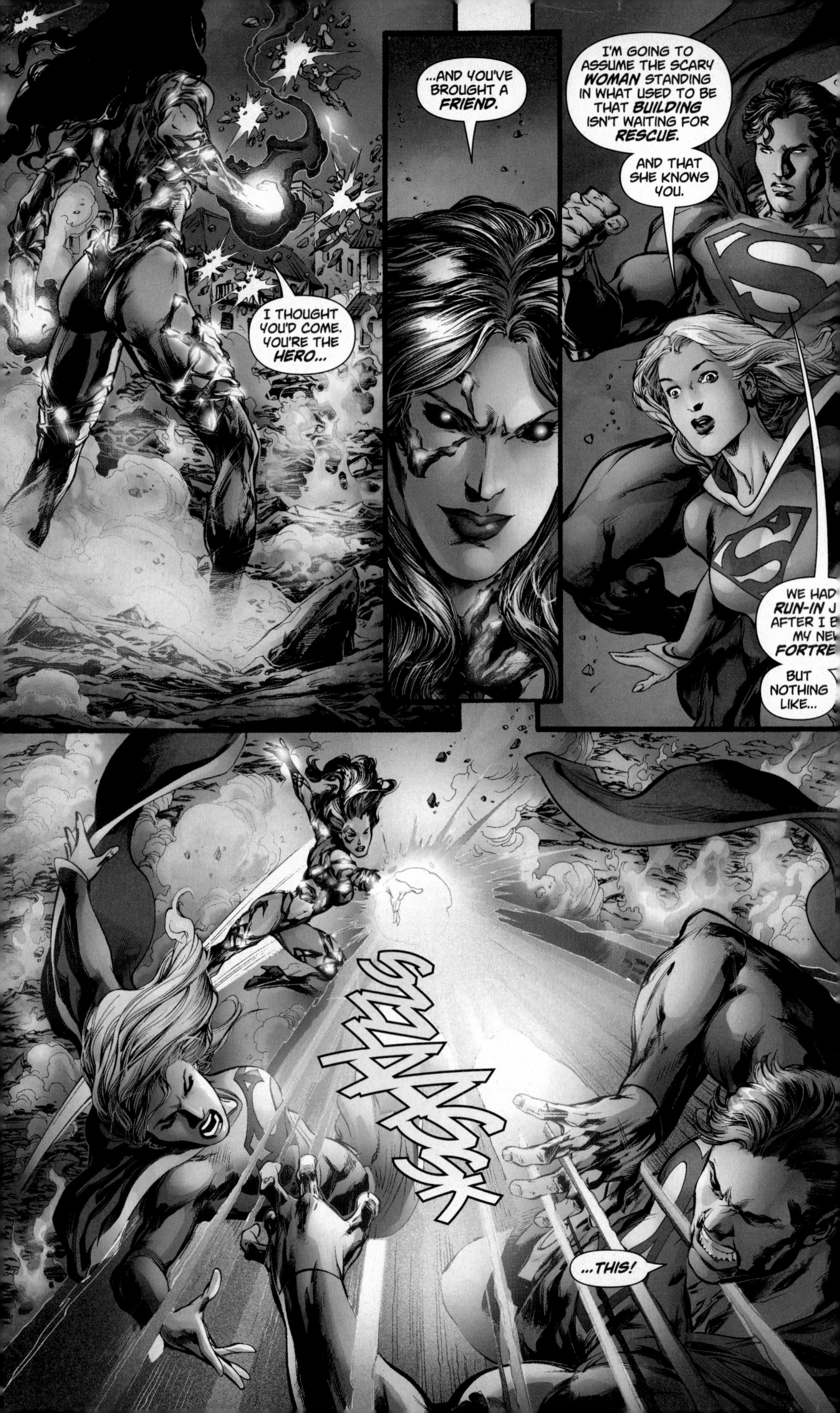
I THOUGHT YOU'D COME. YOU'RE THE HERO...
...AND YOU'VE BROUGHT A FRIEND.
I'M GOING TO ASSUME THE SCARY WOMAN STANDING IN WHAT USED TO BE THAT BUILDING ISN'T WAITING FOR RESCUE.
AND THAT SHE KNOWS YOU.
WE HAD RUN-IN J AFTER I B MY NEW FORTRE
BUT NOTHING LIKE...
...THIS!

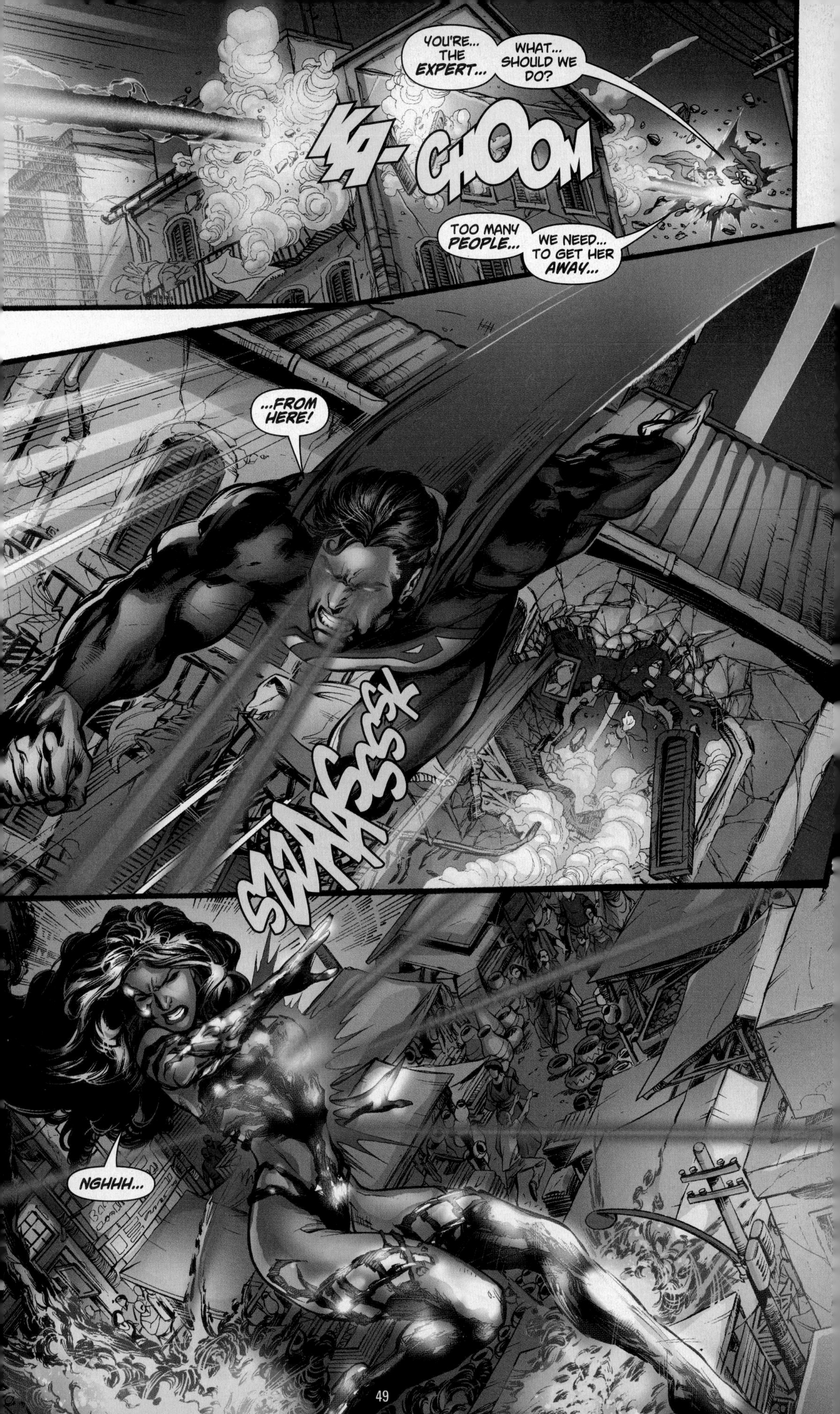
YOU'RE... THE EXPERT...
WHAT... SHOULD WE DO?
KA-CHOOM
TOO MANY PEOPLE...
WE NEED... TO GET HER AWAY...
...FROM HERE!
SZZAKSSSK
NGHHH...

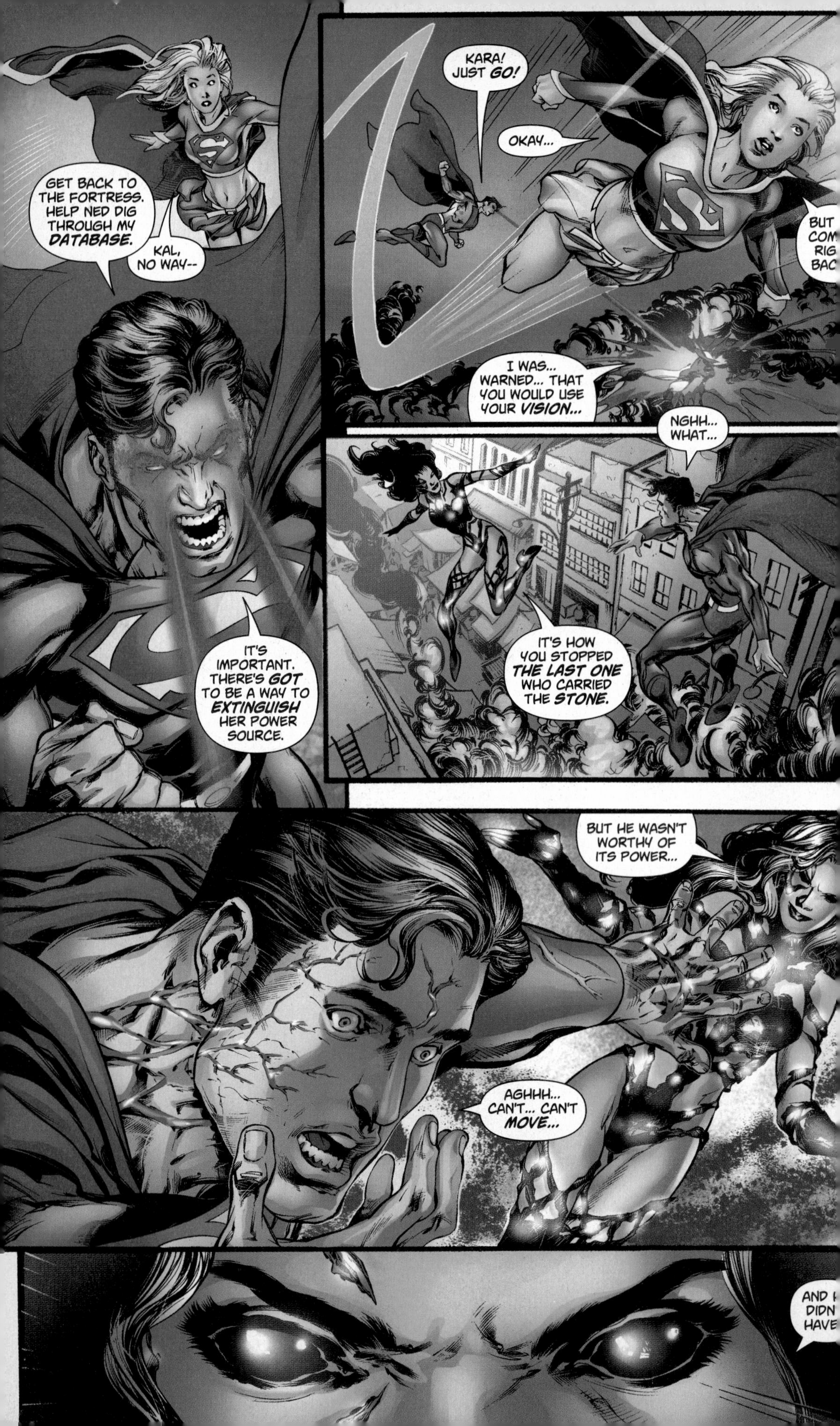

GET BACK TO THE FORTRESS. HELP NED DIG THROUGH MY DATABASE.
KAL, NO WAY--
IT'S IMPORTANT. THERE'S GOT TO BE A WAY TO EXTINGUISH HER POWER SOURCE.
KARA! JUST GO!
OKAY...
I WAS... WARNED... THAT YOU WOULD USE YOUR VISION...
NGHH... WHAT...
IT'S HOW YOU STOPPED THE LAST ONE WHO CARRIED THE STONE.
BUT HE WASN'T WORTHY OF ITS POWER...
AGHHH... CAN'T... CAN'T MOVE...

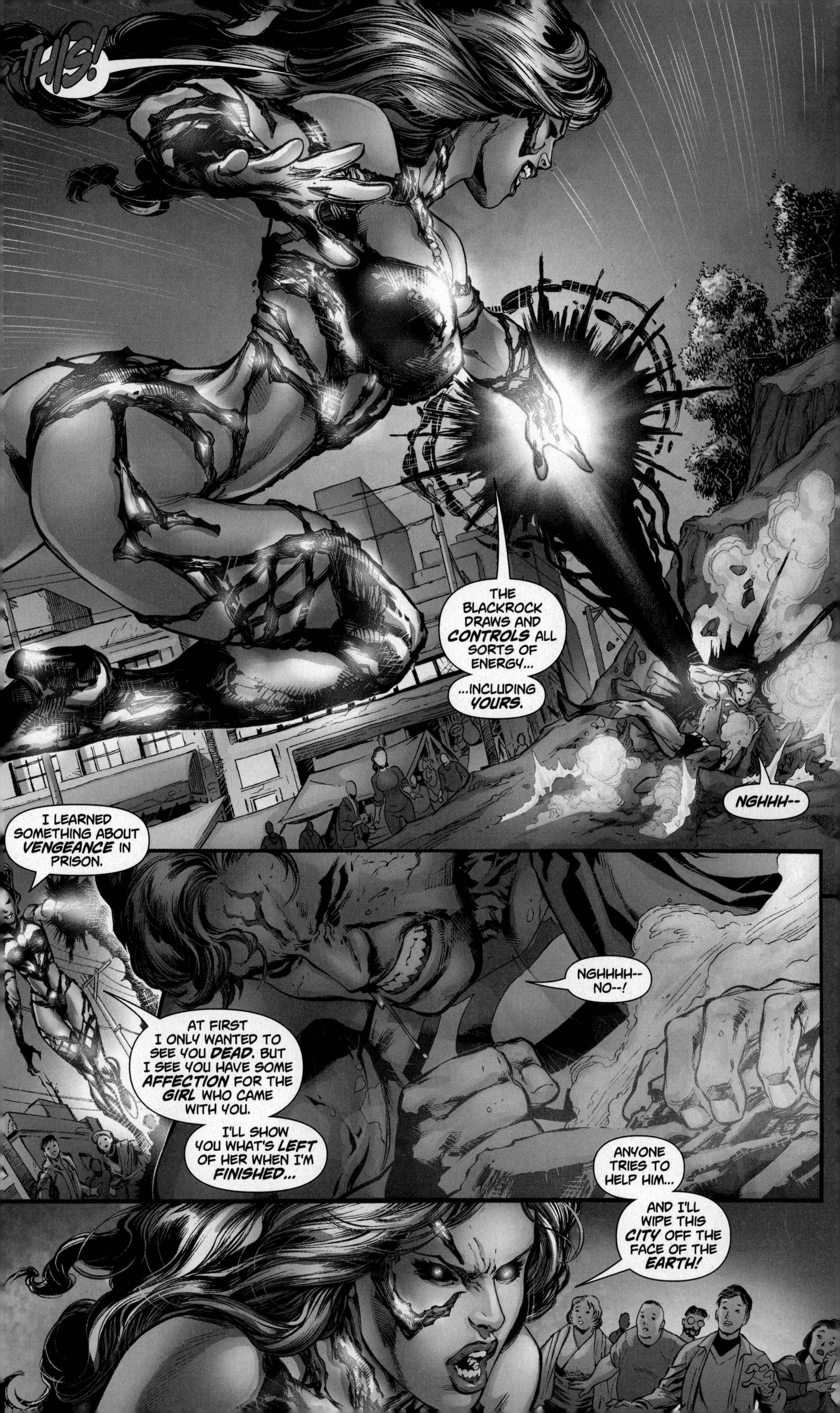
...THIS!
THE BLACKROCK DRAWS AND CONTROLS ALL SORTS OF ENERGY...
...INCLUDING YOURS.
NGHHH--
I LEARNED SOMETHING ABOUT VENGEANCE IN PRISON.
NGHHHH-- NO--!
AT FIRST I ONLY WANTED TO SEE YOU DEAD. BUT I SEE YOU HAVE SOME AFFECTION FOR THE GIRL WHO CAME WITH YOU.
I'LL SHOW YOU WHAT'S LEFT OF HER WHEN I'M FINISHED...
ANYONE TRIES TO HELP HIM...
AND I'LL WIPE THIS CITY OFF THE FACE OF THE EARTH!

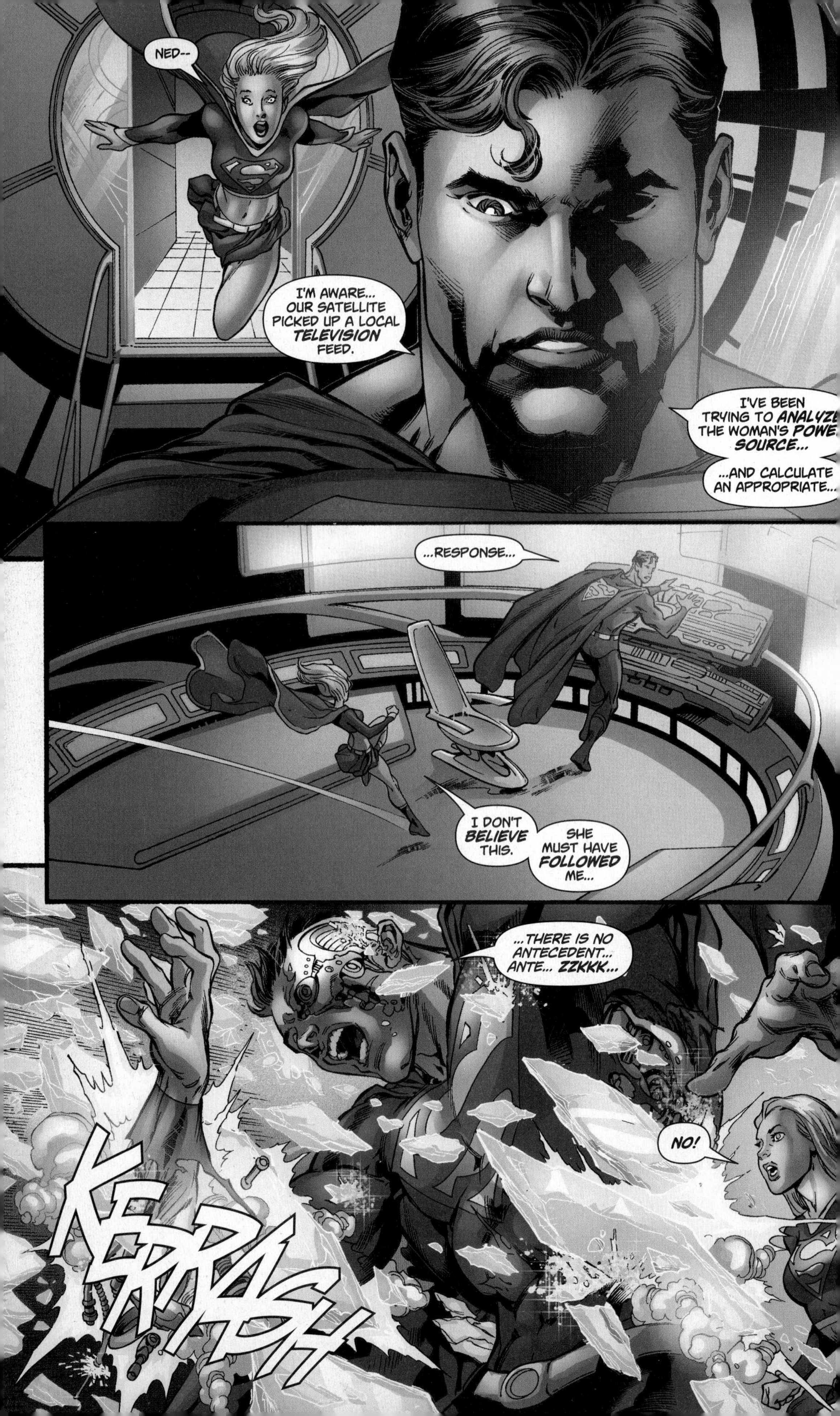

NED--
I'M AWARE... OUR SATELLITE PICKED UP A LOCAL TELEVISION FEED.
I'VE BEEN TRYING TO ANALYZE THE WOMAN'S POWER SOURCE...
...AND CALCULATE AN APPROPRIATE...
...RESPONSE...
I DON'T BELIEVE THIS.
SHE MUST HAVE FOLLOWED ME...
...THERE IS NO ANTECEDENT... ANTE... ZZKKK...
NO!
KERRASH

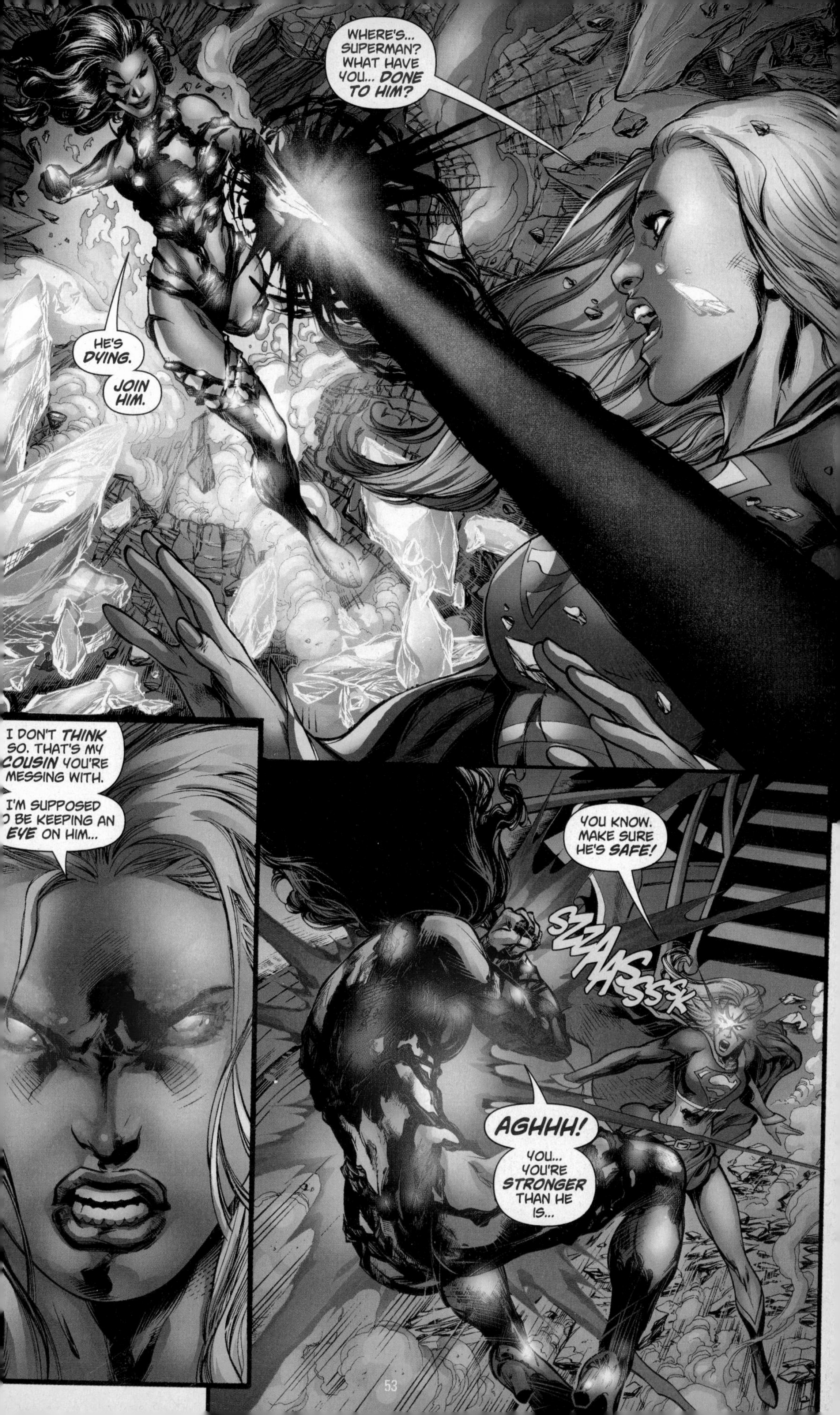
WHERE'S... SUPERMAN? WHAT HAVE YOU... DONE TO HIM?
HE'S DYING.
JOIN HIM.
I DON'T THINK SO. THAT'S MY COUSIN YOU'RE MESSING WITH.
I'M SUPPOSED TO BE KEEPING AN EYE ON HIM...
YOU KNOW. MAKE SURE HE'S SAFE!
SZZAASSSSK
AGHHH!
YOU... YOU'RE STRONGER THAN HE IS...

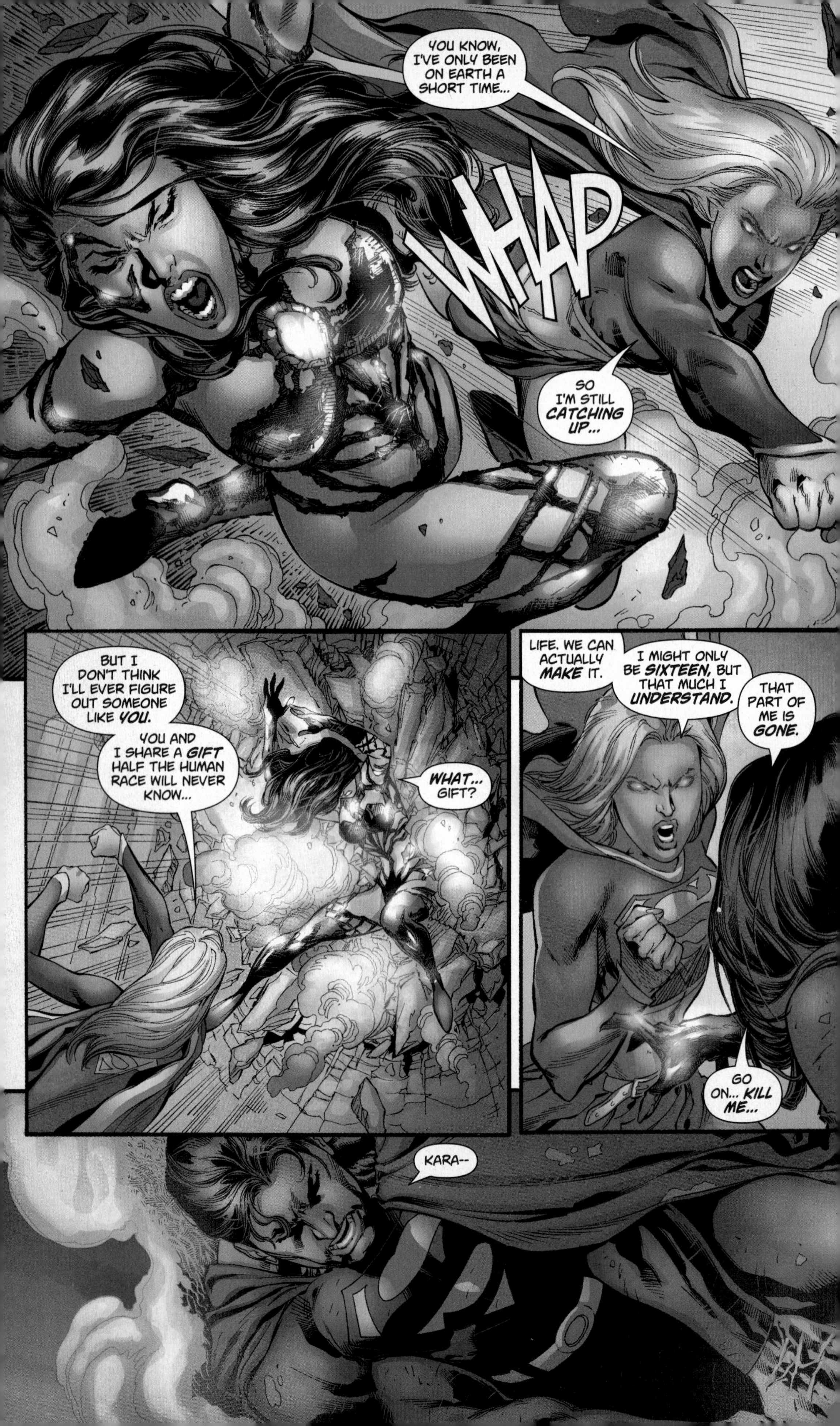
YOU KNOW, I'VE ONLY BEEN ON EARTH A SHORT TIME...
WHAP
SO I'M STILL CATCHING UP...
BUT I DON'T THINK I'LL EVER FIGURE OUT SOMEONE LIKE YOU.
YOU AND I SHARE A GIFT HALF THE HUMAN RACE WILL NEVER KNOW...
WHAT... GIFT?
LIFE. WE CAN ACTUALLY MAKE IT.
I MIGHT ONLY BE SIXTEEN, BUT THAT MUCH I UNDERSTAND.
THAT PART OF ME IS GONE.
GO ON... KILL ME...
KARA--

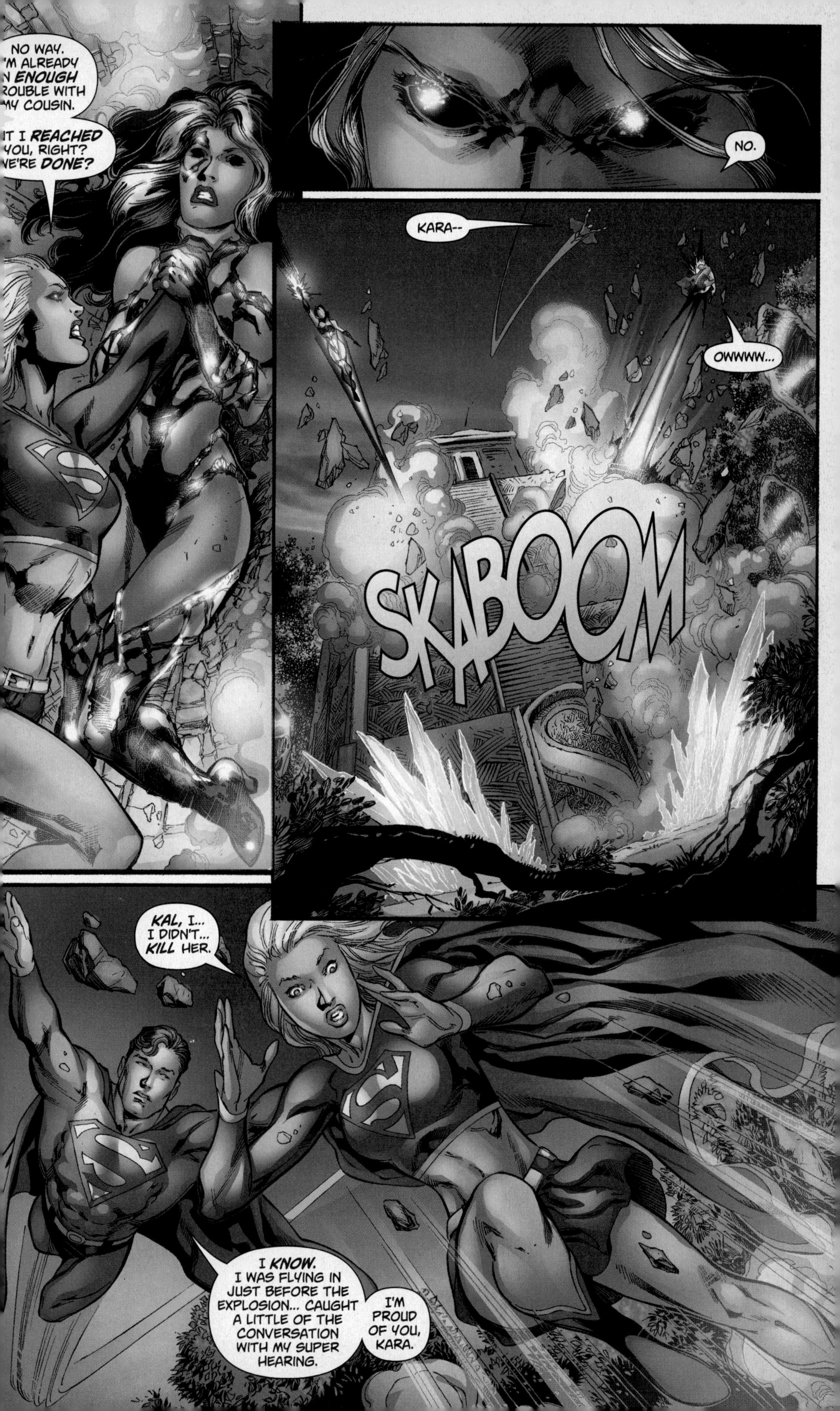

NO WAY. 'M ALREADY N ENOUGH ROUBLE WITH MY COUSIN.
IT I REACHED YOU, RIGHT? WE'RE DONE?
NO.
KARA--
OWWWW...
SKABOOM
KAL, I... I DIDN'T... KILL HER.
I KNOW. I WAS FLYING IN JUST BEFORE THE EXPLOSION... CAUGHT A LITTLE OF THE CONVERSATION WITH MY SUPER HEARING.
I'M PROUD OF YOU, KARA.

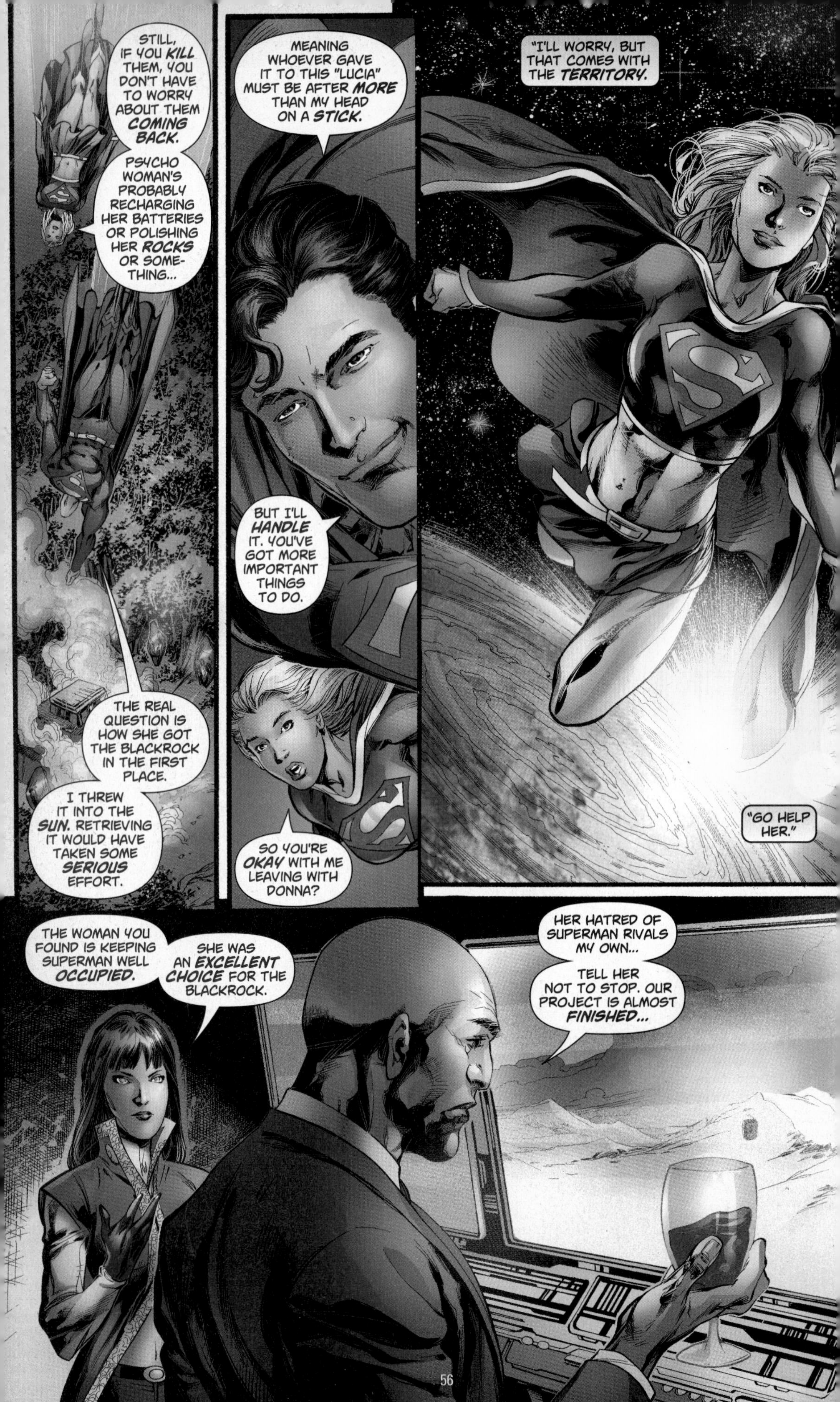
STILL, IF YOU KILL THEM, YOU DON'T HAVE TO WORRY ABOUT THEM COMING BACK.
PSYCHO WOMAN'S PROBABLY RECHARGING HER BATTERIES OR POLISHING HER ROCKS OR SOME-THING...
THE REAL QUESTION IS HOW SHE GOT THE BLACKROCK IN THE FIRST PLACE.
I THREW IT INTO THE SUN. RETRIEVING IT WOULD HAVE TAKEN SOME SERIOUS EFFORT.
MEANING WHOEVER GAVE IT TO THIS "LUCIA" MUST BE AFTER MORE THAN MY HEAD ON A STICK.
BUT I'LL HANDLE IT. YOU'VE GOT MORE IMPORTANT THINGS TO DO.
SO YOU'RE OKAY WITH ME LEAVING WITH DONNA?
"I'LL WORRY, BUT THAT COMES WITH THE TERRITORY.
"GO HELP HER."
THE WOMAN YOU FOUND IS KEEPING SUPERMAN WELL OCCUPIED.
SHE WAS AN EXCELLENT CHOICE FOR THE BLACKROCK.
HER HATRED OF SUPERMAN RIVALS MY OWN...
TELL HER NOT TO STOP. OUR PROJECT IS ALMOST FINISHED...

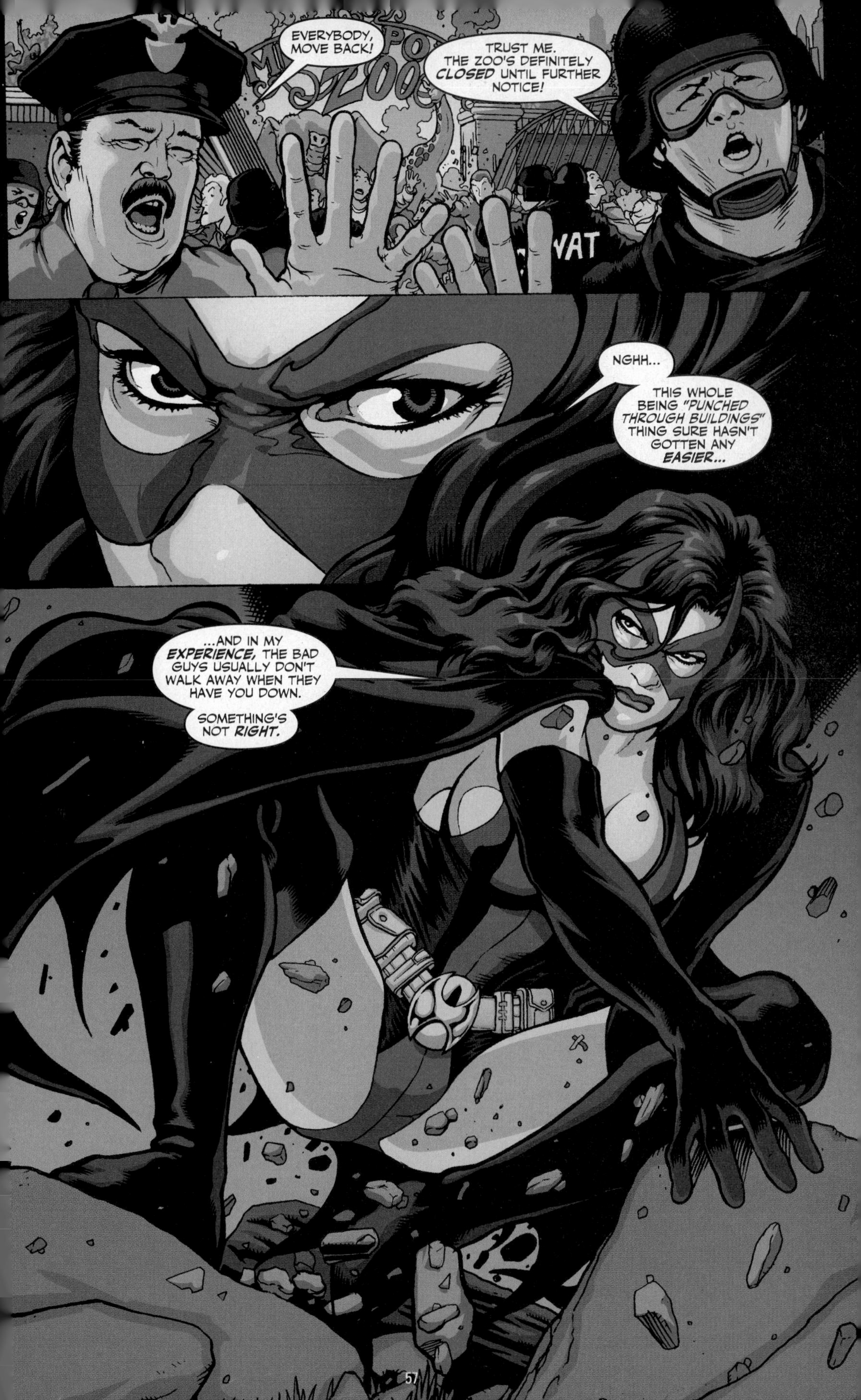
EVERYBODY, MOVE BACK!
TRUST ME. THE ZOO'S DEFINITELY CLOSED UNTIL FURTHER NOTICE!
NGHH...
THIS WHOLE BEING "PUNCHED THROUGH BUILDINGS" THING SURE HASN'T GOTTEN ANY EASIER...
...AND IN MY EXPERIENCE, THE BAD GUYS USUALLY DON'T WALK AWAY WHEN THEY HAVE YOU DOWN.
SOMETHING'S NOT RIGHT.

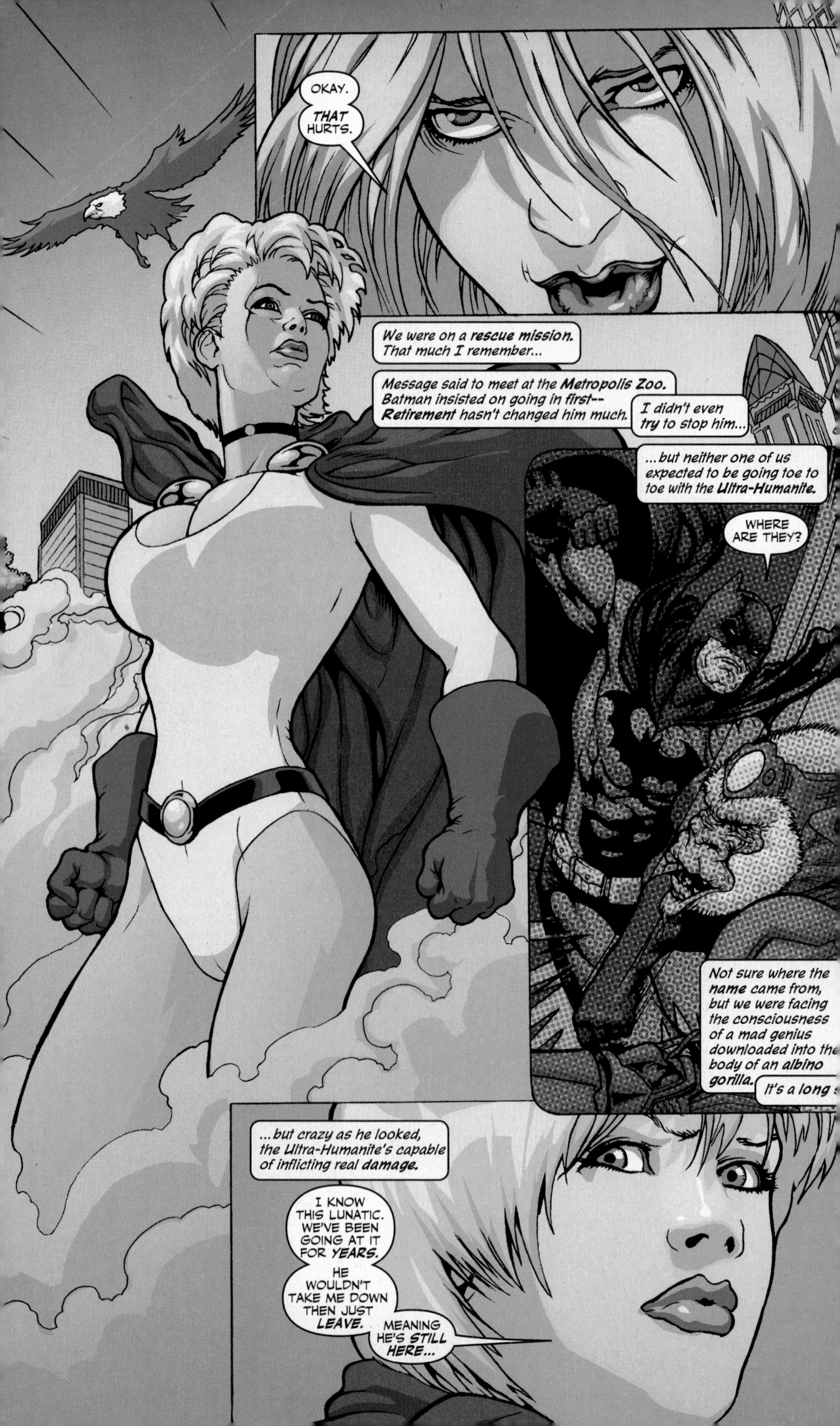

OKAY.
THAT HURTS.
We were on a rescue mission. That much I remember...
Message said to meet at the Metropolis Zoo. Batman insisted on going in first-- Retirement hasn't changed him much.
I didn't even try to stop him...
...but neither one of us expected to be going toe to toe with the Ultra-Humanite.
WHERE ARE THEY?
Not sure where the name came from, but we were facing the consciousness of a mad genius downloaded into the body of an albino gorilla.
...but crazy as he looked, the Ultra-Humanite's capable of inflicting real damage.
I KNOW THIS LUNATIC. WE'VE BEEN GOING AT IT FOR YEARS.
HE WOULDN'T TAKE ME DOWN THEN JUST LEAVE.
MEANING HE'S STILL HERE...

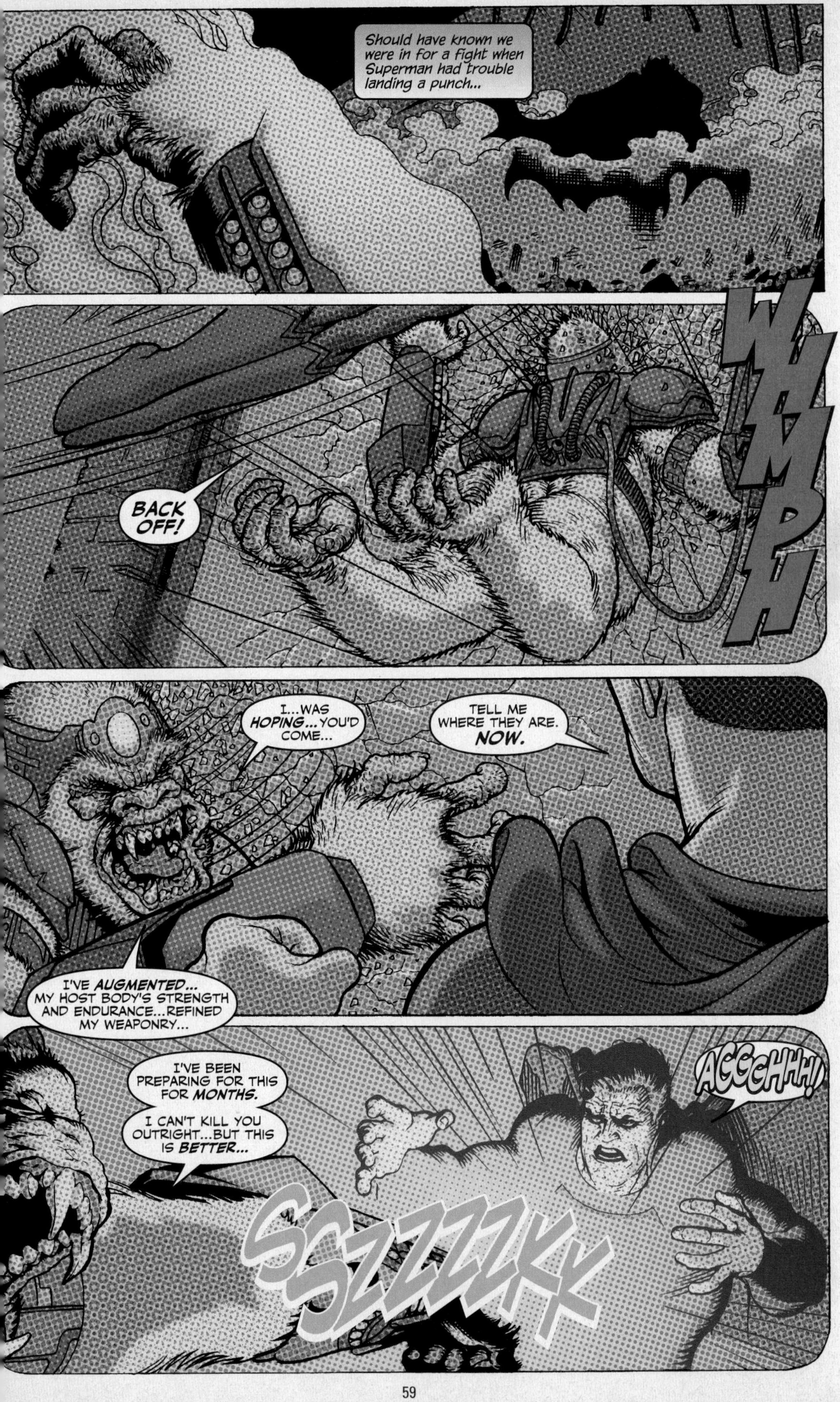
Should have known we were in for a fight when Superman had trouble landing a punch...
WHUMPH
BACK OFF!
I...WAS HOPING...YOU'D COME...
TELL ME WHERE THEY ARE. NOW.
I'VE AUGMENTED... MY HOST BODY'S STRENGTH AND ENDURANCE...REFINED MY WEAPONRY...
I'VE BEEN PREPARING FOR THIS FOR MONTHS.
I CAN'T KILL YOU OUTRIGHT...BUT THIS IS BETTER...
AGGGHHH!
SSZZZZKK

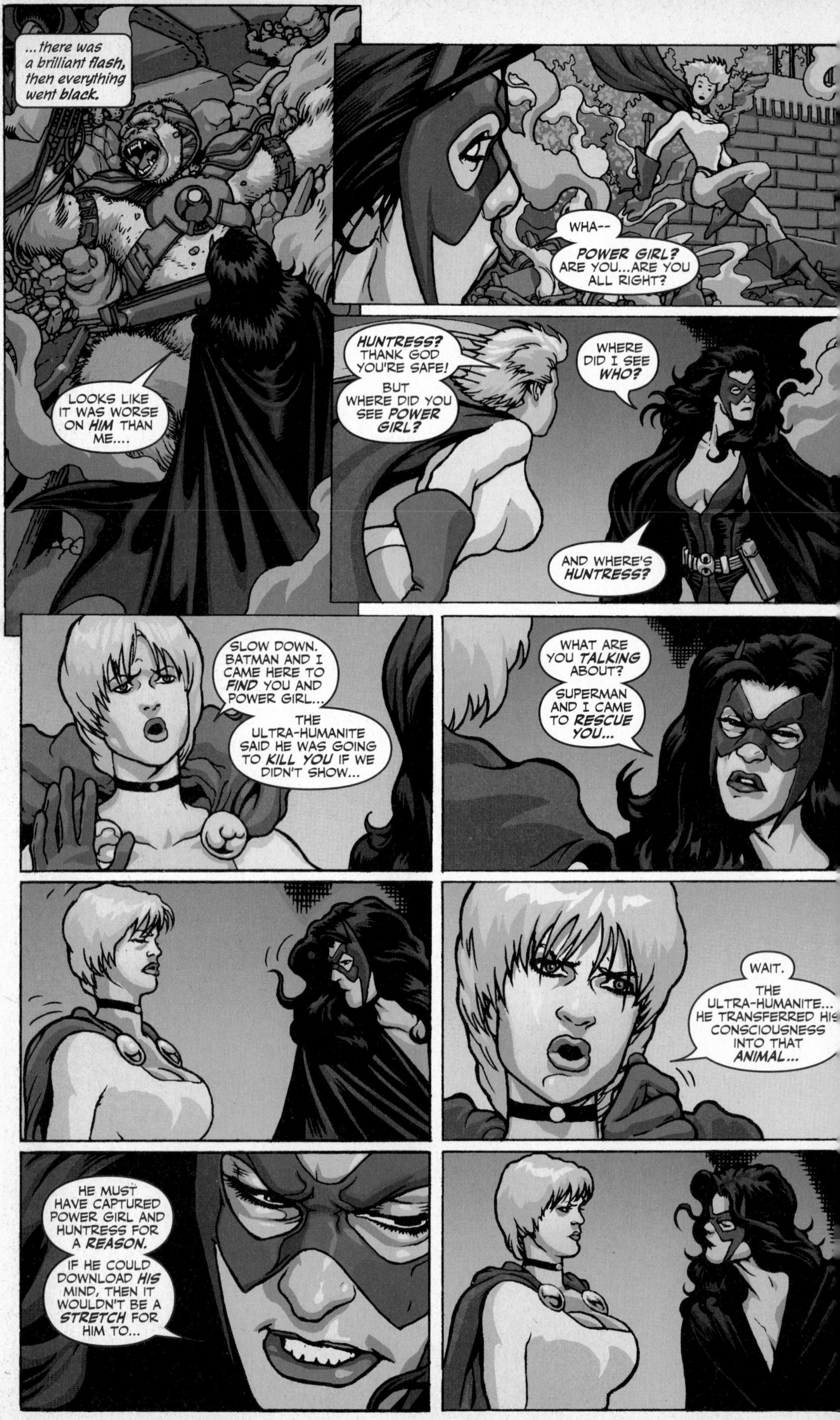
...there was a brilliant flash, then everything went black.
LOOKS LIKE IT WAS WORSE ON HIM THAN ME....
WHA--
POWER GIRL? ARE YOU...ARE YOU ALL RIGHT?
HUNTRESS? THANK GOD YOU'RE SAFE!
BUT WHERE DID YOU SEE POWER GIRL?
WHERE DID I SEE WHO?
AND WHERE'S HUNTRESS?
SLOW DOWN. BATMAN AND I CAME HERE TO FIND YOU AND POWER GIRL...
THE ULTRA-HUMANITE SAID HE WAS GOING TO KILL YOU IF WE DIDN'T SHOW...
WHAT ARE YOU TALKING ABOUT?
SUPERMAN AND I CAME TO RESCUE YOU...
WAIT.
THE ULTRA-HUMANITE... HE TRANSFERRED HIS CONSCIOUSNESS INTO THAT ANIMAL...
HE MUST HAVE CAPTURED POWER GIRL AND HUNTRESS FOR A REASON.
IF HE COULD DOWNLOAD HIS MIND, THEN IT WOULDN'T BE A STRETCH FOR HIM TO...

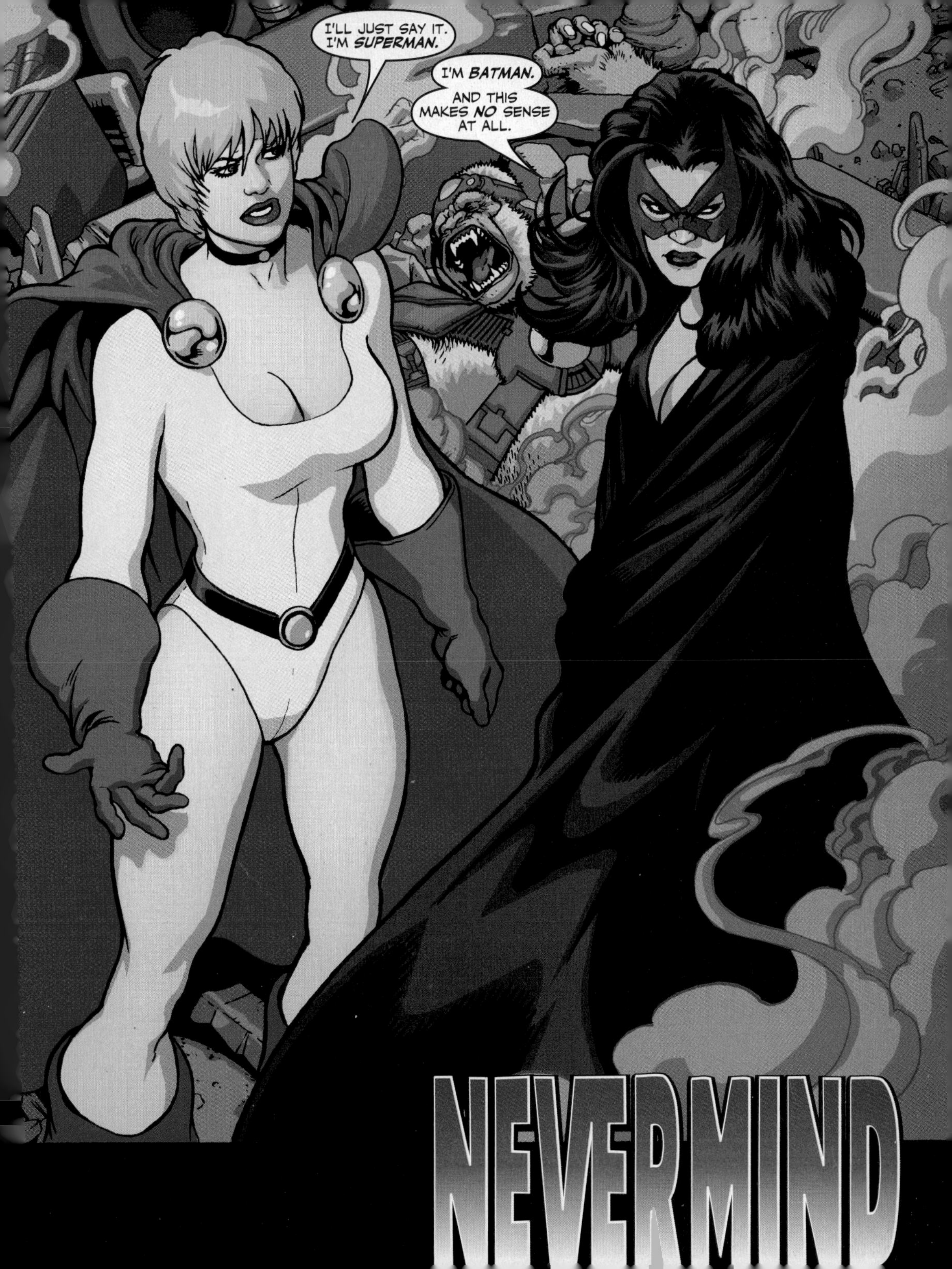
I'LL JUST SAY IT. I'M SUPERMAN.
I'M BATMAN.
AND THIS MAKES NO SENSE AT ALL.
NEVERMIND

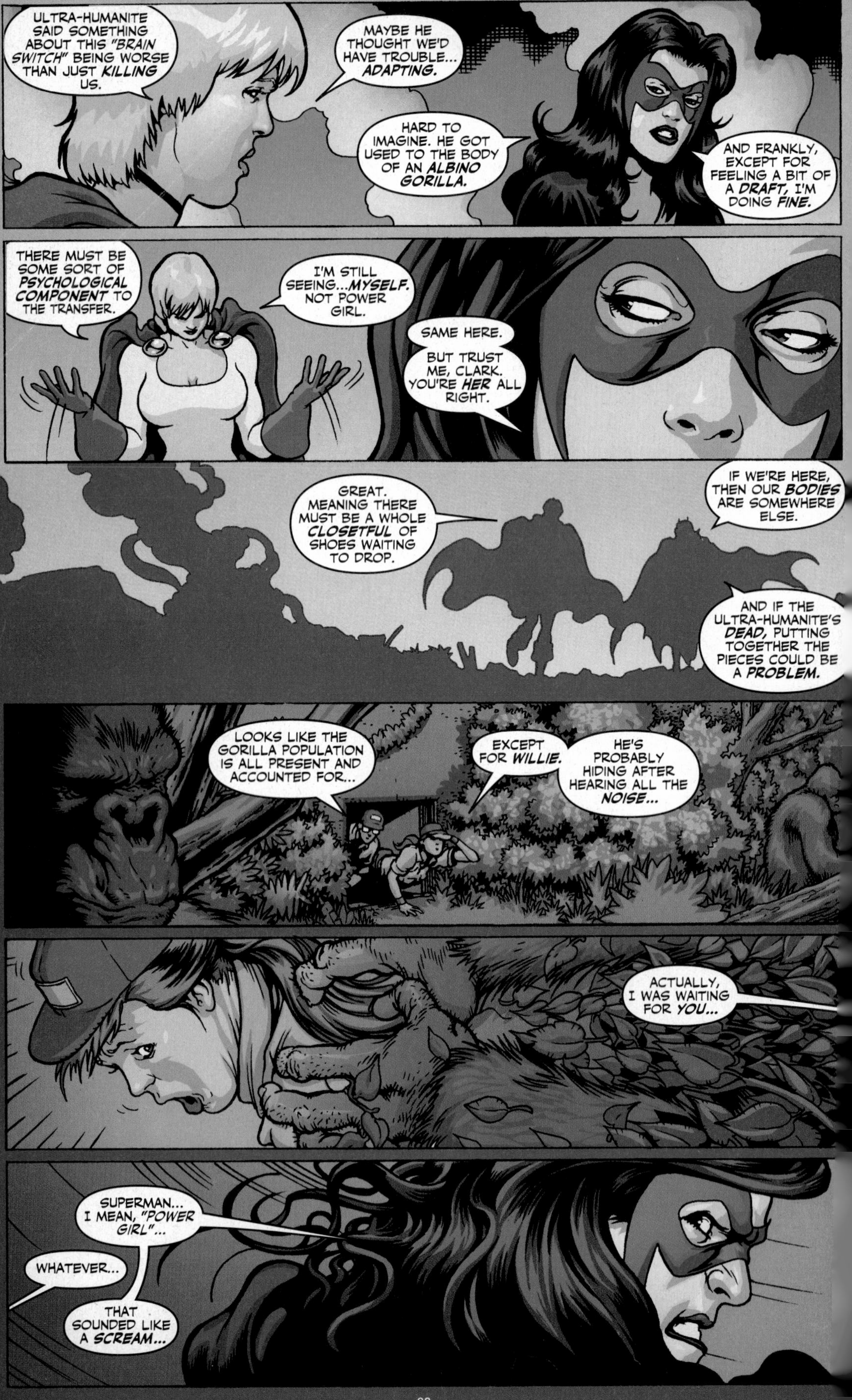

ULTRA-HUMANITE SAID SOMETHING ABOUT THIS "BRAIN SWITCH" BEING WORSE THAN JUST KILLING US.
MAYBE HE THOUGHT WE'D HAVE TROUBLE... ADAPTING.
HARD TO IMAGINE. HE GOT USED TO THE BODY OF AN ALBINO GORILLA.
AND FRANKLY, EXCEPT FOR FEELING A BIT OF A DRAFT, I'M DOING FINE.
THERE MUST BE SOME SORT OF PSYCHOLOGICAL COMPONENT TO THE TRANSFER.
I'M STILL SEEING...MYSELF. NOT POWER GIRL.
SAME HERE.
BUT TRUST ME, CLARK. YOU'RE HER ALL RIGHT.
GREAT. MEANING THERE MUST BE A WHOLE CLOSETFUL OF SHOES WAITING TO DROP.
IF WE'RE HERE, THEN OUR BODIES ARE SOMEWHERE ELSE.
AND IF THE ULTRA-HUMANITE'S DEAD, PUTTING TOGETHER THE PIECES COULD BE A PROBLEM.
LOOKS LIKE THE GORILLA POPULATION IS ALL PRESENT AND ACCOUNTED FOR...
EXCEPT FOR WILLIE.
HE'S PROBABLY HIDING AFTER HEARING ALL THE NOISE...
ACTUALLY, I WAS WAITING FOR YOU...
SUPERMAN... I MEAN, "POWER GIRL"...
WHATEVER...
THAT SOUNDED LIKE A SCREAM...

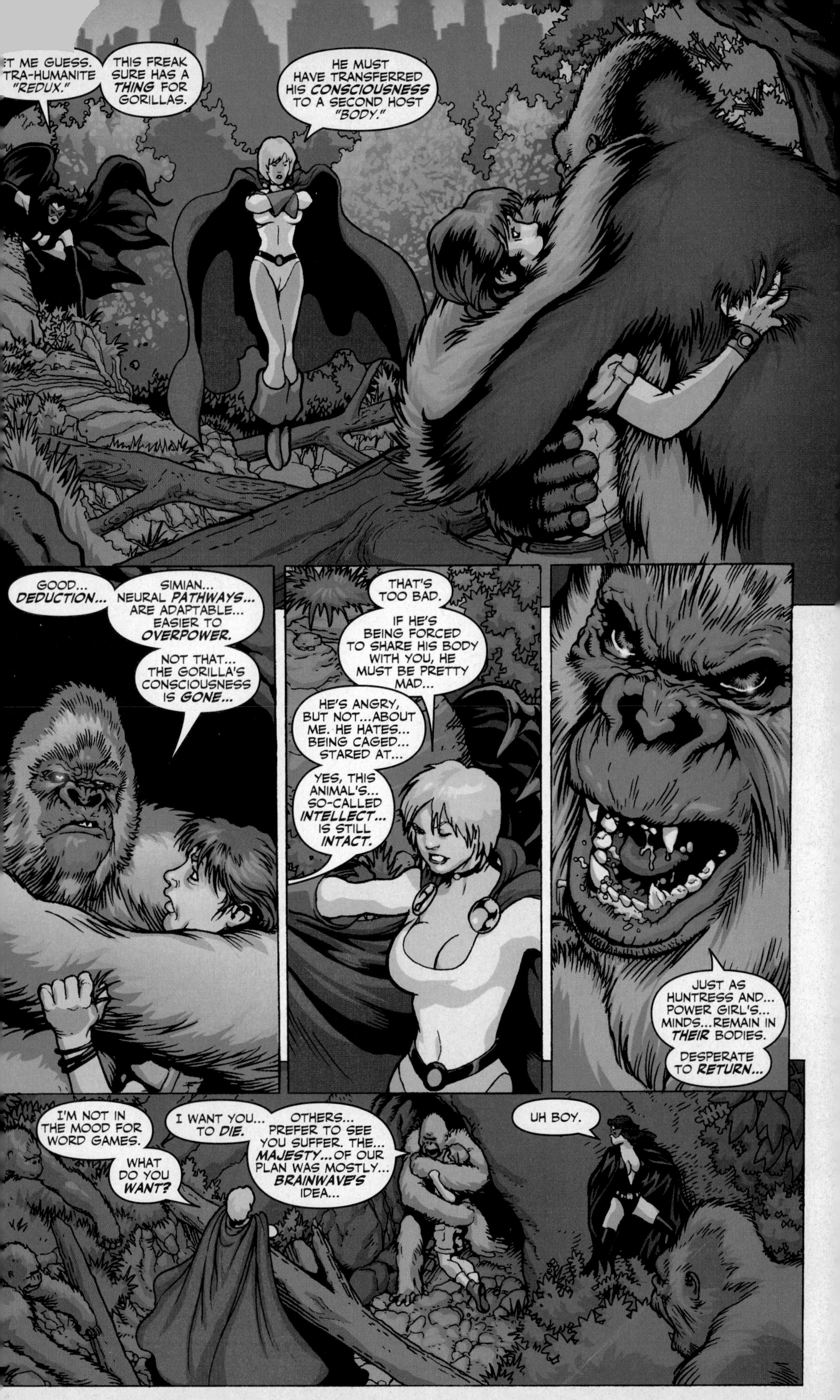
ET ME GUESS. TRA-HUMANITE "REDUX."
THIS FREAK SURE HAS A THING FOR GORILLAS.
HE MUST HAVE TRANSFERRED HIS CONSCIOUSNESS TO A SECOND HOST "BODY."
GOOD... DEDUCTION...
SIMIAN... NEURAL PATHWAYS... ARE ADAPTABLE... EASIER TO OVERPOWER.
NOT THAT... THE GORILLA'S CONSCIOUSNESS IS GONE...
THAT'S TOO BAD.
IF HE'S BEING FORCED TO SHARE HIS BODY WITH YOU, HE MUST BE PRETTY MAD...
HE'S ANGRY, BUT NOT...ABOUT ME. HE HATES... BEING CAGED... STARED AT...
YES, THIS ANIMAL'S... SO-CALLED INTELLECT... IS STILL INTACT.
JUST AS HUNTRESS AND... POWER GIRL'S... MINDS...REMAIN IN THEIR BODIES.
DESPERATE TO RETURN...
I'M NOT IN THE MOOD FOR WORD GAMES.
WHAT DO YOU WANT?
I WANT YOU... TO DIE.
OTHERS... PREFER TO SEE YOU SUFFER. THE... MAJESTY...OF OUR PLAN WAS MOSTLY... BRAINWAVE'S IDEA...
UH BOY.

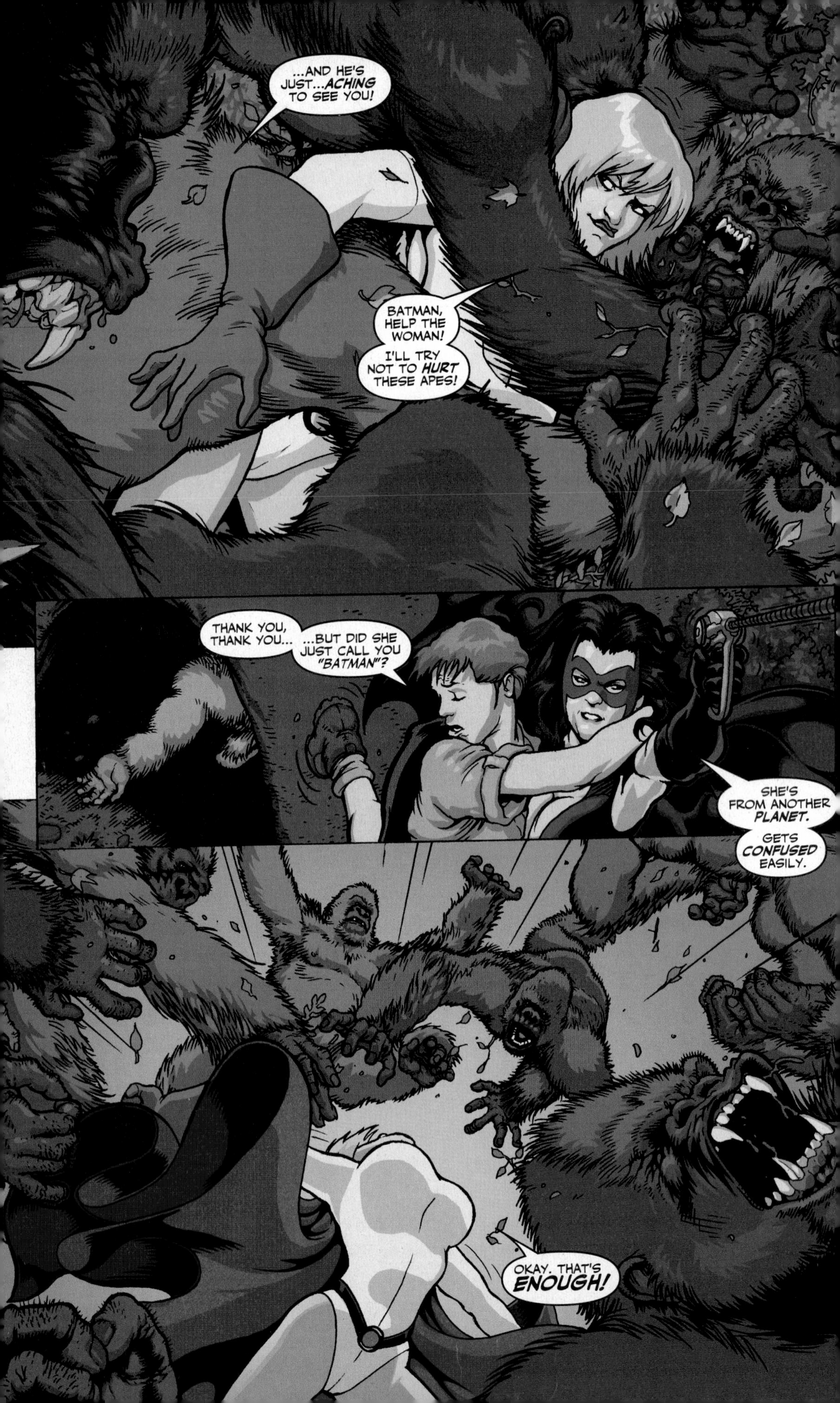
...AND HE'S JUST...ACHING TO SEE YOU!
BATMAN, HELP THE WOMAN!
I'LL TRY NOT TO HURT THESE APES!
THANK YOU, THANK YOU...
...BUT DID SHE JUST CALL YOU "BATMAN"?
SHE'S FROM ANOTHER PLANET.
GETS CONFUSED EASILY.
OKAY. THAT'S ENOUGH!

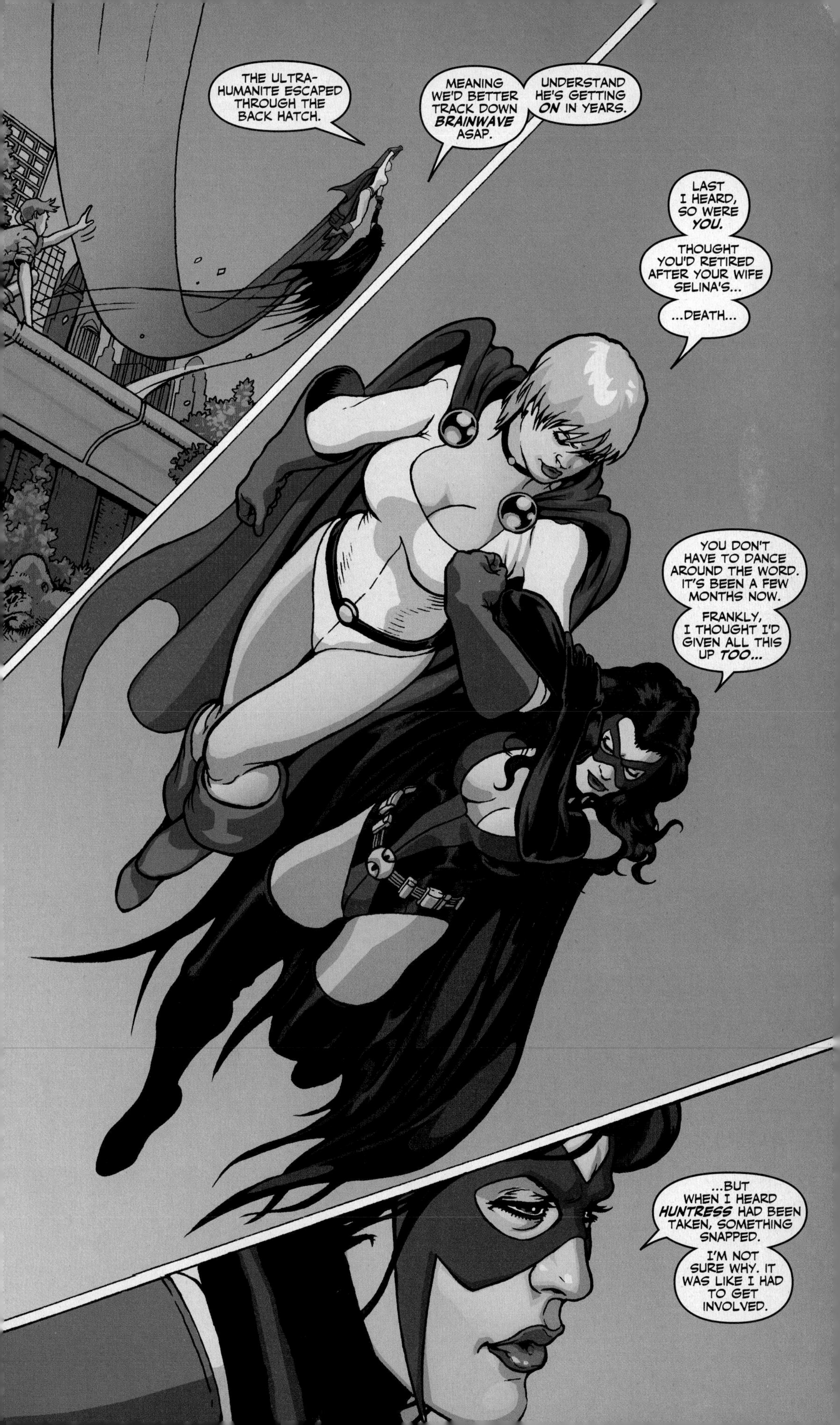
THE ULTRA-HUMANITE ESCAPED THROUGH THE BACK HATCH.
MEANING WE'D BETTER TRACK DOWN BRAINWAVE ASAP.
UNDERSTAND HE'S GETTING ON IN YEARS.
LAST I HEARD, SO WERE YOU.
THOUGHT YOU'D RETIRED AFTER YOUR WIFE SELINA'S...
...DEATH...
YOU DON'T HAVE TO DANCE AROUND THE WORD. IT'S BEEN A FEW MONTHS NOW.
FRANKLY, I THOUGHT I'D GIVEN ALL THIS UP TOO...
...BUT WHEN I HEARD HUNTRESS HAD BEEN TAKEN, SOMETHING SNAPPED.
I'M NOT SURE WHY. IT WAS LIKE I HAD TO GET INVOLVED.

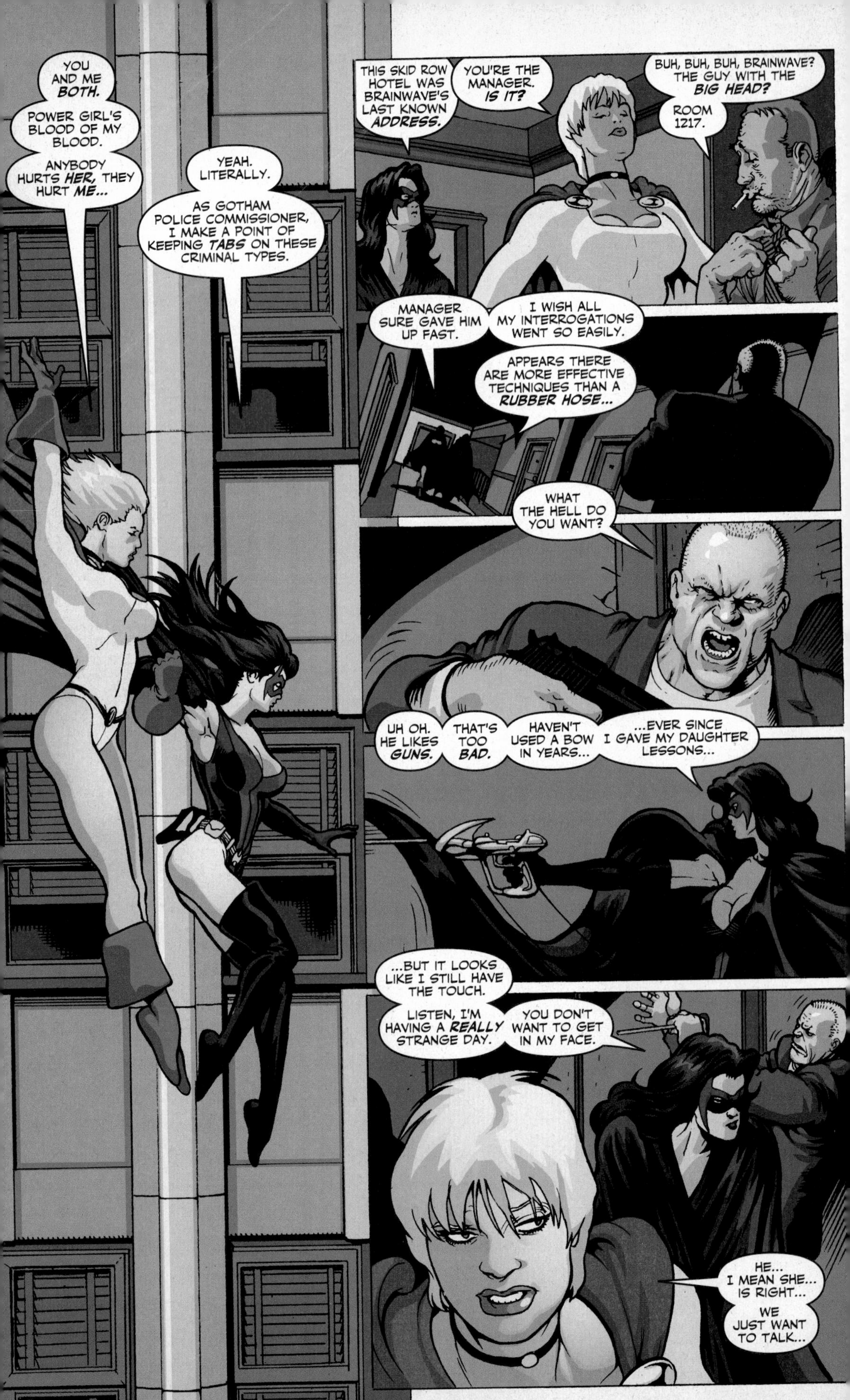
YOU AND ME BOTH.
POWER GIRL'S BLOOD OF MY BLOOD.
ANYBODY HURTS HER, THEY HURT ME...
YEAH. LITERALLY.
AS GOTHAM POLICE COMMISSIONER, I MAKE A POINT OF KEEPING TABS ON THESE CRIMINAL TYPES.
THIS SKID ROW HOTEL WAS BRAINWAVE'S LAST KNOWN ADDRESS.
YOU'RE THE MANAGER. IS IT?
BUH, BUH, BUH, BRAINWAVE? THE GUY WITH THE BIG HEAD?
ROOM 1217.
MANAGER SURE GAVE HIM UP FAST.
I WISH ALL MY INTERROGATIONS WENT SO EASILY.
APPEARS THERE ARE MORE EFFECTIVE TECHNIQUES THAN A RUBBER HOSE...
WHAT THE HELL DO YOU WANT?
UH OH. HE LIKES GUNS.
THAT'S TOO BAD.
HAVEN'T USED A BOW IN YEARS...
...EVER SINCE I GAVE MY DAUGHTER LESSONS...
...BUT IT LOOKS LIKE I STILL HAVE THE TOUCH.
LISTEN, I'M HAVING A REALLY STRANGE DAY.
YOU DON'T WANT TO GET IN MY FACE.
HE... I MEAN SHE... IS RIGHT...
WE JUST WANT TO TALK...

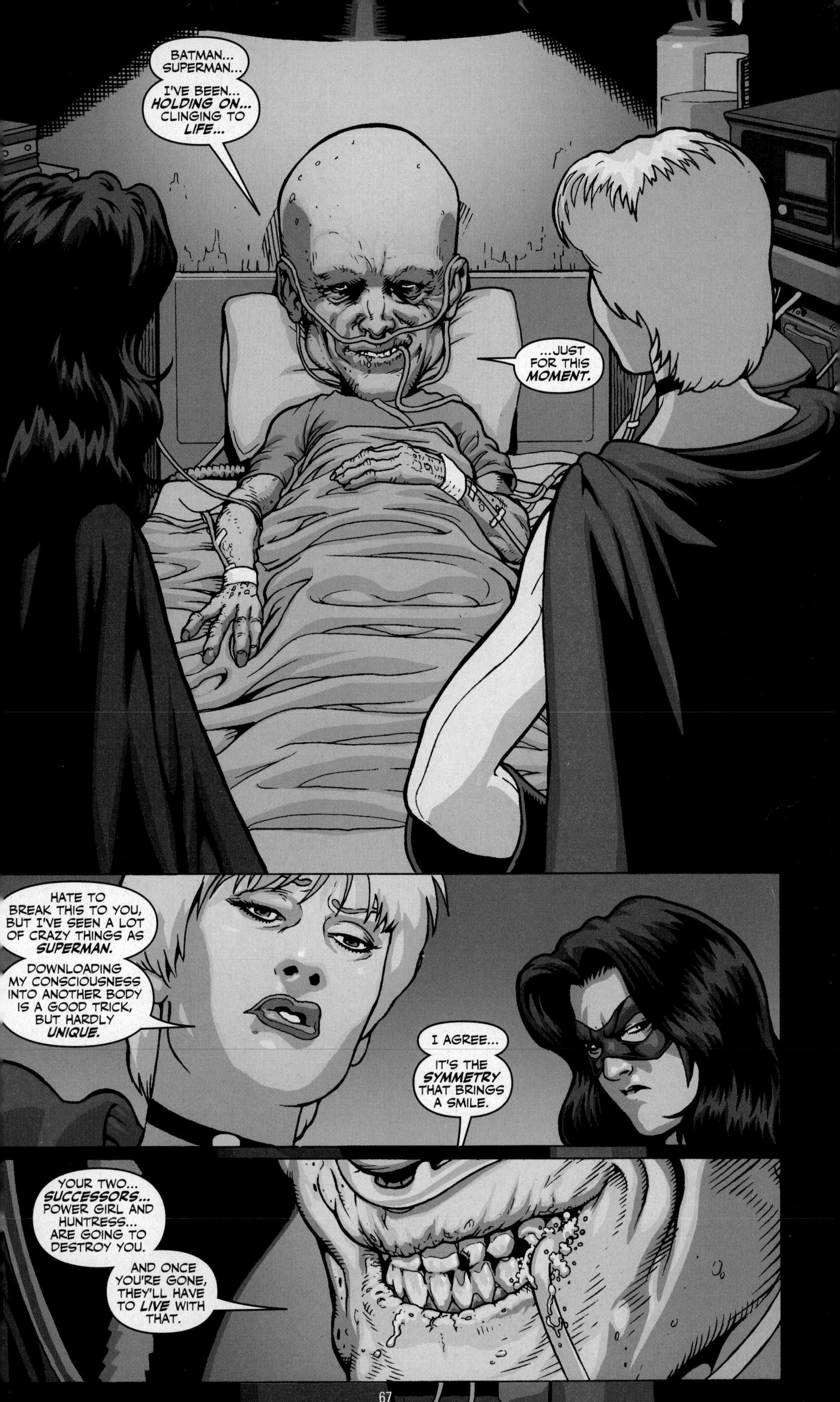
BATMAN... SUPERMAN...
I'VE BEEN... HOLDING ON... CLINGING TO LIFE...
...JUST FOR THIS MOMENT.
HATE TO BREAK THIS TO YOU, BUT I'VE SEEN A LOT OF CRAZY THINGS AS SUPERMAN.
DOWNLOADING MY CONSCIOUSNESS INTO ANOTHER BODY IS A GOOD TRICK, BUT HARDLY UNIQUE.
I AGREE...
IT'S THE SYMMETRY THAT BRINGS A SMILE.
YOUR TWO... SUCCESSORS... POWER GIRL AND HUNTRESS... ARE GOING TO DESTROY YOU.
AND ONCE YOU'RE GONE, THEY'LL HAVE TO LIVE WITH THAT.

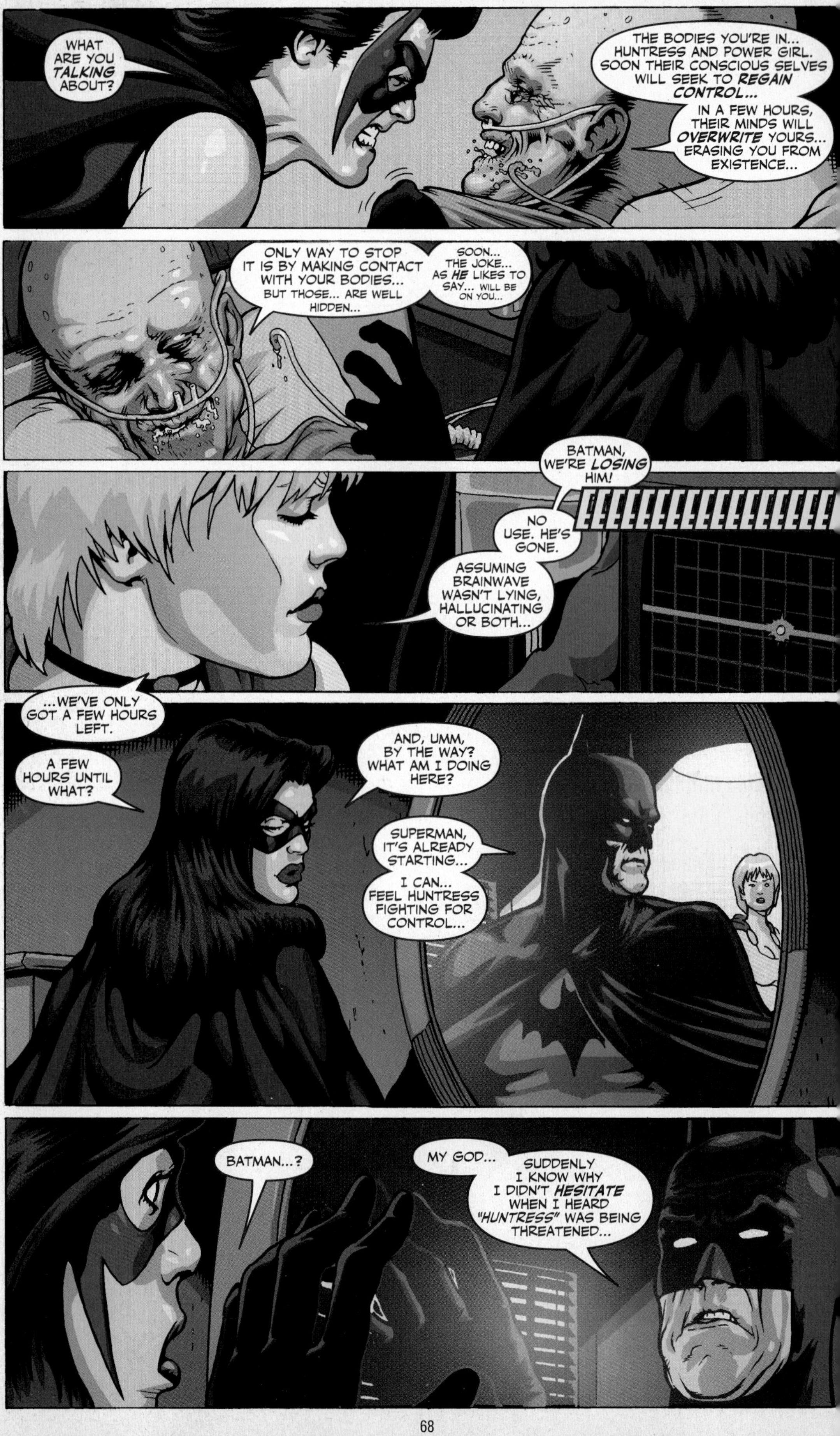
WHAT ARE YOU *TALKING* ABOUT?
THE BODIES YOU'RE IN... HUNTRESS AND POWER GIRL. SOON THEIR CONSCIOUS SELVES WILL SEEK TO *REGAIN CONTROL...*
IN A FEW HOURS, THEIR MINDS WILL *OVERWRITE* YOURS... ERASING YOU FROM EXISTENCE...
ONLY WAY TO STOP IT IS BY MAKING CONTACT WITH YOUR BODIES... BUT THOSE... ARE WELL HIDDEN...
SOON... THE JOKE... AS *HE* LIKES TO SAY... WILL BE ON YOU...
BATMAN, WE'RE *LOSING* HIM!
EEEEEEEEEEEEEEEEEEE
NO USE. HE'S GONE.
ASSUMING BRAINWAVE WASN'T LYING, HALLUCINATING OR BOTH...
...WE'VE ONLY GOT A FEW HOURS LEFT.
A FEW HOURS UNTIL WHAT?
AND, UMM, BY THE WAY? WHAT AM I DOING HERE?
SUPERMAN, IT'S ALREADY STARTING...
I CAN... FEEL HUNTRESS FIGHTING FOR CONTROL...
BATMAN...?
MY GOD...
SUDDENLY I KNOW WHY I DIDN'T *HESITATE* WHEN I HEARD *"HUNTRESS"* WAS BEING THREATENED...

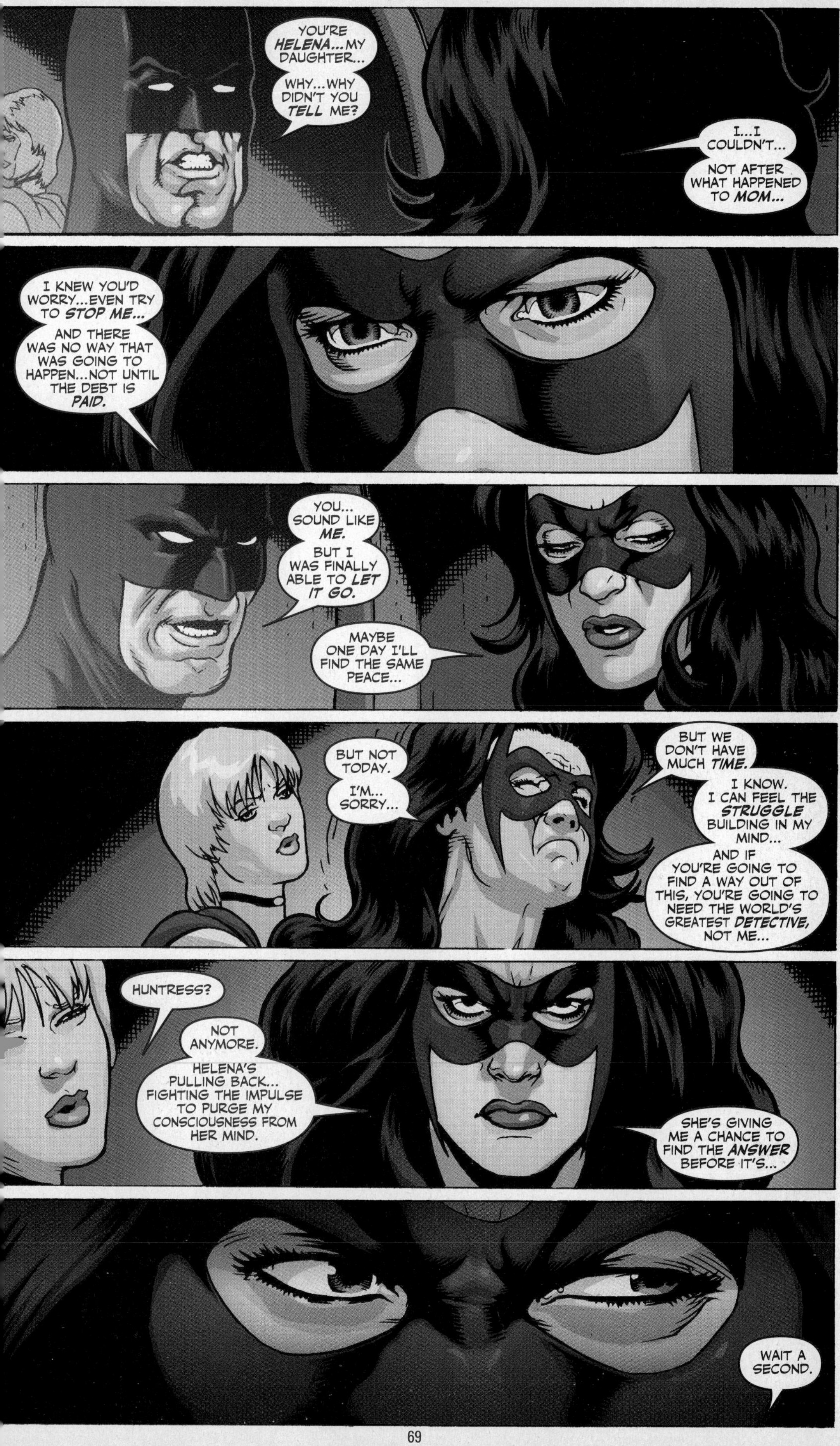
YOU'RE HELENA...MY DAUGHTER...
WHY...WHY DIDN'T YOU TELL ME?
I...I COULDN'T...
NOT AFTER WHAT HAPPENED TO MOM...
I KNEW YOU'D WORRY...EVEN TRY TO STOP ME...
AND THERE WAS NO WAY THAT WAS GOING TO HAPPEN...NOT UNTIL THE DEBT IS PAID.
YOU... SOUND LIKE ME.
BUT I WAS FINALLY ABLE TO LET IT GO.
MAYBE ONE DAY I'LL FIND THE SAME PEACE...
BUT NOT TODAY.
I'M... SORRY...
BUT WE DON'T HAVE MUCH TIME.
I KNOW. I CAN FEEL THE STRUGGLE BUILDING IN MY MIND...
AND IF YOU'RE GOING TO FIND A WAY OUT OF THIS, YOU'RE GOING TO NEED THE WORLD'S GREATEST DETECTIVE, NOT ME...
HUNTRESS?
NOT ANYMORE.
HELENA'S PULLING BACK... FIGHTING THE IMPULSE TO PURGE MY CONSCIOUSNESS FROM HER MIND.
SHE'S GIVING ME A CHANCE TO FIND THE ANSWER BEFORE IT'S...
WAIT A SECOND.

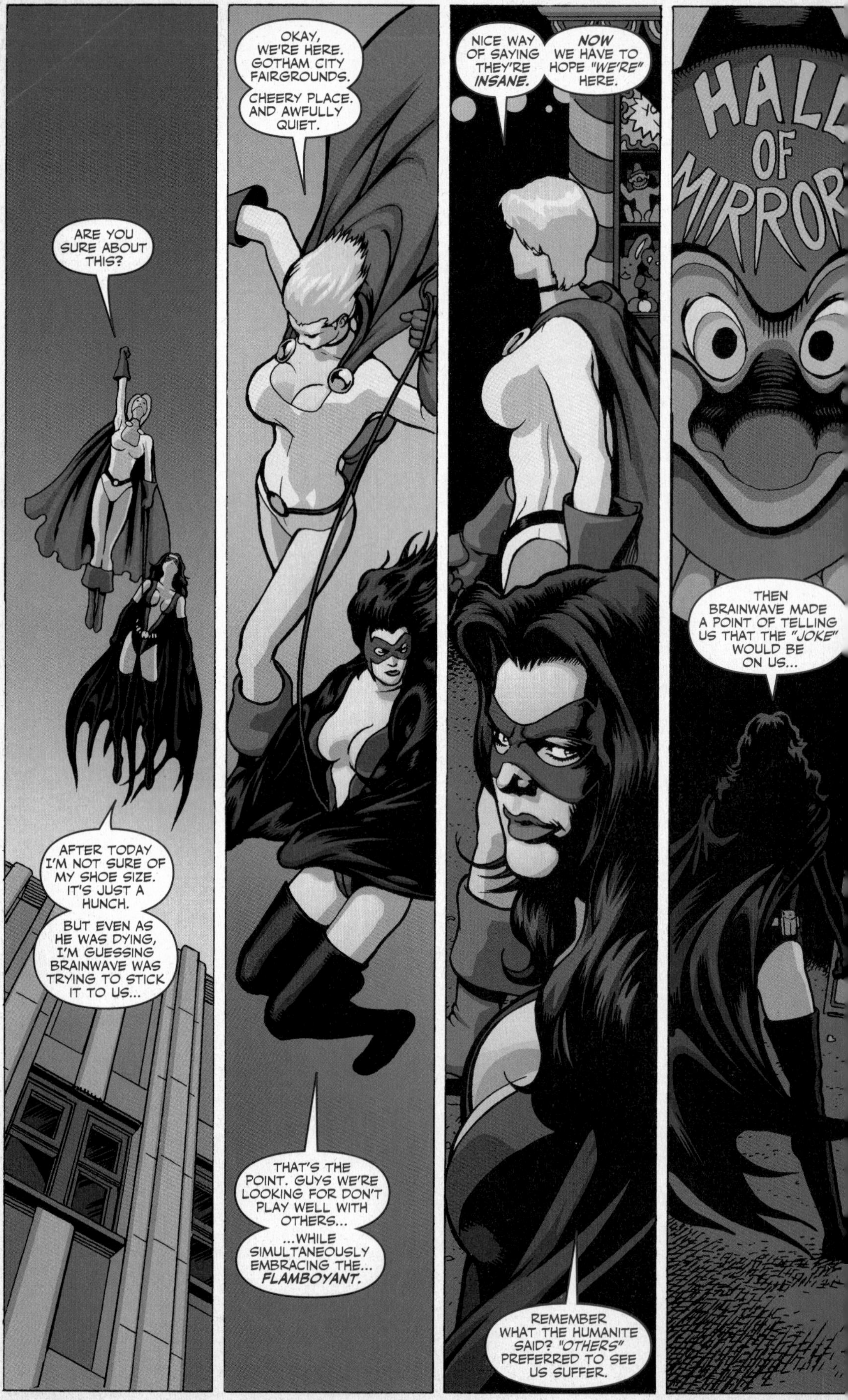
ARE YOU SURE ABOUT THIS?
AFTER TODAY I'M NOT SURE OF MY SHOE SIZE. IT'S JUST A HUNCH.
BUT EVEN AS HE WAS DYING, I'M GUESSING BRAINWAVE WAS TRYING TO STICK IT TO US...
OKAY, WE'RE HERE. GOTHAM CITY FAIRGROUNDS.
CHEERY PLACE. AND AWFULLY QUIET.
THAT'S THE POINT. GUYS WE'RE LOOKING FOR DON'T PLAY WELL WITH OTHERS...
...WHILE SIMULTANEOUSLY EMBRACING THE... FLAMBOYANT.
NICE WAY OF SAYING THEY'RE INSANE.
NOW WE HAVE TO HOPE "WE'RE" HERE.
REMEMBER WHAT THE HUMANITE SAID? "OTHERS" PREFERRED TO SEE US SUFFER.
HALL OF MIRROR
THEN BRAINWAVE MADE A POINT OF TELLING US THAT THE "JOKE" WOULD BE ON US...

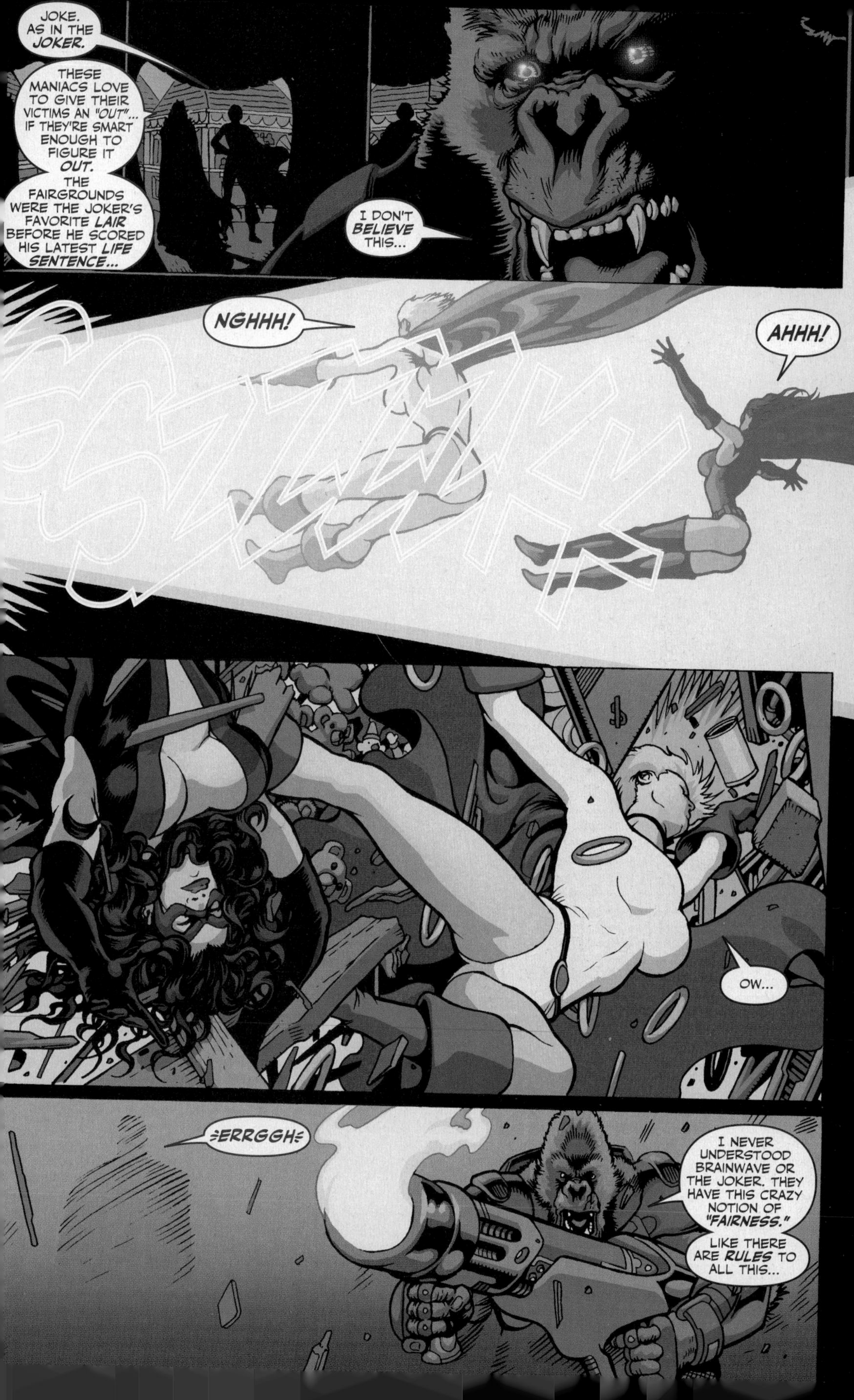
JOKE. AS IN THE JOKER.
THESE MANIACS LOVE TO GIVE THEIR VICTIMS AN "OUT"... IF THEY'RE SMART ENOUGH TO FIGURE IT OUT.
THE FAIRGROUNDS WERE THE JOKER'S FAVORITE LAIR BEFORE HE SCORED HIS LATEST LIFE SENTENCE...
I DON'T BELIEVE THIS...
NGHHH!
AHHH!
OW...
ERRGGH
I NEVER UNDERSTOOD BRAINWAVE OR THE JOKER. THEY HAVE THIS CRAZY NOTION OF "FAIRNESS."
LIKE THERE ARE RULES TO ALL THIS...

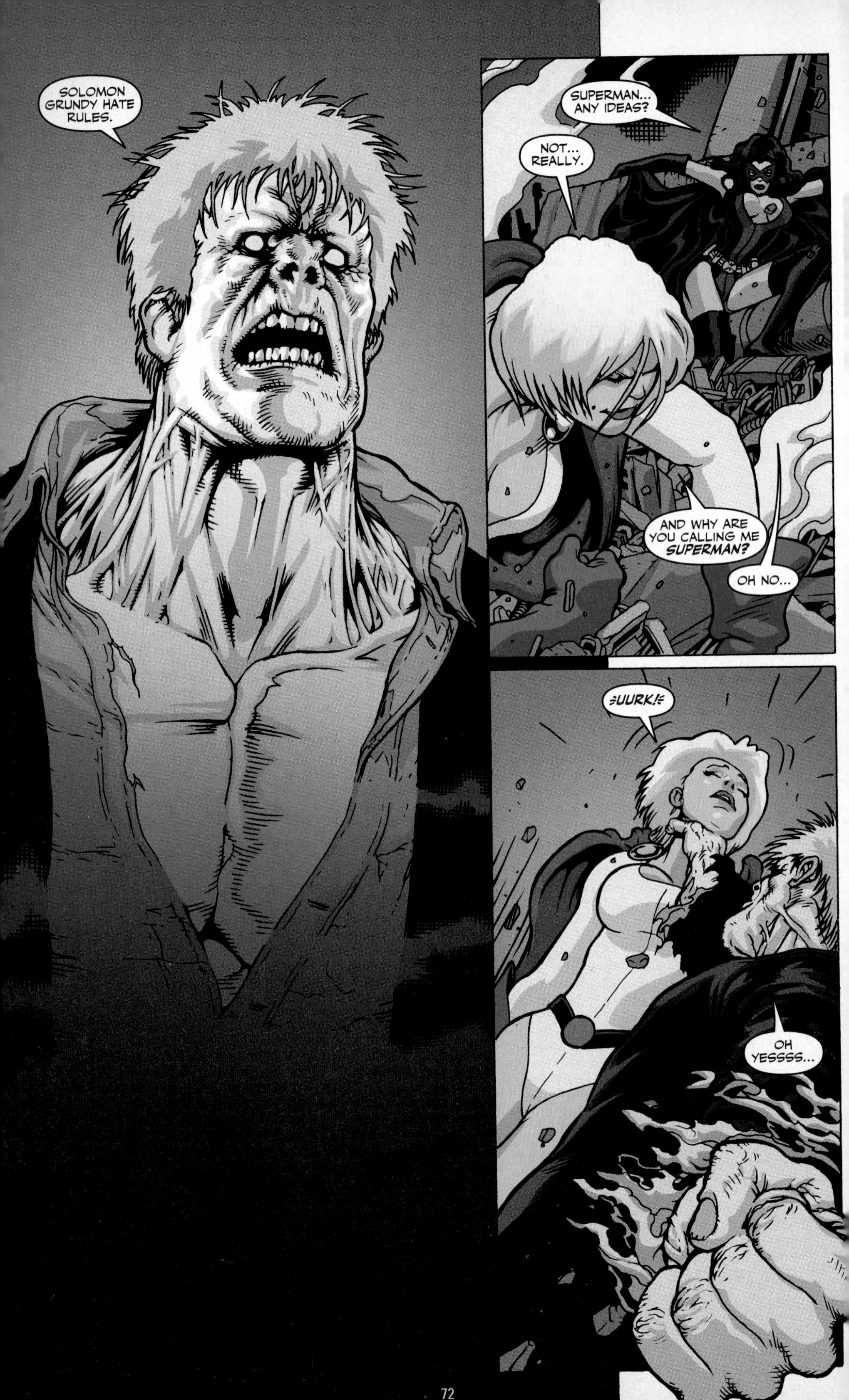
SOLOMON GRUNDY HATE RULES.
SUPERMAN... ANY IDEAS?
NOT... REALLY.
AND WHY ARE YOU CALLING ME SUPERMAN?
OH NO...
UURK!
OH YESSSS...

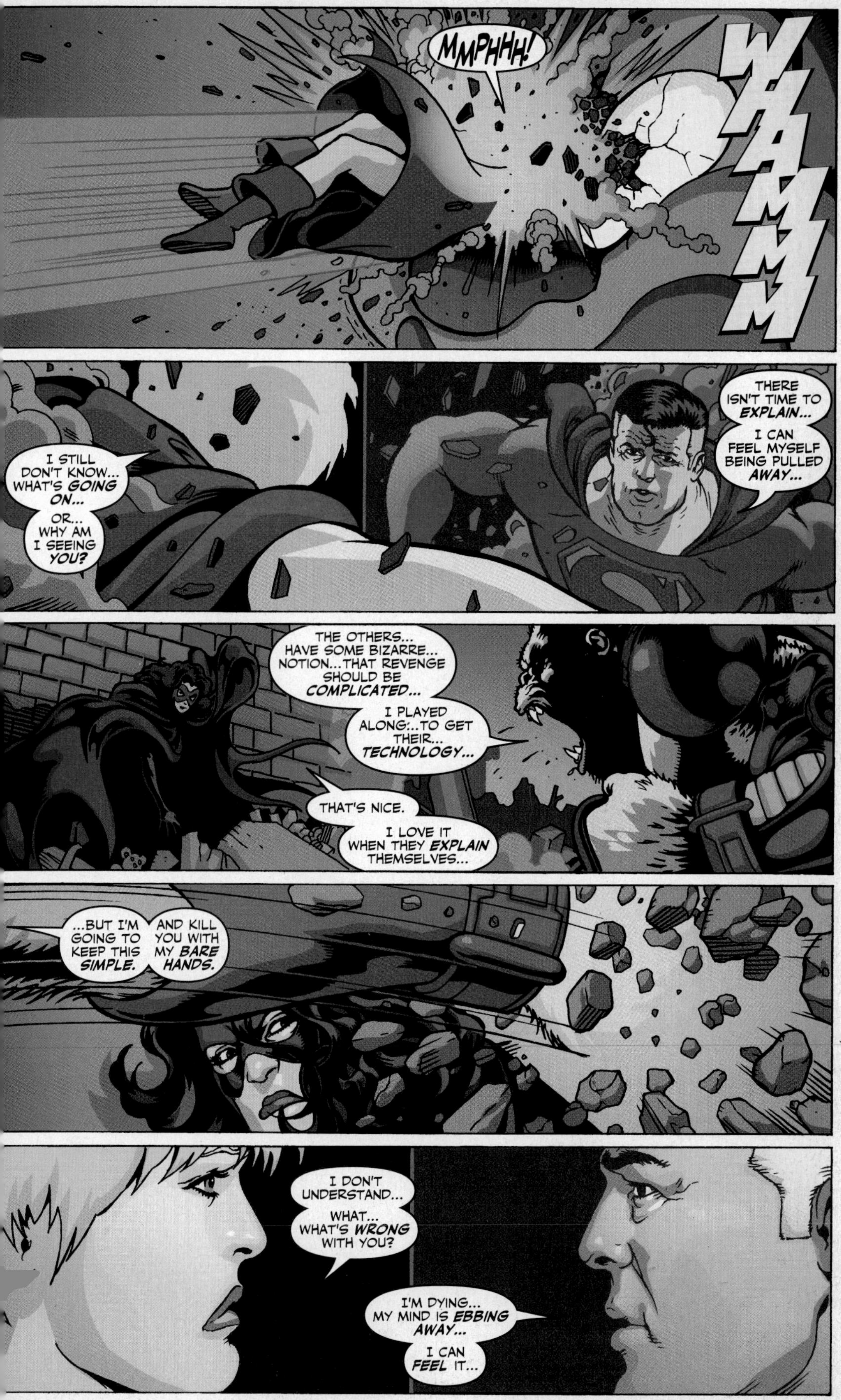
MMPHHH!
WHAMMM
I STILL DON'T KNOW... WHAT'S *GOING ON*... OR... WHY AM I SEEING *YOU*?
THERE ISN'T TIME TO *EXPLAIN*...
I CAN FEEL MYSELF BEING PULLED *AWAY*...
THE OTHERS... HAVE SOME BIZARRE... NOTION...THAT REVENGE SHOULD BE *COMPLICATED*...
I PLAYED ALONG:..TO GET THEIR... *TECHNOLOGY*...
THAT'S NICE.
I LOVE IT WHEN THEY *EXPLAIN* THEMSELVES...
...BUT I'M GOING TO KEEP THIS *SIMPLE*.
AND KILL YOU WITH MY *BARE HANDS*.
I DON'T UNDERSTAND...
WHAT... WHAT'S *WRONG* WITH YOU?
I'M DYING... MY MIND IS *EBBING AWAY*...
I CAN *FEEL* IT...

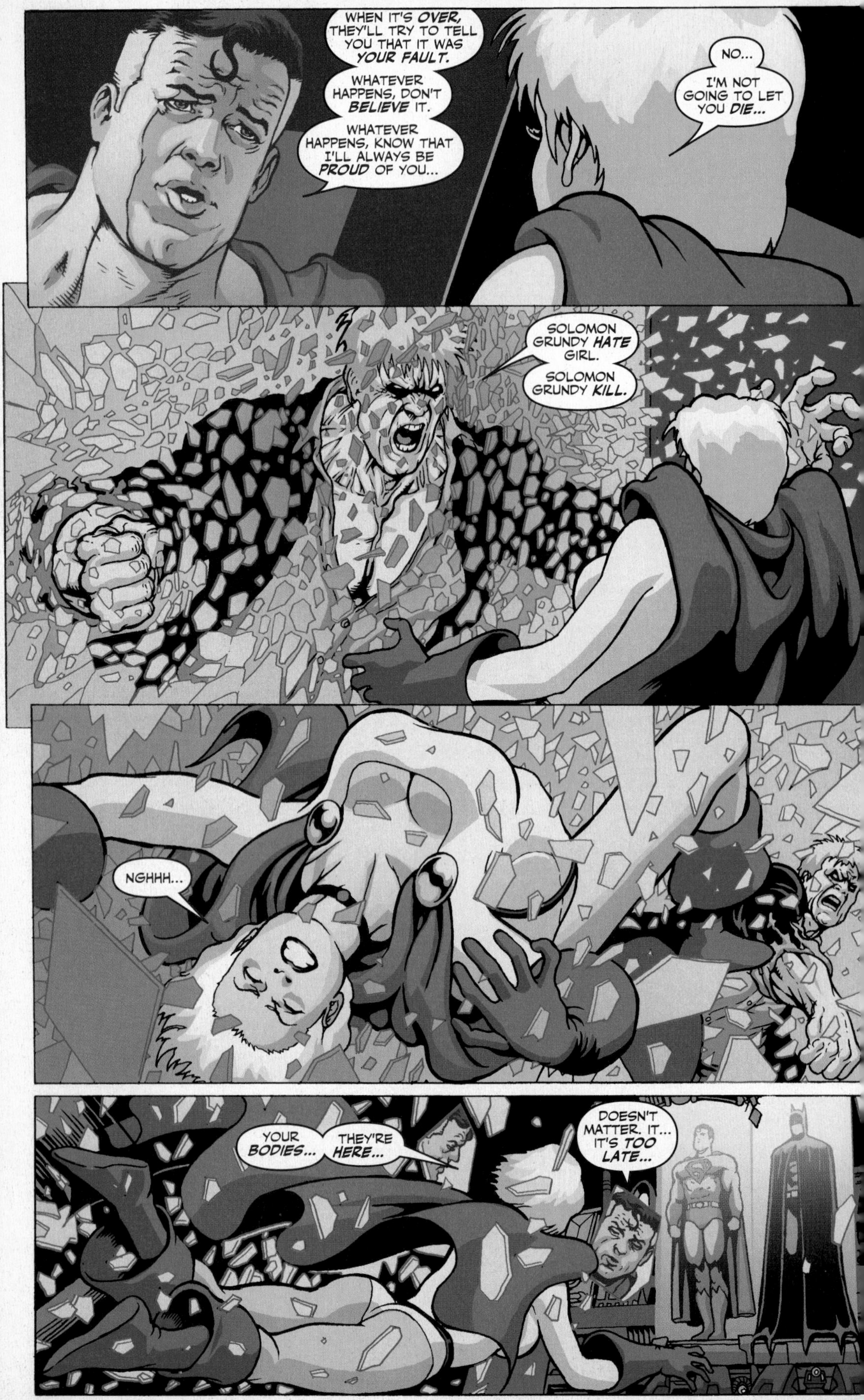
WHEN IT'S OVER, THEY'LL TRY TO TELL YOU THAT IT WAS YOUR FAULT.
WHATEVER HAPPENS, DON'T BELIEVE IT.
WHATEVER HAPPENS, KNOW THAT I'LL ALWAYS BE PROUD OF YOU...
NO...
I'M NOT GOING TO LET YOU DIE...
SOLOMON GRUNDY HATE GIRL.
SOLOMON GRUNDY KILL.
NGHHH...
YOUR BODIES...
THEY'RE HERE...
DOESN'T MATTER. IT... IT'S TOO LATE...

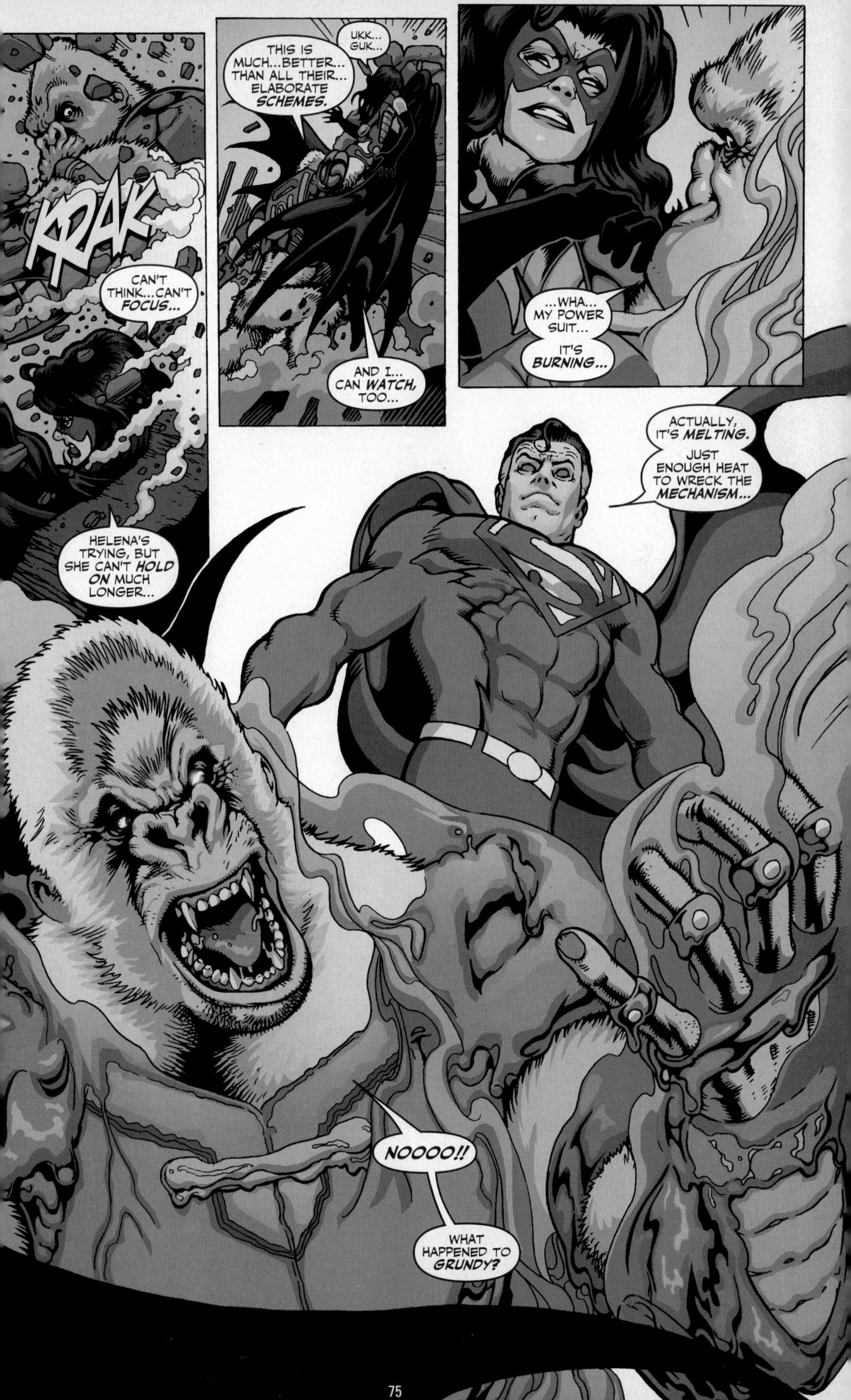
KRAK
CAN'T THINK...CAN'T FOCUS...
UKK... GUK...
THIS IS MUCH...BETTER... THAN ALL THEIR... ELABORATE SCHEMES.
AND I... CAN WATCH, TOO...
...WHA... MY POWER SUIT...
IT'S BURNING...
ACTUALLY, IT'S MELTING.
JUST ENOUGH HEAT TO WRECK THE MECHANISM...
HELENA'S TRYING, BUT SHE CAN'T HOLD ON MUCH LONGER...
NOOOO!!
WHAT HAPPENED TO GRUNDY?

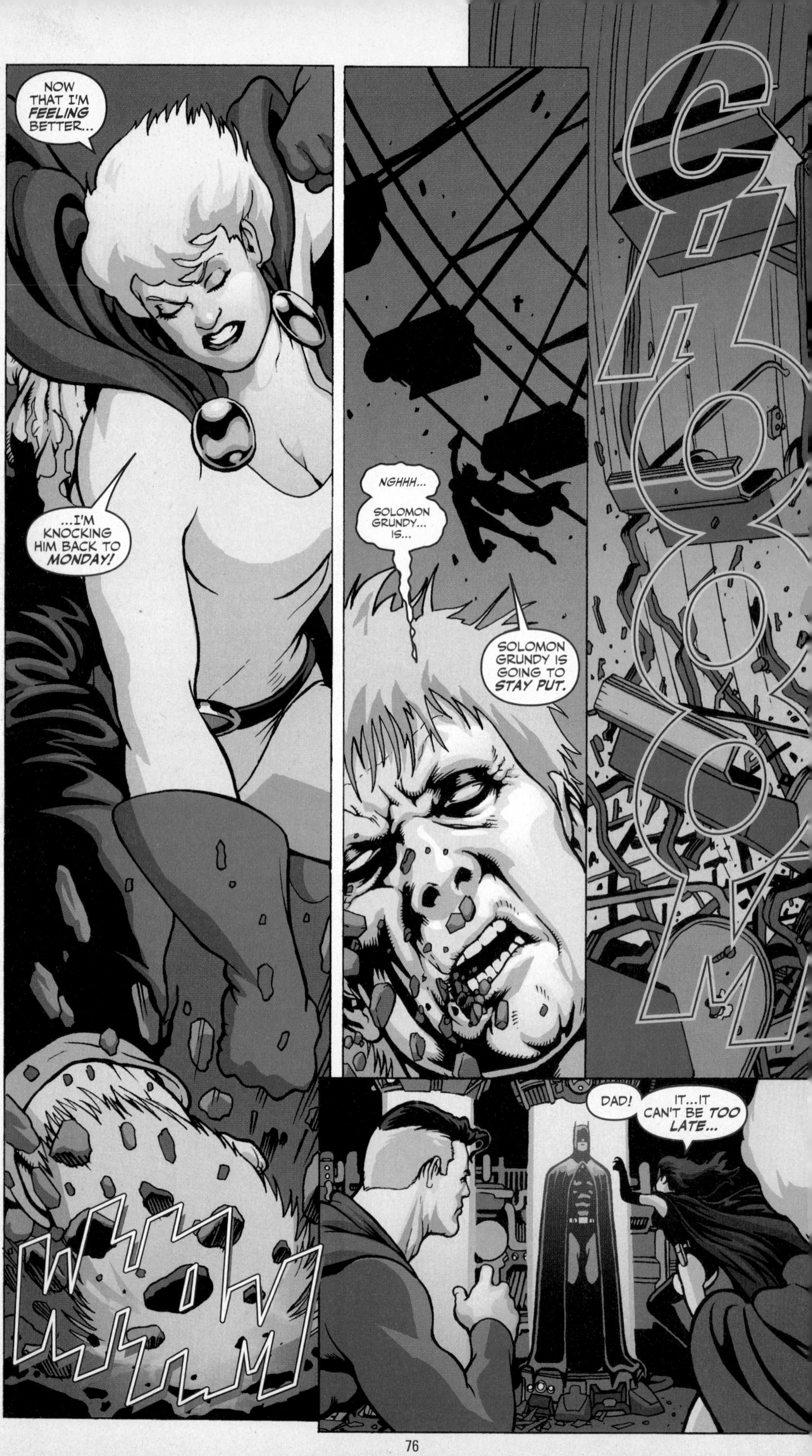
NOW THAT I'M *FEELING* BETTER...
...I'M KNOCKING HIM BACK TO *MONDAY!*
WHAM
NGHHH...
SOLOMON GRUNDY... IS...
SOLOMON GRUNDY IS GOING TO *STAY PUT.*
CHOOOOM
DAD!
IT...IT CAN'T BE *TOO LATE...*

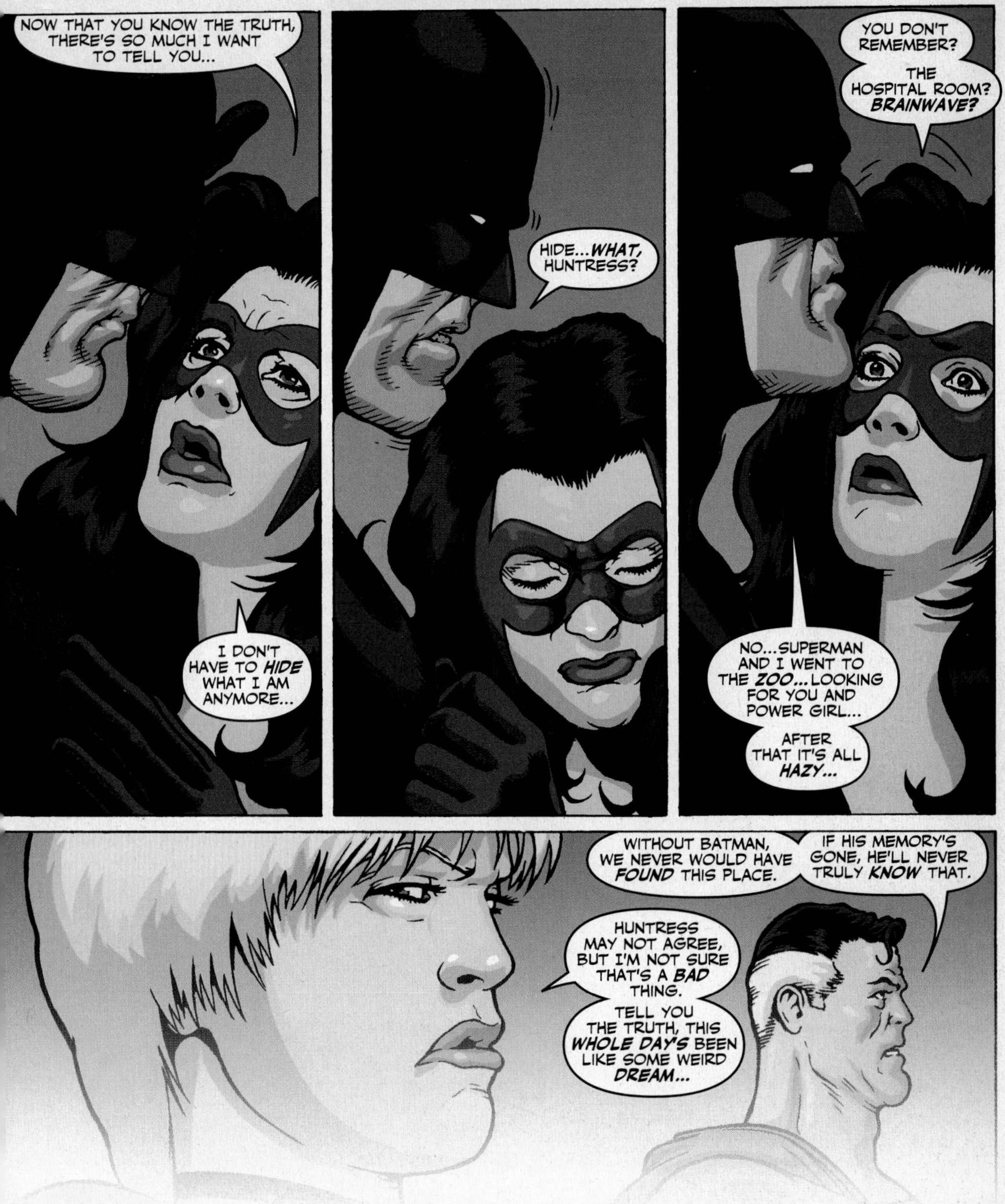
NOW THAT YOU KNOW THE TRUTH, THERE'S SO MUCH I WANT TO TELL YOU...
I DON'T HAVE TO *HIDE* WHAT I AM ANYMORE...
HIDE...*WHAT,* HUNTRESS?
YOU DON'T REMEMBER?
THE HOSPITAL ROOM? *BRAINWAVE?*
NO...SUPERMAN AND I WENT TO THE *ZOO*...LOOKING FOR YOU AND POWER GIRL...
AFTER THAT IT'S ALL *HAZY*...
WITHOUT BATMAN, WE NEVER WOULD HAVE *FOUND* THIS PLACE.
IF HIS MEMORY'S GONE, HE'LL NEVER TRULY *KNOW* THAT.
HUNTRESS MAY NOT AGREE, BUT I'M NOT SURE THAT'S A *BAD* THING.
TELL YOU THE TRUTH, THIS *WHOLE DAY'S* BEEN LIKE SOME WEIRD *DREAM*...

Following the world-shattering events known as the Infinite Crisis,

the stories of the DC Universe catapulted ahead one year where

the World's Greatest Super-Heroes continue their adventures in new settings and situations!

BOTTLE CITY
KANDOR.
WOW.
I JUST HAD THE MOST INSANE DREAM.
GREAT. YOU CAN SLEEP WHEN YOU'RE DEAD.
HURRY UP AND GET DRESSED. WE NEED TO GET OUT ON PATROL.

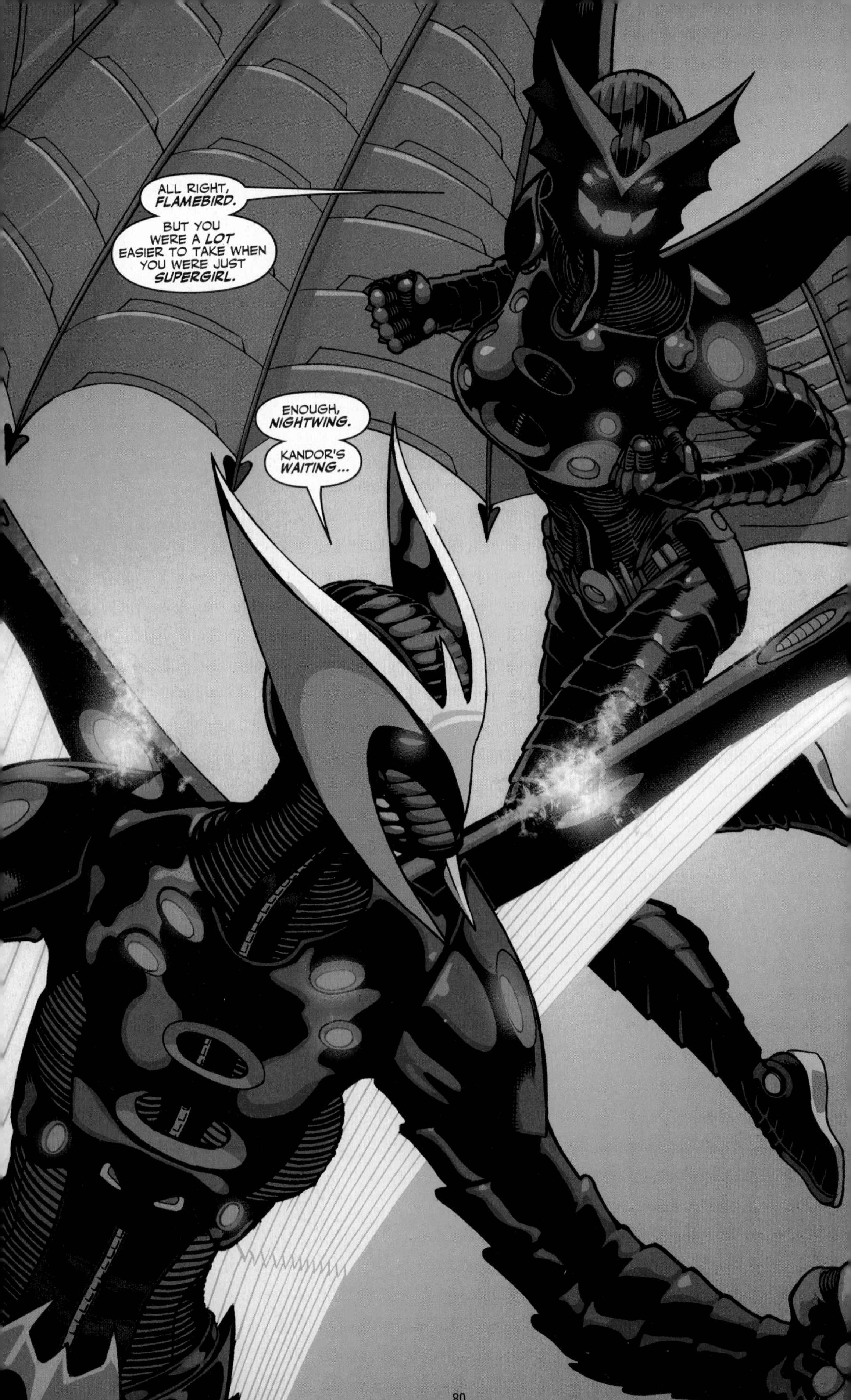
ALL RIGHT, FLAMEBIRD.
BUT YOU WERE A LOT EASIER TO TAKE WHEN YOU WERE JUST SUPERGIRL.
ENOUGH, NIGHTWING.
KANDOR'S WAITING...

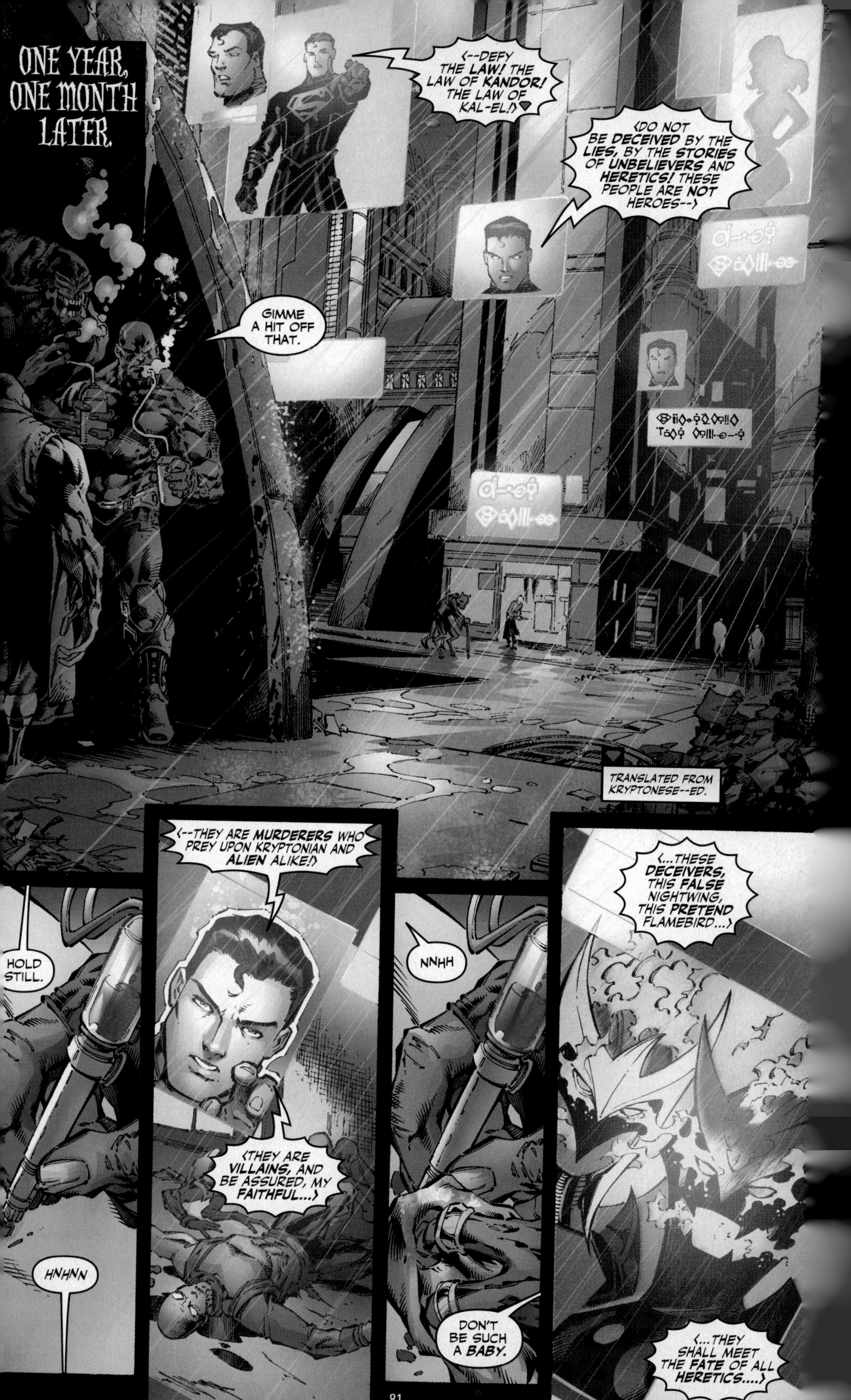
ONE YEAR, ONE MONTH LATER.
‹--DEFY THE LAW! THE LAW OF KANDOR! THE LAW OF KAL-EL!›
‹DO NOT BE DECEIVED BY THE LIES, BY THE STORIES OF UNBELIEVERS AND HERETICS! THESE PEOPLE ARE NOT HEROES--›
GIMME A HIT OFF THAT.
TRANSLATED FROM KRYPTONESE--ED.
HOLD STILL.
HNHNN
‹--THEY ARE MURDERERS WHO PREY UPON KRYPTONIAN AND ALIEN ALIKE!›
‹THEY ARE VILLAINS, AND BE ASSURED, MY FAITHFUL...›
NNHH
DON'T BE SUCH A BABY.
‹...THESE DECEIVERS, THIS FALSE NIGHTWING, THIS PRETEND FLAMEBIRD...›
‹...THEY SHALL MEET THE FATE OF ALL HERETICS....›

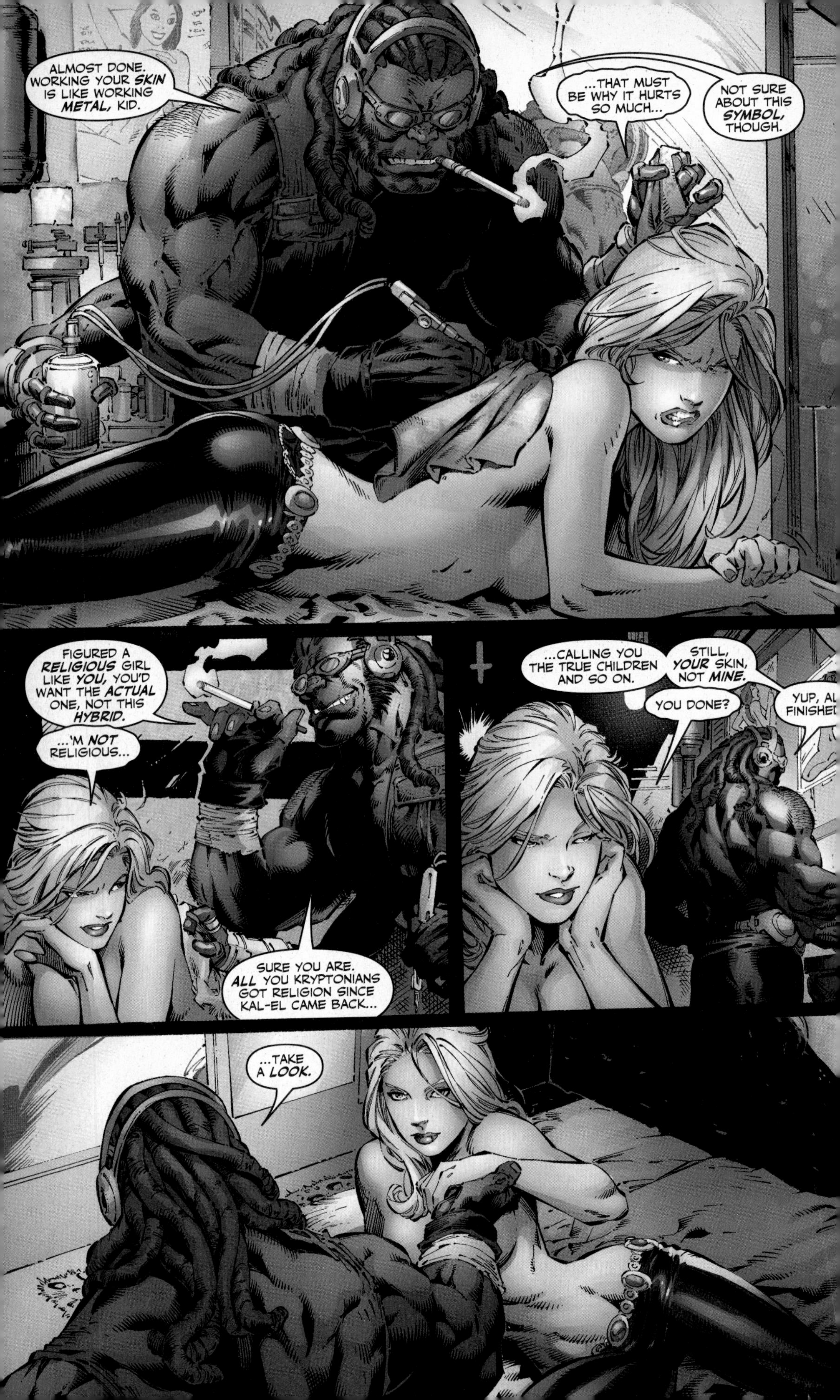
ALMOST DONE. WORKING YOUR SKIN IS LIKE WORKING METAL, KID.
...THAT MUST BE WHY IT HURTS SO MUCH...
NOT SURE ABOUT THIS SYMBOL, THOUGH.
FIGURED A RELIGIOUS GIRL LIKE YOU, YOU'D WANT THE ACTUAL ONE, NOT THIS HYBRID.
...'M NOT RELIGIOUS...
SURE YOU ARE. ALL YOU KRYPTONIANS GOT RELIGION SINCE KAL-EL CAME BACK...
...CALLING YOU THE TRUE CHILDREN AND SO ON.
STILL, YOUR SKIN, NOT MINE.
YOU DONE?
YUP, AL FINISHED
...TAKE A LOOK.

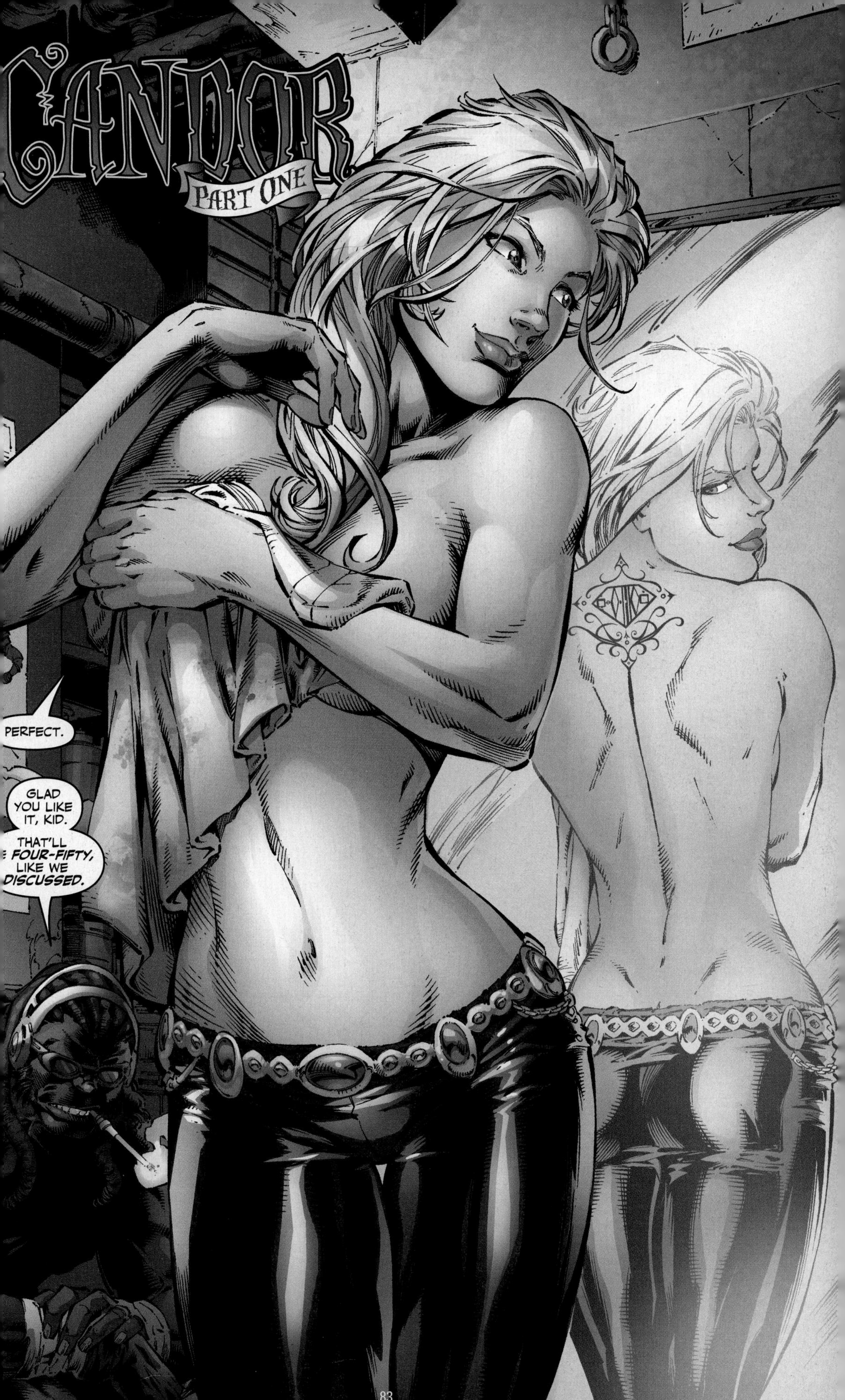
CANDOR
PART ONE
PERFECT.
GLAD YOU LIKE IT, KID.
THAT'LL FOUR-FIFTY, LIKE WE DISCUSSED.

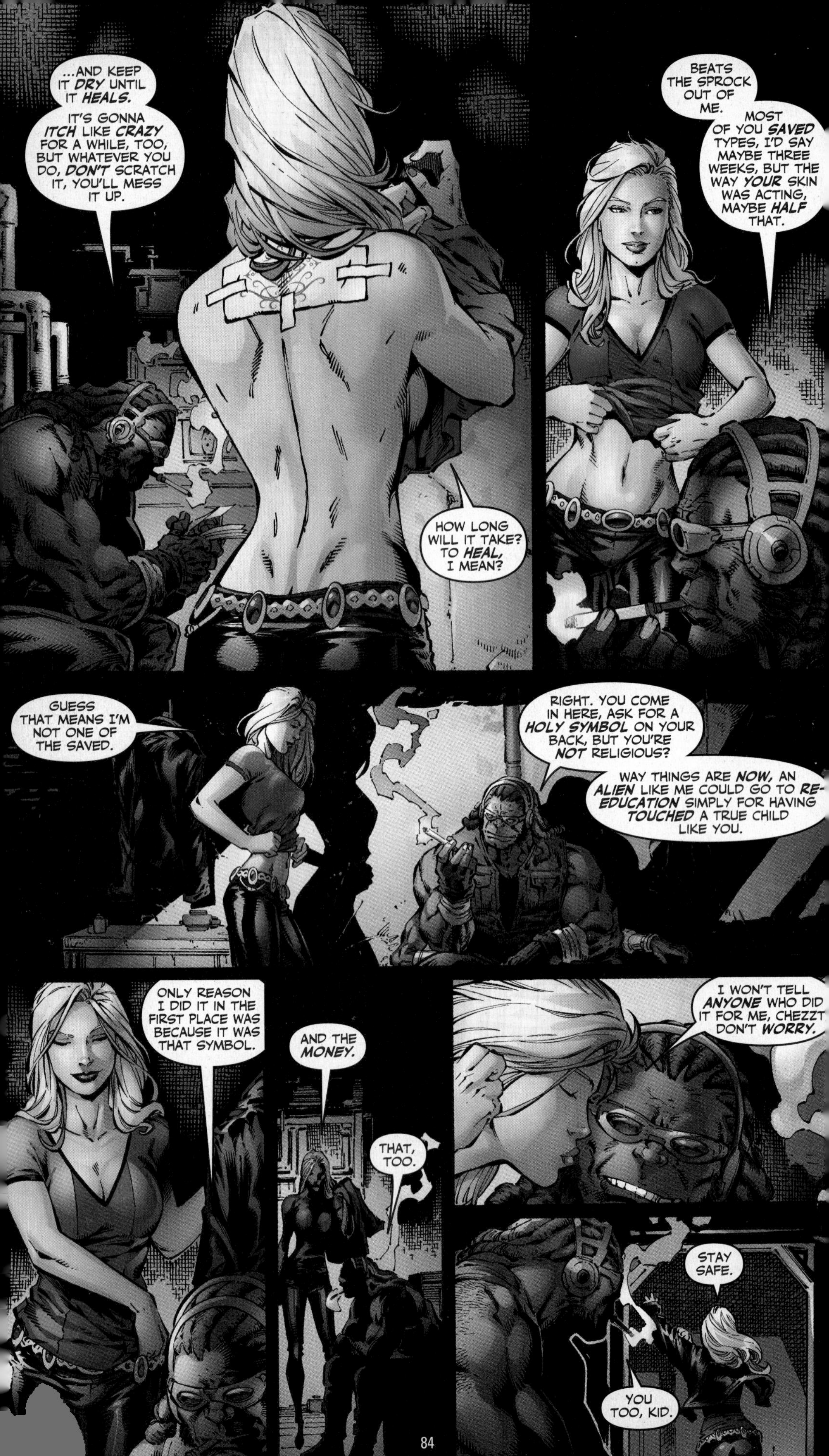
...AND KEEP IT DRY UNTIL IT HEALS.
IT'S GONNA ITCH LIKE CRAZY FOR A WHILE, TOO, BUT WHATEVER YOU DO, DON'T SCRATCH IT, YOU'LL MESS IT UP.
HOW LONG WILL IT TAKE? TO HEAL, I MEAN?
BEATS THE SPROCK OUT OF ME.
MOST OF YOU SAVED TYPES, I'D SAY MAYBE THREE WEEKS, BUT THE WAY YOUR SKIN WAS ACTING, MAYBE HALF THAT.
GUESS THAT MEANS I'M NOT ONE OF THE SAVED.
RIGHT. YOU COME IN HERE, ASK FOR A HOLY SYMBOL ON YOUR BACK, BUT YOU'RE NOT RELIGIOUS?
WAY THINGS ARE NOW, AN ALIEN LIKE ME COULD GO TO RE-EDUCATION SIMPLY FOR HAVING TOUCHED A TRUE CHILD LIKE YOU.
ONLY REASON I DID IT IN THE FIRST PLACE WAS BECAUSE IT WAS THAT SYMBOL.
AND THE MONEY.
THAT, TOO.
I WON'T TELL ANYONE WHO DID IT FOR ME, CHEZZT. DON'T WORRY.
STAY SAFE.
YOU TOO, KID.

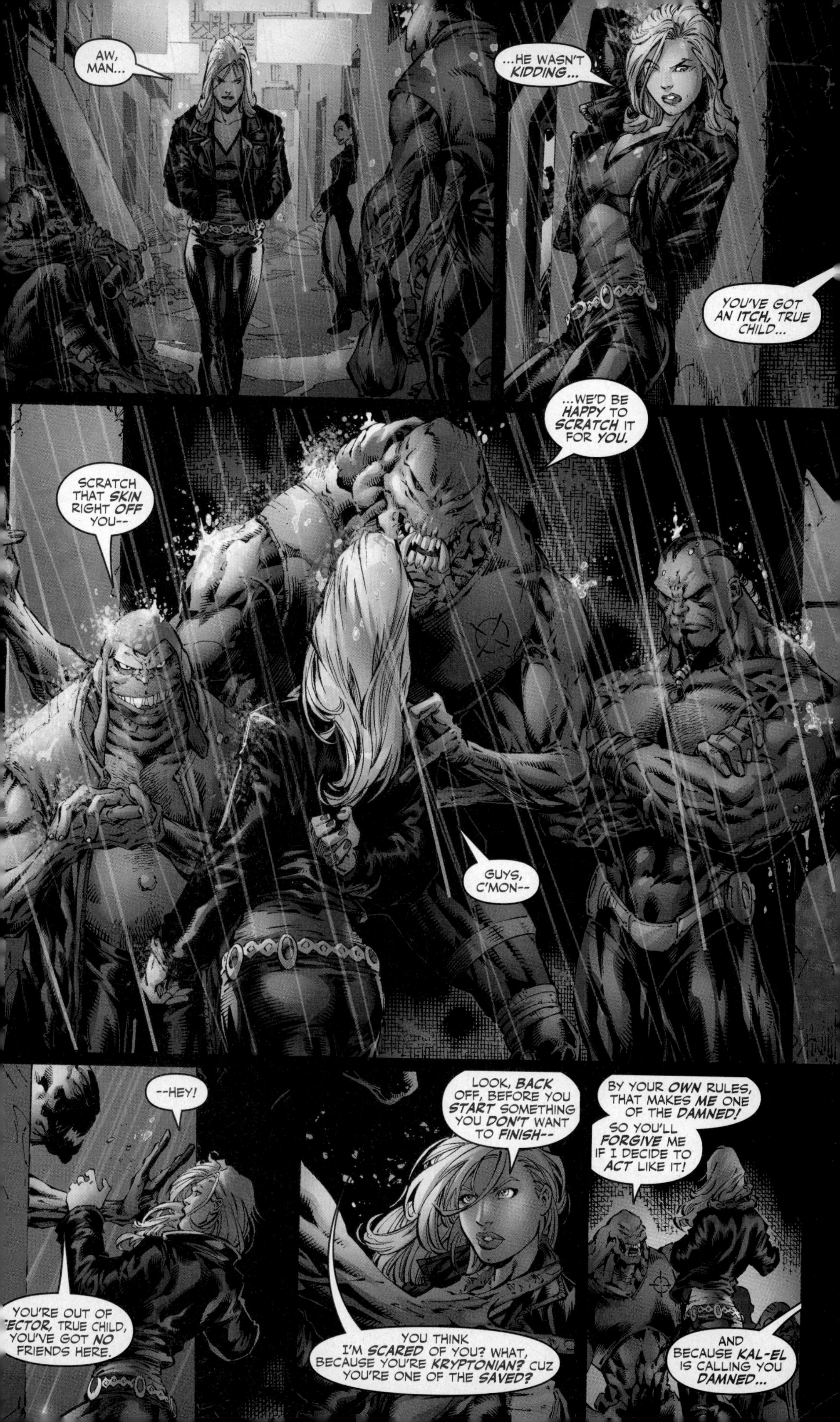

AW, MAN...
...HE WASN'T KIDDING...
YOU'VE GOT AN ITCH, TRUE CHILD...
...WE'D BE HAPPY TO SCRATCH IT FOR YOU.
SCRATCH THAT SKIN RIGHT OFF YOU--
GUYS, C'MON--
--HEY!
YOU'RE OUT OF ECTOR, TRUE CHILD, YOU'VE GOT NO FRIENDS HERE.
LOOK, BACK OFF, BEFORE YOU START SOMETHING YOU DON'T WANT TO FINISH--
YOU THINK I'M SCARED OF YOU? WHAT, BECAUSE YOU'RE KRYPTONIAN? CUZ YOU'RE ONE OF THE SAVED?
BY YOUR OWN RULES, THAT MAKES ME ONE OF THE DAMNED!
SO YOU'LL FORGIVE ME IF I DECIDE TO ACT LIKE IT!
AND BECAUSE KAL-EL IS CALLING YOU DAMNED...

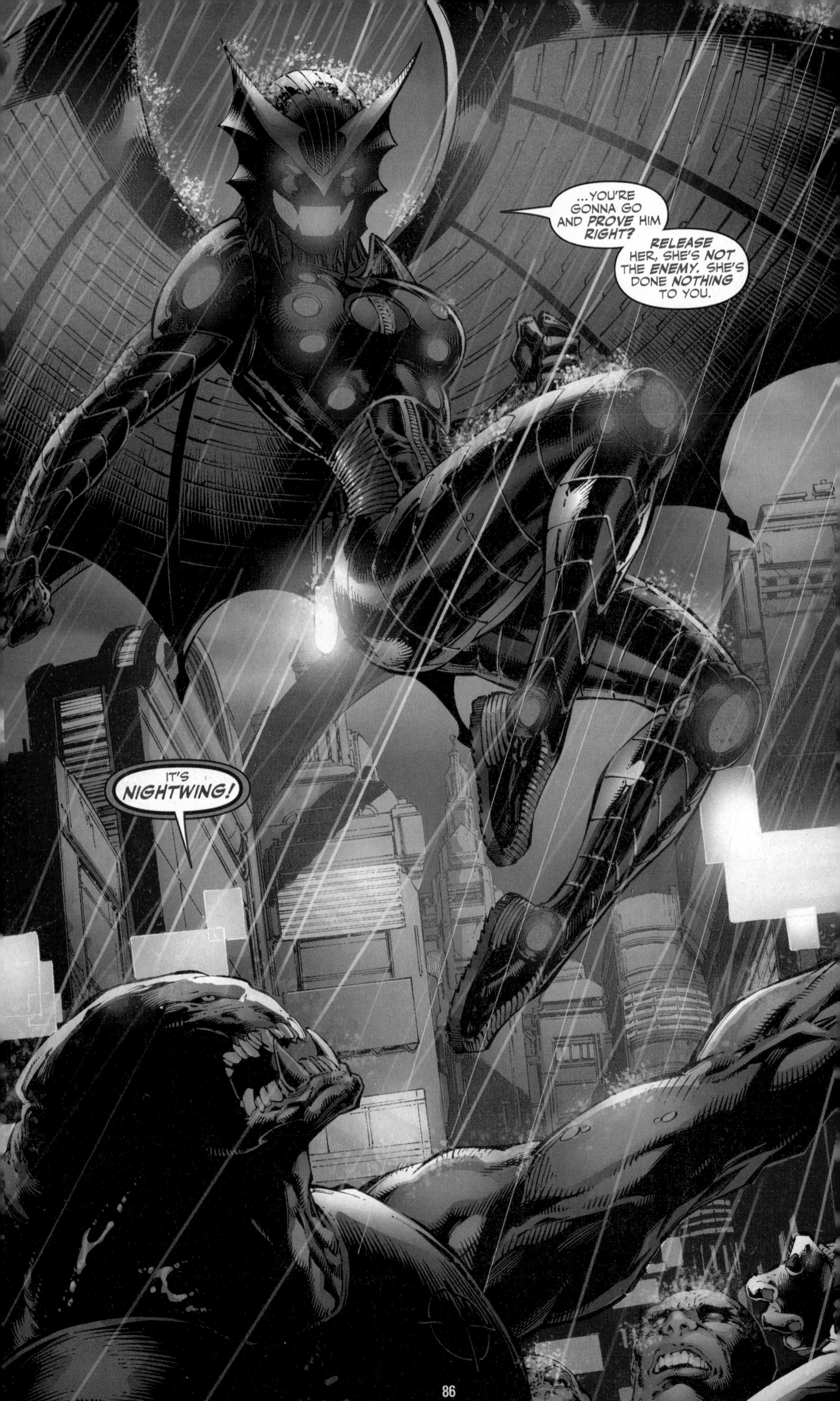
...YOU'RE GONNA GO AND PROVE HIM RIGHT? RELEASE HER, SHE'S NOT THE ENEMY. SHE'S DONE NOTHING TO YOU.
IT'S NIGHTWING!

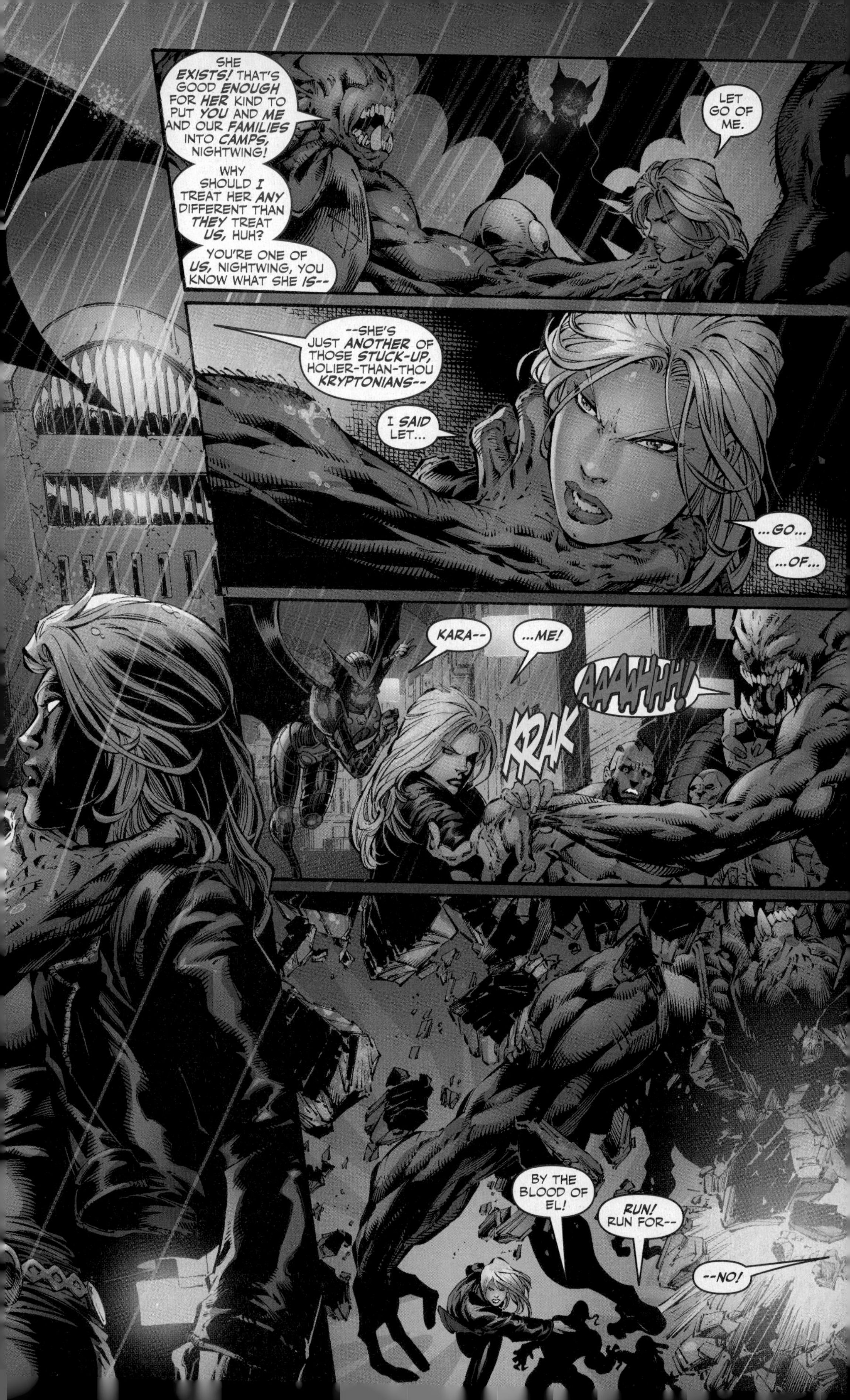
SHE EXISTS! THAT'S GOOD ENOUGH FOR HER KIND TO PUT YOU AND ME AND OUR FAMILIES INTO CAMPS, NIGHTWING!
WHY SHOULD I TREAT HER ANY DIFFERENT THAN THEY TREAT US, HUH?
YOU'RE ONE OF US, NIGHTWING, YOU KNOW WHAT SHE IS--
LET GO OF ME.
--SHE'S JUST ANOTHER OF THOSE STUCK-UP, HOLIER-THAN-THOU KRYPTONIANS--
I SAID LET...
...GO...
...OF...
KARA--
...ME!
KRAK
AAAAHHH!
BY THE BLOOD OF EL!
RUN! RUN FOR--
--NO!

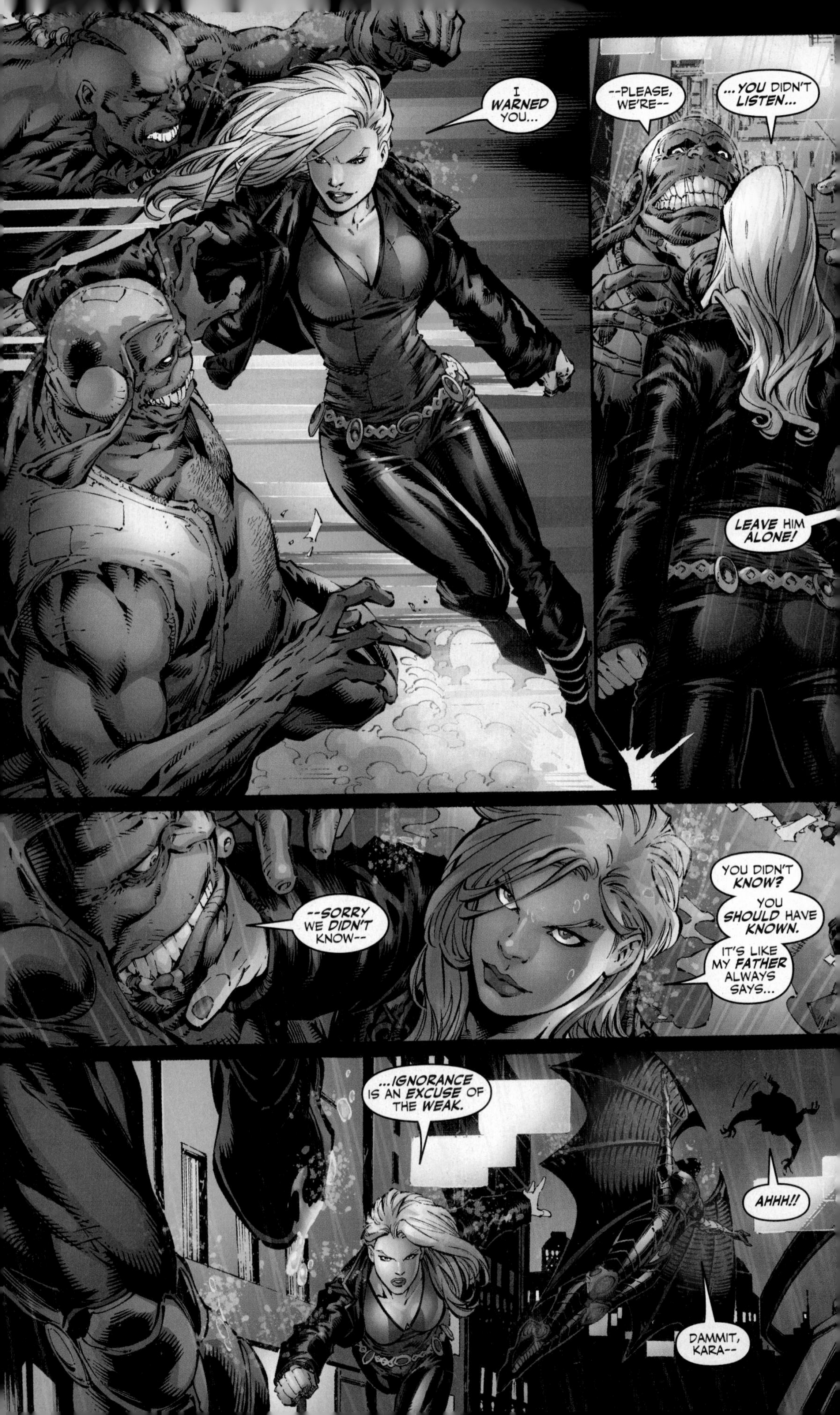
I WARNED YOU...
--PLEASE, WE'RE--
...YOU DIDN'T LISTEN...
LEAVE HIM ALONE!
--SORRY WE DIDN'T KNOW--
YOU DIDN'T KNOW?
YOU SHOULD HAVE KNOWN.
IT'S LIKE MY FATHER ALWAYS SAYS...
...IGNORANCE IS AN EXCUSE OF THE WEAK.
AHHH!!
DAMMIT, KARA--

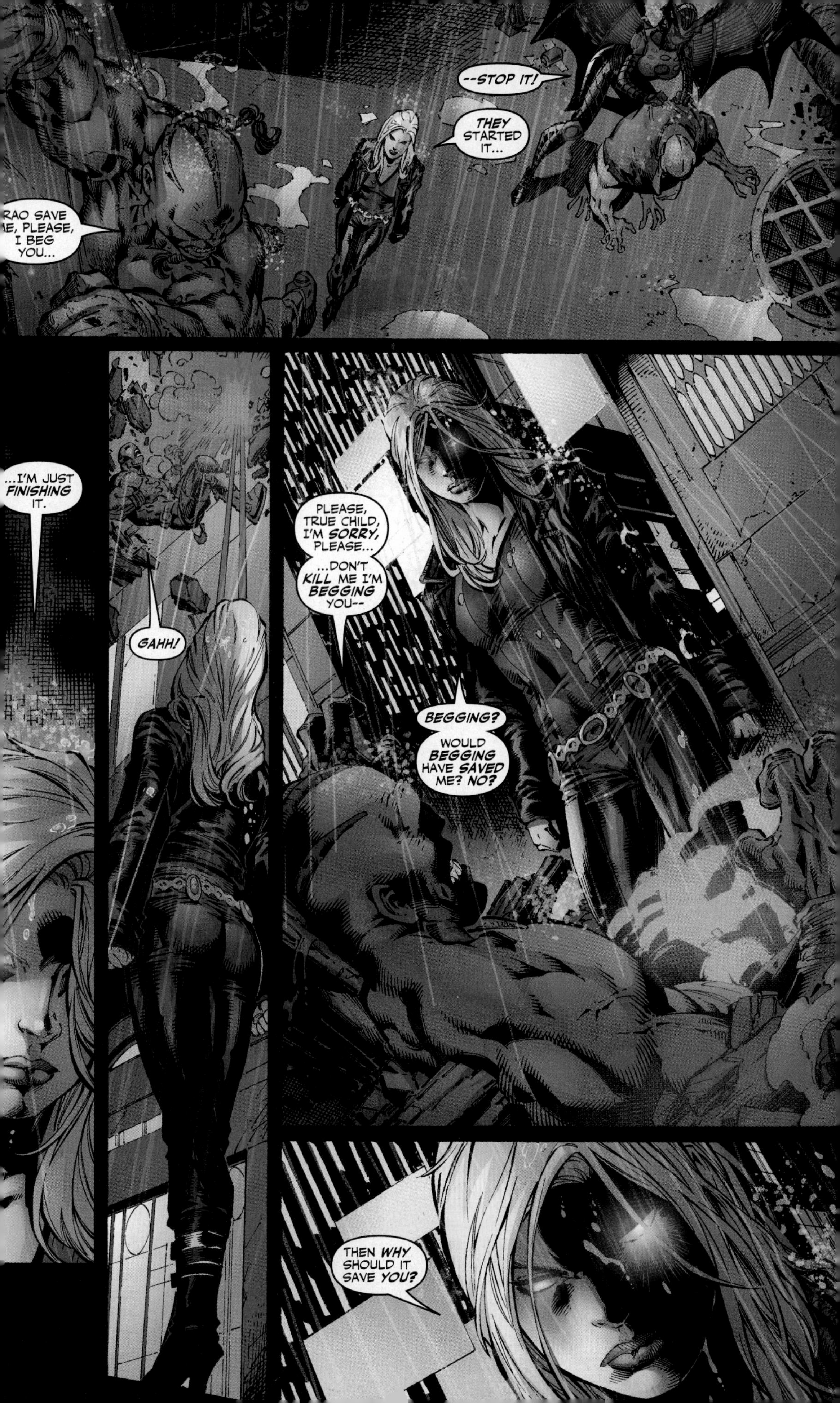
RAO SAVE ME, PLEASE, I BEG YOU...
--STOP IT!
THEY STARTED IT...
...I'M JUST FINISHING IT.
GAHH!
PLEASE, TRUE CHILD, I'M SORRY, PLEASE...
...DON'T KILL ME I'M BEGGING YOU--
BEGGING?
WOULD BEGGING HAVE SAVED ME? NO?
THEN WHY SHOULD IT SAVE YOU?

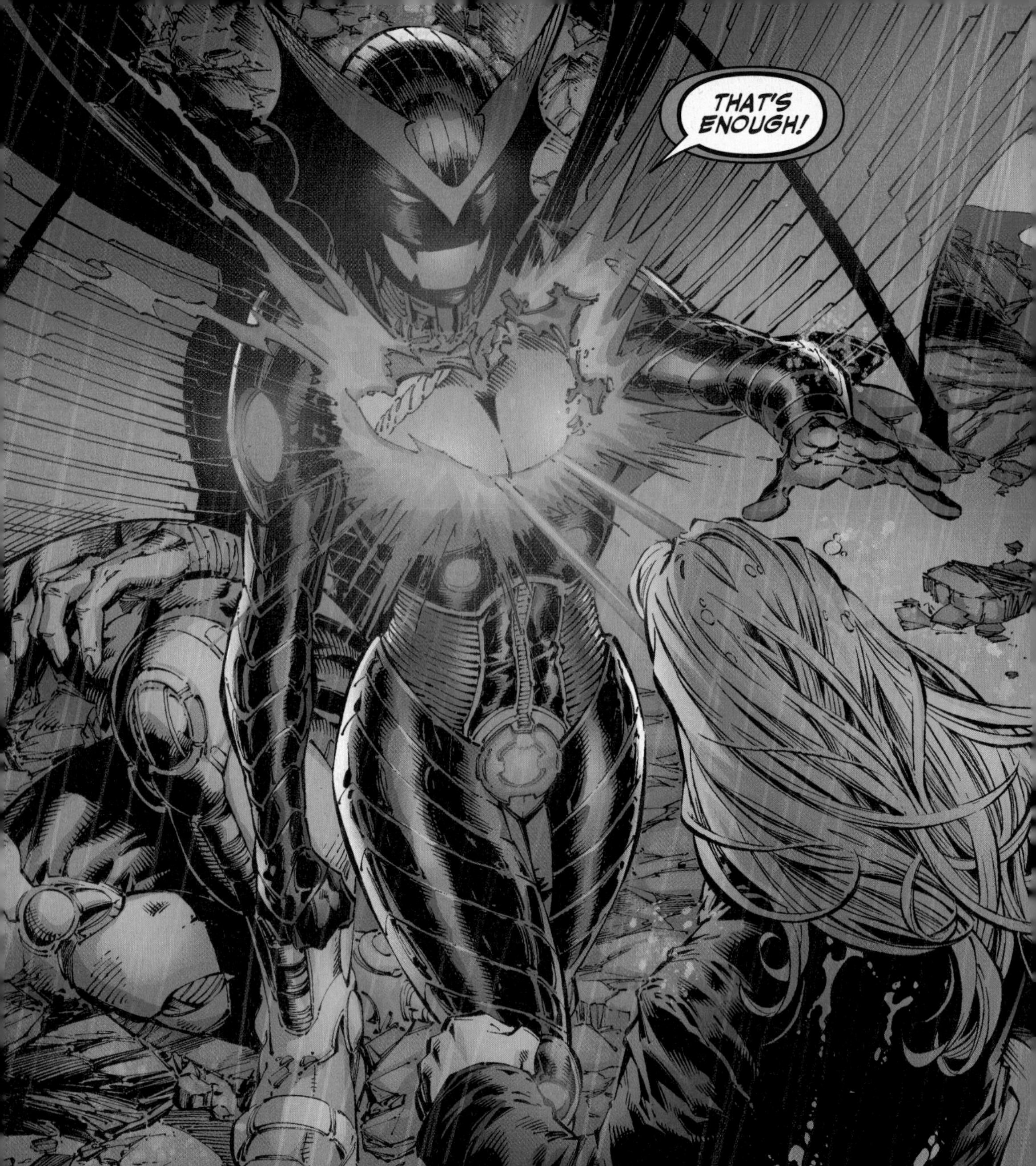
THAT'S
ENOUGH!

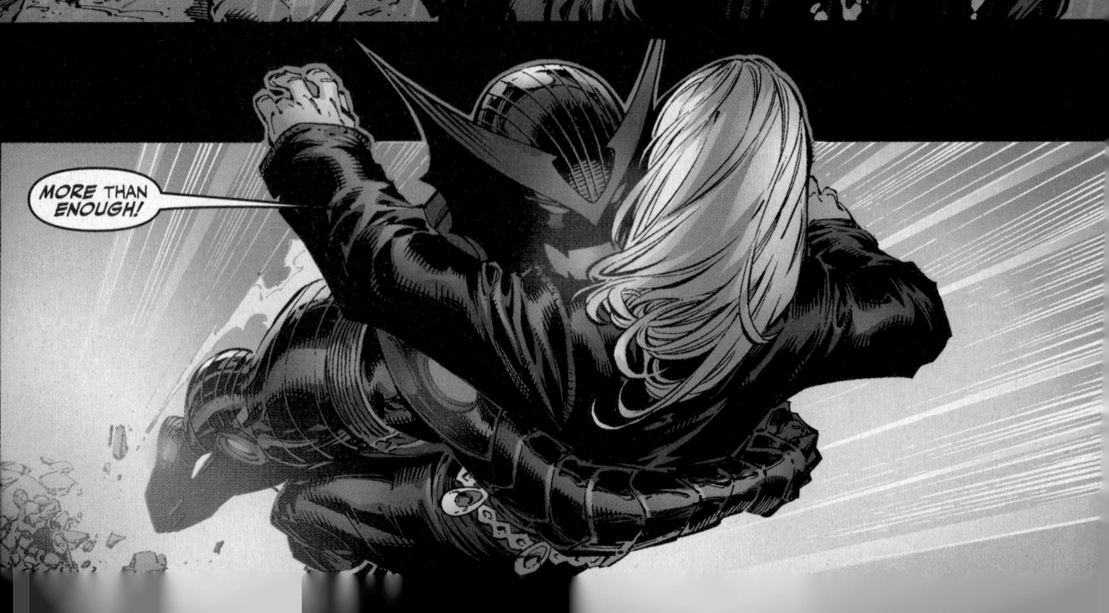
MORE THAN
ENOUGH!

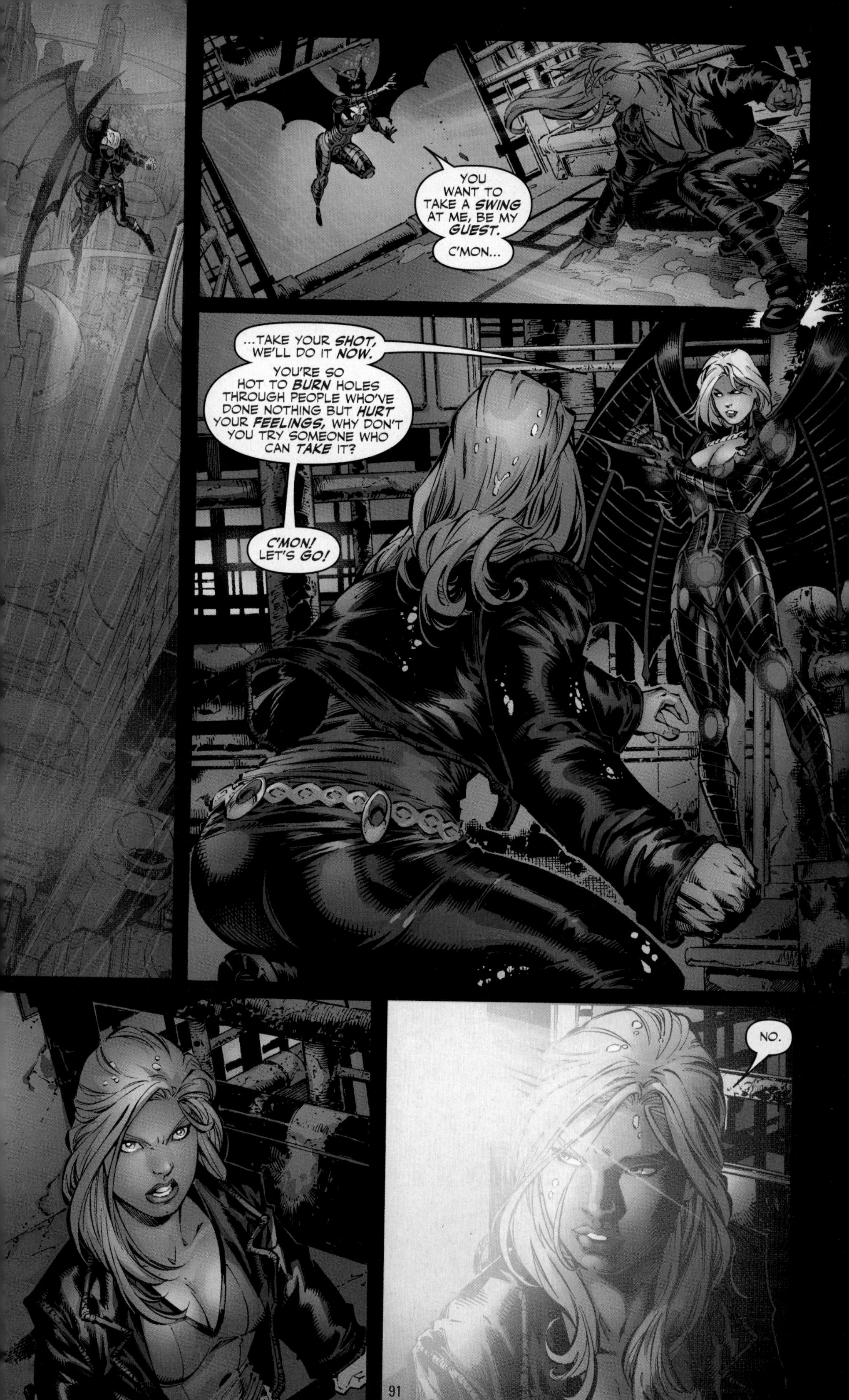
YOU WANT TO TAKE A SWING AT ME, BE MY GUEST.
C'MON...
...TAKE YOUR SHOT, WE'LL DO IT NOW.
YOU'RE SO HOT TO BURN HOLES THROUGH PEOPLE WHO'VE DONE NOTHING BUT HURT YOUR FEELINGS, WHY DON'T YOU TRY SOMEONE WHO CAN TAKE IT?
C'MON! LET'S GO!
NO.

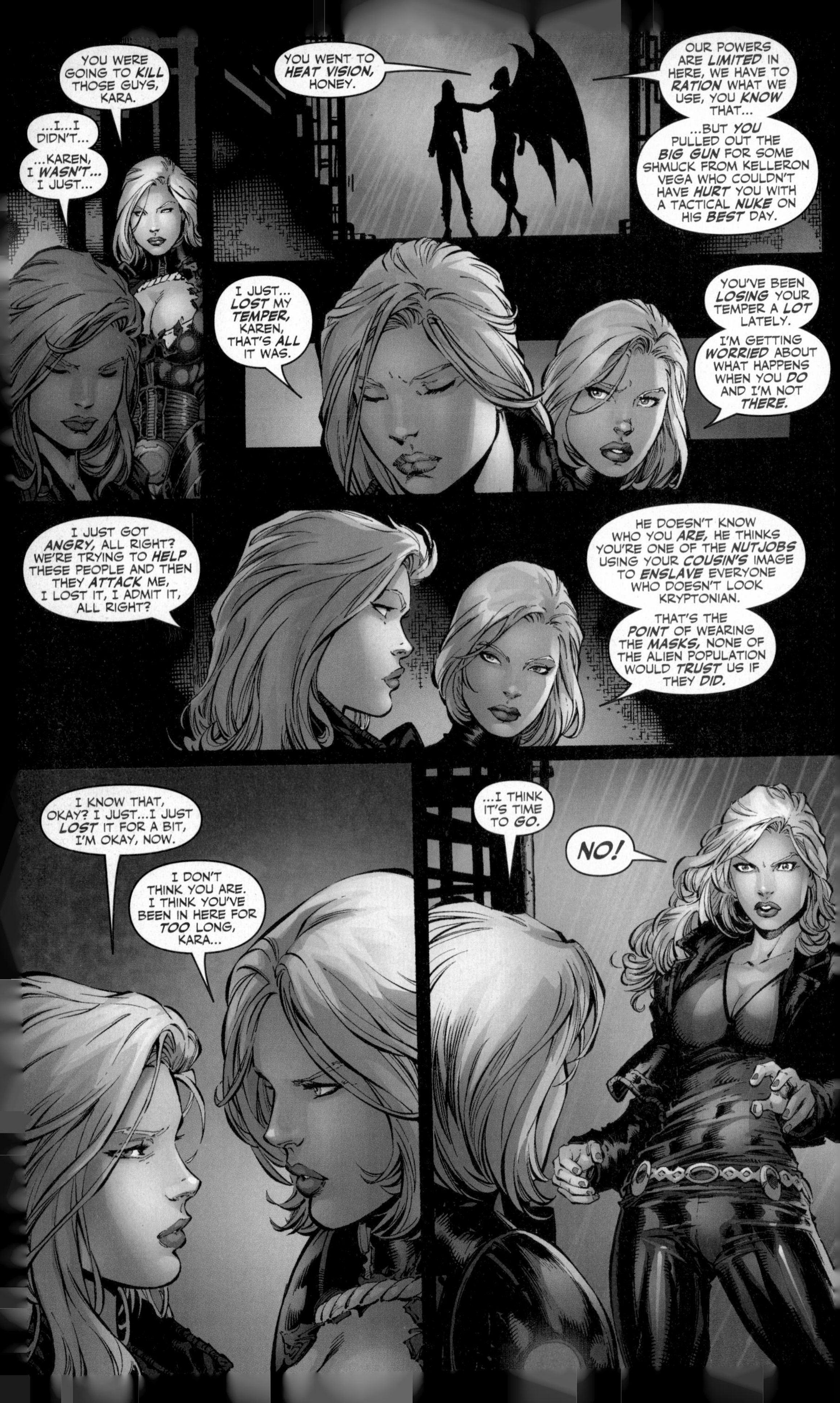
YOU WERE GOING TO KILL THOSE GUYS, KARA.
...I...I DIDN'T...
...KAREN, I WASN'T... I JUST...
YOU WENT TO HEAT VISION, HONEY.
OUR POWERS ARE LIMITED IN HERE, WE HAVE TO RATION WHAT WE USE, YOU KNOW THAT...
...BUT YOU PULLED OUT THE BIG GUN FOR SOME SHMUCK FROM KELLERON VEGA WHO COULDN'T HAVE HURT YOU WITH A TACTICAL NUKE ON HIS BEST DAY.
I JUST... LOST MY TEMPER, KAREN, THAT'S ALL IT WAS.
YOU'VE BEEN LOSING YOUR TEMPER A LOT LATELY.
I'M GETTING WORRIED ABOUT WHAT HAPPENS WHEN YOU DO AND I'M NOT THERE.
I JUST GOT ANGRY, ALL RIGHT? WE'RE TRYING TO HELP THESE PEOPLE AND THEN THEY ATTACK ME, I LOST IT, I ADMIT IT, ALL RIGHT?
HE DOESN'T KNOW WHO YOU ARE, HE THINKS YOU'RE ONE OF THE NUTJOBS USING YOUR COUSIN'S IMAGE TO ENSLAVE EVERYONE WHO DOESN'T LOOK KRYPTONIAN.
THAT'S THE POINT OF WEARING THE MASKS, NONE OF THE ALIEN POPULATION WOULD TRUST US IF THEY DID.
I KNOW THAT, OKAY? I JUST...I JUST LOST IT FOR A BIT, I'M OKAY, NOW.
I DON'T THINK YOU ARE. I THINK YOU'VE BEEN IN HERE FOR TOO LONG, KARA...
...I THINK IT'S TIME TO GO.
NO!

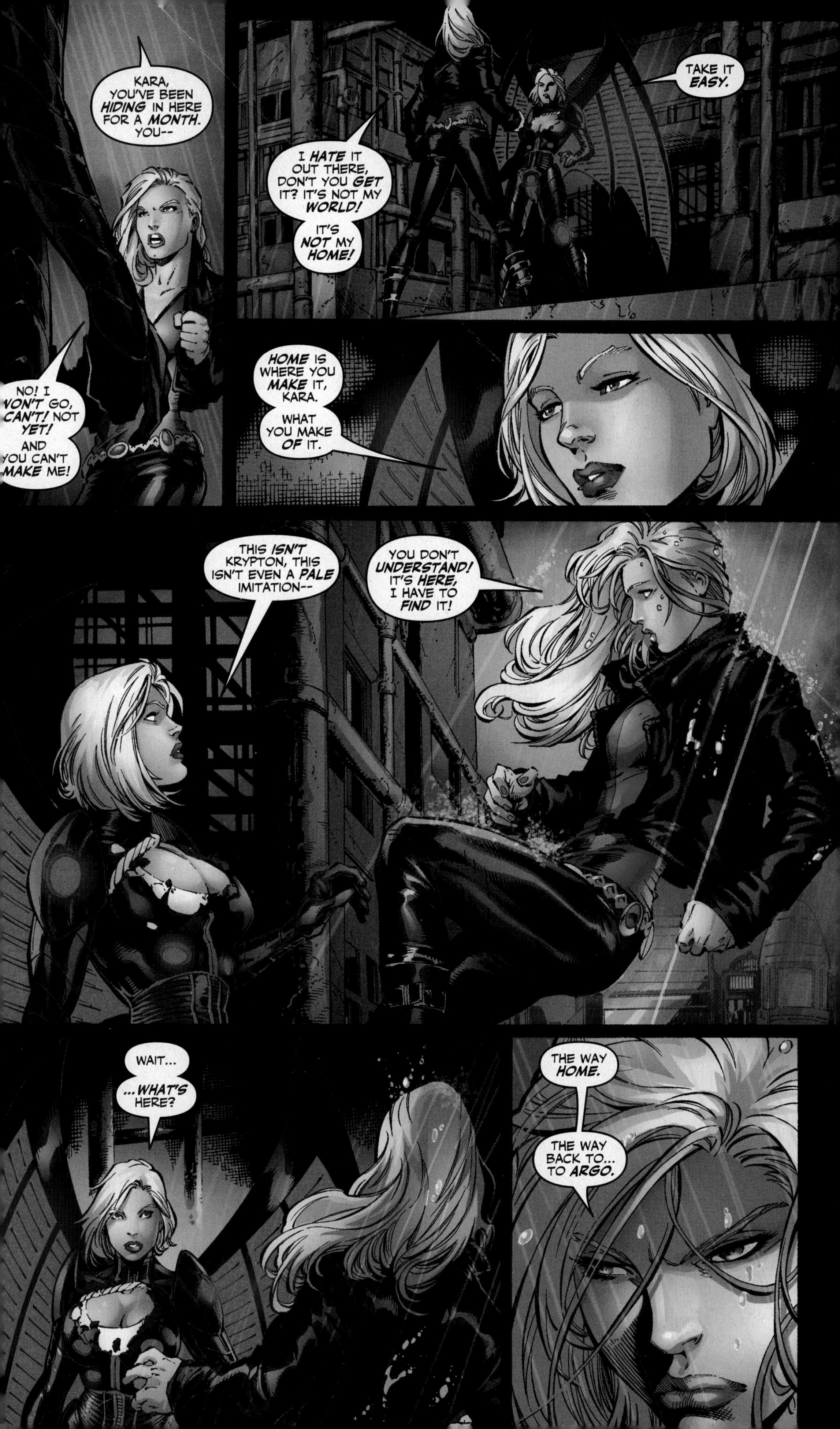

KARA, YOU'VE BEEN HIDING IN HERE FOR A MONTH. YOU--
I HATE IT OUT THERE, DON'T YOU GET IT? IT'S NOT MY WORLD!
IT'S NOT MY HOME!
TAKE IT EASY.
NO! I WON'T GO, CAN'T! NOT YET!
AND YOU CAN'T MAKE ME!
HOME IS WHERE YOU MAKE IT, KARA.
WHAT YOU MAKE OF IT.
THIS ISN'T KRYPTON, THIS ISN'T EVEN A PALE IMITATION--
YOU DON'T UNDERSTAND! IT'S HERE, I HAVE TO FIND IT!
WAIT...
...WHAT'S HERE?
THE WAY HOME.
THE WAY BACK TO... TO ARGO.

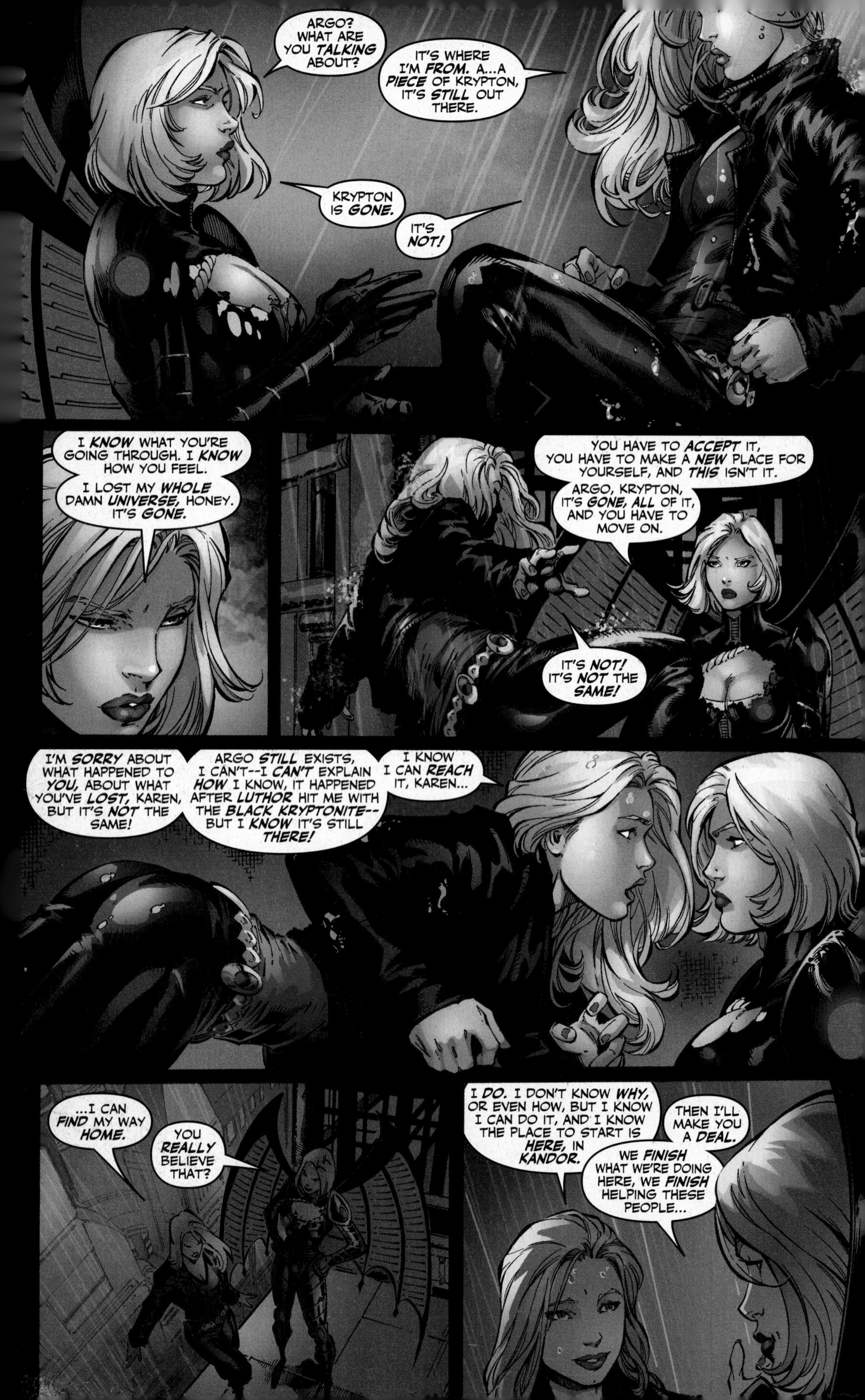
ARGO? WHAT ARE YOU TALKING ABOUT?
IT'S WHERE I'M FROM. A...A PIECE OF KRYPTON, IT'S STILL OUT THERE.
KRYPTON IS GONE.
IT'S NOT!
I KNOW WHAT YOU'RE GOING THROUGH. I KNOW HOW YOU FEEL.
I LOST MY WHOLE DAMN UNIVERSE, HONEY. IT'S GONE.
YOU HAVE TO ACCEPT IT, YOU HAVE TO MAKE A NEW PLACE FOR YOURSELF, AND THIS ISN'T IT.
ARGO, KRYPTON, IT'S GONE, ALL OF IT, AND YOU HAVE TO MOVE ON.
IT'S NOT! IT'S NOT THE SAME!
I'M SORRY ABOUT WHAT HAPPENED TO YOU, ABOUT WHAT YOU'VE LOST, KAREN, BUT IT'S NOT THE SAME!
ARGO STILL EXISTS, I CAN'T--I CAN'T EXPLAIN HOW I KNOW, IT HAPPENED AFTER LUTHOR HIT ME WITH THE BLACK KRYPTONITE-- BUT I KNOW IT'S STILL THERE!
I KNOW I CAN REACH IT, KAREN...
...I CAN FIND MY WAY HOME.
YOU REALLY BELIEVE THAT?
I DO. I DON'T KNOW WHY, OR EVEN HOW, BUT I KNOW I CAN DO IT, AND I KNOW THE PLACE TO START IS HERE, IN KANDOR.
THEN I'LL MAKE YOU A DEAL.
WE FINISH WHAT WE'RE DOING HERE, WE FINISH HELPING THESE PEOPLE...

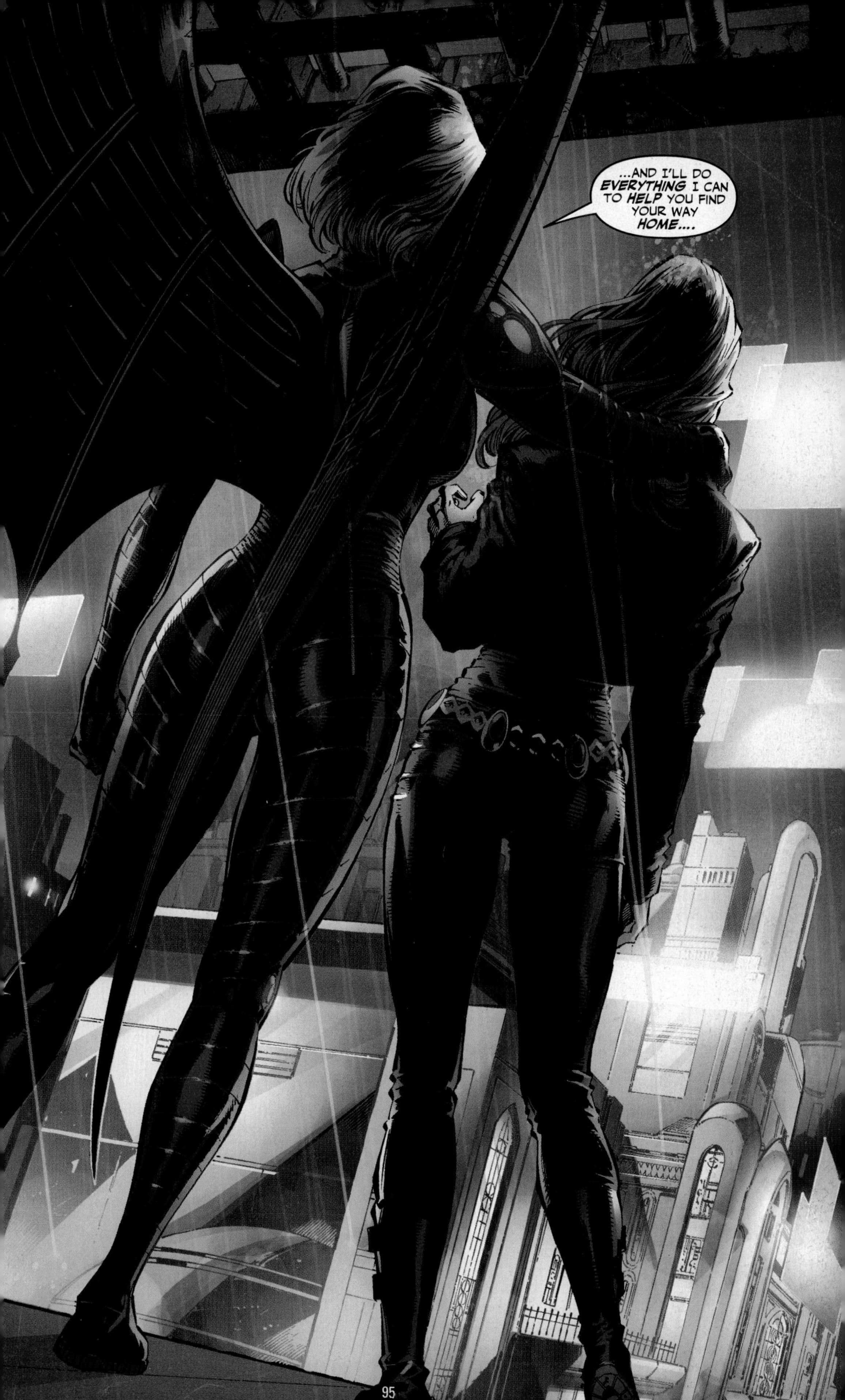
...AND I'LL DO EVERYTHING I CAN TO HELP YOU FIND YOUR WAY HOME....

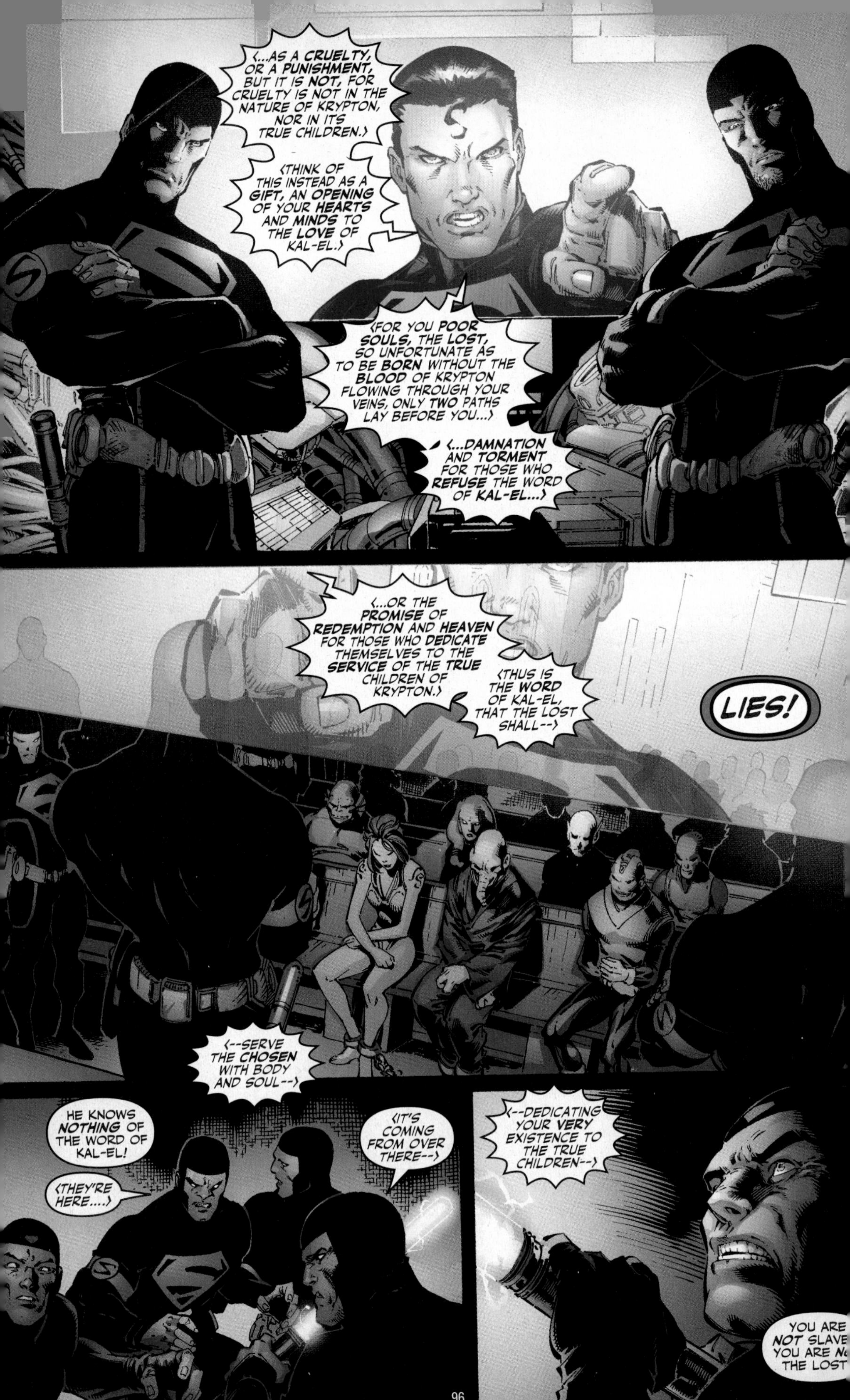

⟨...AS A CRUELTY, OR A PUNISHMENT, BUT IT IS NOT, FOR CRUELTY IS NOT IN THE NATURE OF KRYPTON, NOR IN ITS TRUE CHILDREN.⟩
⟨THINK OF THIS INSTEAD AS A GIFT, AN OPENING OF YOUR HEARTS AND MINDS TO THE LOVE OF KAL-EL.⟩
⟨FOR YOU POOR SOULS, THE LOST, SO UNFORTUNATE AS TO BE BORN WITHOUT THE BLOOD OF KRYPTON FLOWING THROUGH YOUR VEINS, ONLY TWO PATHS LAY BEFORE YOU...⟩
⟨...DAMNATION AND TORMENT FOR THOSE WHO REFUSE THE WORD OF KAL-EL...⟩
⟨...OR THE PROMISE OF REDEMPTION AND HEAVEN FOR THOSE WHO DEDICATE THEMSELVES TO THE SERVICE OF THE TRUE CHILDREN OF KRYPTON.⟩
⟨THUS IS THE WORD OF KAL-EL, THAT THE LOST SHALL--⟩
LIES!
⟨--SERVE THE CHOSEN WITH BODY AND SOUL--⟩
HE KNOWS NOTHING OF THE WORD OF KAL-EL!
⟨THEY'RE HERE....⟩
⟨IT'S COMING FROM OVER THERE--⟩
⟨--DEDICATING YOUR VERY EXISTENCE TO THE TRUE CHILDREN--⟩
YOU ARE NOT SLAVE YOU ARE N THE LOST

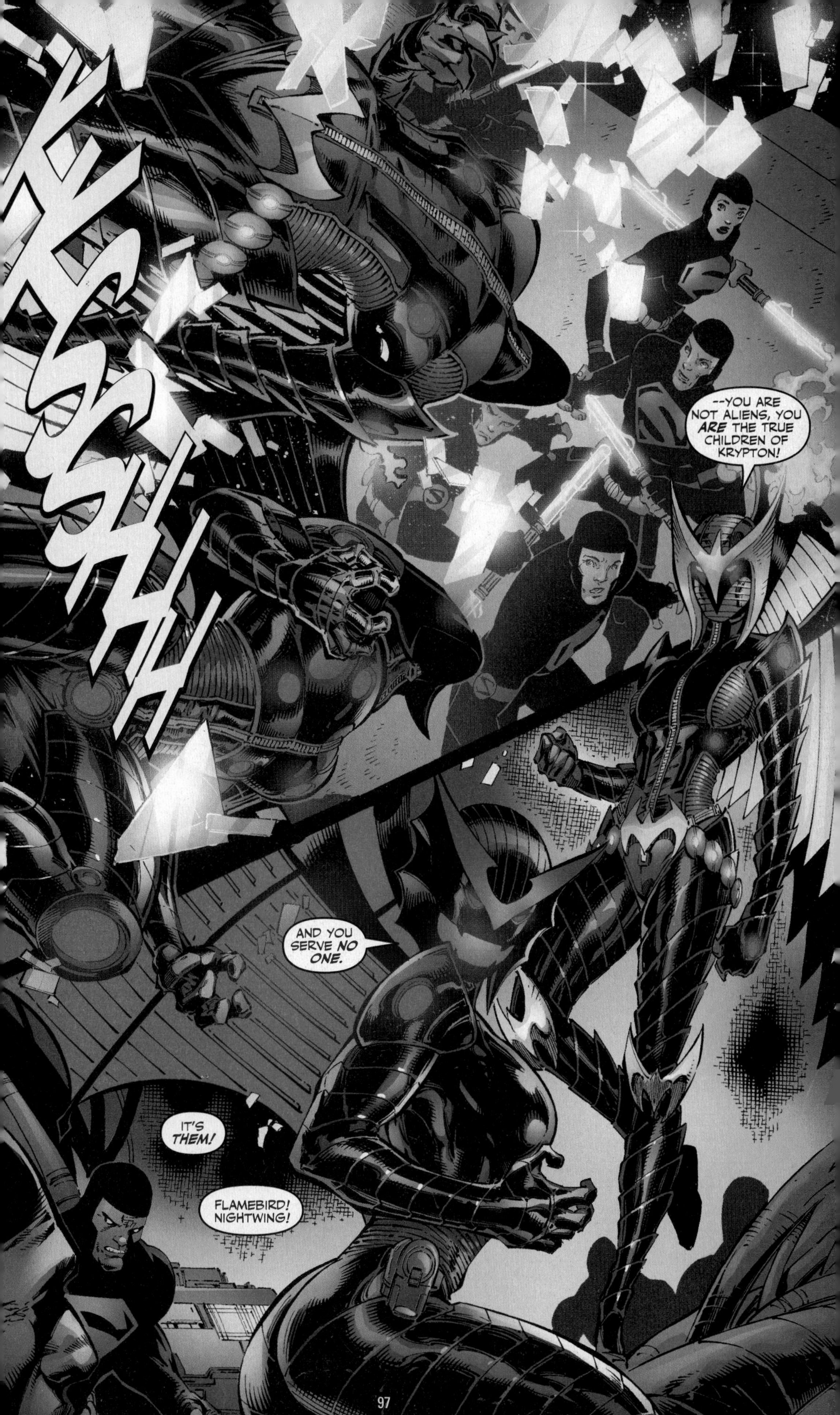
KRSSSHHH
--YOU ARE NOT ALIENS, YOU ARE THE TRUE CHILDREN OF KRYPTON!
AND YOU SERVE NO ONE.
IT'S THEM!
FLAMEBIRD! NIGHTWING!

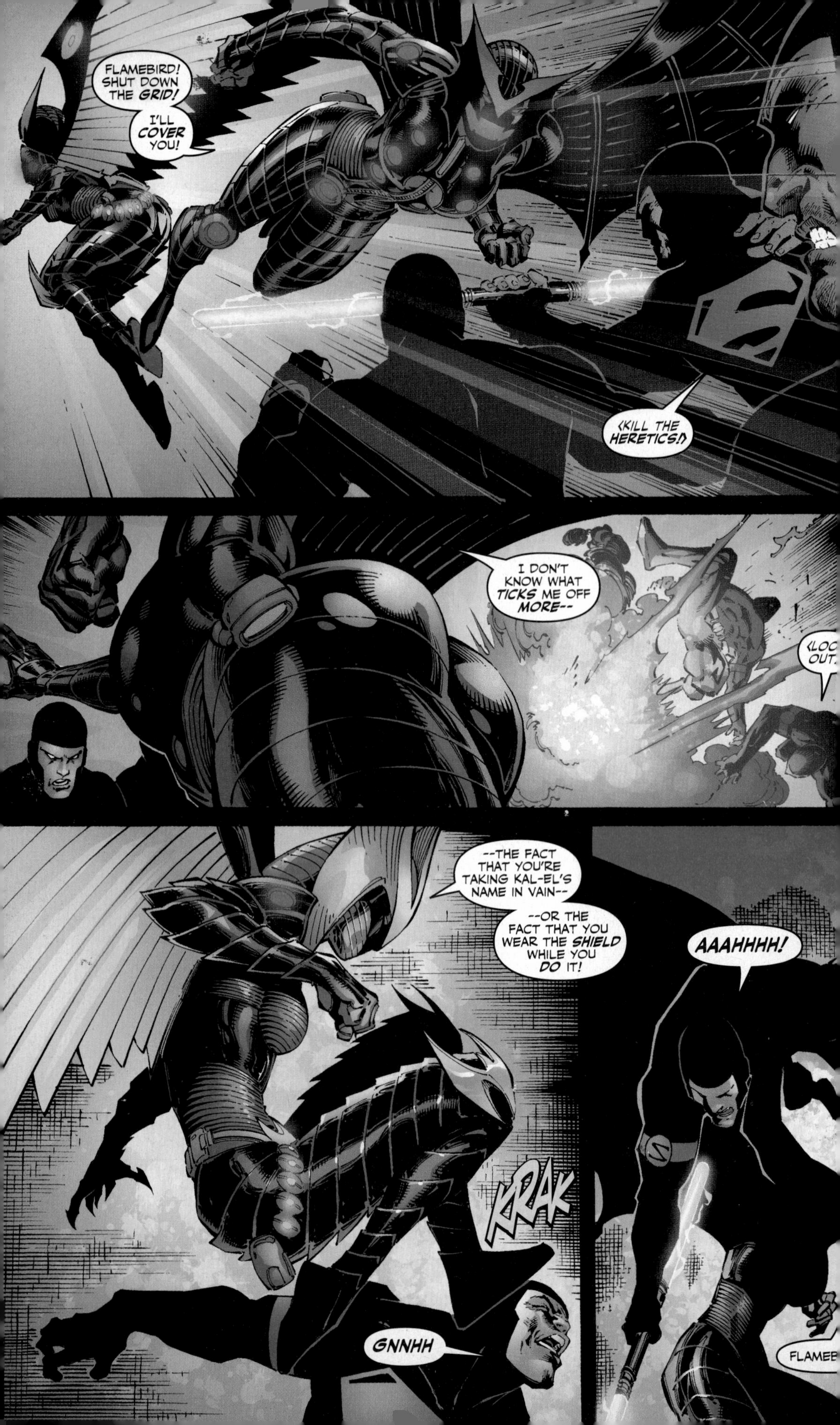
FLAMEBIRD! SHUT DOWN THE GRID!
I'LL COVER YOU!
‹KILL THE HERETICS!›
I DON'T KNOW WHAT TICKS ME OFF MORE--
‹LOO OUT.
--THE FACT THAT YOU'RE TAKING KAL-EL'S NAME IN VAIN--
--OR THE FACT THAT YOU WEAR THE SHIELD WHILE YOU DO IT!
AAAHHHH!
KRAK
GNNHH
FLAMEB

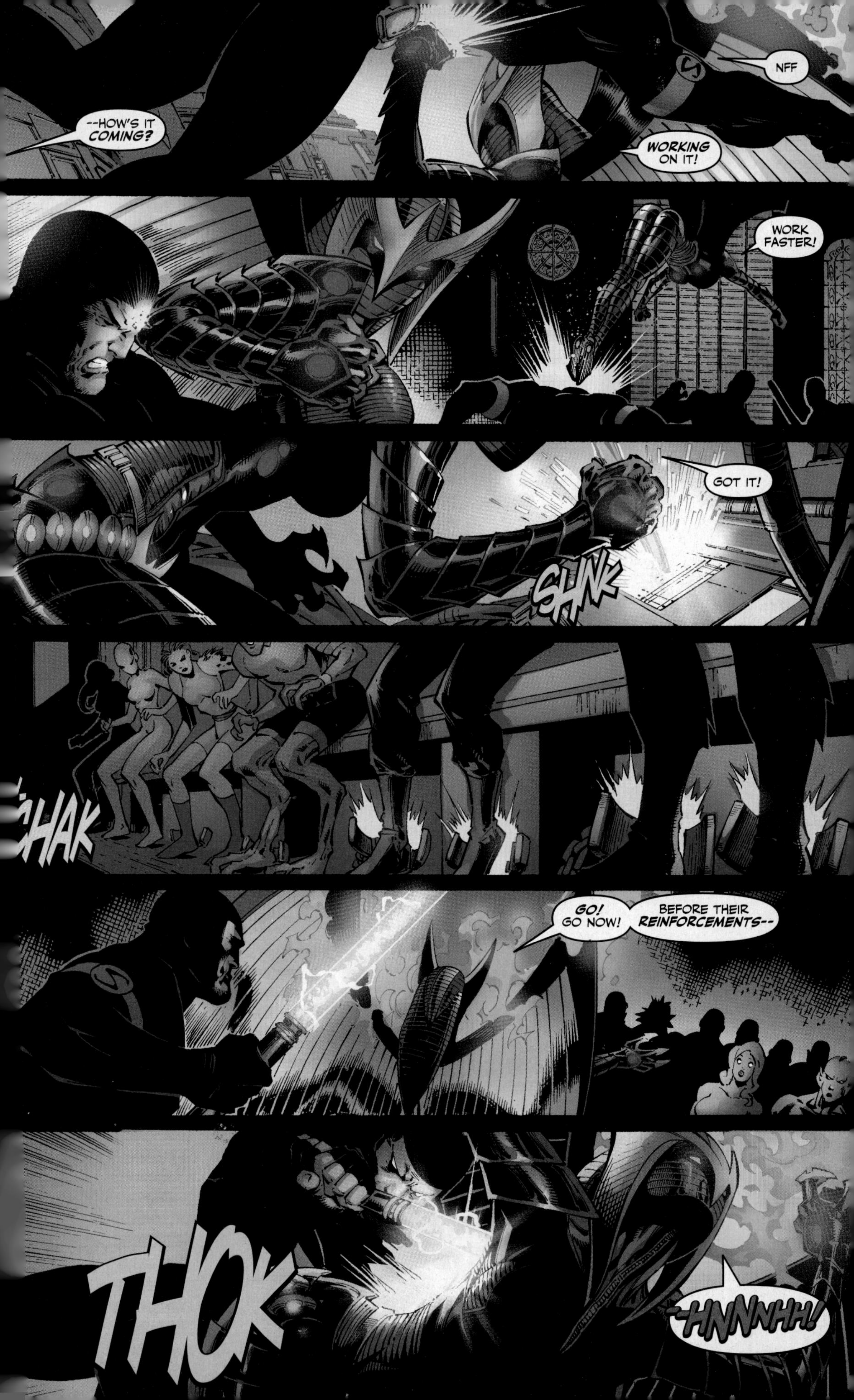
NFF
--HOW'S IT COMING?
WORKING ON IT!
WORK FASTER!
GOT IT!
SHNK
CHAK
GO! GO NOW!
BEFORE THEIR REINFORCEMENTS--
THOK
-HNNNHH!

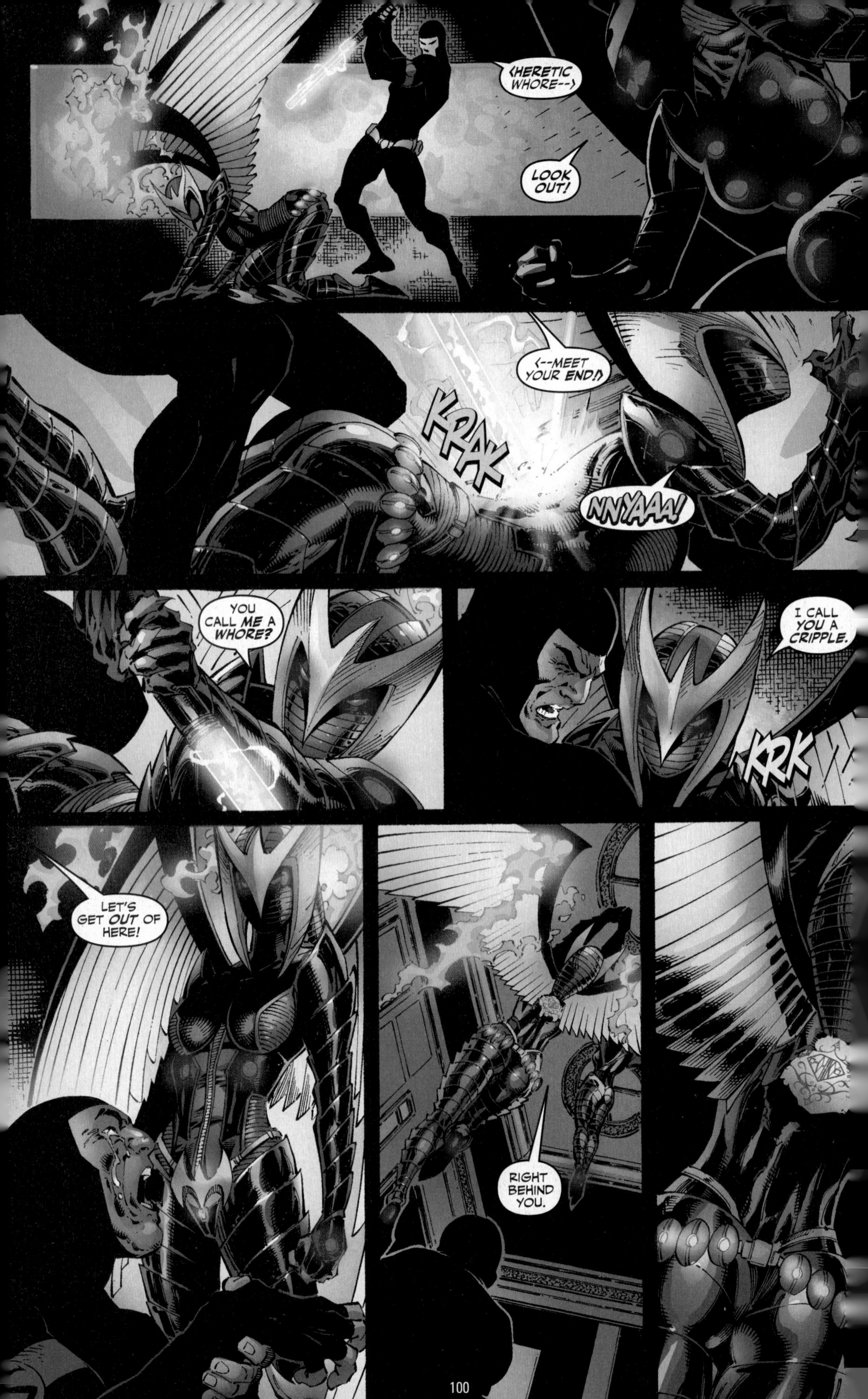

‹HERETIC WHORE--›
LOOK OUT!
‹--MEET YOUR END!›
KRAK
NNYAAA!
YOU CALL ME A WHORE?
I CALL YOU A CRIPPLE.
KRK
LET'S GET OUT OF HERE!
RIGHT BEHIND YOU.

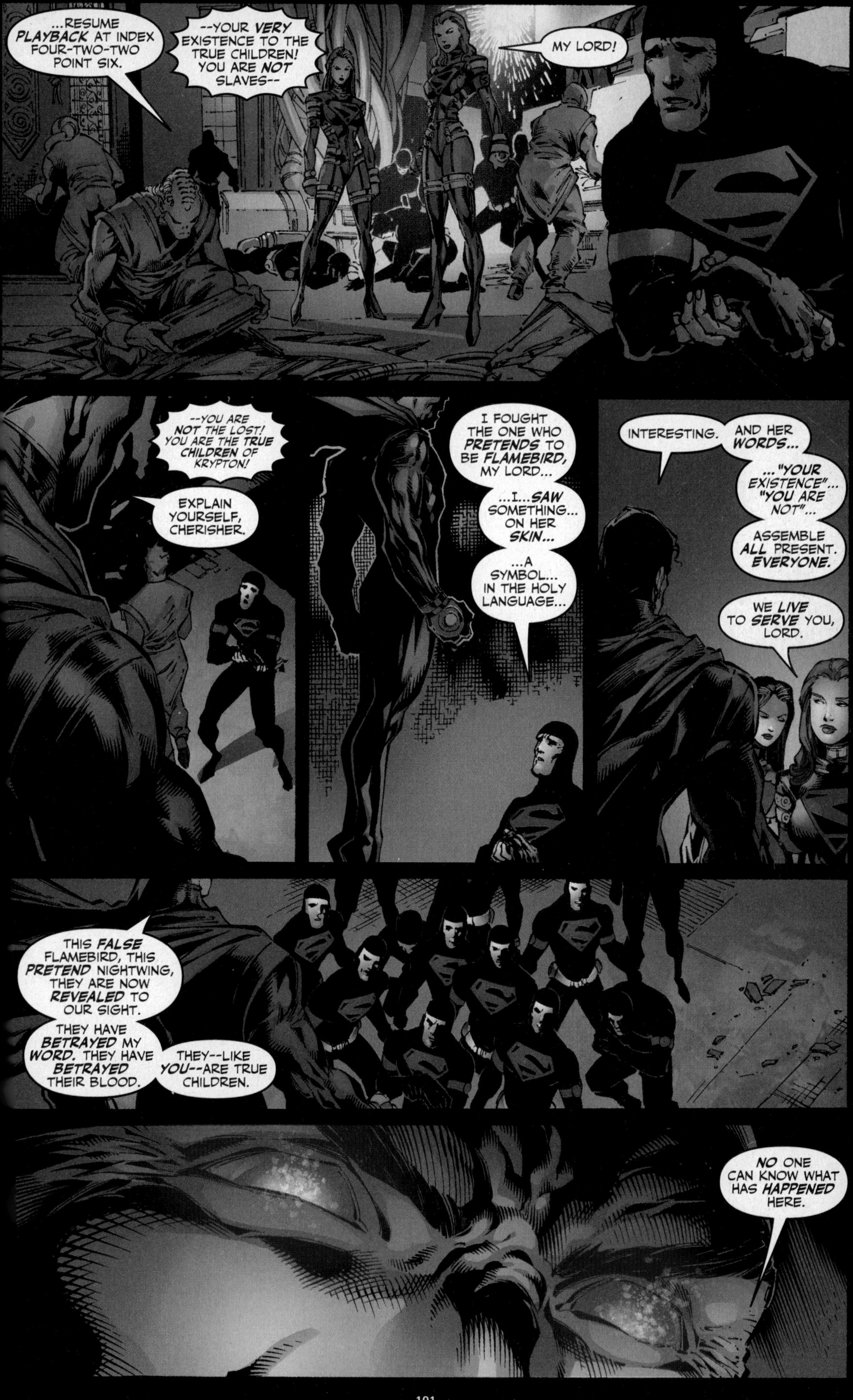
...RESUME PLAYBACK AT INDEX FOUR-TWO-TWO POINT SIX.
--YOUR VERY EXISTENCE TO THE TRUE CHILDREN! YOU ARE NOT SLAVES--
MY LORD!
--YOU ARE NOT THE LOST! YOU ARE THE TRUE CHILDREN OF KRYPTON!
EXPLAIN YOURSELF, CHERISHER.
I FOUGHT THE ONE WHO PRETENDS TO BE FLAMEBIRD, MY LORD...
...I...SAW SOMETHING... ON HER SKIN...
...A SYMBOL... IN THE HOLY LANGUAGE...
INTERESTING.
AND HER WORDS...
..."YOUR EXISTENCE"... "YOU ARE NOT"...
ASSEMBLE ALL PRESENT. EVERYONE.
WE LIVE TO SERVE YOU, LORD.
THIS FALSE FLAMEBIRD, THIS PRETEND NIGHTWING, THEY ARE NOW REVEALED TO OUR SIGHT.
THEY HAVE BETRAYED MY WORD. THEY HAVE BETRAYED THEIR BLOOD.
THEY--LIKE YOU--ARE TRUE CHILDREN.
NO ONE CAN KNOW WHAT HAS HAPPENED HERE.

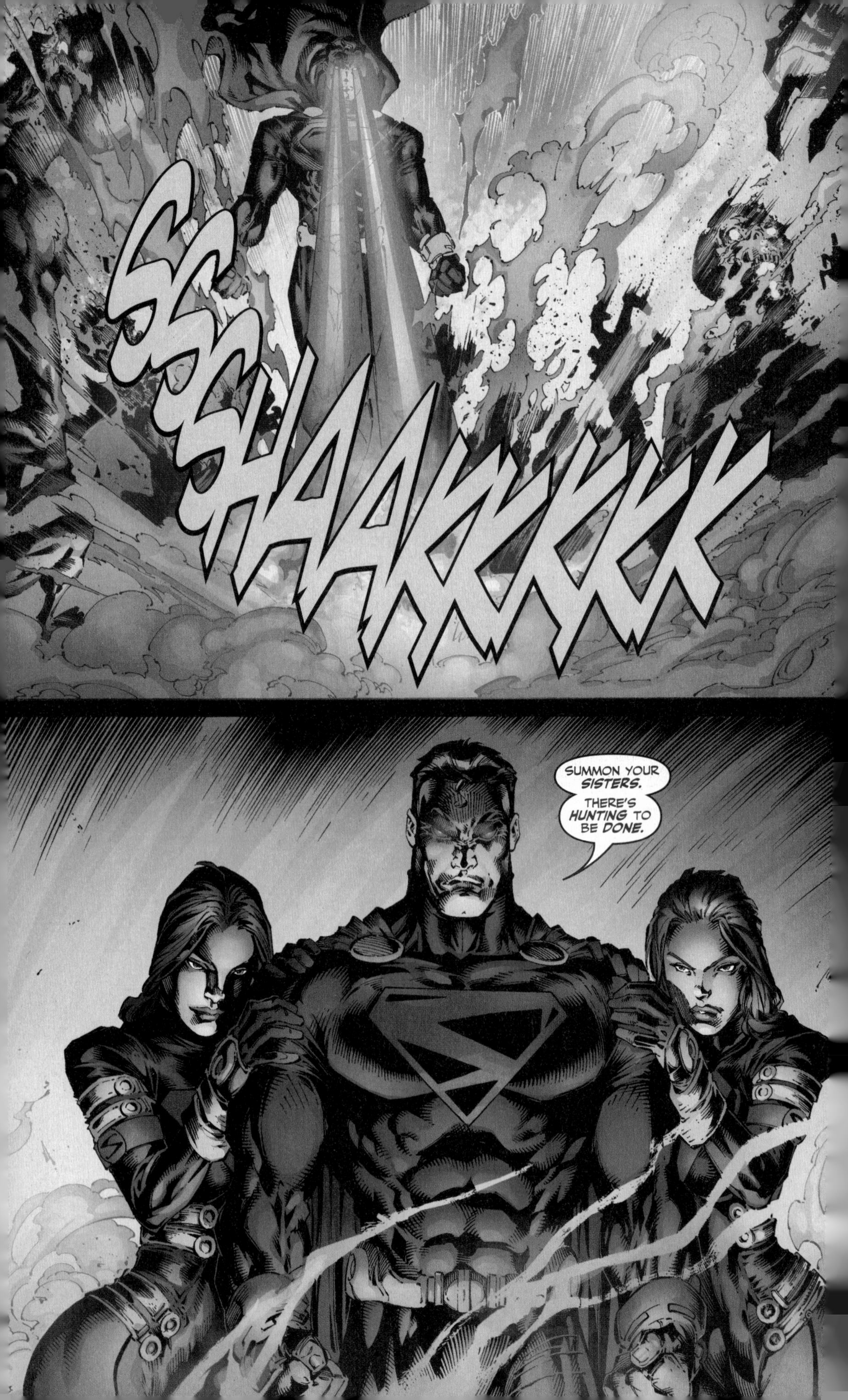
SUMMON YOUR *SISTERS*. THERE'S *HUNTING* TO BE *DONE*.

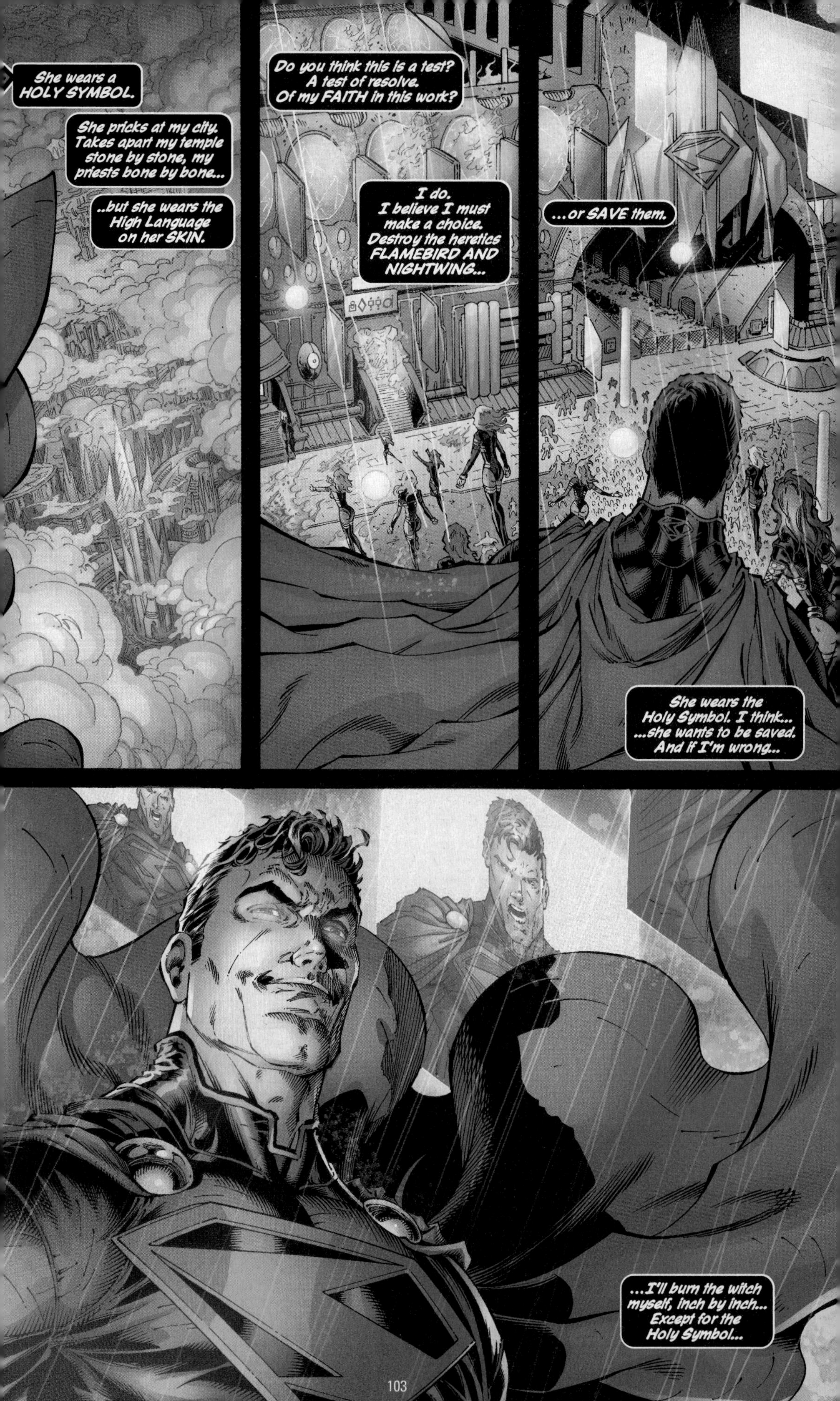

She wears a HOLY SYMBOL.
She pricks at my city. Takes apart my temple stone by stone, my priests bone by bone...
..but she wears the High Language on her SKIN.
Do you think this is a test? A test of resolve. Of my FAITH in this work?
I do. I believe I must make a choice. Destroy the heretics FLAMEBIRD AND NIGHTWING...
...or SAVE them.
She wears the Holy Symbol. I think... ...she wants to be saved. And if I'm wrong...
...I'll burn the witch myself, inch by inch... Except for the Holy Symbol...

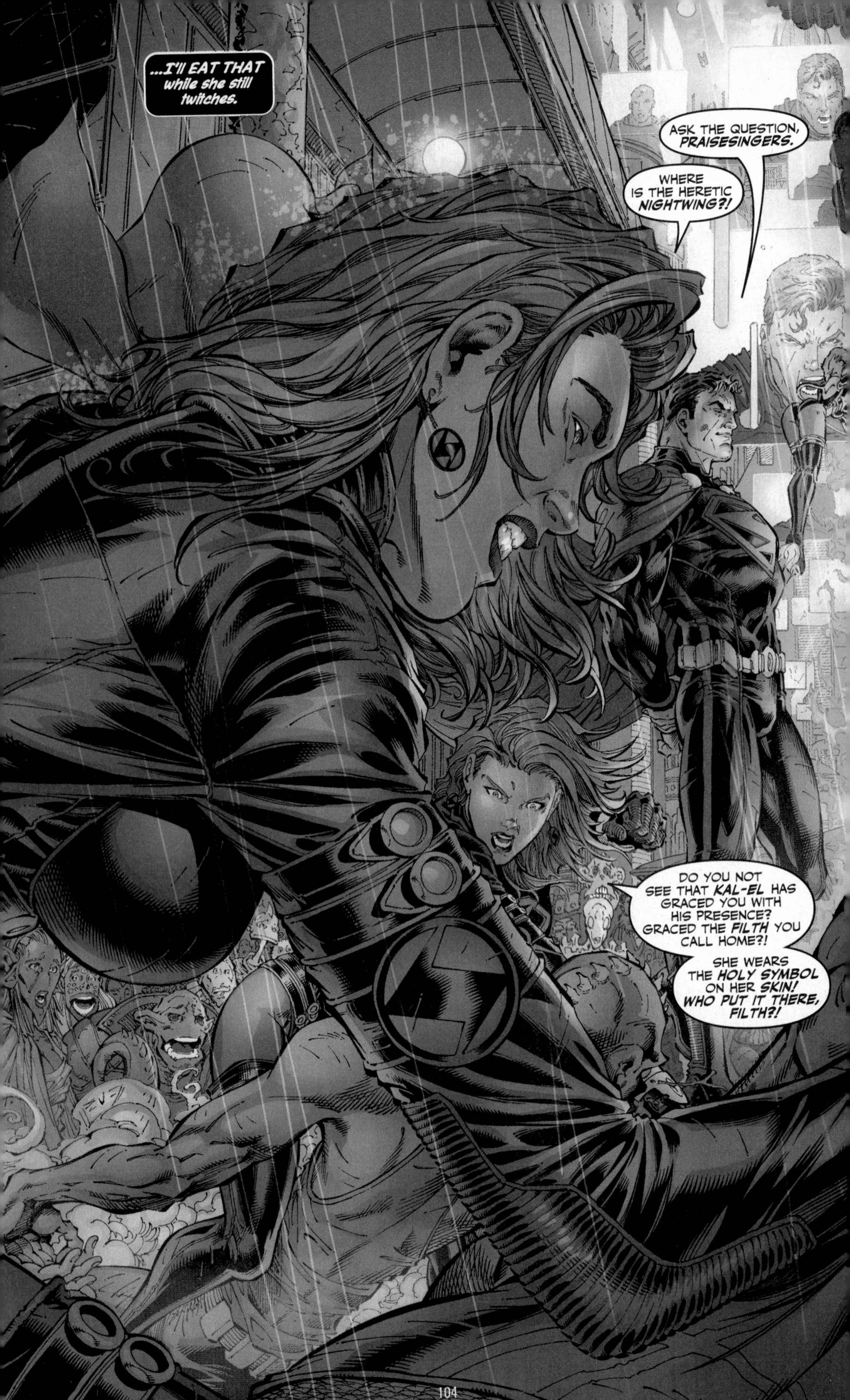

...I'LL EAT THAT while she still twitches.
ASK THE QUESTION, PRAISESINGERS.
WHERE IS THE HERETIC NIGHTWING?!
DO YOU NOT SEE THAT KAL-EL HAS GRACED YOU WITH HIS PRESENCE? GRACED THE FILTH YOU CALL HOME?!
SHE WEARS THE HOLY SYMBOL ON HER SKIN! WHO PUT IT THERE, FILTH?!

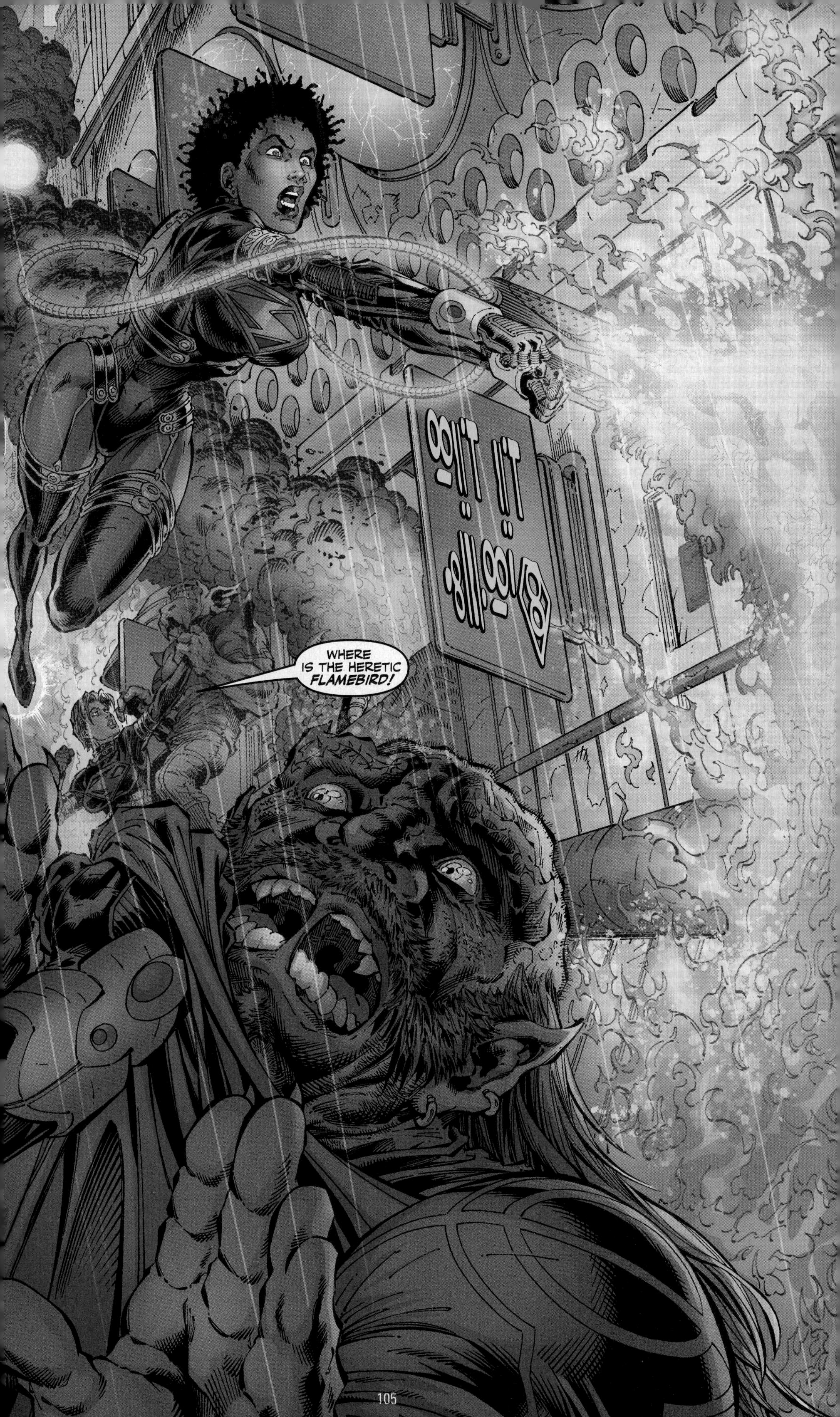
WHERE IS THE HERETIC *FLAMEBIRD!*

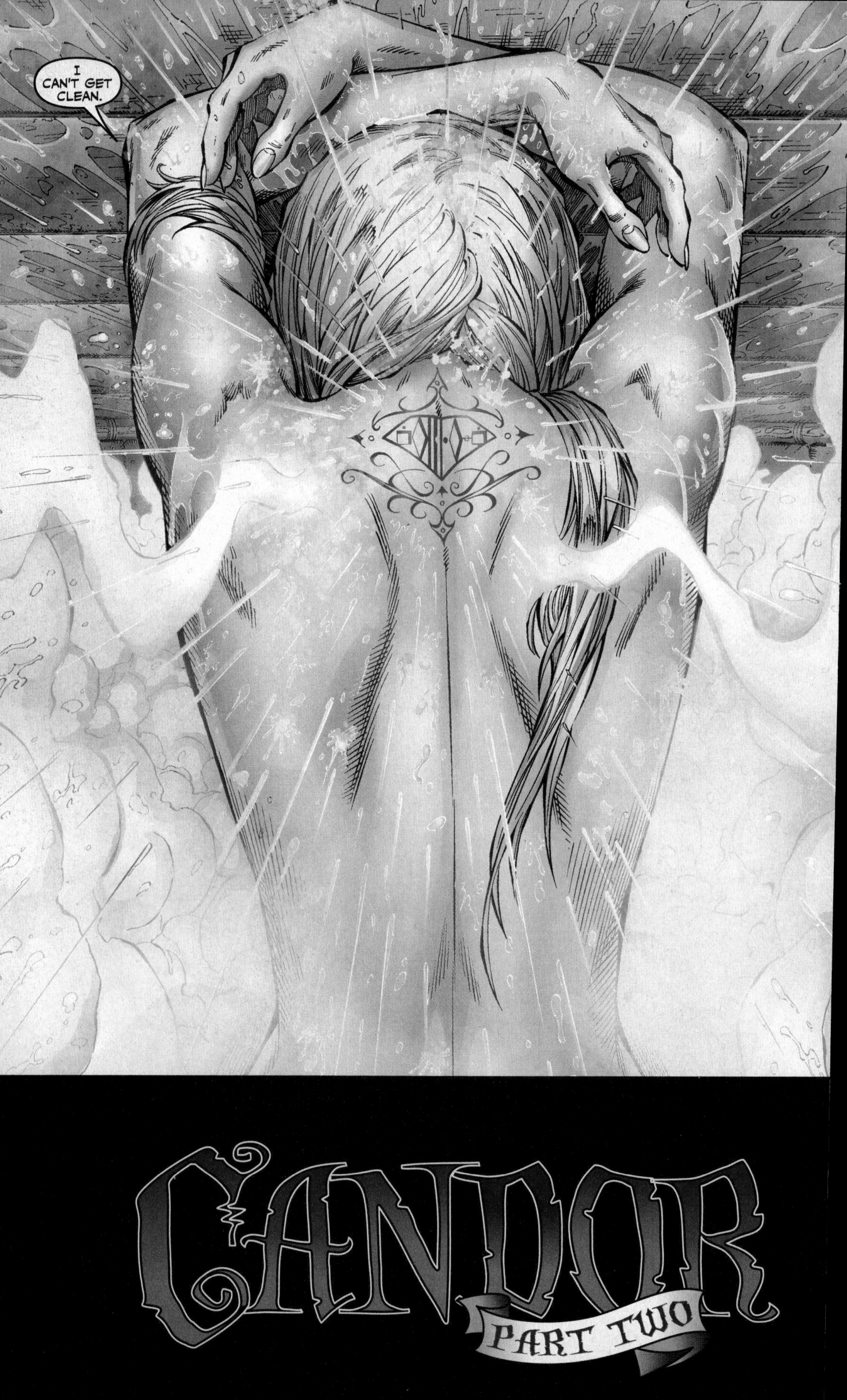
I CAN'T GET CLEAN.
CANDOR
PART TWO

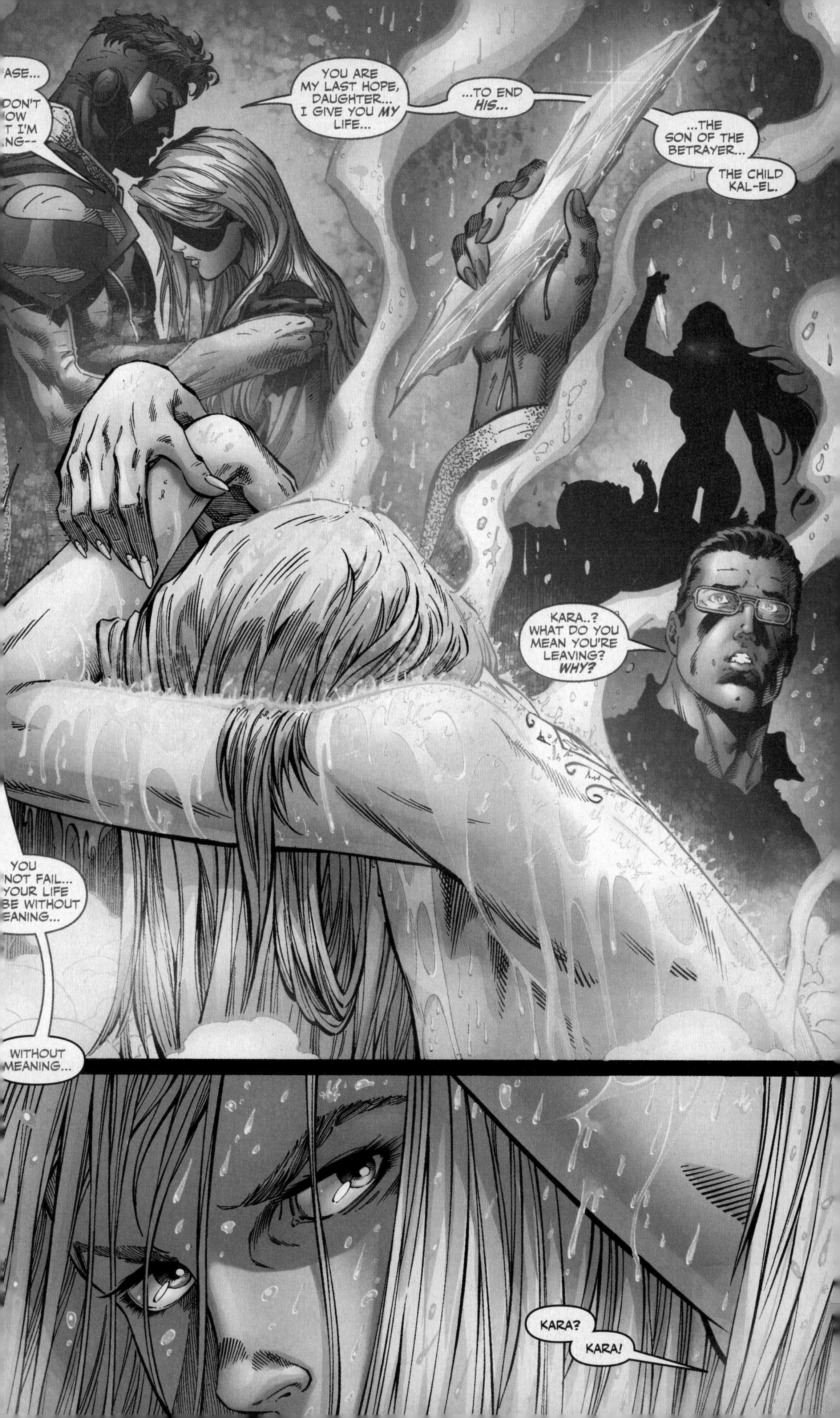

ASE...
DON'T
NOW
T I'M
NG--
YOU ARE MY LAST HOPE, DAUGHTER... I GIVE YOU MY LIFE...
...TO END HIS...
...THE SON OF THE BETRAYER...
THE CHILD KAL-EL.
KARA..? WHAT DO YOU MEAN YOU'RE LEAVING? WHY?
YOU
NOT FAIL...
YOUR LIFE
BE WITHOUT
EANING...
WITHOUT MEANING...
KARA?
KARA!

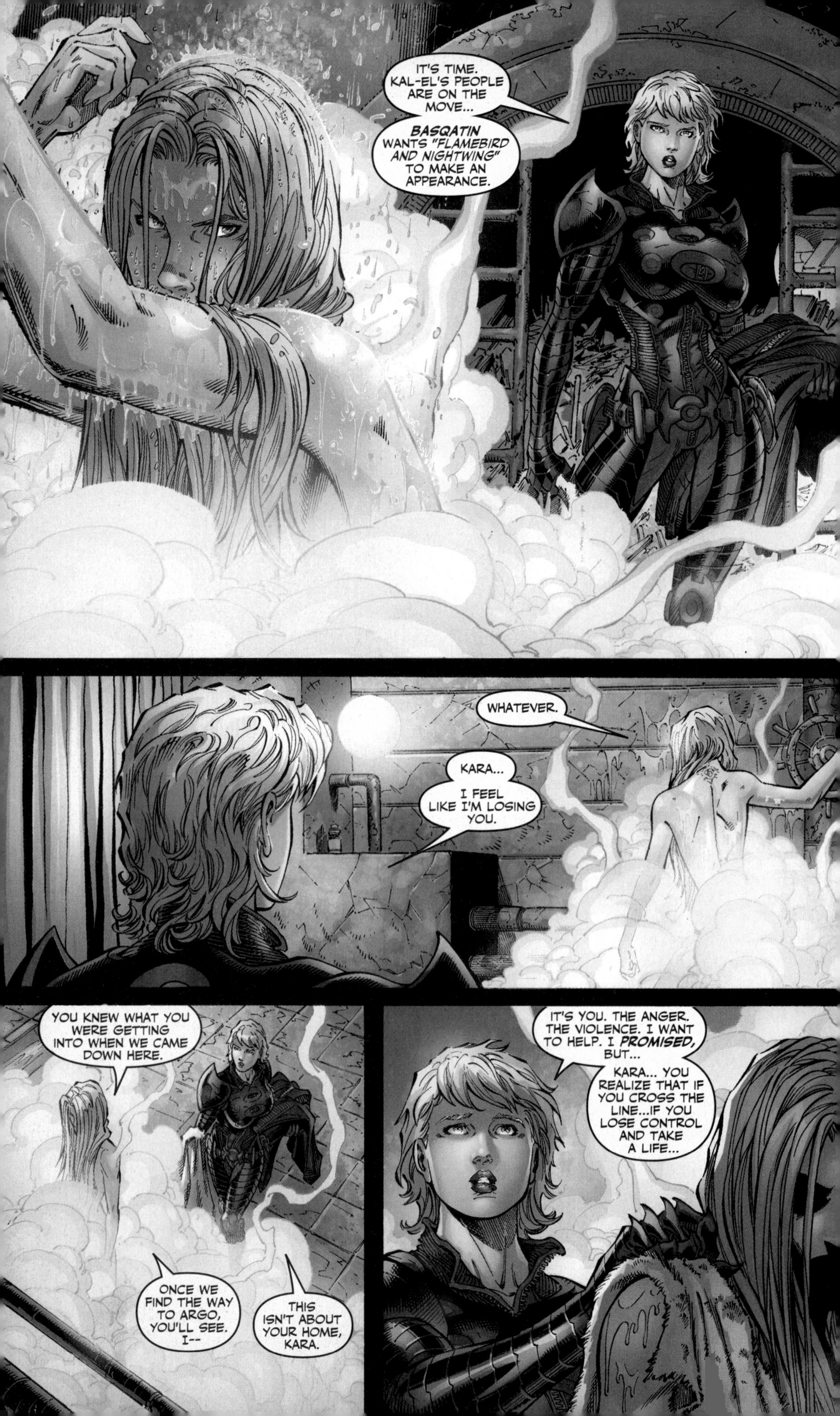
IT'S TIME. KAL-EL'S PEOPLE ARE ON THE MOVE...
BASQATIN WANTS "*FLAMEBIRD AND NIGHTWING*" TO MAKE AN APPEARANCE.
WHATEVER.
KARA...
I FEEL LIKE I'M LOSING YOU.
YOU KNEW WHAT YOU WERE GETTING INTO WHEN WE CAME DOWN HERE.
ONCE WE FIND THE WAY TO ARGO, YOU'LL SEE. I--
THIS ISN'T ABOUT YOUR HOME, KARA.
IT'S YOU. THE ANGER. THE VIOLENCE. I WANT TO HELP. I *PROMISED,* BUT...
KARA... YOU REALIZE THAT IF YOU CROSS THE LINE...IF YOU LOSE CONTROL AND TAKE A LIFE...

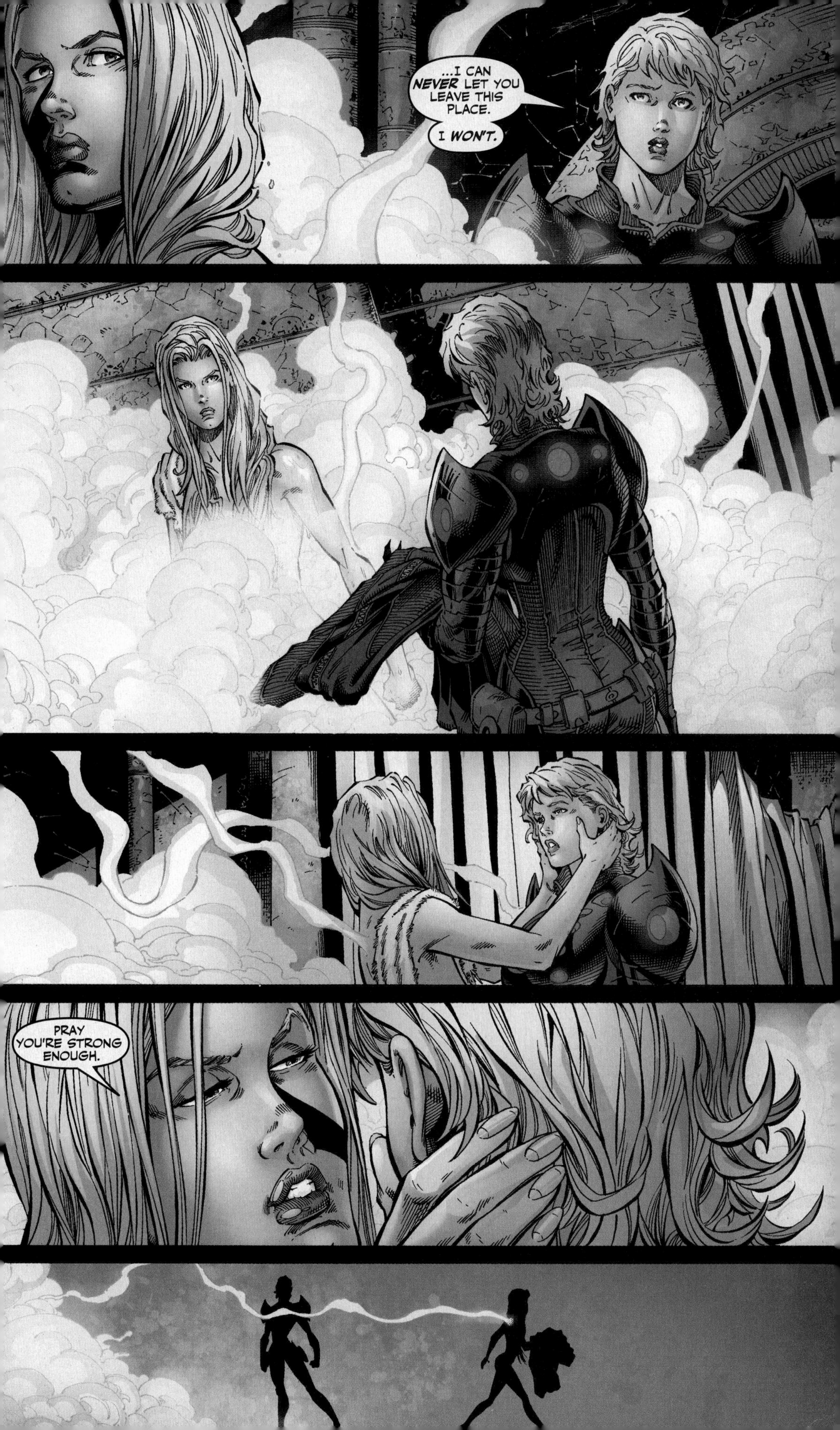
...I CAN NEVER LET YOU LEAVE THIS PLACE.
I WON'T.
PRAY YOU'RE STRONG ENOUGH.

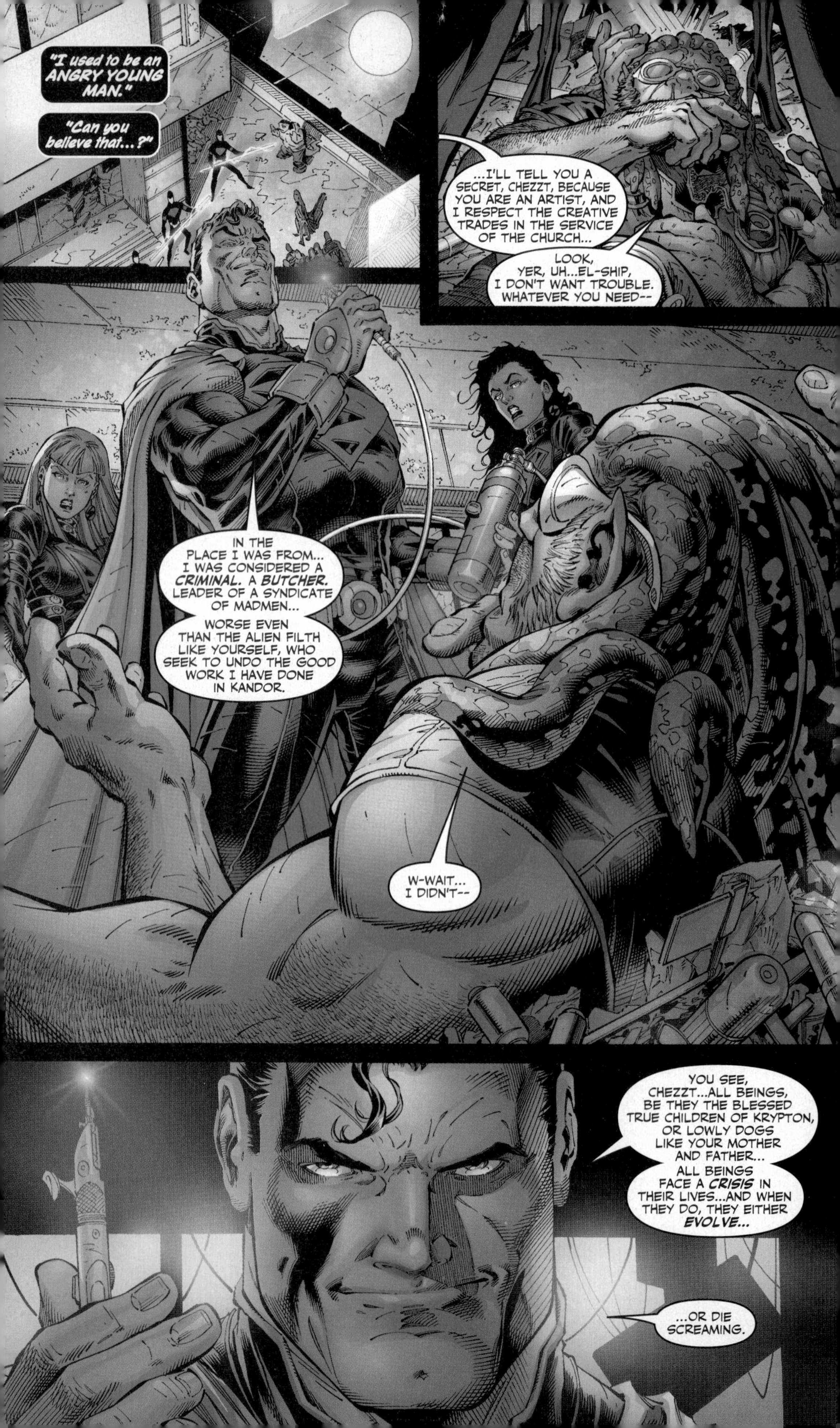
"I used to be an ANGRY YOUNG MAN."
"Can you believe that...?"
...I'LL TELL YOU A SECRET, CHEZZT, BECAUSE YOU ARE AN ARTIST, AND I RESPECT THE CREATIVE TRADES IN THE SERVICE OF THE CHURCH...
LOOK, YER, UH...EL-SHIP, I DON'T WANT TROUBLE. WHATEVER YOU NEED--
IN THE PLACE I WAS FROM... I WAS CONSIDERED A CRIMINAL. A BUTCHER. LEADER OF A SYNDICATE OF MADMEN...
WORSE EVEN THAN THE ALIEN FILTH LIKE YOURSELF, WHO SEEK TO UNDO THE GOOD WORK I HAVE DONE IN KANDOR.
W-WAIT... I DIDN'T--
YOU SEE, CHEZZT...ALL BEINGS, BE THEY THE BLESSED TRUE CHILDREN OF KRYPTON, OR LOWLY DOGS LIKE YOUR MOTHER AND FATHER...
ALL BEINGS FACE A CRISIS IN THEIR LIVES...AND WHEN THEY DO, THEY EITHER EVOLVE...
...OR DIE SCREAMING.

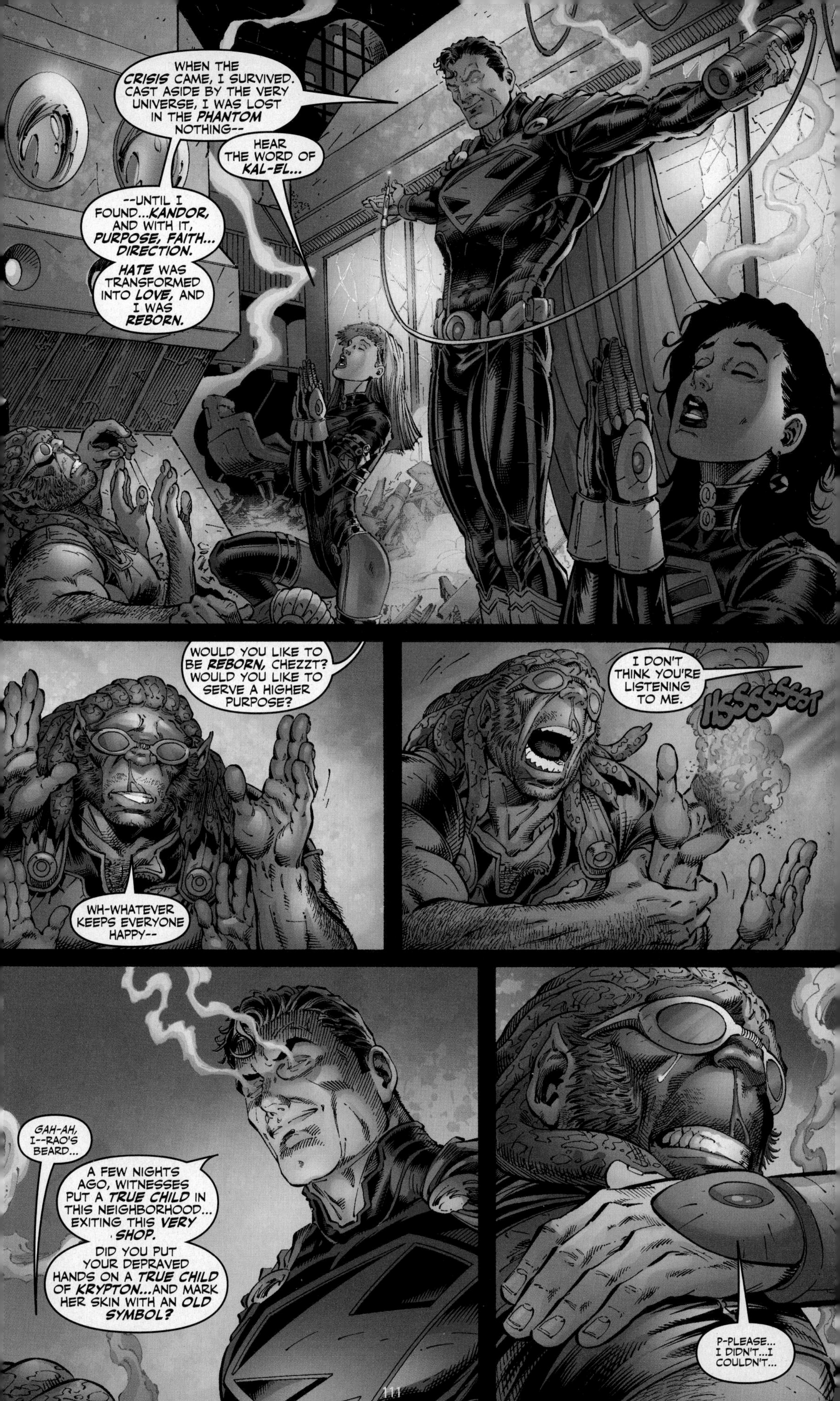
WHEN THE CRISIS CAME, I SURVIVED. CAST ASIDE BY THE VERY UNIVERSE, I WAS LOST IN THE PHANTOM NOTHING--
HEAR THE WORD OF KAL-EL...
--UNTIL I FOUND...KANDOR, AND WITH IT, PURPOSE, FAITH... DIRECTION.
HATE WAS TRANSFORMED INTO LOVE, AND I WAS REBORN.
WOULD YOU LIKE TO BE REBORN, CHEZZT? WOULD YOU LIKE TO SERVE A HIGHER PURPOSE?
WH-WHATEVER KEEPS EVERYONE HAPPY--
I DON'T THINK YOU'RE LISTENING TO ME.
HSSSSSSST
GAH-AH, I--RAO'S BEARD...
A FEW NIGHTS AGO, WITNESSES PUT A TRUE CHILD IN THIS NEIGHBORHOOD... EXITING THIS VERY SHOP.
DID YOU PUT YOUR DEPRAVED HANDS ON A TRUE CHILD OF KRYPTON...AND MARK HER SKIN WITH AN OLD SYMBOL?
P-PLEASE... I DIDN'T...I COULDN'T...

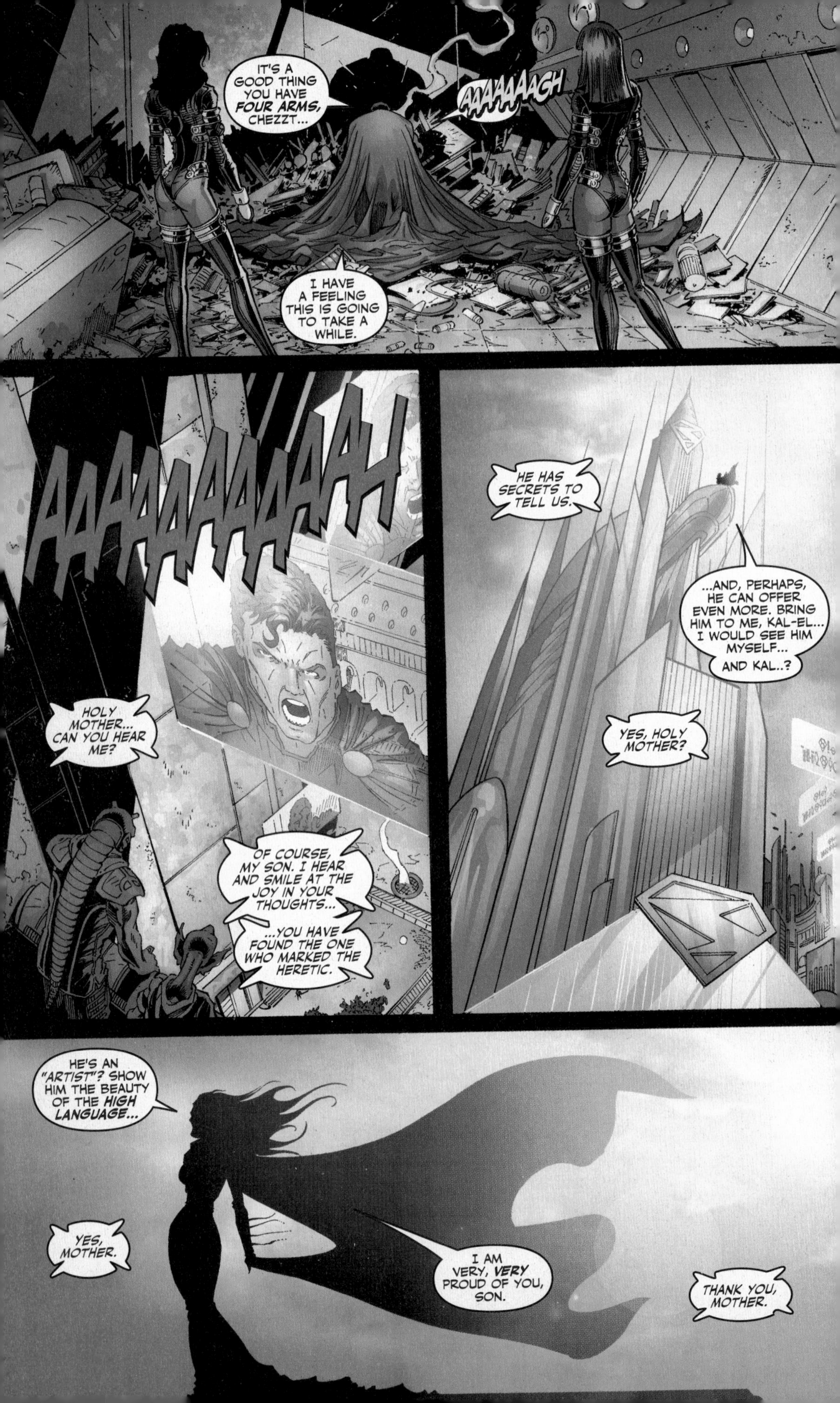

IT'S A GOOD THING YOU HAVE FOUR ARMS, CHEZZT...
AAAAAAAGH
I HAVE A FEELING THIS IS GOING TO TAKE A WHILE.
AAAAAAAAAAH
HOLY MOTHER... CAN YOU HEAR ME?
OF COURSE, MY SON. I HEAR AND SMILE AT THE JOY IN YOUR THOUGHTS...
...YOU HAVE FOUND THE ONE WHO MARKED THE HERETIC.
HE HAS SECRETS TO TELL US.
...AND, PERHAPS, HE CAN OFFER EVEN MORE. BRING HIM TO ME, KAL-EL... I WOULD SEE HIM MYSELF...
AND KAL..?
YES, HOLY MOTHER?
HE'S AN "ARTIST"? SHOW HIM THE BEAUTY OF THE HIGH LANGUAGE...
YES, MOTHER.
I AM VERY, VERY PROUD OF YOU, SON.
THANK YOU, MOTHER.

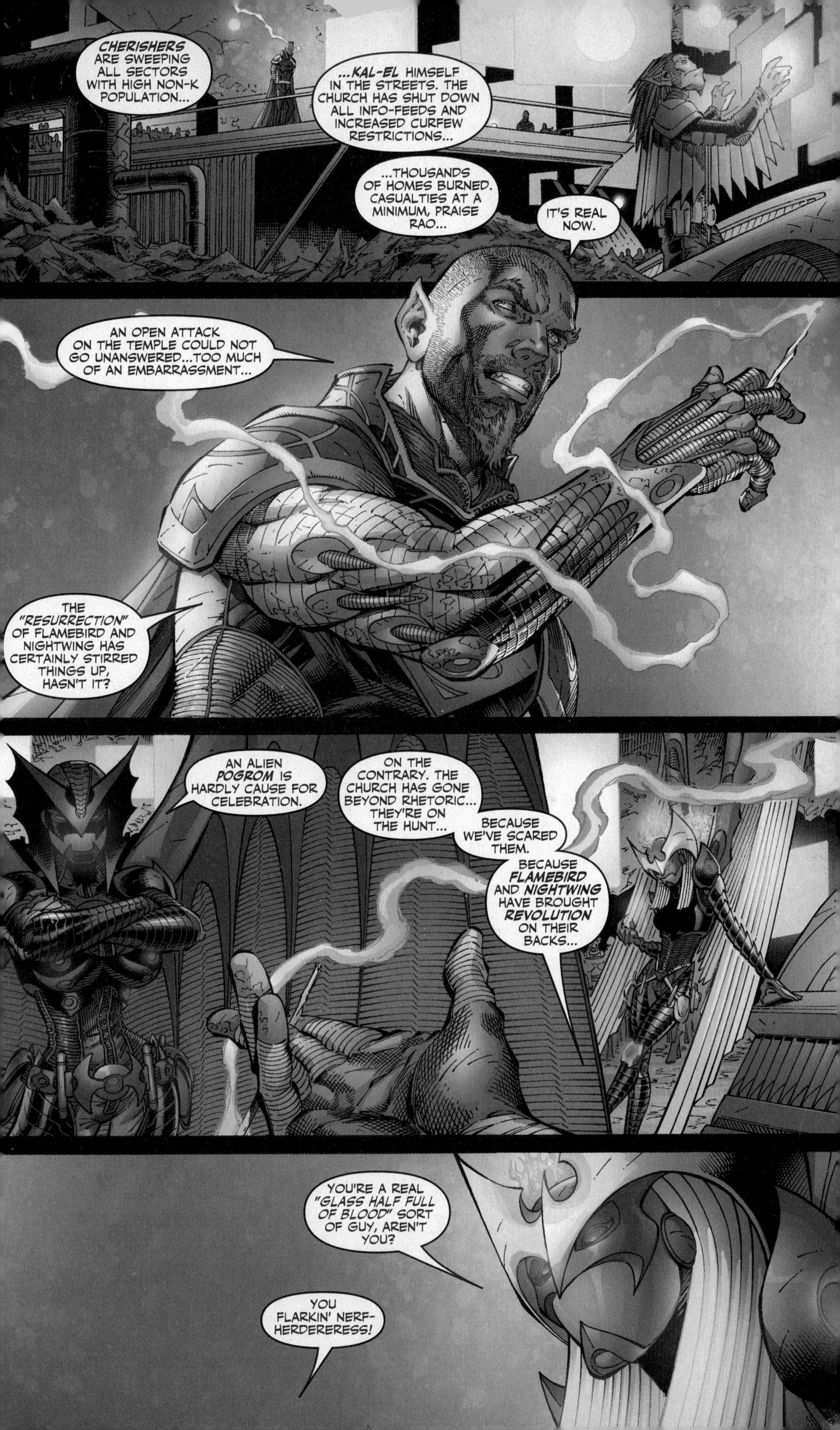
CHERISHERS ARE SWEEPING ALL SECTORS WITH HIGH NON-K POPULATION...
...KAL-EL HIMSELF IN THE STREETS. THE CHURCH HAS SHUT DOWN ALL INFO-FEEDS AND INCREASED CURFEW RESTRICTIONS...
...THOUSANDS OF HOMES BURNED. CASUALTIES AT A MINIMUM, PRAISE RAO...
IT'S REAL NOW.
AN OPEN ATTACK ON THE TEMPLE COULD NOT GO UNANSWERED...TOO MUCH OF AN EMBARRASSMENT...
THE "RESURRECTION" OF FLAMEBIRD AND NIGHTWING HAS CERTAINLY STIRRED THINGS UP, HASN'T IT?
AN ALIEN POGROM IS HARDLY CAUSE FOR CELEBRATION.
ON THE CONTRARY. THE CHURCH HAS GONE BEYOND RHETORIC... THEY'RE ON THE HUNT...
BECAUSE WE'VE SCARED THEM.
BECAUSE FLAMEBIRD AND NIGHTWING HAVE BROUGHT REVOLUTION ON THEIR BACKS...
YOU'RE A REAL "GLASS HALF FULL OF BLOOD" SORT OF GUY, AREN'T YOU?
YOU FLARKIN' NERF-HERDERERESS!

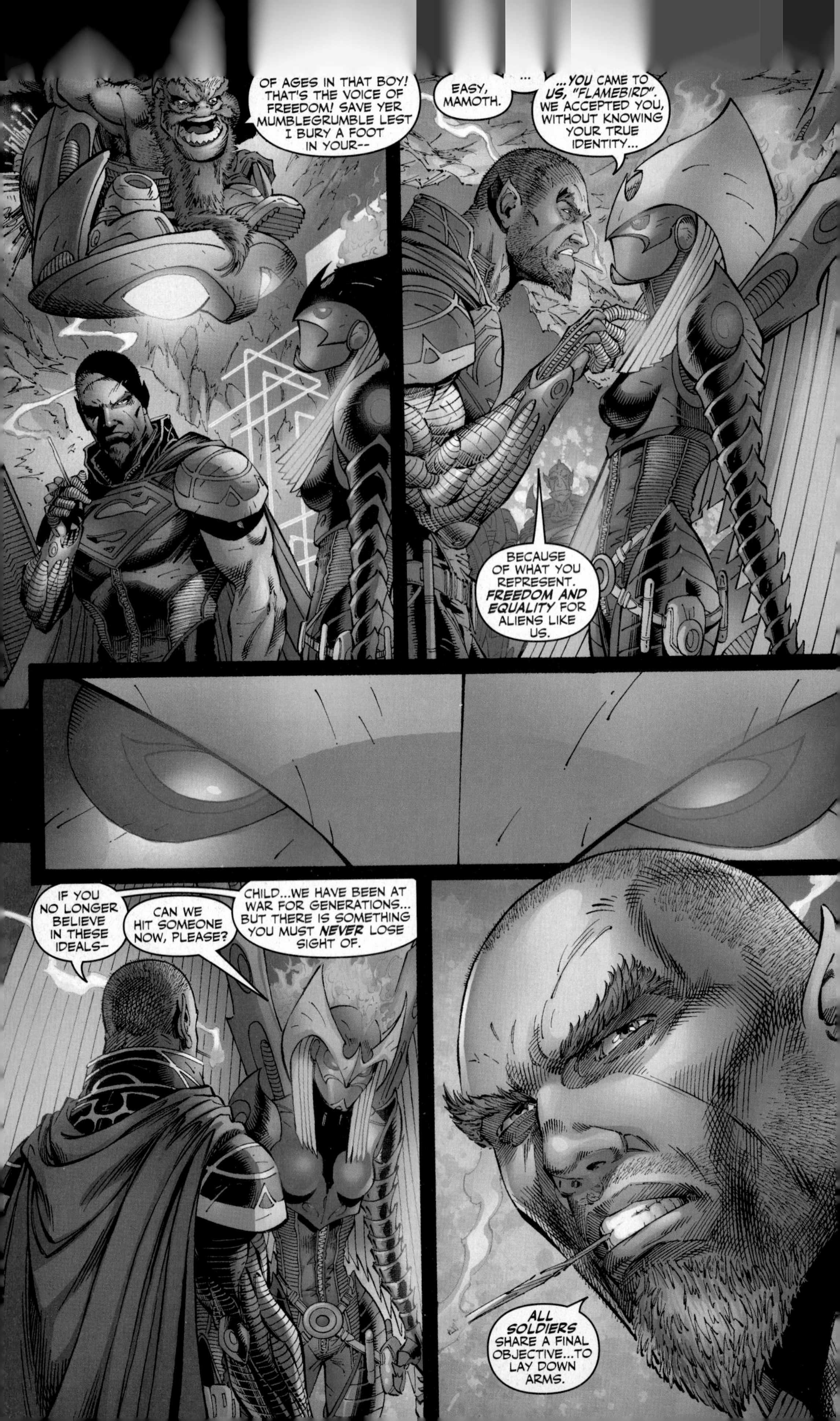
OF AGES IN THAT BOY! THAT'S THE VOICE OF FREEDOM! SAVE YER MUMBLEGRUMBLE LEST I BURY A FOOT IN YOUR--
EASY, MAMOTH.
...
...YOU CAME TO US, "FLAMEBIRD". WE ACCEPTED YOU, WITHOUT KNOWING YOUR TRUE IDENTITY...
BECAUSE OF WHAT YOU REPRESENT. FREEDOM AND EQUALITY FOR ALIENS LIKE US.
IF YOU NO LONGER BELIEVE IN THESE IDEALS–
CAN WE HIT SOMEONE NOW, PLEASE?
CHILD...WE HAVE BEEN AT WAR FOR GENERATIONS... BUT THERE IS SOMETHING YOU MUST NEVER LOSE SIGHT OF.
ALL SOLDIERS SHARE A FINAL OBJECTIVE...TO LAY DOWN ARMS.

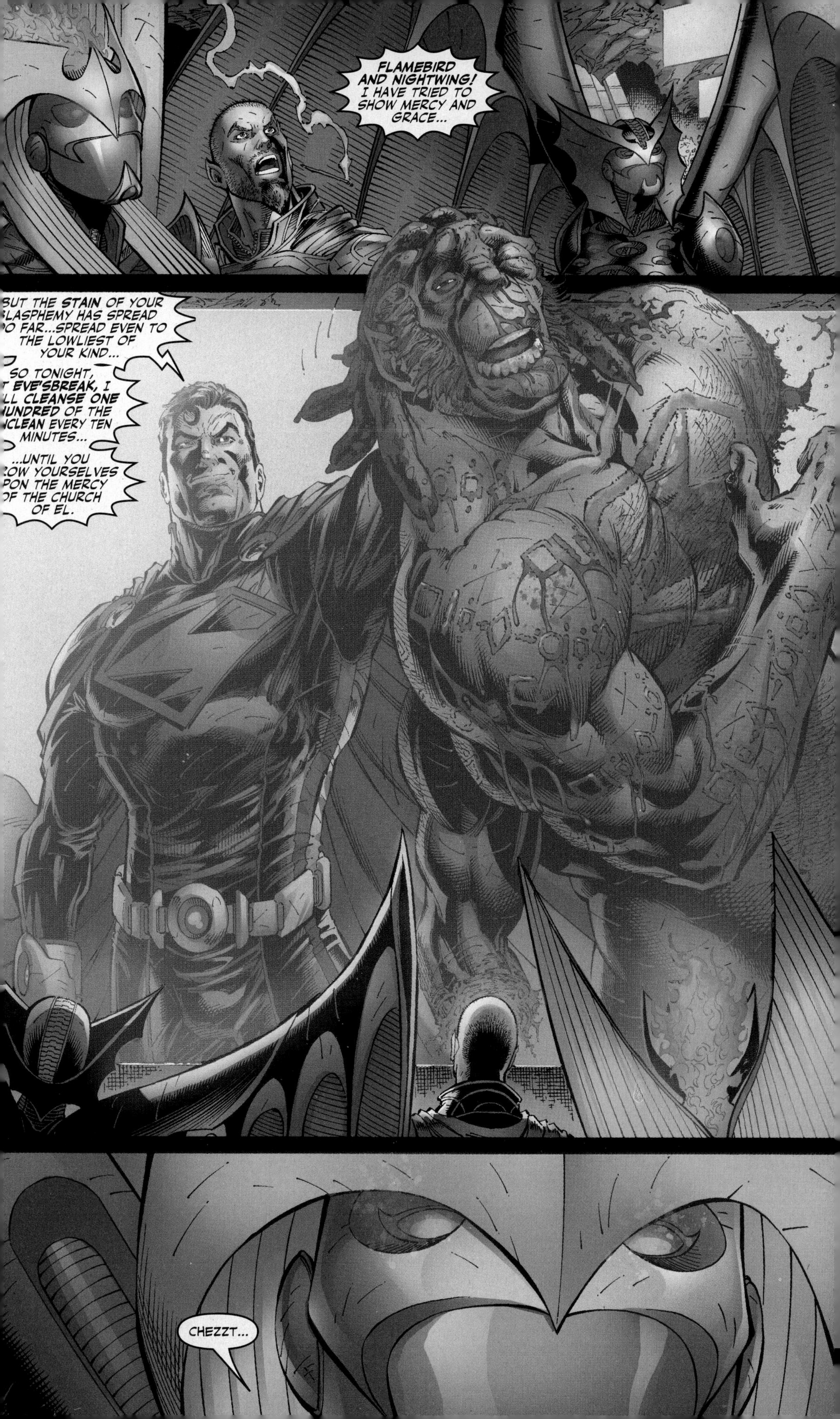
FLAMEBIRD AND NIGHTWING! I HAVE TRIED TO SHOW MERCY AND GRACE...
BUT THE STAIN OF YOUR BLASPHEMY HAS SPREAD TOO FAR...SPREAD EVEN TO THE LOWLIEST OF YOUR KIND...
SO TONIGHT, T EVE'SBREAK, I LL CLEANSE ONE HUNDRED OF THE NCLEAN EVERY TEN MINUTES...
...UNTIL YOU ROW YOURSELVES PON THE MERCY OF THE CHURCH OF EL.
CHEZZT...

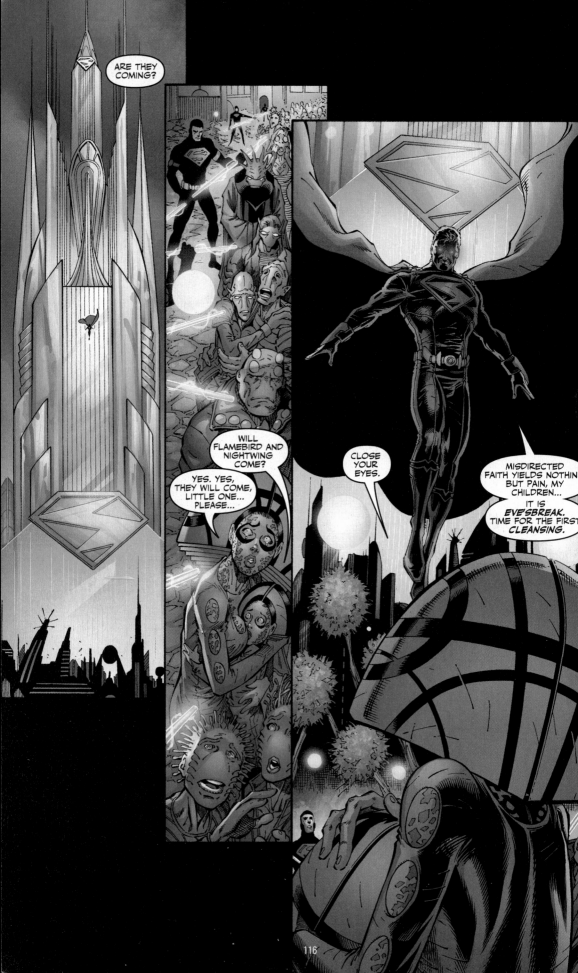

ARE THEY COMING?

WILL FLAMEBIRD AND NIGHTWING COME?

YES. YES, THEY WILL COME, LITTLE ONE... PLEASE...

CLOSE YOUR EYES.

MISDIRECTED FAITH YIELDS NOTHING BUT PAIN, MY CHILDREN... IT IS *EVE'SBREAK.* TIME FOR THE FIRST *CLEANSING.*

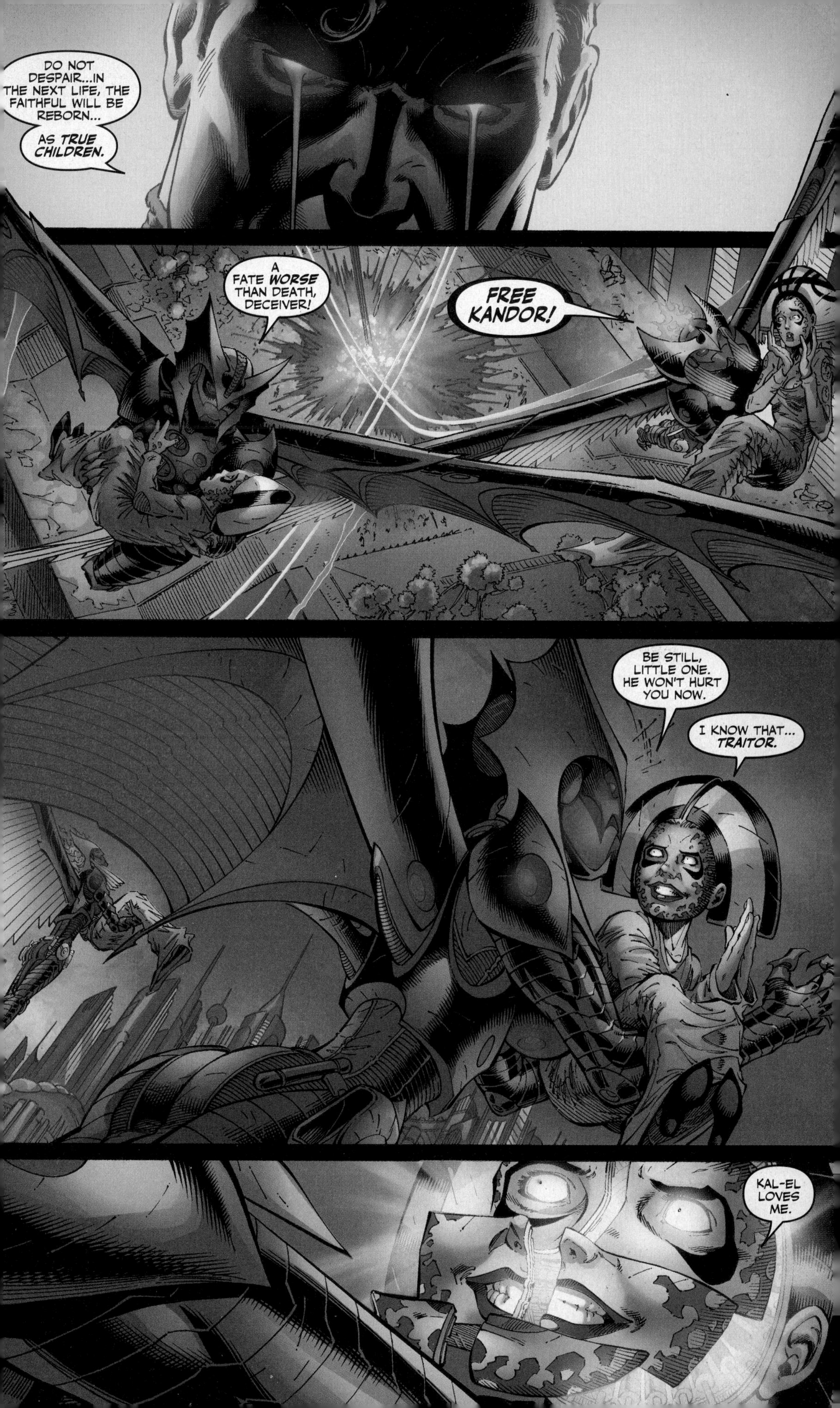
DO NOT DESPAIR...IN THE NEXT LIFE, THE FAITHFUL WILL BE REBORN...
AS TRUE CHILDREN.
A FATE WORSE THAN DEATH, DECEIVER!
FREE KANDOR!
BE STILL, LITTLE ONE. HE WON'T HURT YOU NOW.
I KNOW THAT... TRAITOR.
KAL-EL LOVES ME.

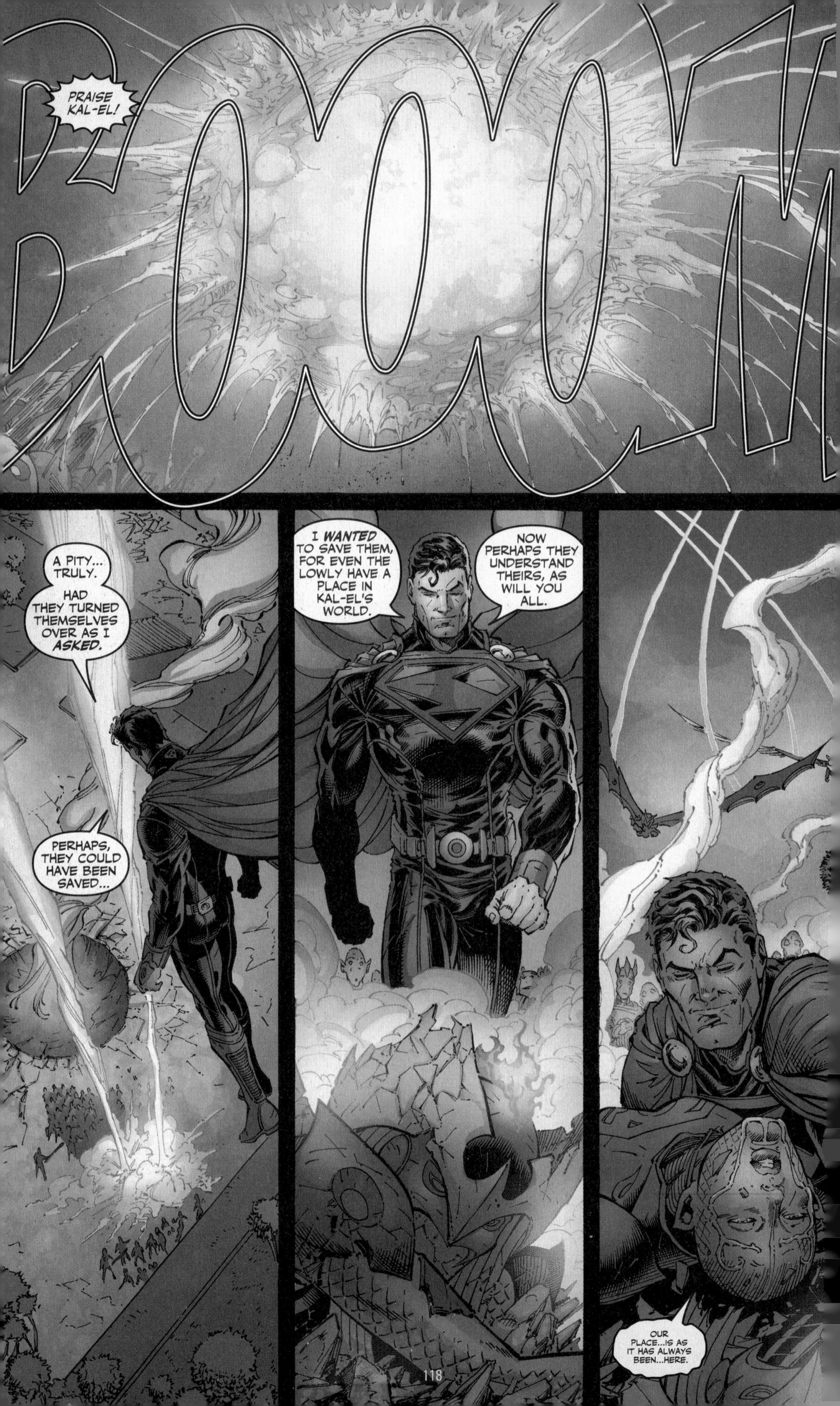
PRAISE KAL-EL!
BOOOOM
A PITY... TRULY.
HAD THEY TURNED THEMSELVES OVER AS I *ASKED.*
PERHAPS, THEY COULD HAVE BEEN SAVED...
I *WANTED* TO SAVE THEM, FOR EVEN THE LOWLY HAVE A PLACE IN KAL-EL'S WORLD.
NOW PERHAPS THEY UNDERSTAND THEIRS, AS WILL YOU ALL.
OUR PLACE...IS AS IT HAS ALWAYS BEEN...HERE.

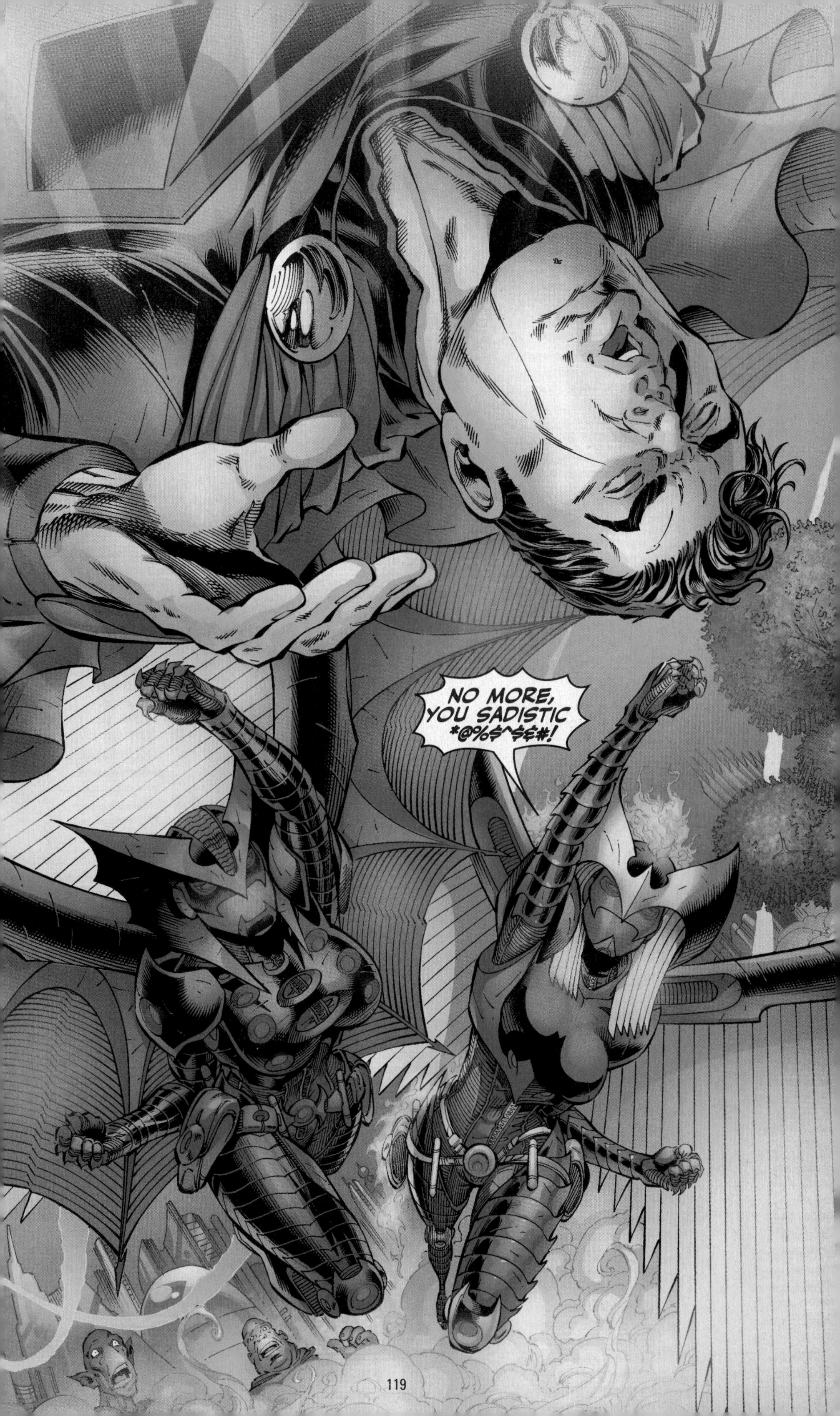
NO MORE, YOU SADISTIC *@%$^$&#!

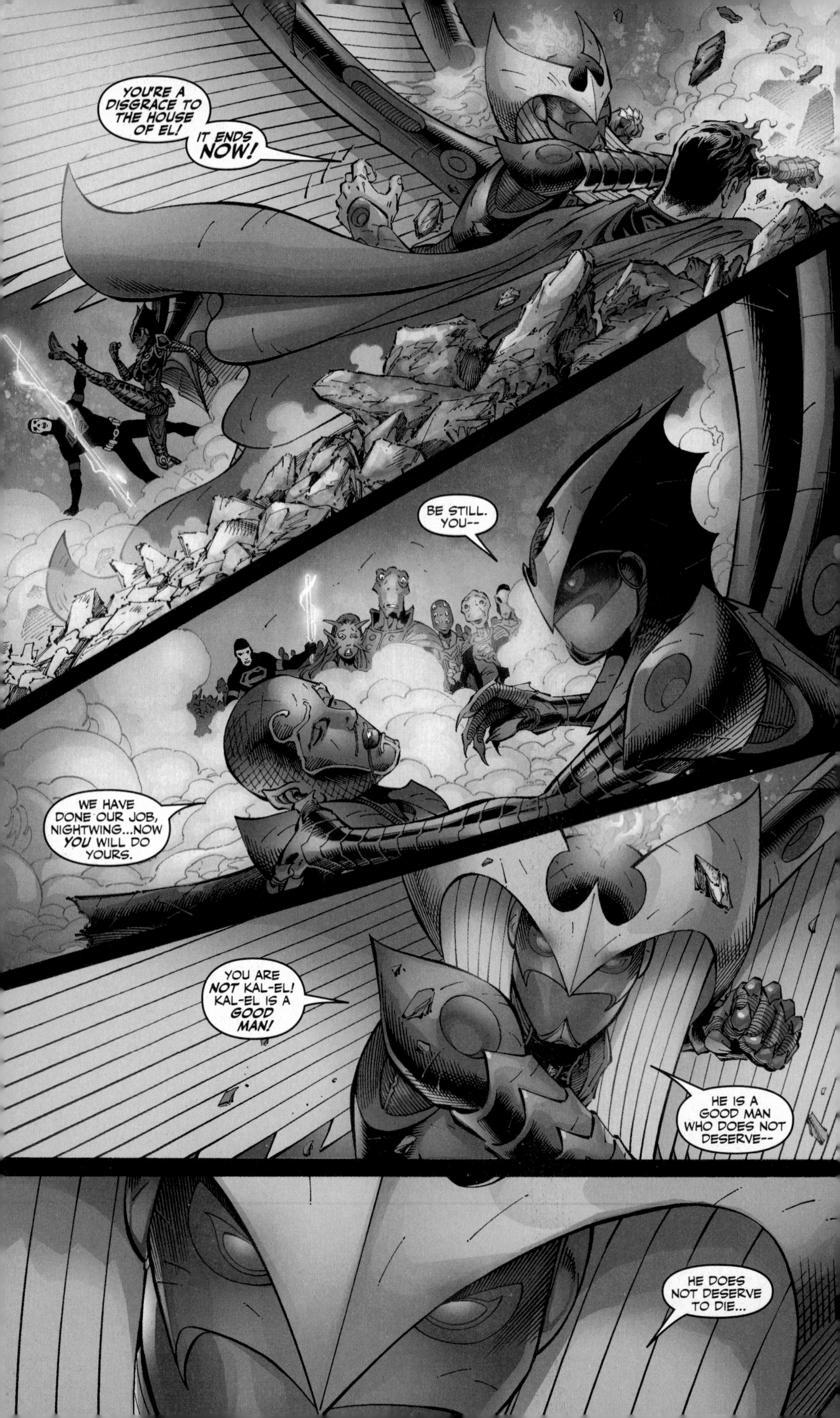
YOU'RE A DISGRACE TO THE HOUSE OF EL!
IT ENDS NOW!
BE STILL. YOU--
WE HAVE DONE OUR JOB, NIGHTWING...NOW YOU WILL DO YOURS.
YOU ARE NOT KAL-EL! KAL-EL IS A GOOD MAN!
HE IS A GOOD MAN WHO DOES NOT DESERVE--
HE DOES NOT DESERVE TO DIE...

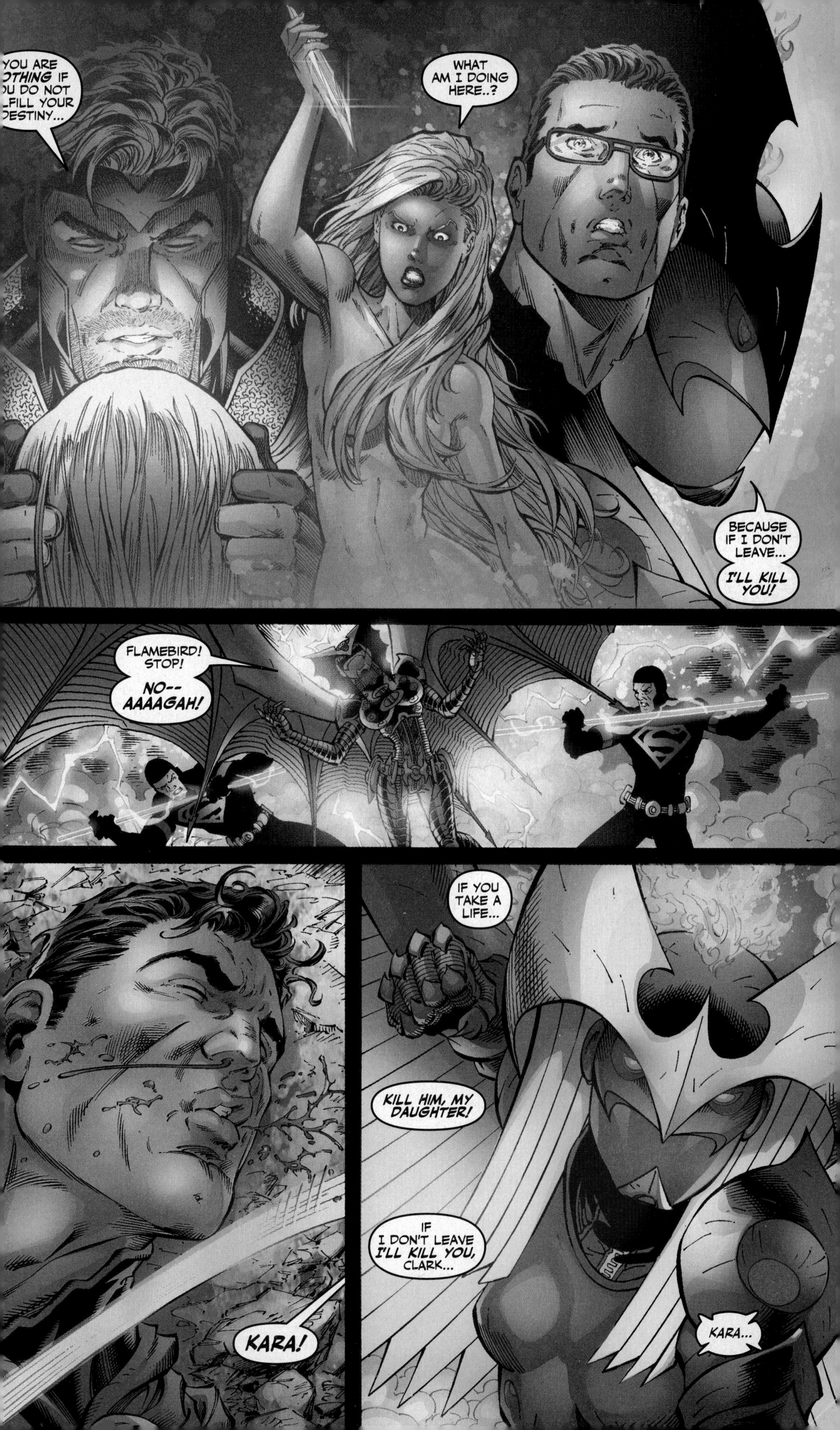
YOU ARE OTHING IF OU DO NOT LFILL YOUR DESTINY...
WHAT AM I DOING HERE..?
BECAUSE IF I DON'T LEAVE...
I'LL KILL YOU!
FLAMEBIRD! STOP!
NO-- AAAAGAH!
IF YOU TAKE A LIFE...
KILL HIM, MY DAUGHTER!
IF I DON'T LEAVE I'LL KILL YOU, CLARK...
KARA!
KARA...

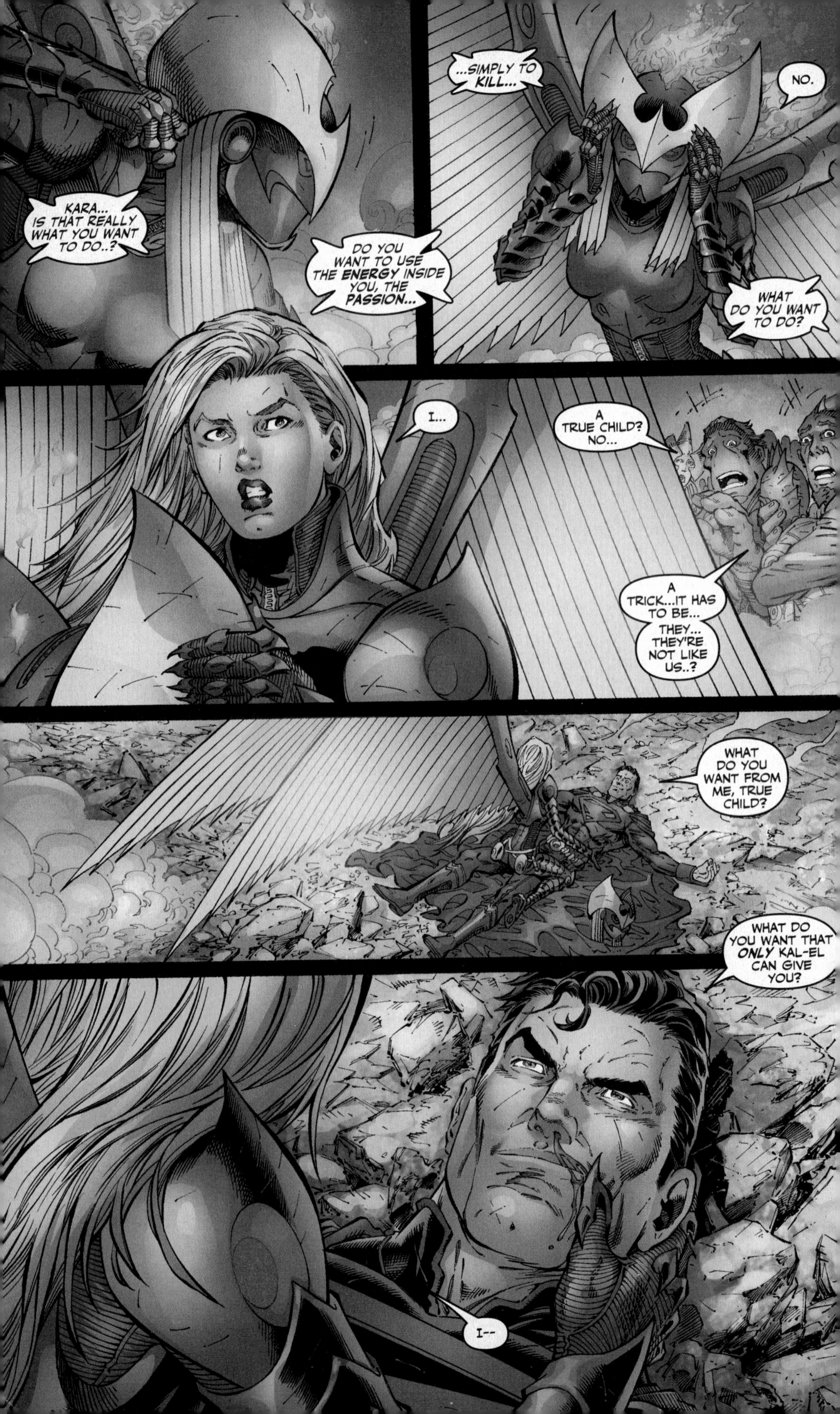
KARA... IS THAT REALLY WHAT YOU WANT TO DO..?
DO YOU WANT TO USE THE ENERGY INSIDE YOU, THE PASSION...
...SIMPLY TO KILL...
NO.
WHAT DO YOU WANT TO DO?
I...
A TRUE CHILD? NO...
A TRICK...IT HAS TO BE... THEY... THEY'RE NOT LIKE US..?
WHAT DO YOU WANT FROM ME, TRUE CHILD?
WHAT DO YOU WANT THAT ONLY KAL-EL CAN GIVE YOU?
I--

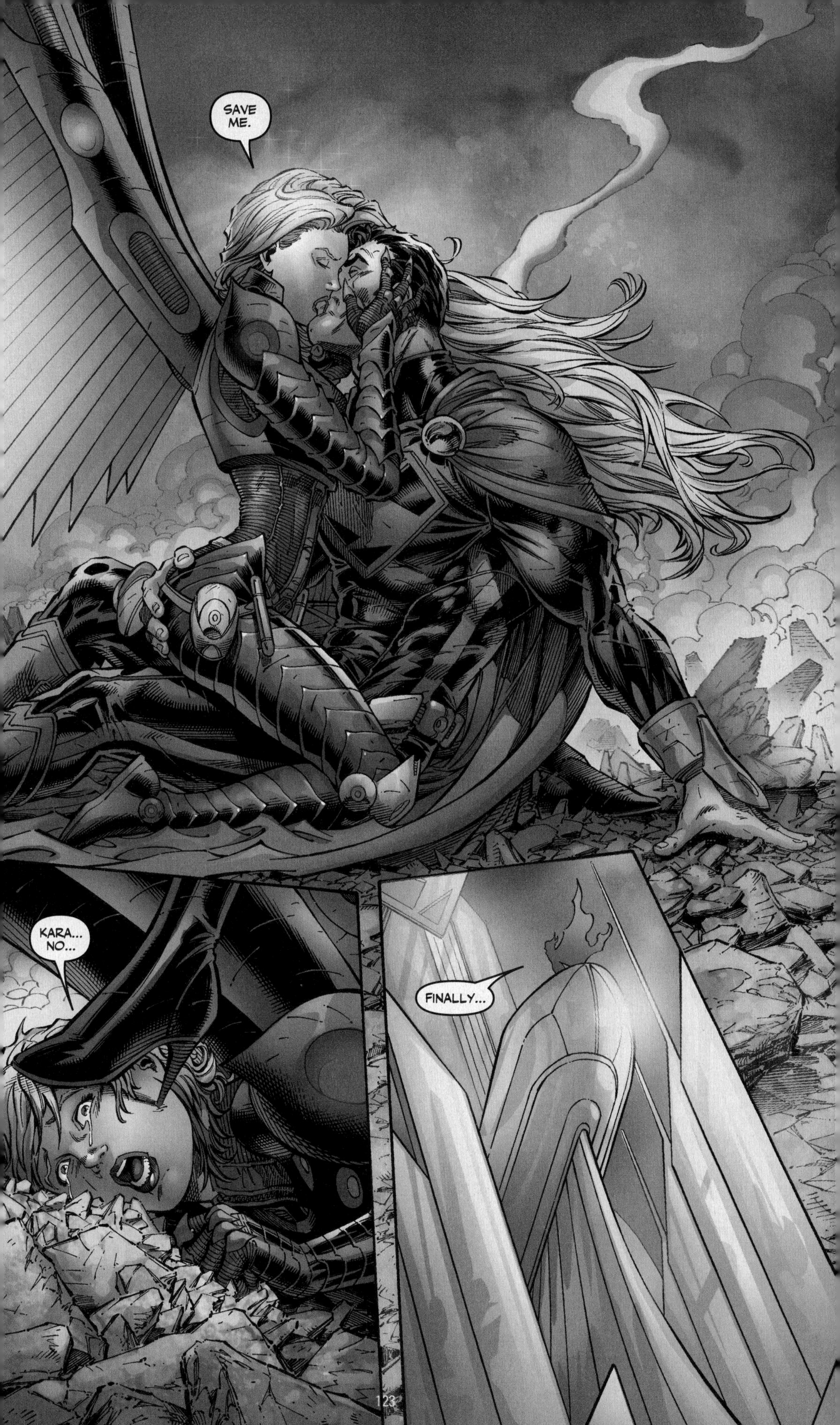
SAVE ME.
KARA... NO...
FINALLY...

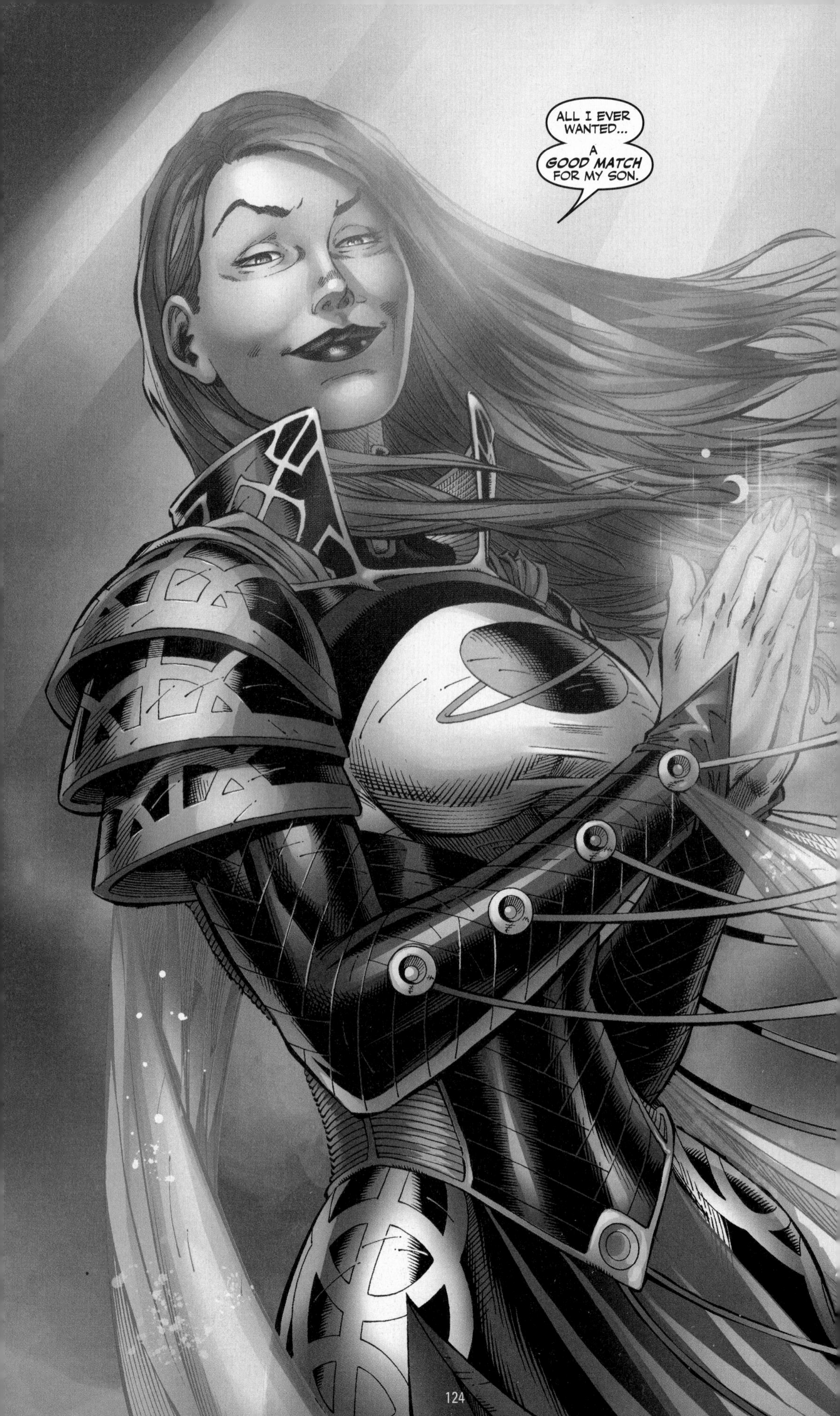
ALL I EVER WANTED... A GOOD MATCH FOR MY SON.

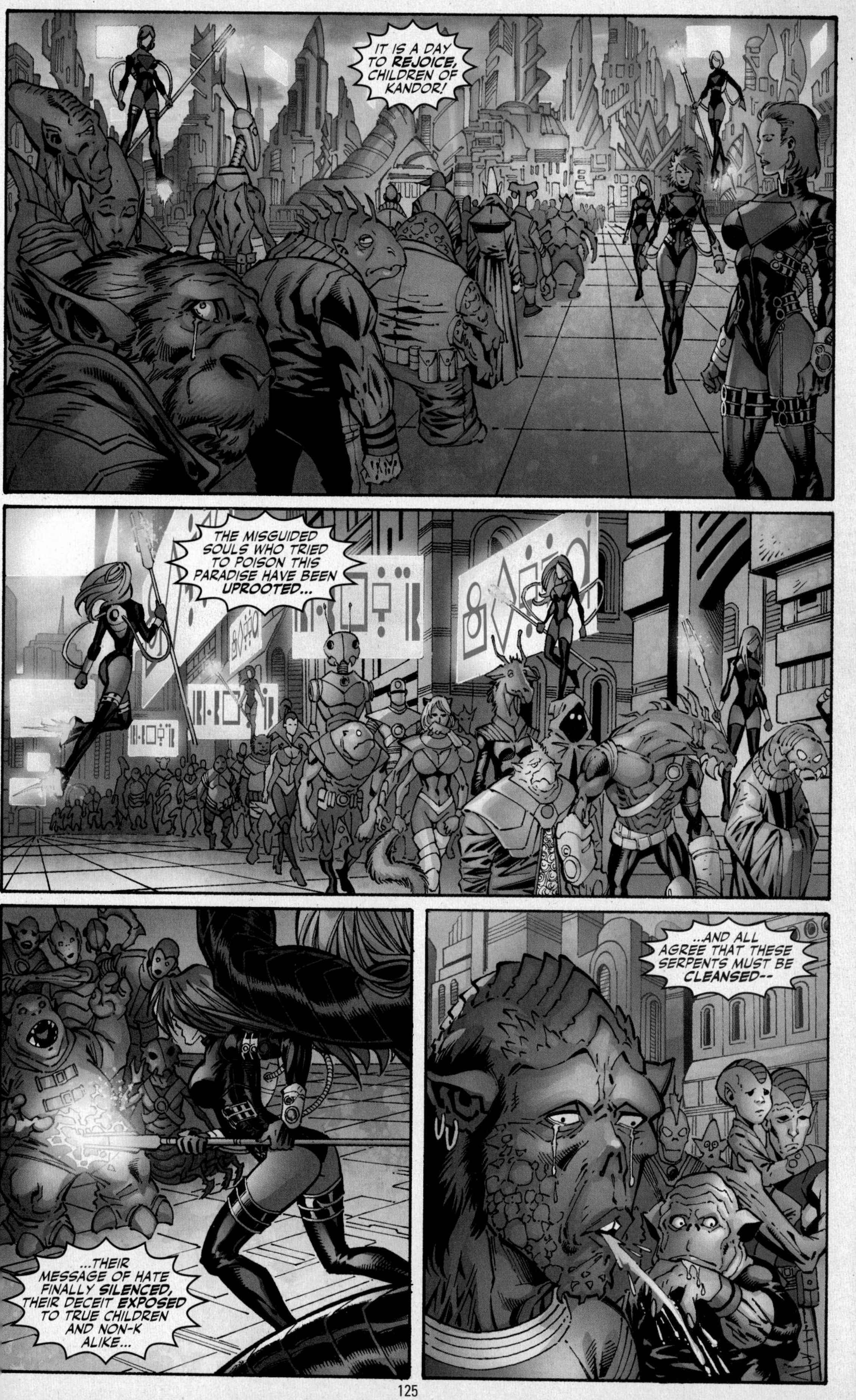
IT IS A DAY TO REJOICE, CHILDREN OF KANDOR!
THE MISGUIDED SOULS WHO TRIED TO POISON THIS PARADISE HAVE BEEN UPROOTED...
...THEIR MESSAGE OF HATE FINALLY SILENCED, THEIR DECEIT EXPOSED TO TRUE CHILDREN AND NON-K ALIKE...
...AND ALL AGREE THAT THESE SERPENTS MUST BE CLEANSED--

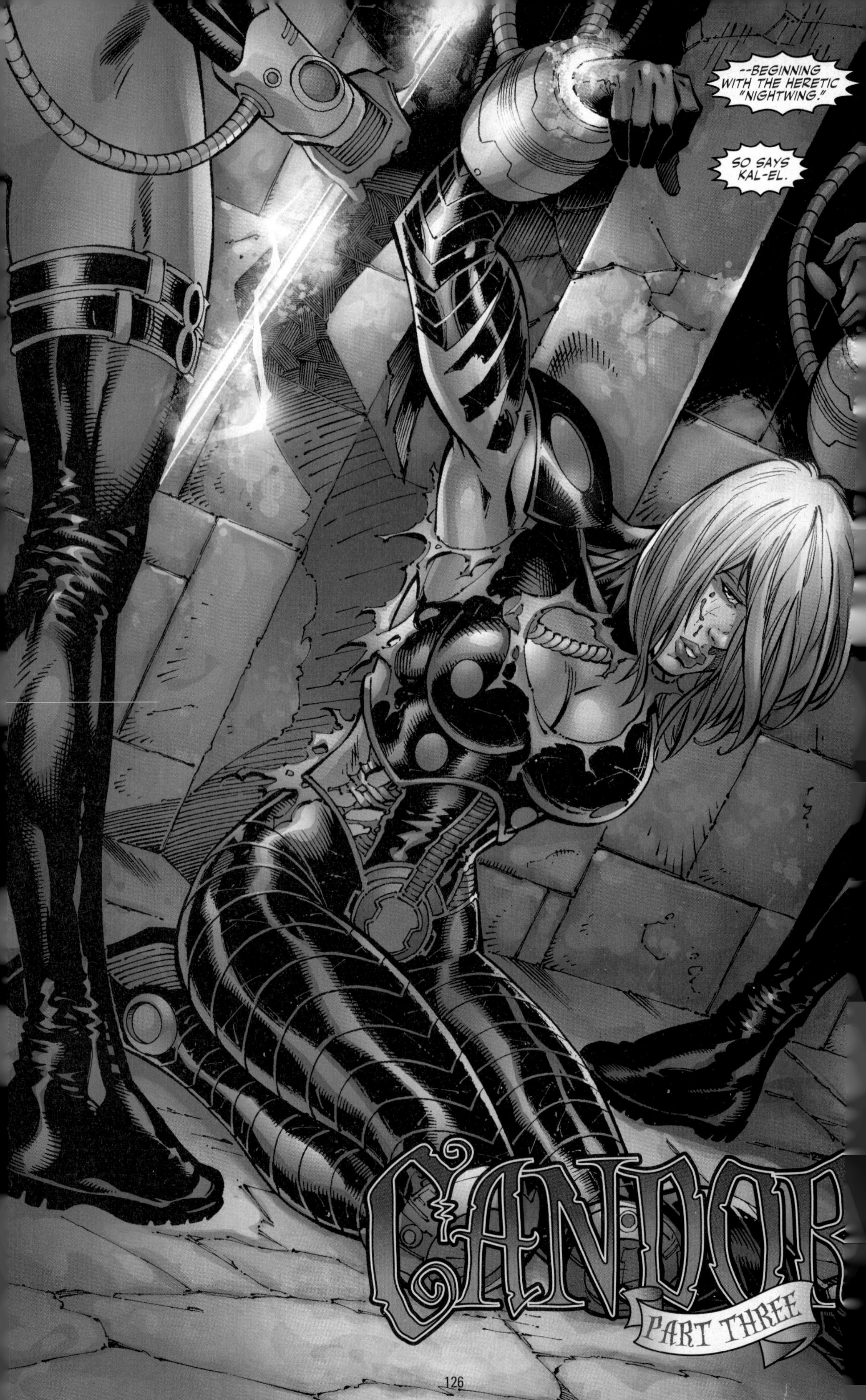
--BEGINNING WITH THE HERETIC "NIGHTWING."
SO SAYS KAL-EL.
CANDOR
PART THREE

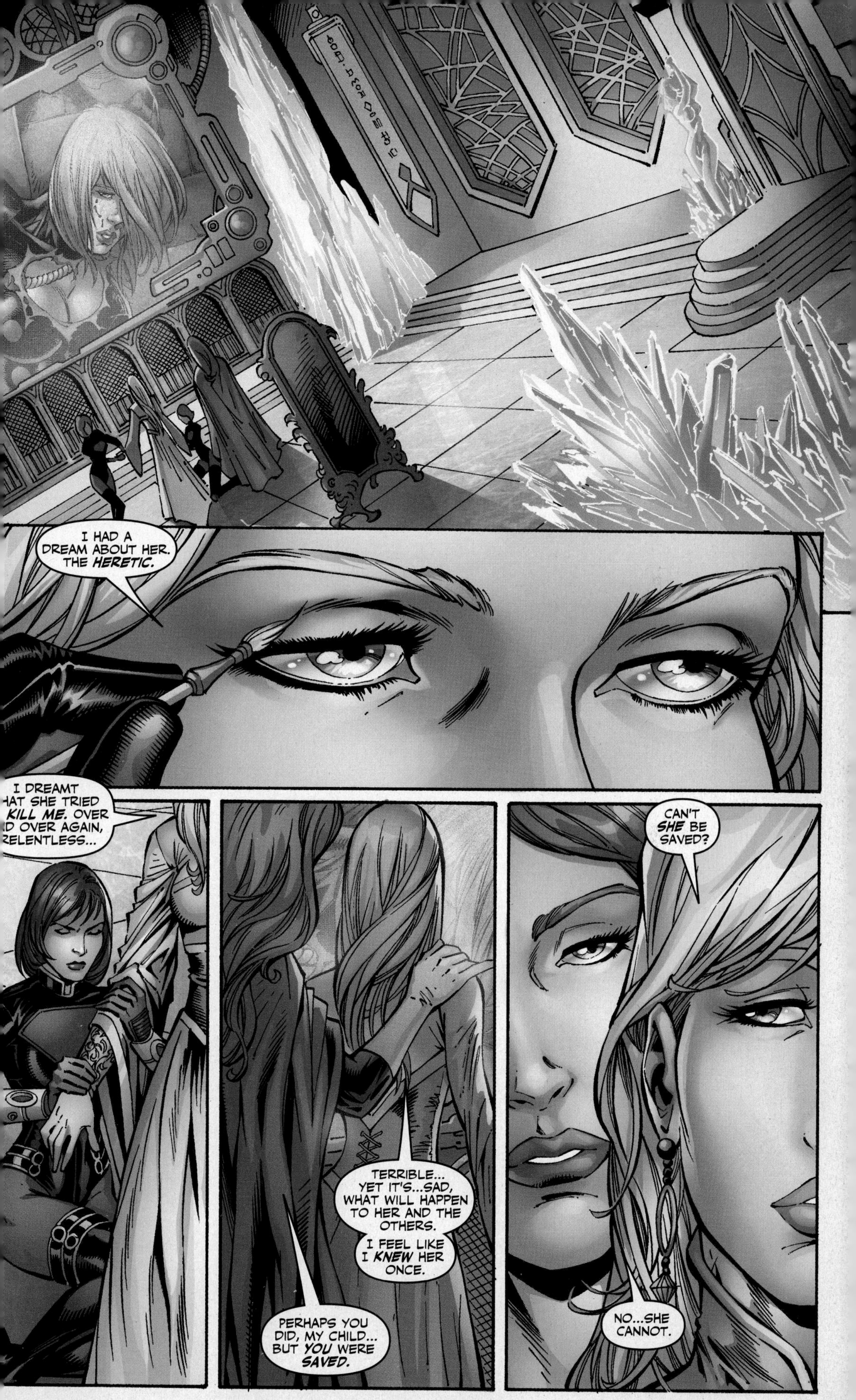
I HAD A DREAM ABOUT HER. THE HERETIC.
I DREAMT HAT SHE TRIED KILL ME. OVER D OVER AGAIN, RELENTLESS...
TERRIBLE... YET IT'S...SAD, WHAT WILL HAPPEN TO HER AND THE OTHERS.
I FEEL LIKE I KNEW HER ONCE.
PERHAPS YOU DID, MY CHILD... BUT YOU WERE SAVED.
CAN'T SHE BE SAVED?
NO...SHE CANNOT.

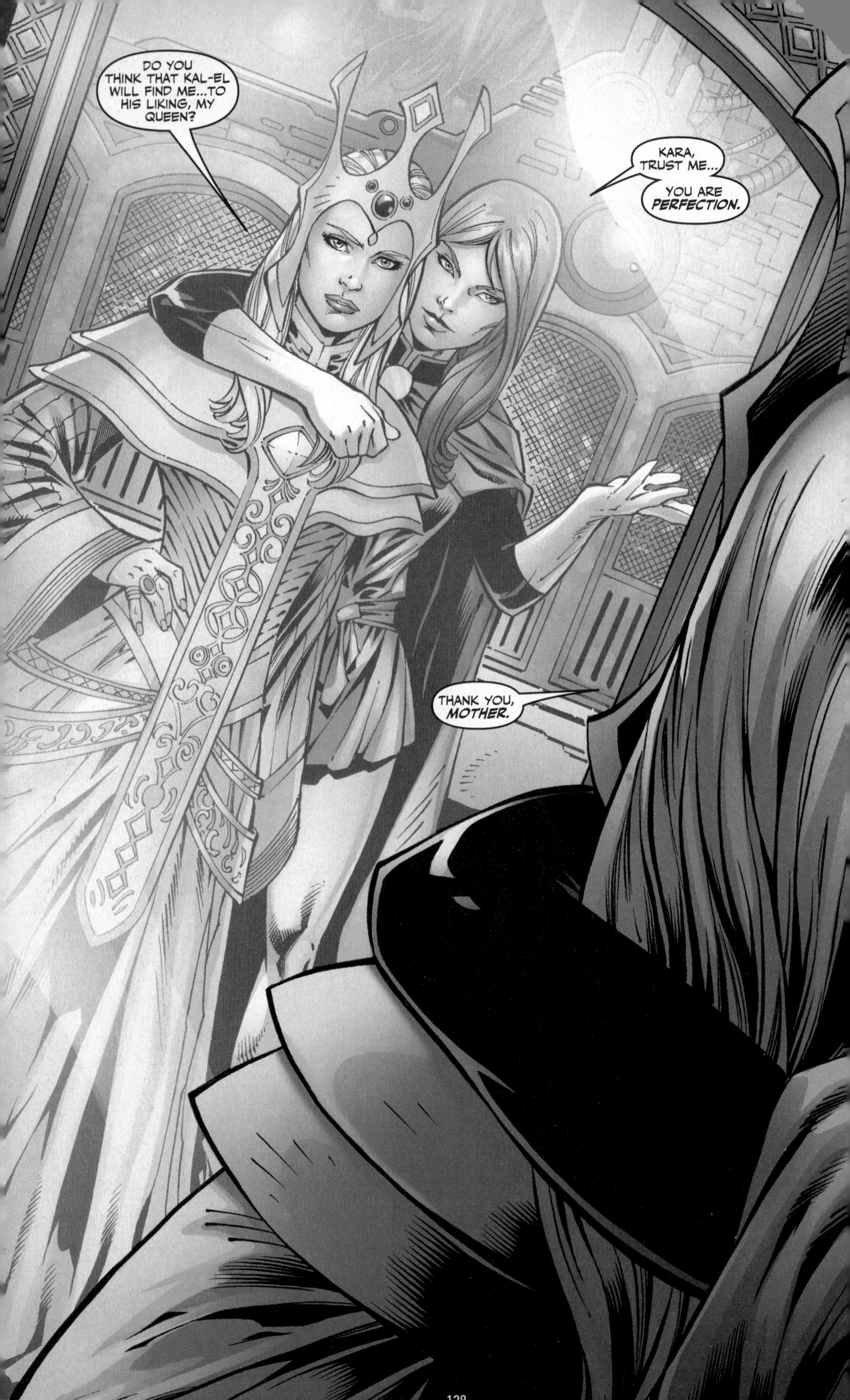
DO YOU THINK THAT KAL-EL WILL FIND ME...TO HIS LIKING, MY QUEEN?
KARA, TRUST ME...
YOU ARE *PERFECTION.*
THANK YOU, *MOTHER.*

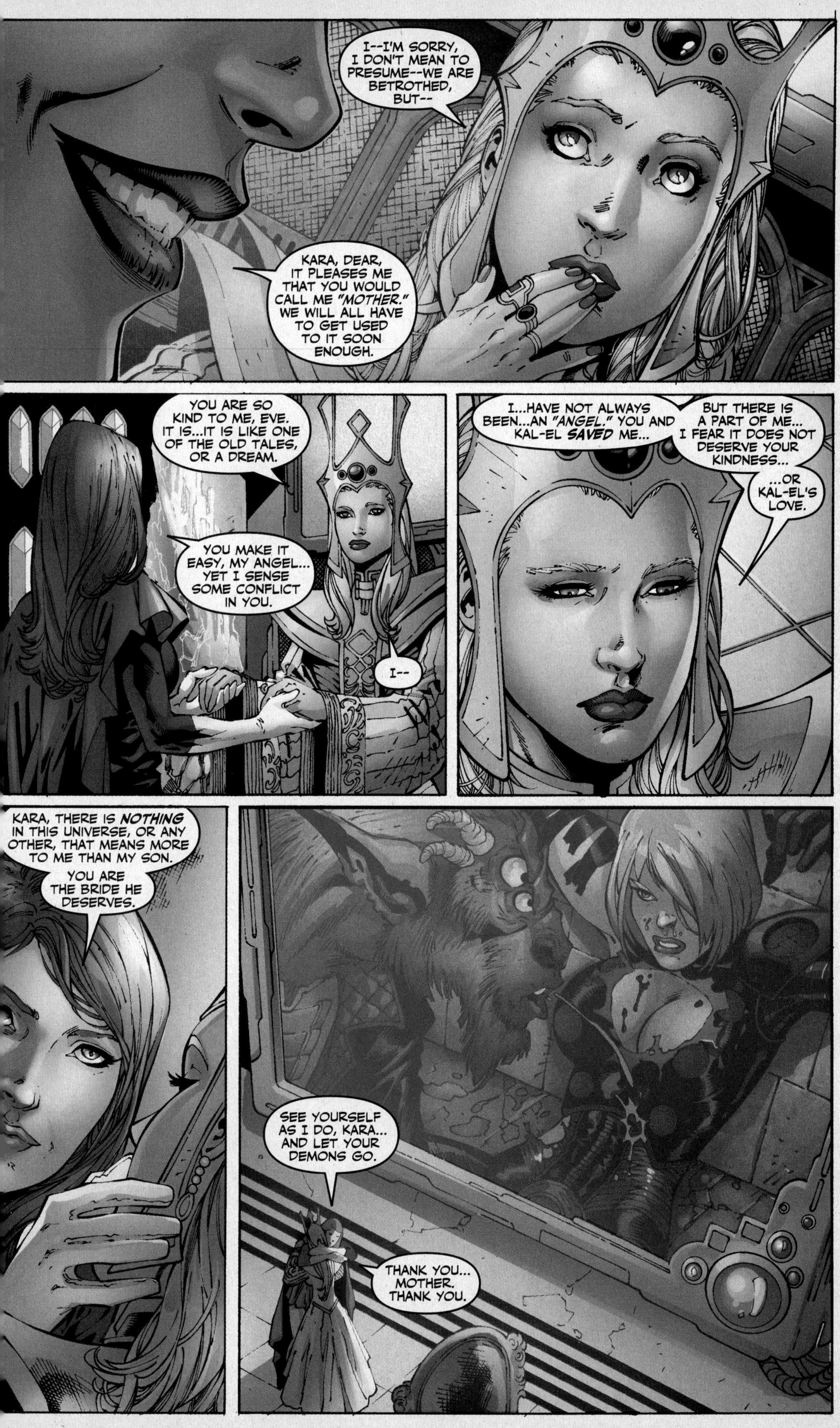
I--I'M SORRY, I DON'T MEAN TO PRESUME--WE ARE BETROTHED, BUT--
KARA, DEAR, IT PLEASES ME THAT YOU WOULD CALL ME "MOTHER." WE WILL ALL HAVE TO GET USED TO IT SOON ENOUGH.
YOU ARE SO KIND TO ME, EVE. IT IS...IT IS LIKE ONE OF THE OLD TALES, OR A DREAM.
YOU MAKE IT EASY, MY ANGEL... YET I SENSE SOME CONFLICT IN YOU.
I--
I...HAVE NOT ALWAYS BEEN...AN "ANGEL." YOU AND KAL-EL ***SAVED*** ME...
BUT THERE IS A PART OF ME... I FEAR IT DOES NOT DESERVE YOUR KINDNESS...
...OR KAL-EL'S LOVE.
KARA, THERE IS ***NOTHING*** IN THIS UNIVERSE, OR ANY OTHER, THAT MEANS MORE TO ME THAN MY SON.
YOU ARE THE BRIDE HE DESERVES.
SEE YOURSELF AS I DO, KARA... AND LET YOUR DEMONS GO.
THANK YOU... MOTHER. THANK YOU.

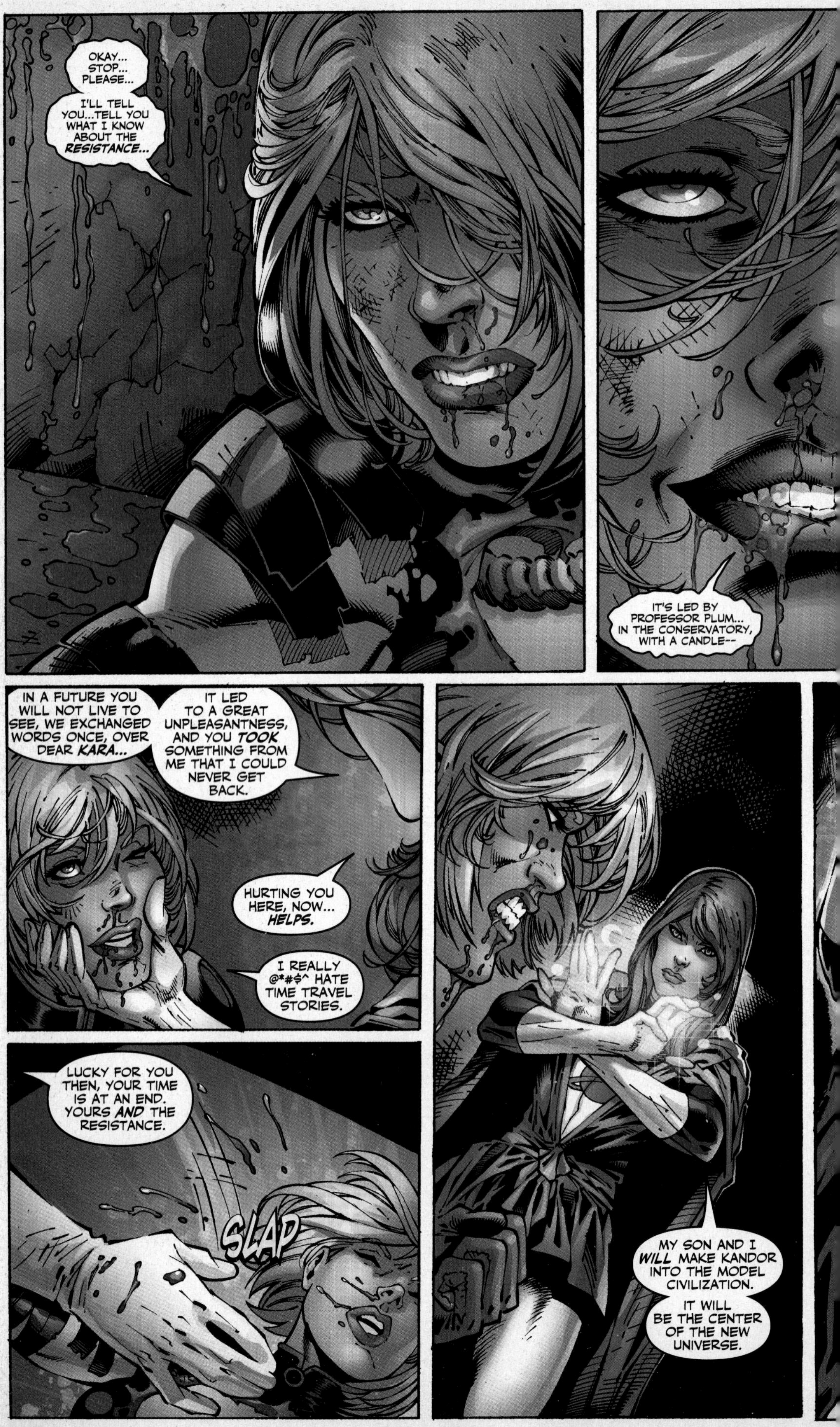
OKAY... STOP... PLEASE...
I'LL TELL YOU...TELL YOU WHAT I KNOW ABOUT THE RESISTANCE...
IT'S LED BY PROFESSOR PLUM... IN THE CONSERVATORY, WITH A CANDLE--
IN A FUTURE YOU WILL NOT LIVE TO SEE, WE EXCHANGED WORDS ONCE, OVER DEAR KARA...
IT LED TO A GREAT UNPLEASANTNESS, AND YOU TOOK SOMETHING FROM ME THAT I COULD NEVER GET BACK.
HURTING YOU HERE, NOW... HELPS.
I REALLY @*#$^ HATE TIME TRAVEL STORIES.
LUCKY FOR YOU THEN, YOUR TIME IS AT AN END. YOURS AND THE RESISTANCE.
SLAP
MY SON AND I WILL MAKE KANDOR INTO THE MODEL CIVILIZATION.
IT WILL BE THE CENTER OF THE NEW UNIVERSE.

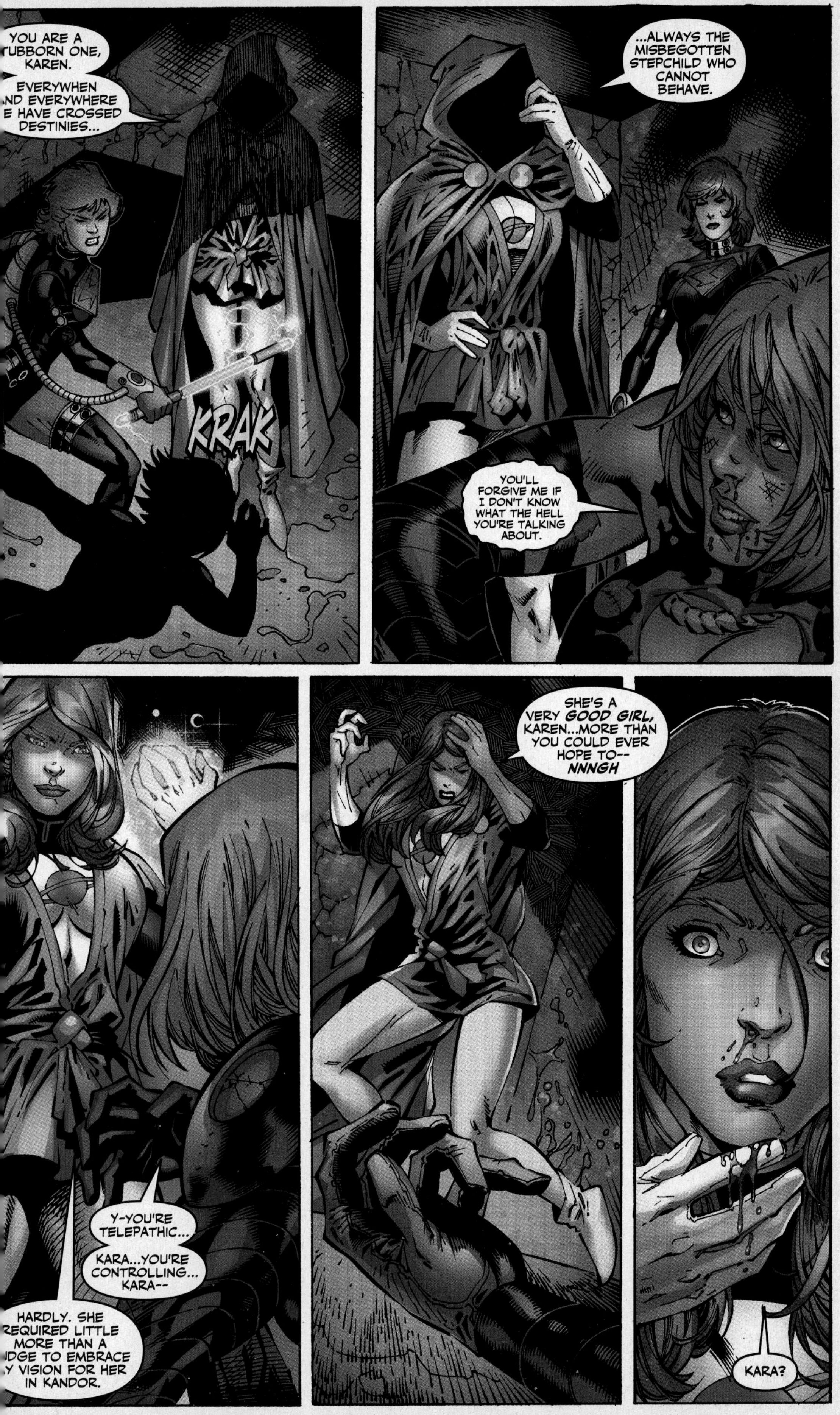
YOU ARE A TUBBORN ONE, KAREN.
EVERYWHEN ND EVERYWHERE E HAVE CROSSED DESTINIES...
KRAK
...ALWAYS THE MISBEGOTTEN STEPCHILD WHO CANNOT BEHAVE.
YOU'LL FORGIVE ME IF I DON'T KNOW WHAT THE HELL YOU'RE TALKING ABOUT.
Y-YOU'RE TELEPATHIC...
KARA...YOU'RE CONTROLLING... KARA--
HARDLY. SHE REQUIRED LITTLE MORE THAN A UDGE TO EMBRACE Y VISION FOR HER IN KANDOR.
SHE'S A VERY GOOD GIRL, KAREN...MORE THAN YOU COULD EVER HOPE TO-- NNNGH
KARA?

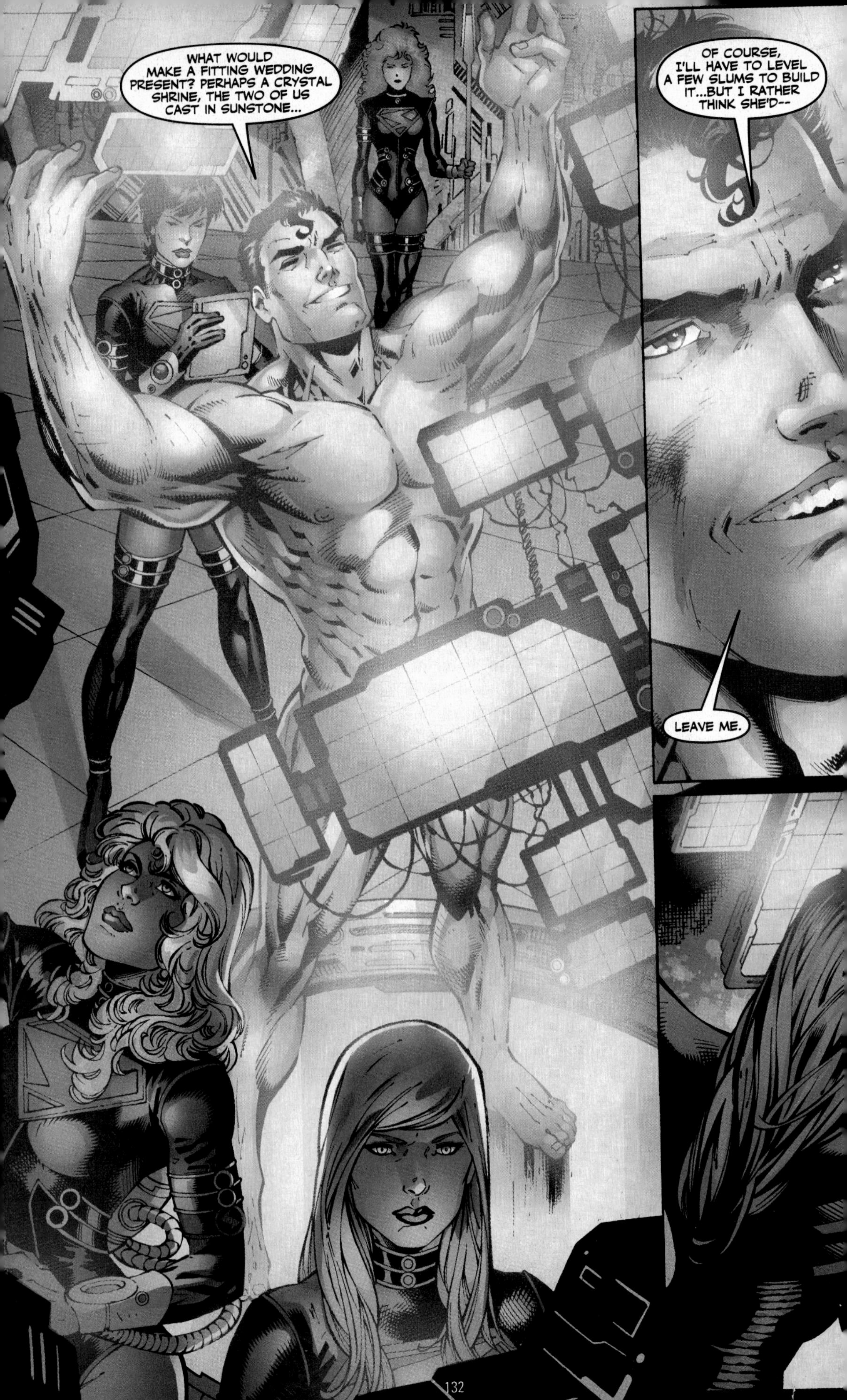
WHAT WOULD MAKE A FITTING WEDDING PRESENT? PERHAPS A CRYSTAL SHRINE, THE TWO OF US CAST IN SUNSTONE...
OF COURSE, I'LL HAVE TO LEVEL A FEW SLUMS TO BUILD IT...BUT I RATHER THINK SHE'D--
LEAVE ME.

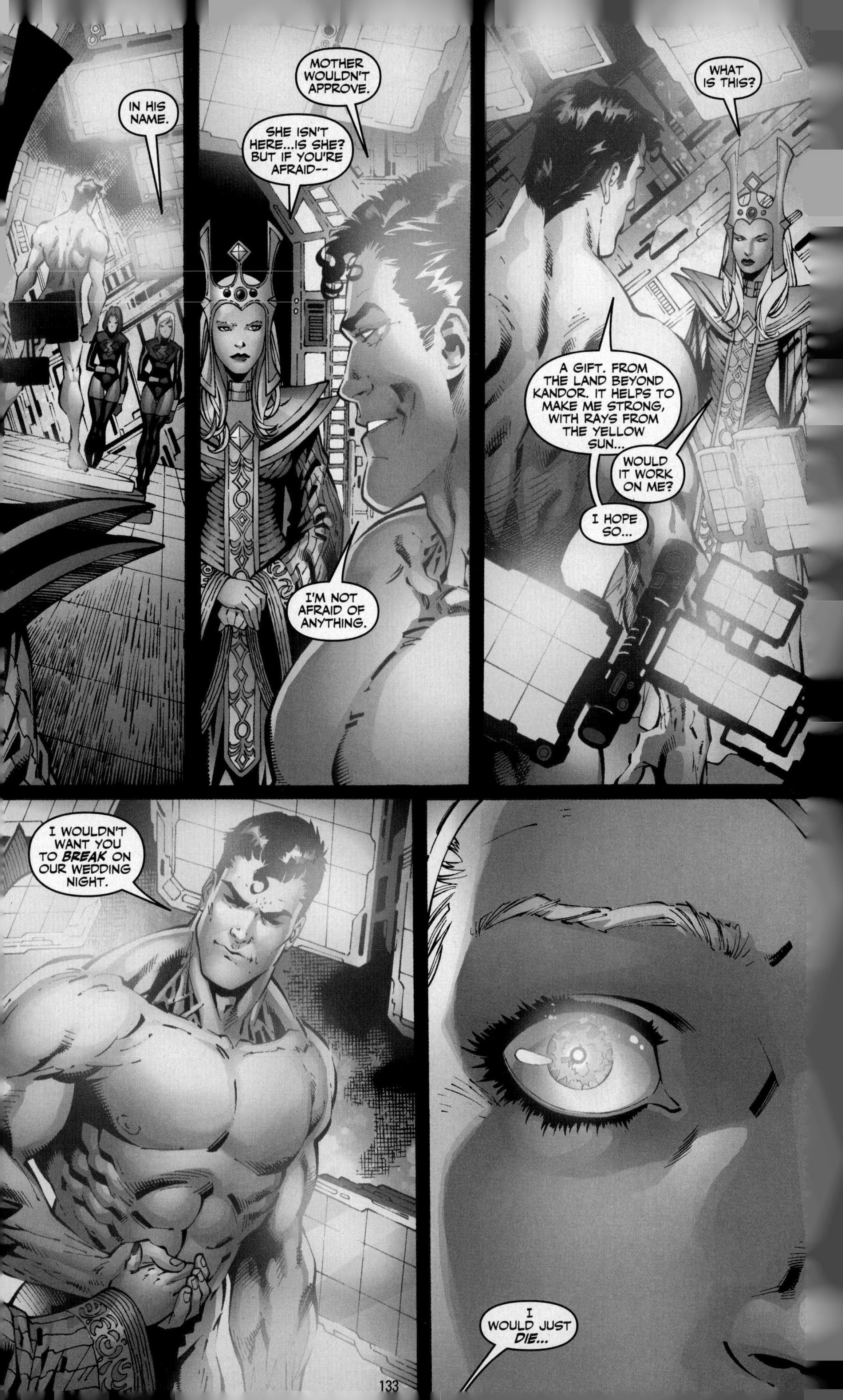
IN HIS NAME.
MOTHER WOULDN'T APPROVE.
SHE ISN'T HERE...IS SHE? BUT IF YOU'RE AFRAID--
I'M NOT AFRAID OF ANYTHING.
WHAT IS THIS?
A GIFT. FROM THE LAND BEYOND KANDOR. IT HELPS TO MAKE ME STRONG, WITH RAYS FROM THE YELLOW SUN...
WOULD IT WORK ON ME?
I HOPE SO...
I WOULDN'T WANT YOU TO BREAK ON OUR WEDDING NIGHT.
I WOULD JUST DIE...

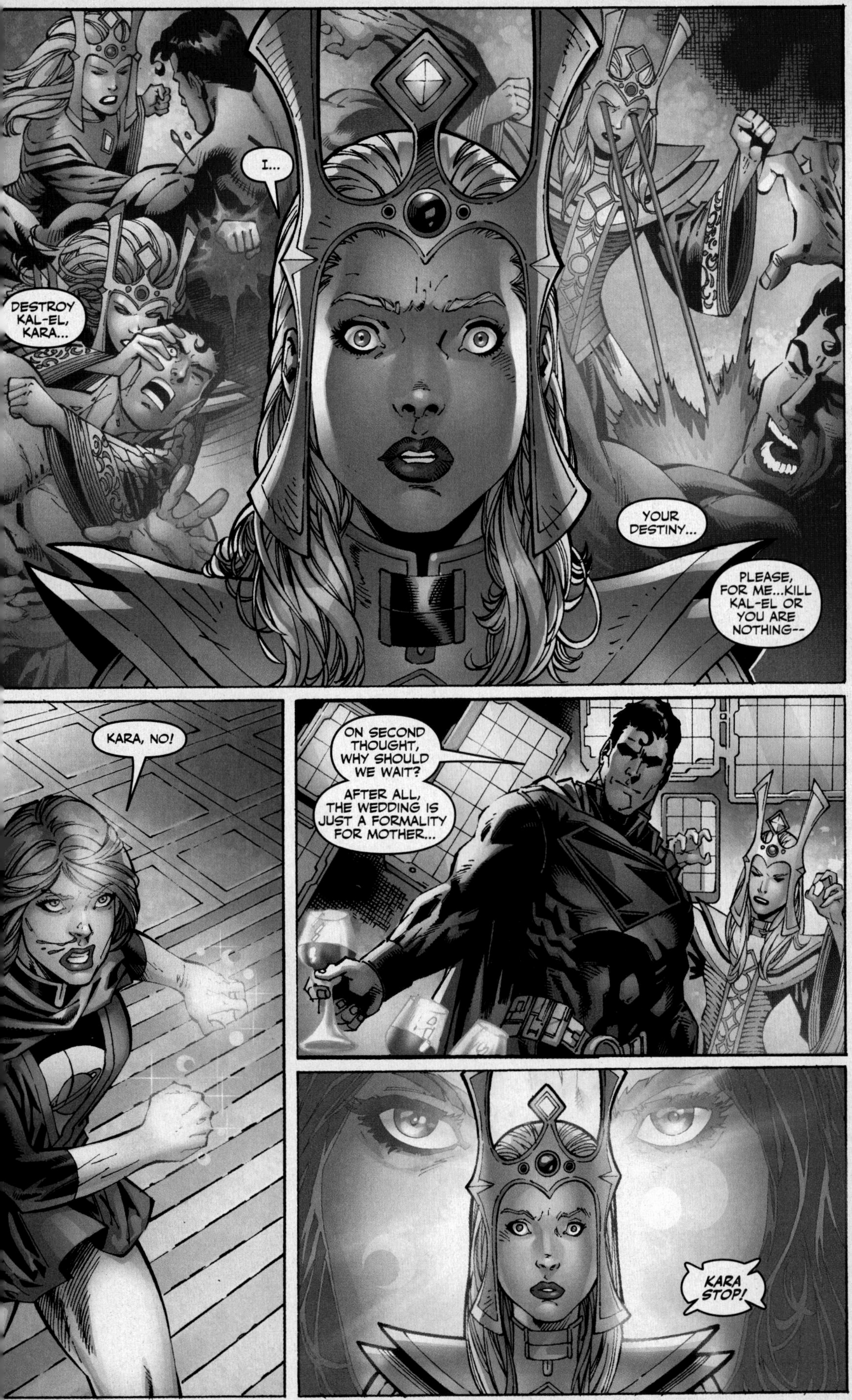
I...
DESTROY KAL-EL, KARA...
YOUR DESTINY...
PLEASE, FOR ME...KILL KAL-EL OR YOU ARE NOTHING--
KARA, NO!
ON SECOND THOUGHT, WHY SHOULD WE WAIT?
AFTER ALL, THE WEDDING IS JUST A FORMALITY FOR MOTHER...
KARA STOP!

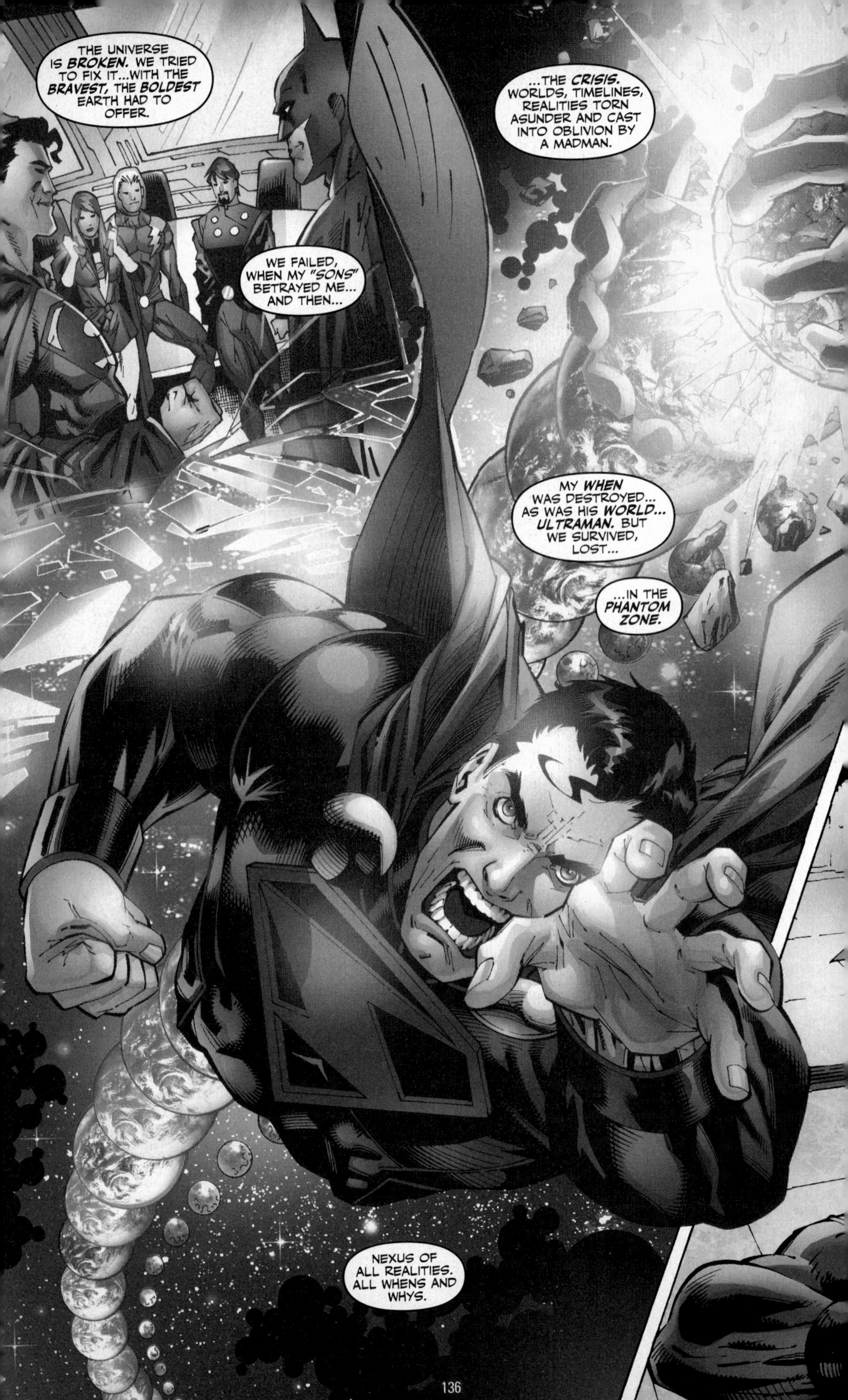
THE UNIVERSE IS BROKEN. WE TRIED TO FIX IT...WITH THE BRAVEST, THE BOLDEST EARTH HAD TO OFFER.
WE FAILED, WHEN MY "SONS" BETRAYED ME... AND THEN...
...THE CRISIS. WORLDS, TIMELINES, REALITIES TORN ASUNDER AND CAST INTO OBLIVION BY A MADMAN.
MY WHEN WAS DESTROYED... AS WAS HIS WORLD... ULTRAMAN. BUT WE SURVIVED, LOST...
...IN THE PHANTOM ZONE.
NEXUS OF ALL REALITIES. ALL WHENS AND WHYS.

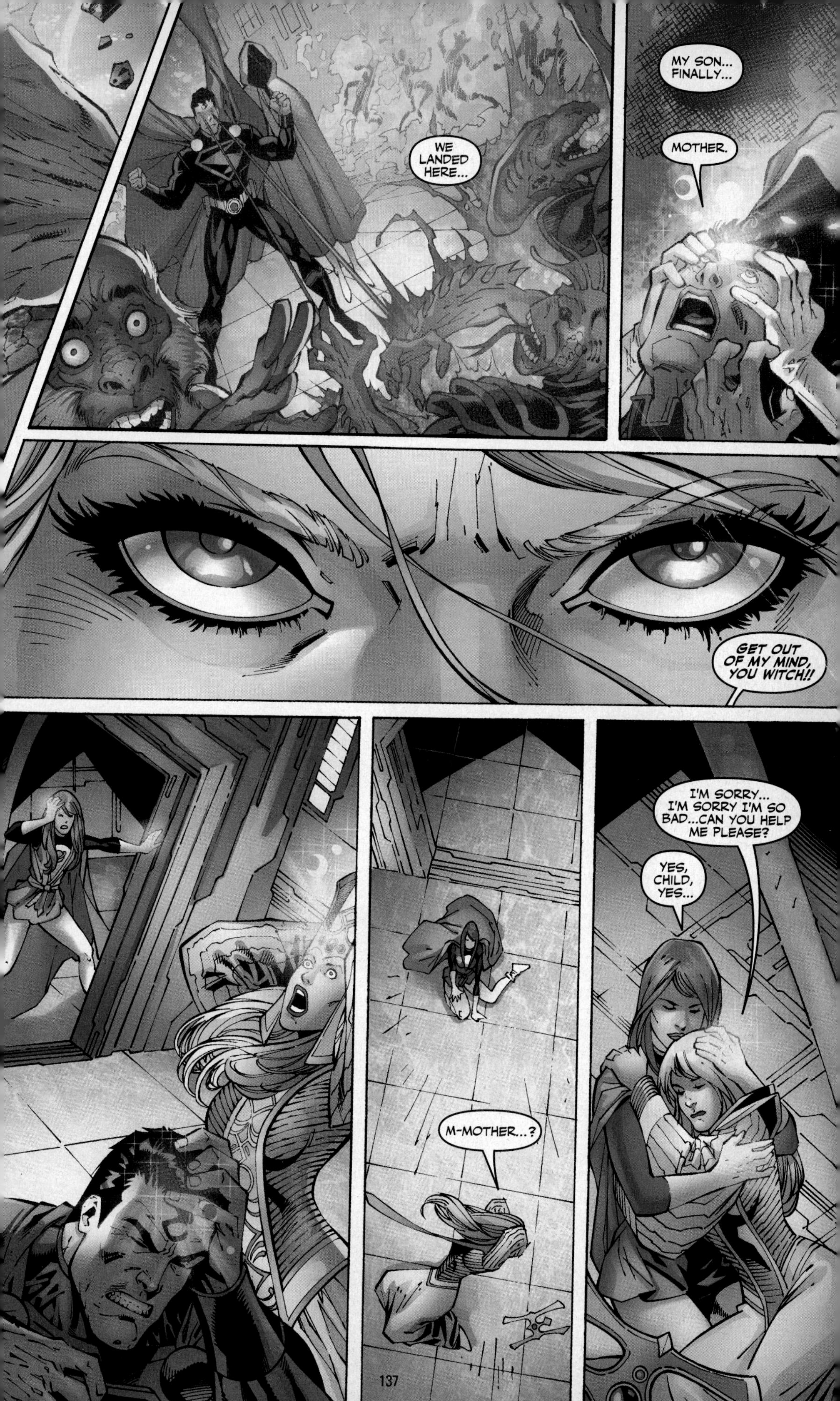
WE LANDED HERE...
MY SON... FINALLY...
MOTHER.
GET OUT OF MY MIND, YOU WITCH!!
M-MOTHER...?
I'M SORRY... I'M SORRY I'M SO BAD...CAN YOU HELP ME PLEASE?
YES, CHILD, YES...

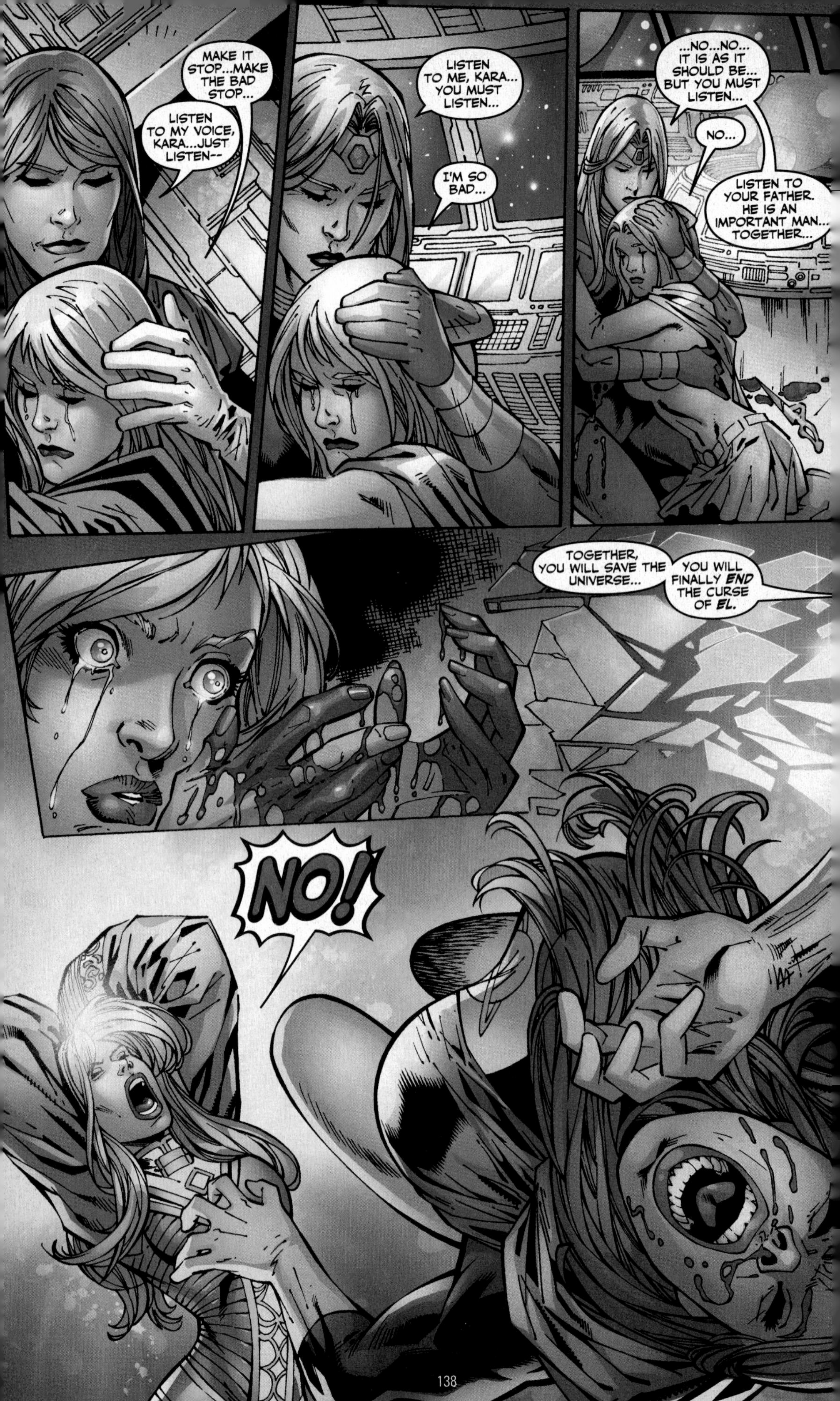
MAKE IT STOP...MAKE THE BAD STOP...
LISTEN TO MY VOICE, KARA...JUST LISTEN--
LISTEN TO ME, KARA... YOU MUST LISTEN...
I'M SO BAD...
...NO...NO... IT IS AS IT SHOULD BE... BUT YOU MUST LISTEN...
NO...
LISTEN TO YOUR FATHER. HE IS AN IMPORTANT MAN... TOGETHER...
TOGETHER, YOU WILL SAVE THE UNIVERSE...
YOU WILL FINALLY END THE CURSE OF EL.
NO!

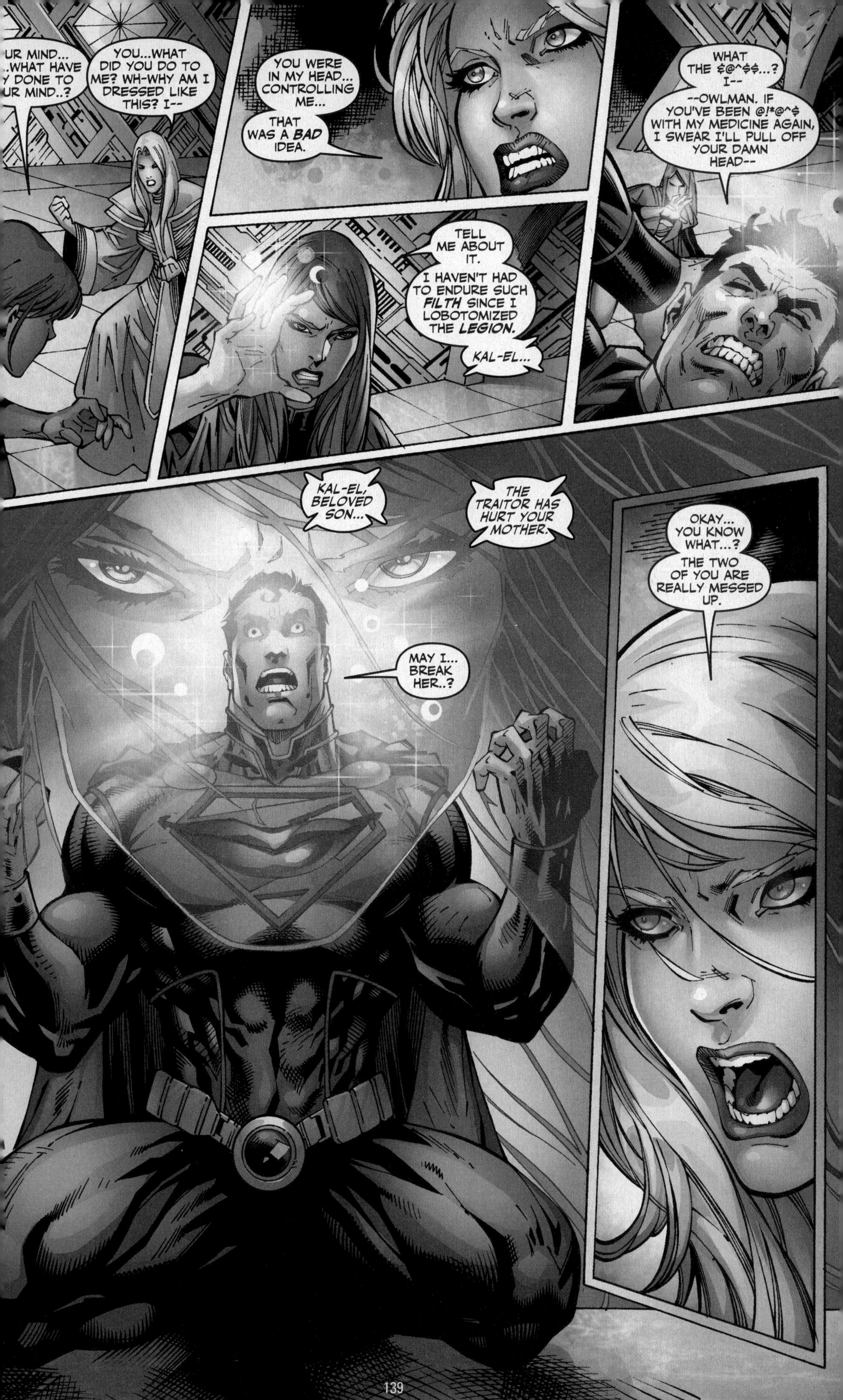
UR MIND... ...WHAT HAVE Y DONE TO UR MIND..?
YOU...WHAT DID YOU DO TO ME? WH-WHY AM I DRESSED LIKE THIS? I--
YOU WERE IN MY HEAD... CONTROLLING ME...
THAT WAS A BAD IDEA.
WHAT THE $@^$$...? I--
--OWLMAN. IF YOU'VE BEEN @!*@^$ WITH MY MEDICINE AGAIN, I SWEAR I'LL PULL OFF YOUR DAMN HEAD--
TELL ME ABOUT IT.
I HAVEN'T HAD TO ENDURE SUCH FILTH SINCE I LOBOTOMIZED THE LEGION.
KAL-EL...
KAL-EL, BELOVED SON...
THE TRAITOR HAS HURT YOUR MOTHER.
MAY I... BREAK HER..?
OKAY... YOU KNOW WHAT...?
THE TWO OF YOU ARE REALLY MESSED UP.

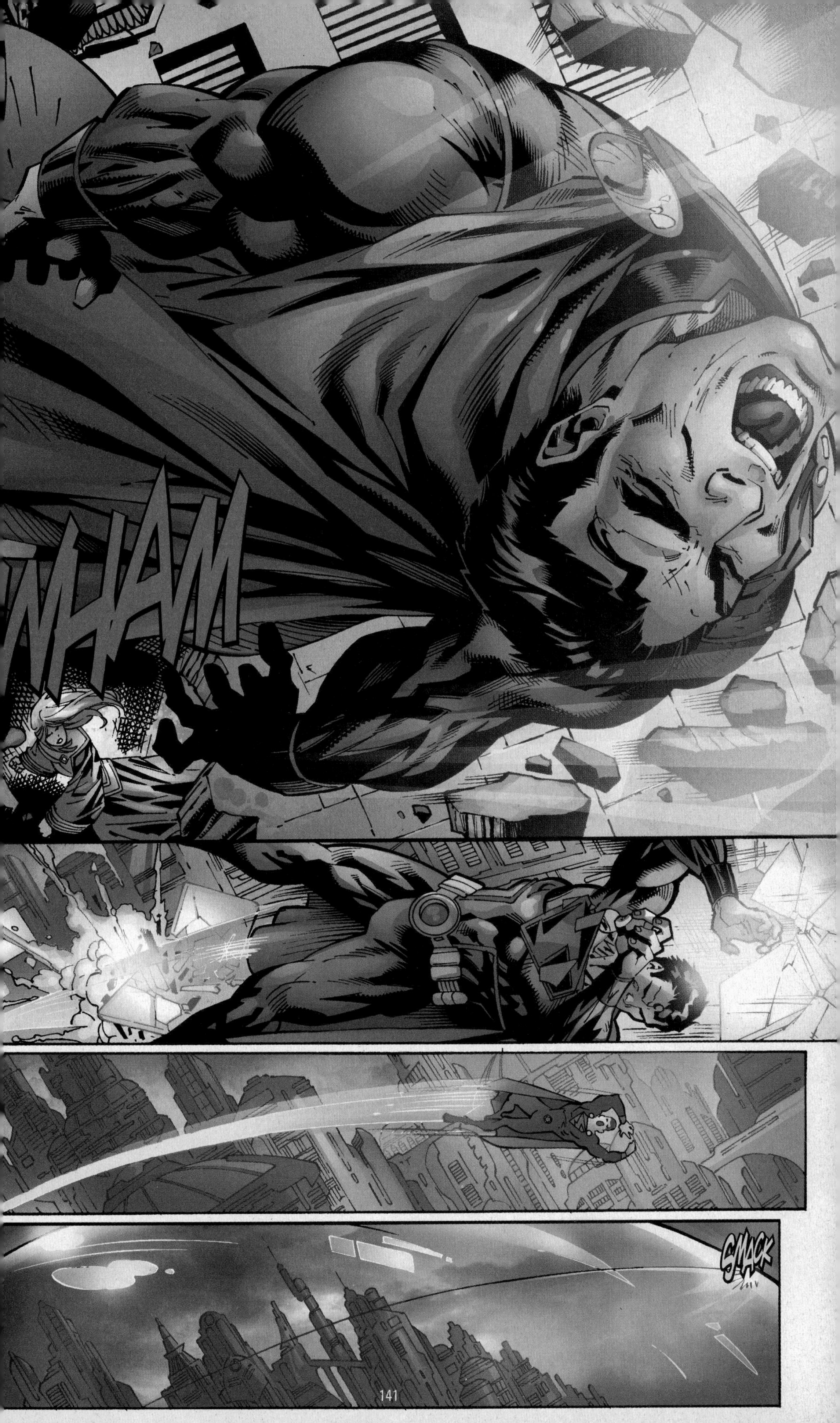
WHAM
SMACK

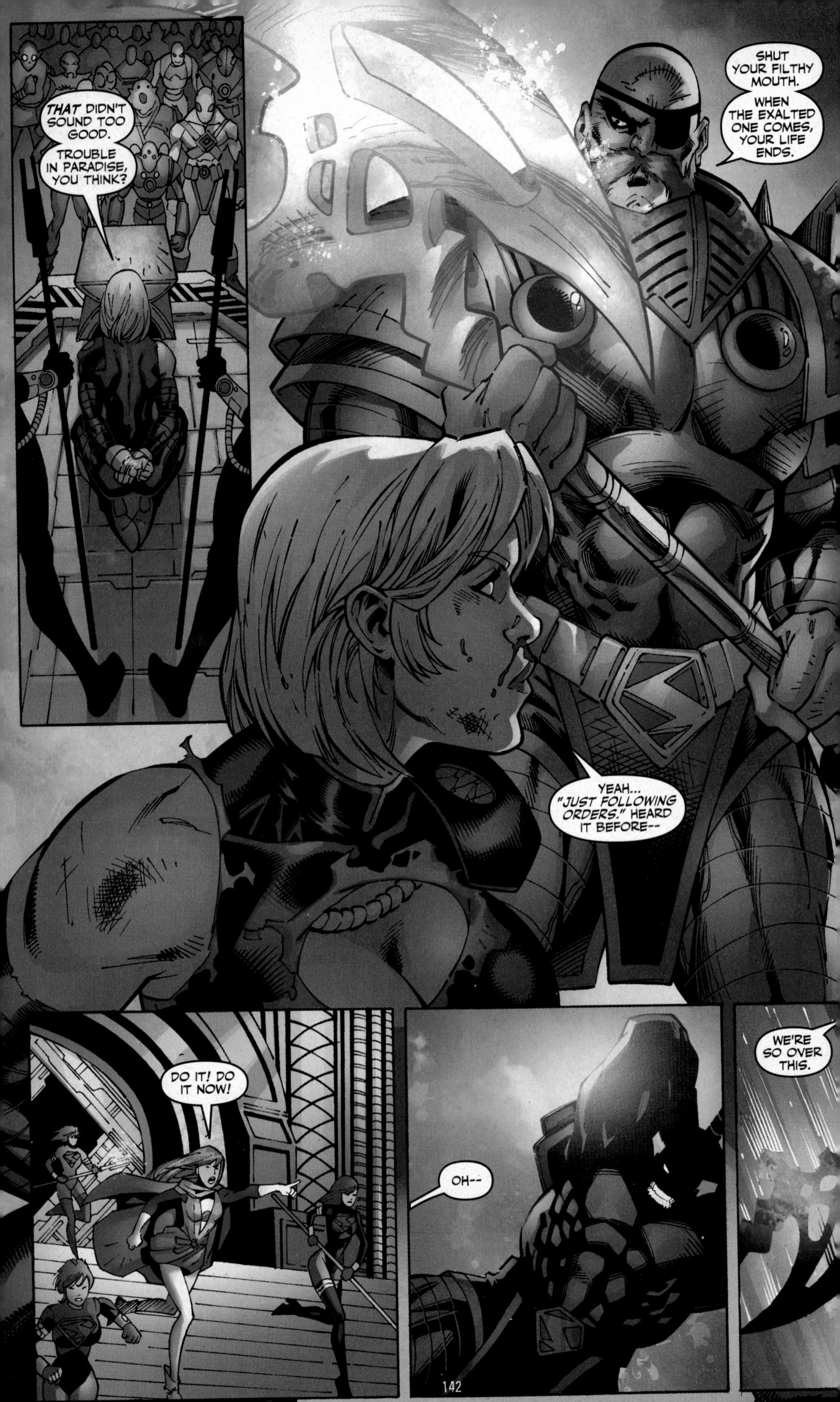
THAT DIDN'T SOUND TOO GOOD.
TROUBLE IN PARADISE, YOU THINK?
SHUT YOUR FILTHY MOUTH.
WHEN THE EXALTED ONE COMES, YOUR LIFE ENDS.
YEAH... "JUST FOLLOWING ORDERS." HEARD IT BEFORE--
DO IT! DO IT NOW!
OH--
WE'RE SO OVER THIS.

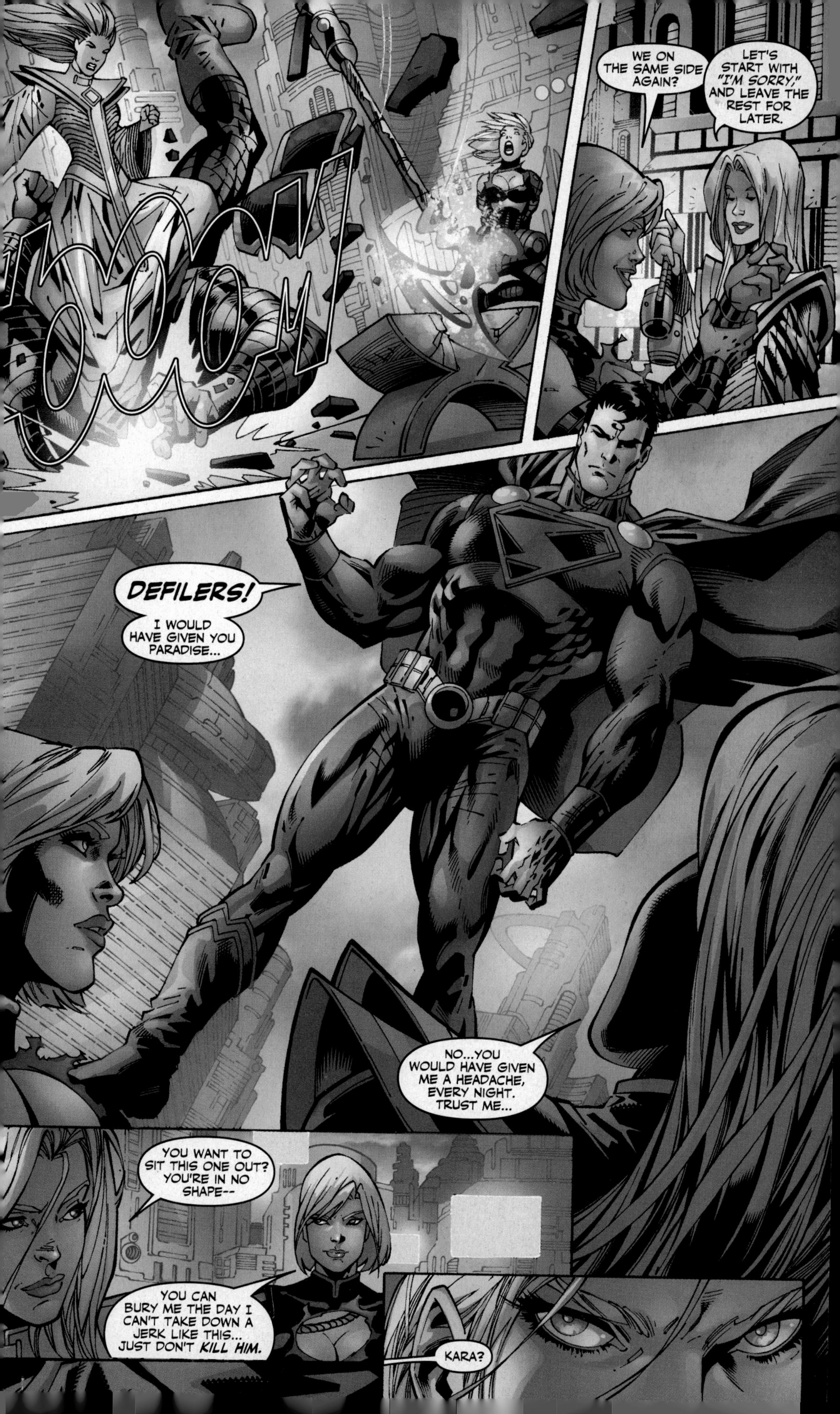

BOOOM
WE ON THE SAME SIDE AGAIN?
LET'S START WITH "I'M SORRY," AND LEAVE THE REST FOR LATER.
DEFILERS!
I WOULD HAVE GIVEN YOU PARADISE...
NO...YOU WOULD HAVE GIVEN ME A HEADACHE, EVERY NIGHT. TRUST ME...
YOU WANT TO SIT THIS ONE OUT? YOU'RE IN NO SHAPE--
YOU CAN BURY ME THE DAY I CAN'T TAKE DOWN A JERK LIKE THIS... JUST DON'T KILL HIM.
KARA?

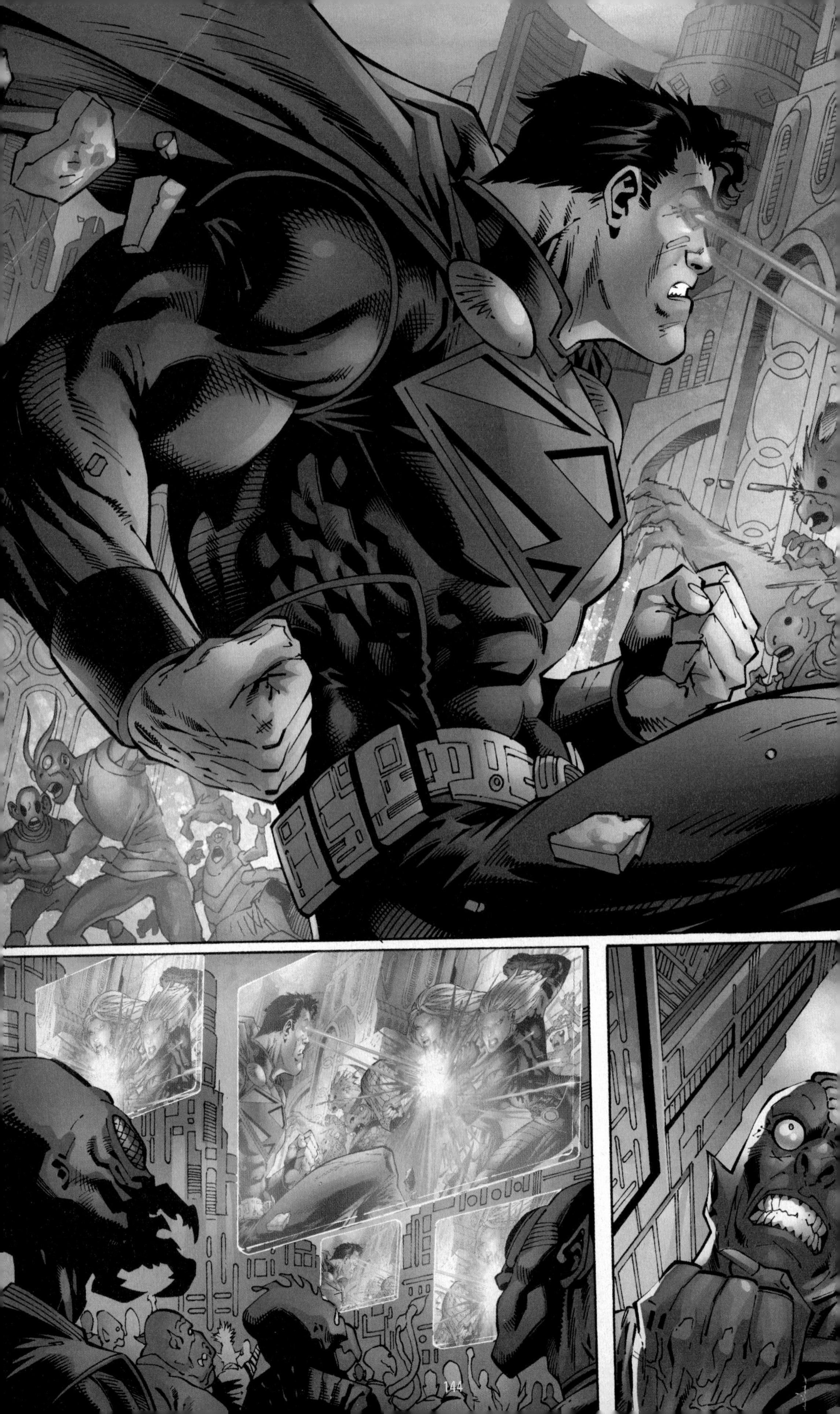

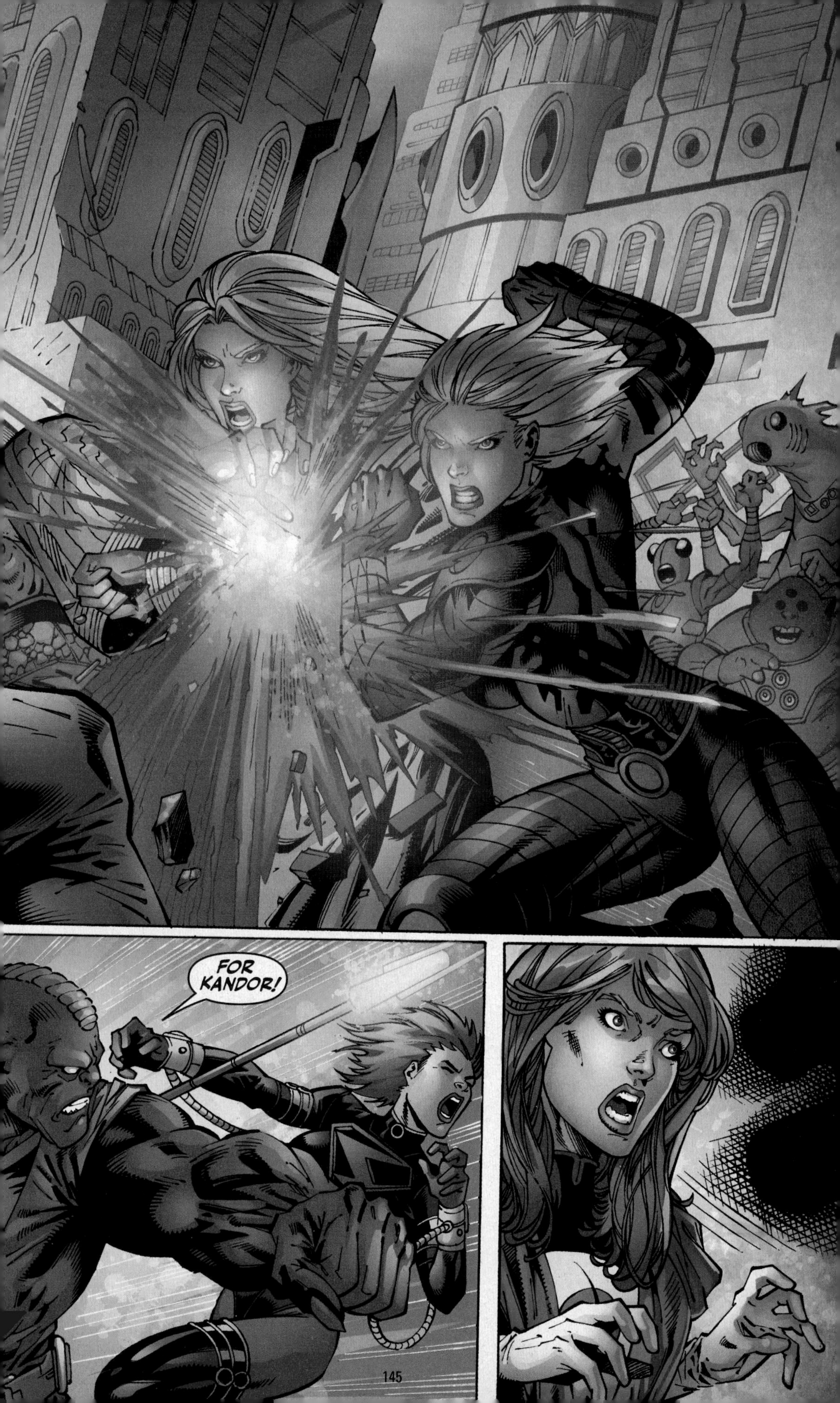
FOR KANDOR!

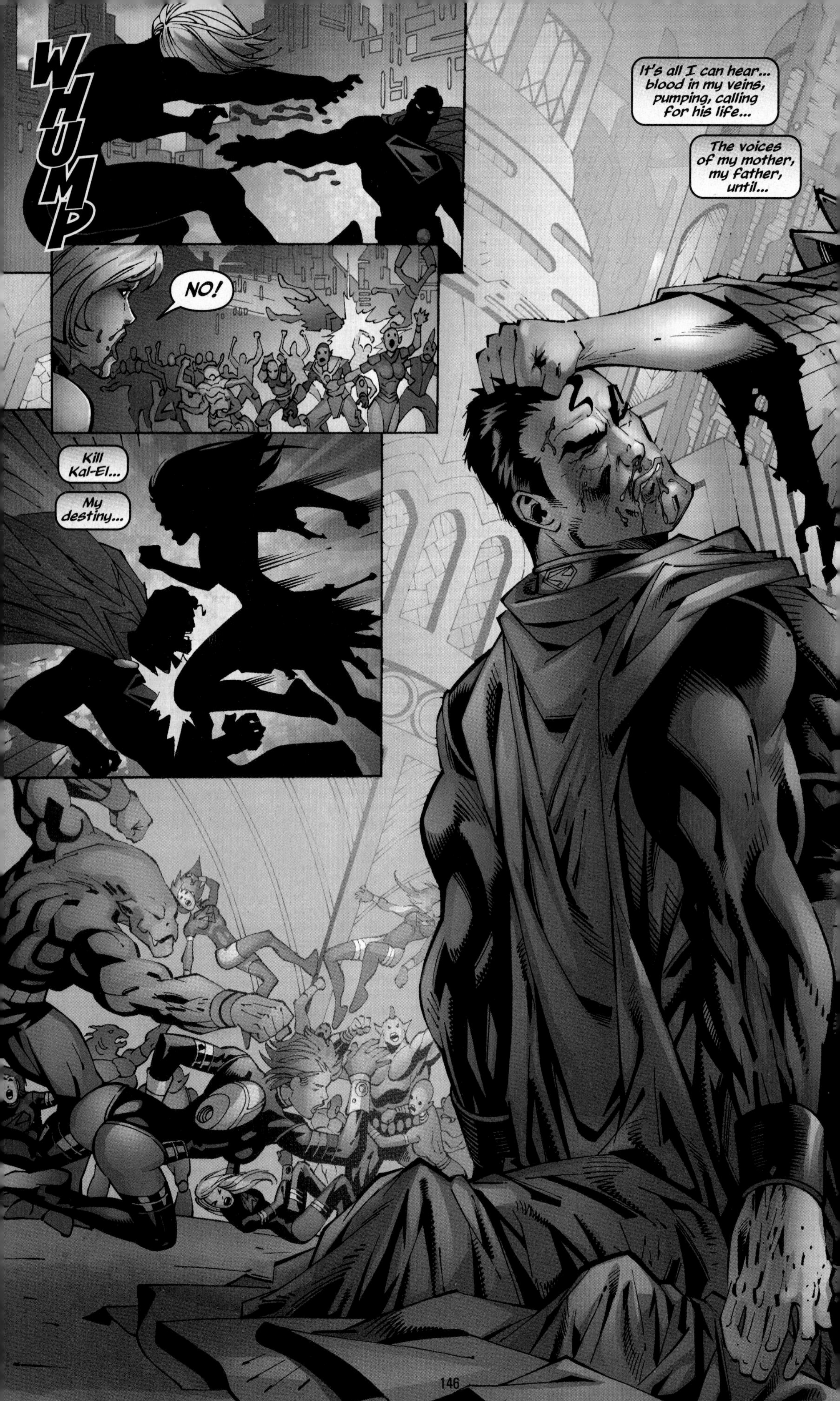
WHUMP
It's all I can hear... blood in my veins, pumping, calling for his life...
The voices of my mother, my father, until...
NO!
Kill Kal-El...
My destiny...

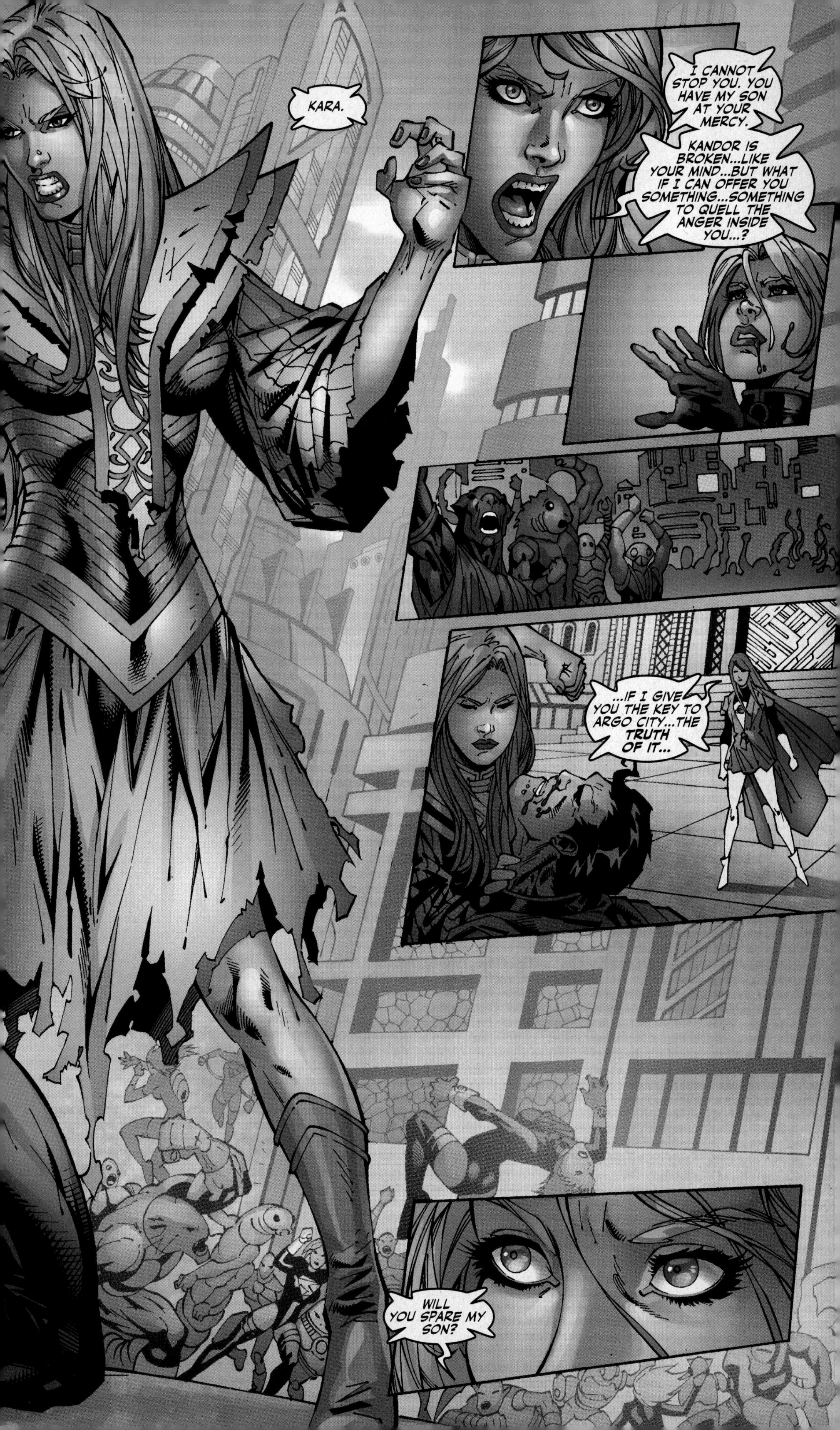
KARA.
I CANNOT STOP YOU. YOU HAVE MY SON AT YOUR MERCY.
KANDOR IS BROKEN...LIKE YOUR MIND...BUT WHAT IF I CAN OFFER YOU SOMETHING...SOMETHING TO QUELL THE ANGER INSIDE YOU...?
...IF I GIVE YOU THE KEY TO ARGO CITY...THE TRUTH OF IT...
WILL YOU SPARE MY SON?

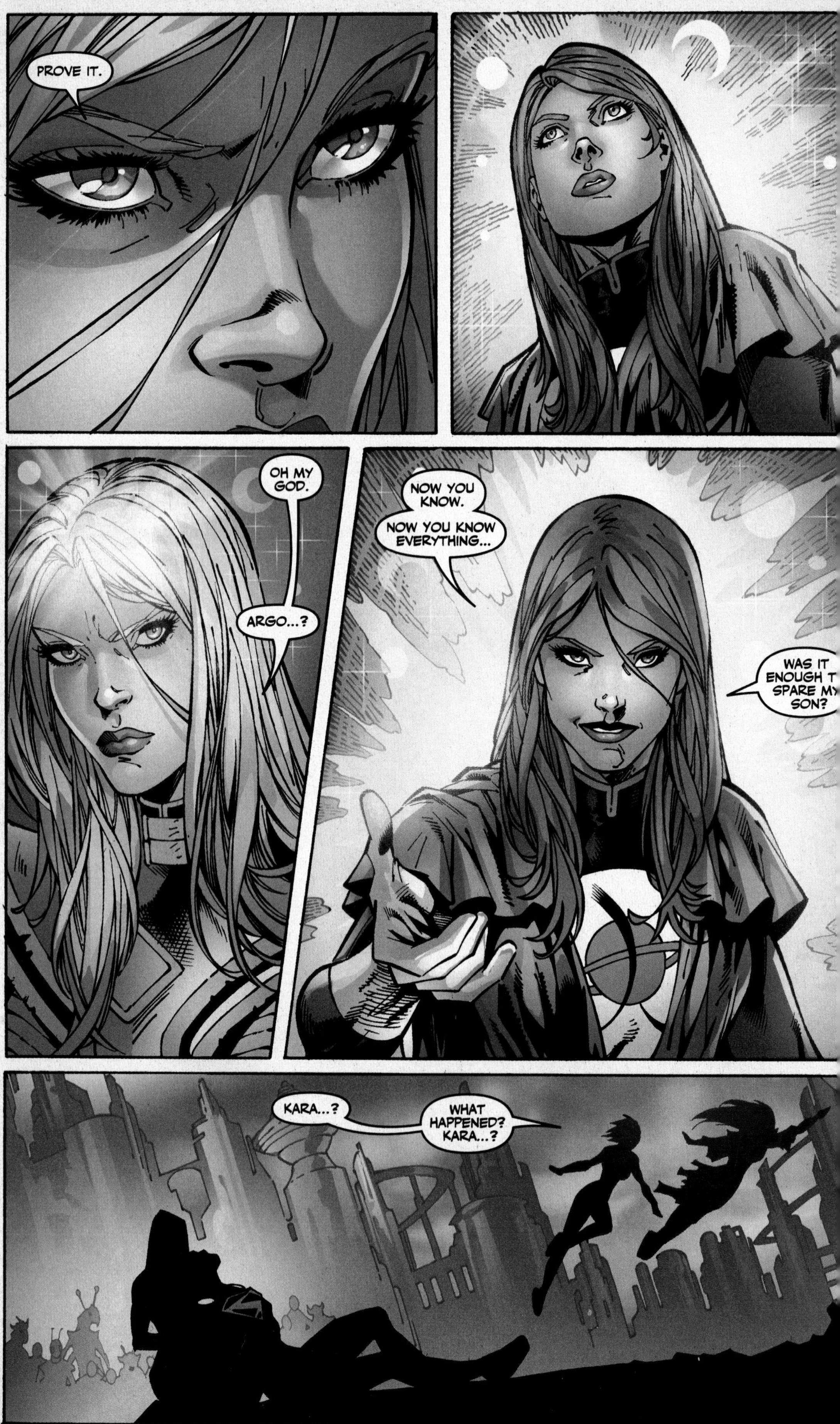
PROVE IT.
OH MY GOD.
ARGO...?
NOW YOU KNOW.
NOW YOU KNOW EVERYTHING...
WAS IT ENOUGH T SPARE MY SON?
KARA...?
WHAT HAPPENED? KARA...?

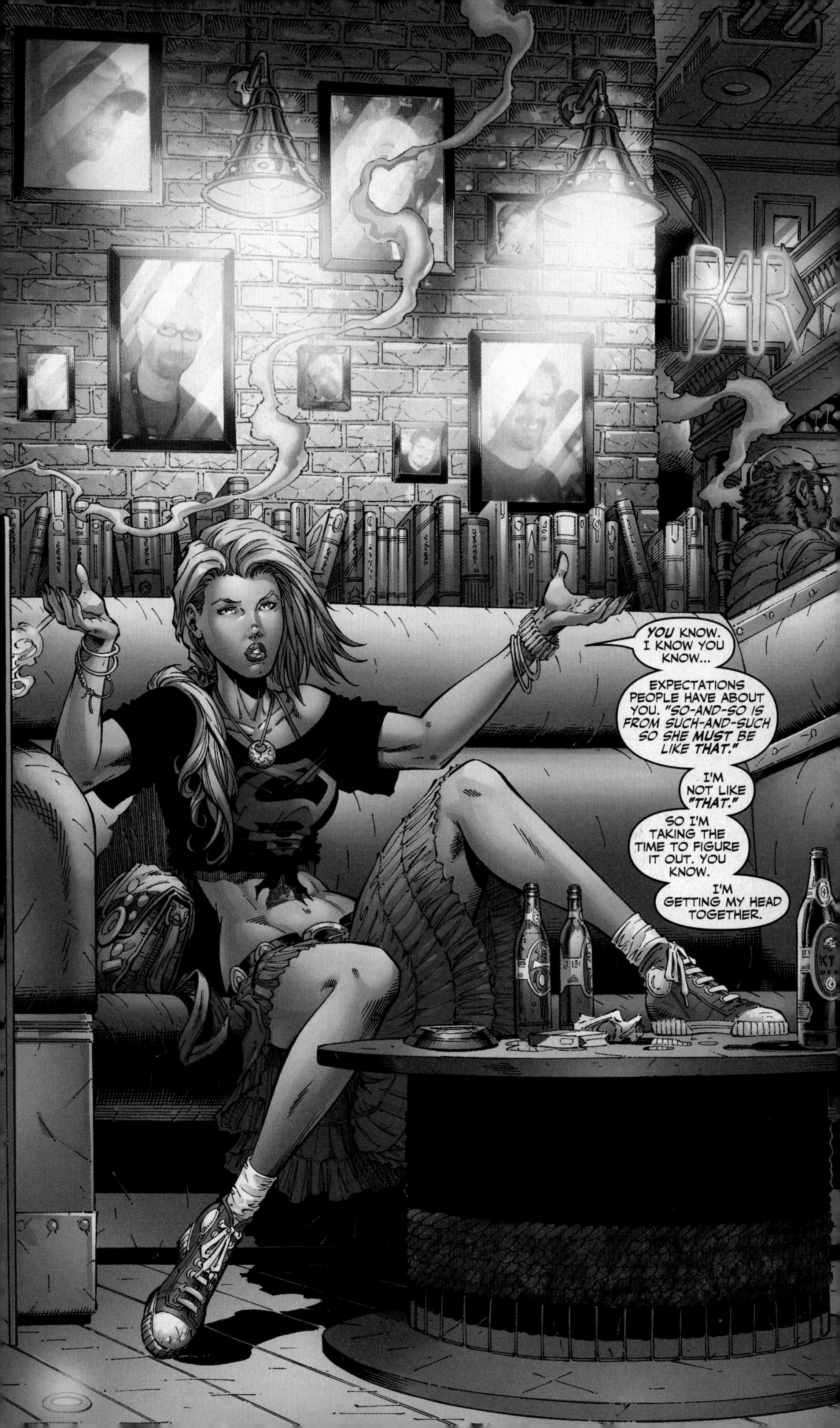
BAR
YOU KNOW. I KNOW YOU KNOW...
EXPECTATIONS PEOPLE HAVE ABOUT YOU. "SO-AND-SO IS FROM SUCH-AND-SUCH SO SHE MUST BE LIKE THAT."
I'M NOT LIKE "THAT."
SO I'M TAKING THE TIME TO FIGURE IT OUT. YOU KNOW.
I'M GETTING MY HEAD TOGETHER.

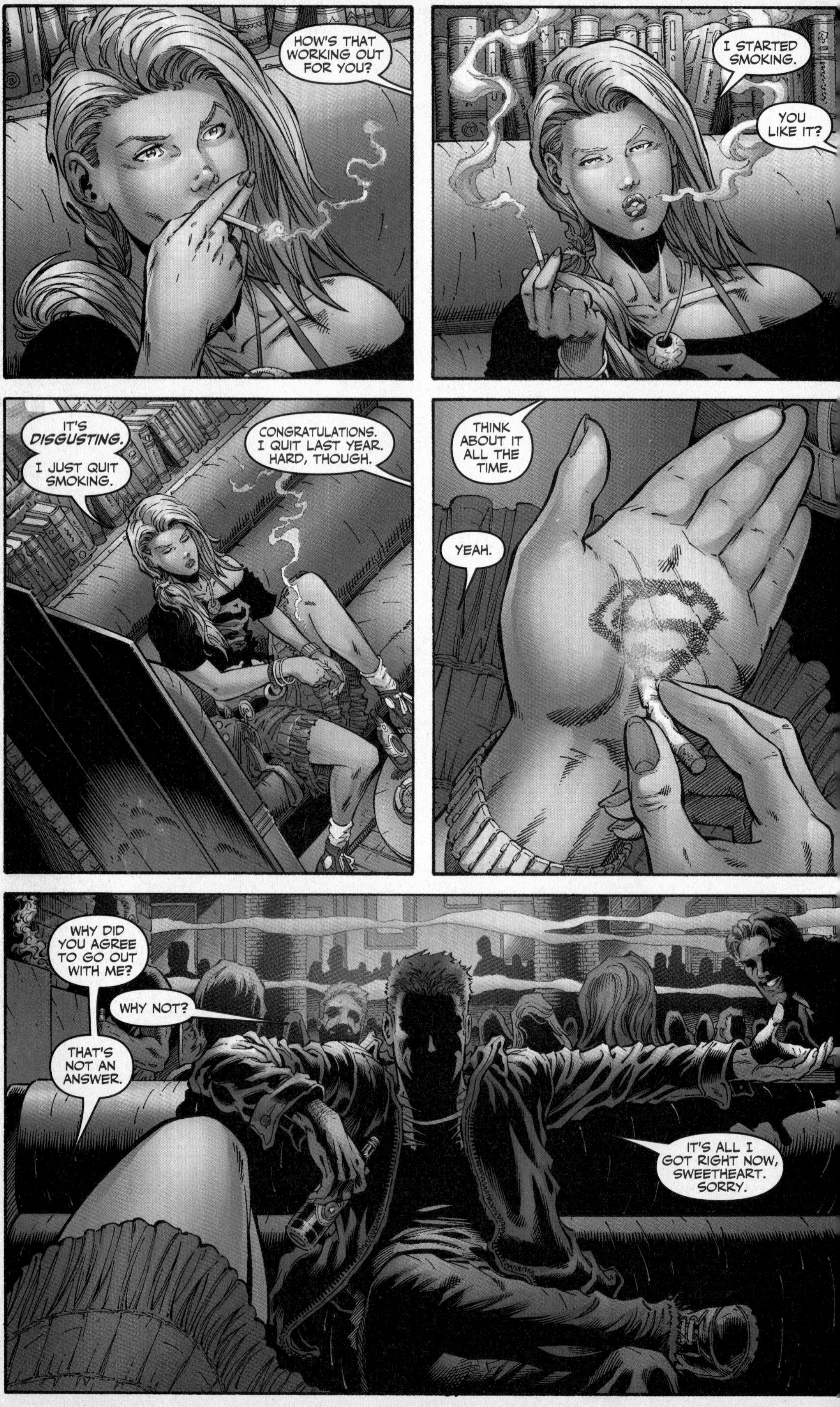
HOW'S THAT WORKING OUT FOR YOU?
I STARTED SMOKING.
YOU LIKE IT?
IT'S DISGUSTING.
I JUST QUIT SMOKING.
CONGRATULATIONS. I QUIT LAST YEAR. HARD, THOUGH.
THINK ABOUT IT ALL THE TIME.
YEAH.
WHY DID YOU AGREE TO GO OUT WITH ME?
WHY NOT?
THAT'S NOT AN ANSWER.
IT'S ALL I GOT RIGHT NOW, SWEETHEART. SORRY.

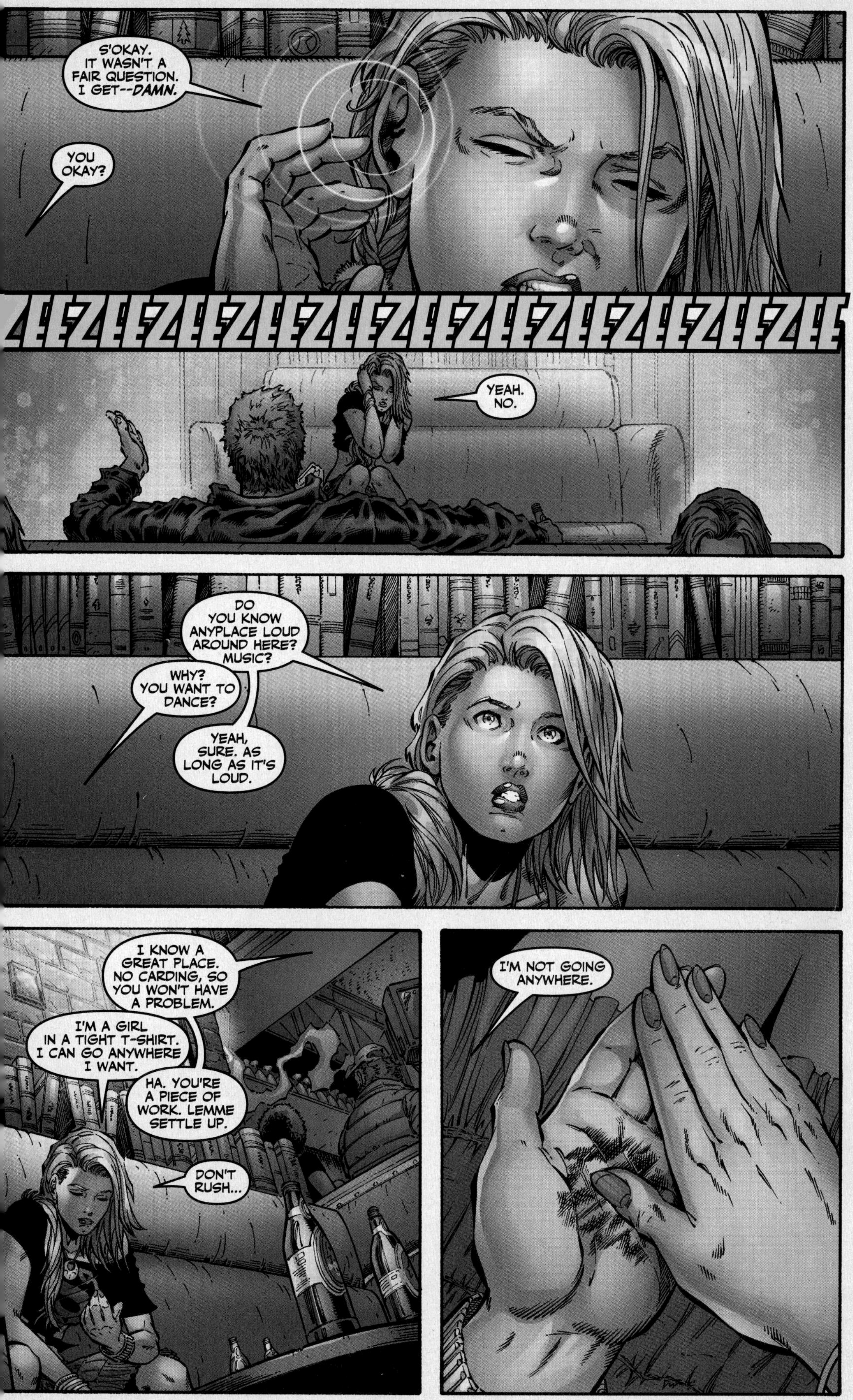
S'OKAY. IT WASN'T A FAIR QUESTION. I GET--DAMN.
YOU OKAY?
ZEEZEEZEEZEEZEEZEEZEEZEEZEEZEE
YEAH. NO.
DO YOU KNOW ANYPLACE LOUD AROUND HERE? MUSIC?
WHY? YOU WANT TO DANCE?
YEAH, SURE. AS LONG AS IT'S LOUD.
I KNOW A GREAT PLACE. NO CARDING, SO YOU WON'T HAVE A PROBLEM.
I'M A GIRL IN A TIGHT T-SHIRT. I CAN GO ANYWHERE I WANT.
HA. YOU'RE A PIECE OF WORK. LEMME SETTLE UP.
DON'T RUSH...
I'M NOT GOING ANYWHERE.

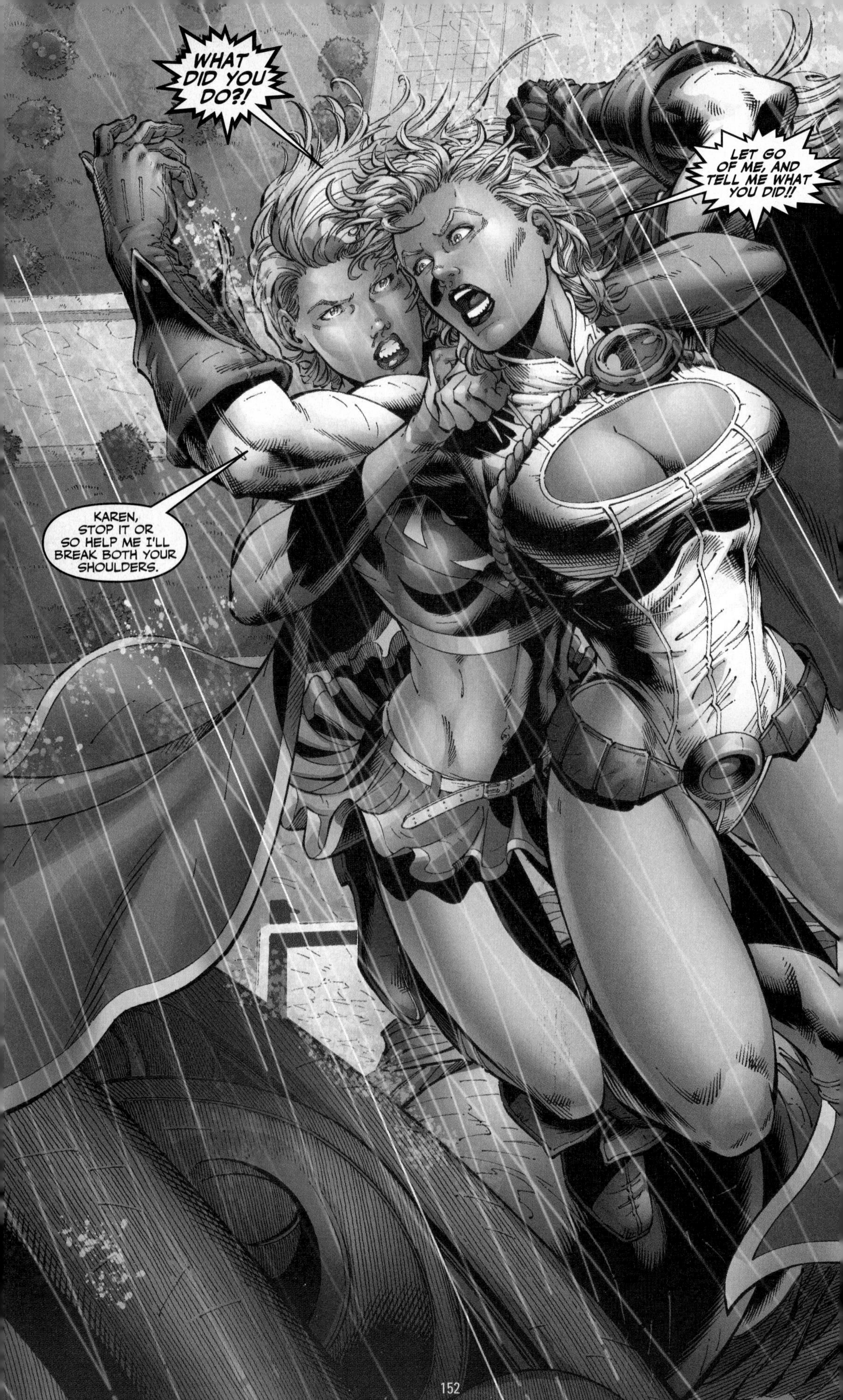
WHAT DID YOU DO?!
LET GO OF ME, AND TELL ME WHAT YOU DID!!
KAREN, STOP IT OR SO HELP ME I'LL BREAK BOTH YOUR SHOULDERS.

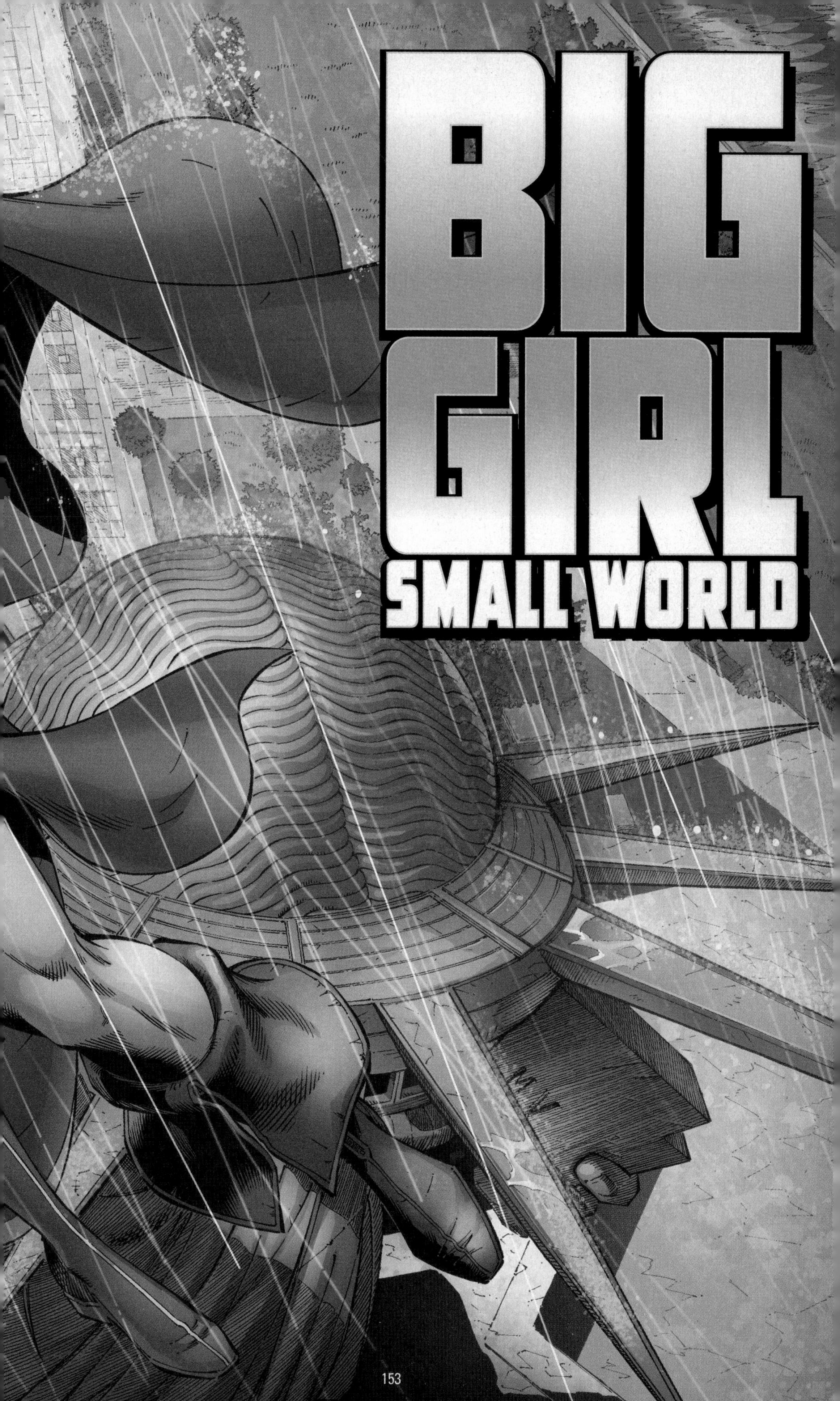
BIG GIRL
SMALL WORLD

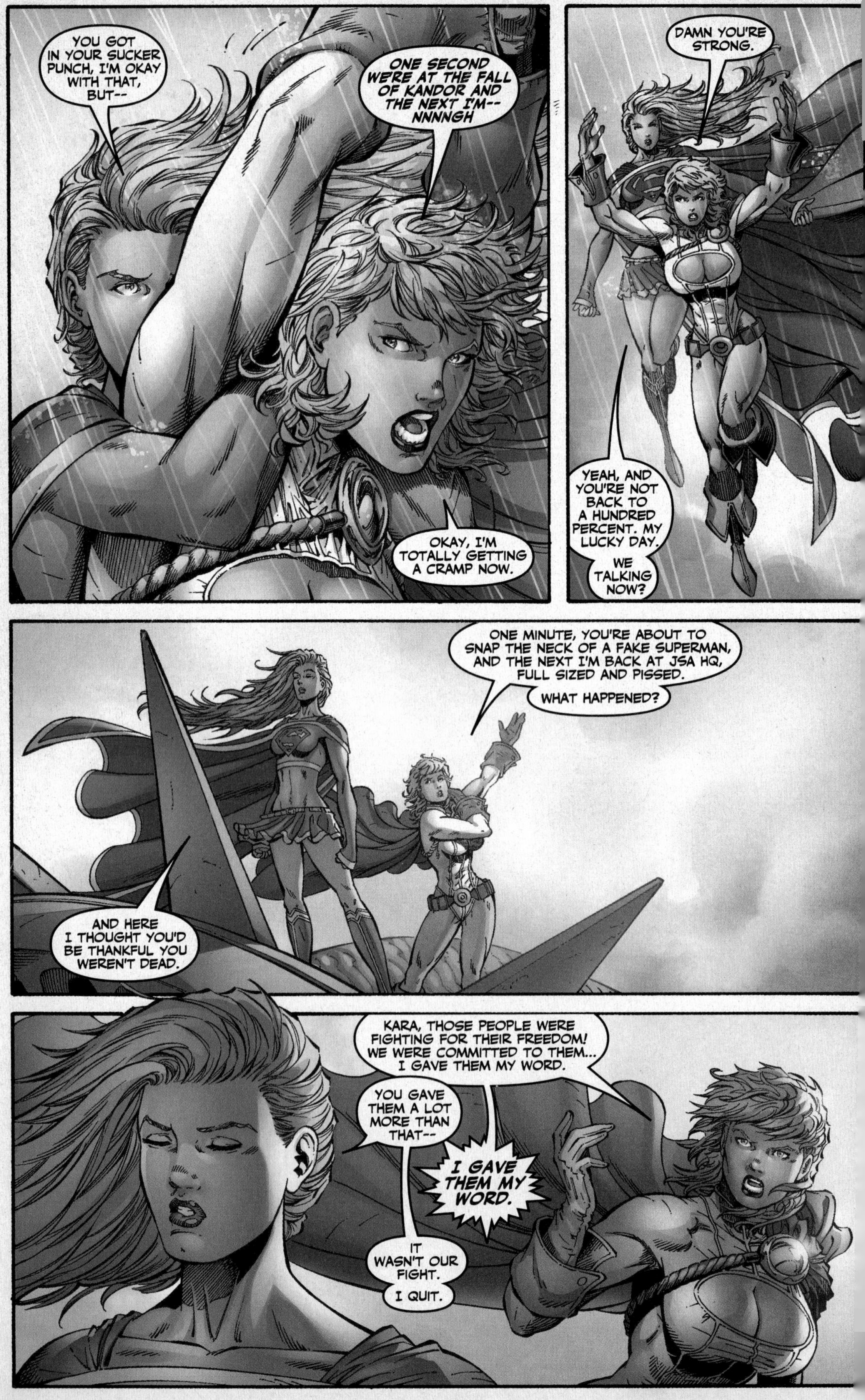
YOU GOT IN YOUR SUCKER PUNCH, I'M OKAY WITH THAT, BUT--
ONE SECOND WE'RE AT THE FALL OF KANDOR AND THE NEXT I'M-- NNNNGH
OKAY, I'M TOTALLY GETTING A CRAMP NOW.
DAMN YOU'RE STRONG.
YEAH, AND YOU'RE NOT BACK TO A HUNDRED PERCENT. MY LUCKY DAY.
WE TALKING NOW?
ONE MINUTE, YOU'RE ABOUT TO SNAP THE NECK OF A FAKE SUPERMAN, AND THE NEXT I'M BACK AT JSA HQ, FULL SIZED AND PISSED.
WHAT HAPPENED?
AND HERE I THOUGHT YOU'D BE THANKFUL YOU WEREN'T DEAD.
KARA, THOSE PEOPLE WERE FIGHTING FOR THEIR FREEDOM! WE WERE COMMITTED TO THEM... I GAVE THEM MY WORD.
YOU GAVE THEM A LOT MORE THAN THAT--
I GAVE THEM MY WORD.
IT WASN'T OUR FIGHT.
I QUIT.

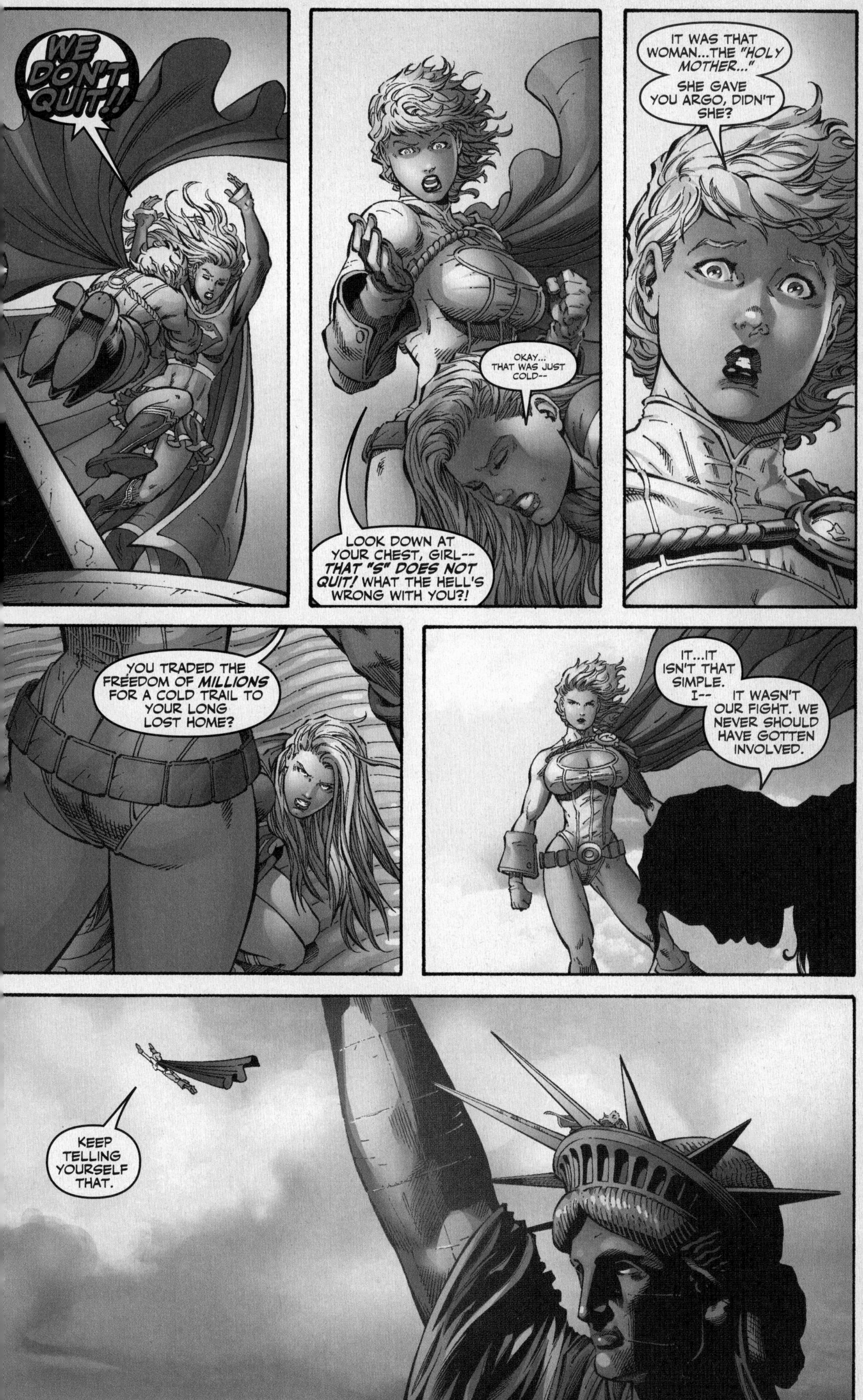
WE DON'T QUIT!!
LOOK DOWN AT YOUR CHEST, GIRL-- THAT "S" DOES NOT QUIT! WHAT THE HELL'S WRONG WITH YOU?!
OKAY... THAT WAS JUST COLD--
IT WAS THAT WOMAN...THE "HOLY MOTHER..."
SHE GAVE YOU ARGO, DIDN'T SHE?
YOU TRADED THE FREEDOM OF MILLIONS FOR A COLD TRAIL TO YOUR LONG LOST HOME?
IT...IT ISN'T THAT SIMPLE. I--
IT WASN'T OUR FIGHT. WE NEVER SHOULD HAVE GOTTEN INVOLVED.
KEEP TELLING YOURSELF THAT.

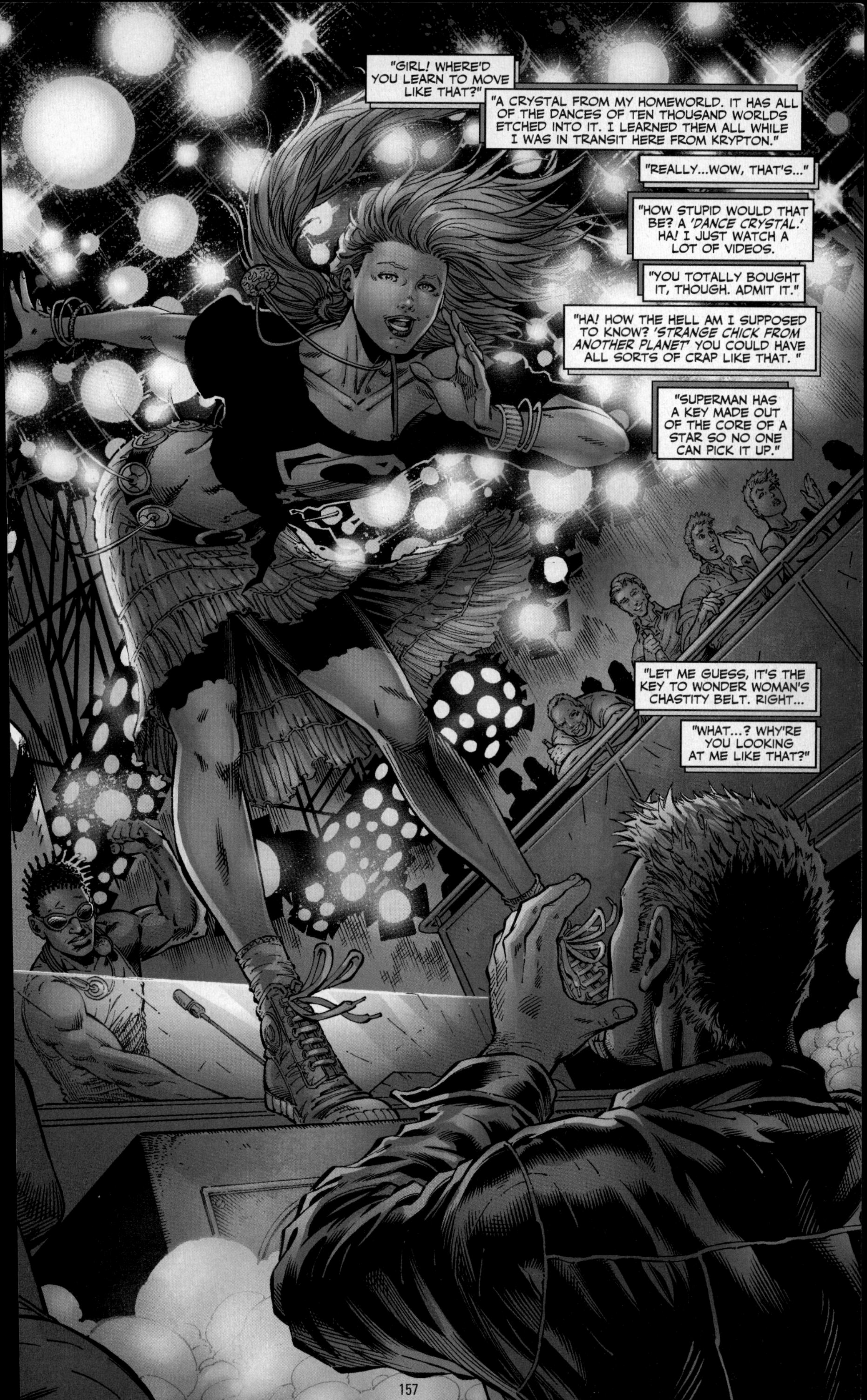
"GIRL! WHERE'D YOU LEARN TO MOVE LIKE THAT?"
"A CRYSTAL FROM MY HOMEWORLD. IT HAS ALL OF THE DANCES OF TEN THOUSAND WORLDS ETCHED INTO IT. I LEARNED THEM ALL WHILE I WAS IN TRANSIT HERE FROM KRYPTON."
"REALLY...WOW, THAT'S..."
"HOW STUPID WOULD THAT BE? A *'DANCE CRYSTAL.'* HA! I JUST WATCH A LOT OF VIDEOS.
"YOU TOTALLY BOUGHT IT, THOUGH. ADMIT IT."
"HA! HOW THE HELL AM I SUPPOSED TO KNOW? *'STRANGE CHICK FROM ANOTHER PLANET'* YOU COULD HAVE ALL SORTS OF CRAP LIKE THAT."
"SUPERMAN HAS A KEY MADE OUT OF THE CORE OF A STAR SO NO ONE CAN PICK IT UP."
"LET ME GUESS, IT'S THE KEY TO WONDER WOMAN'S CHASTITY BELT. RIGHT...
"WHAT...? WHY'RE YOU LOOKING AT ME LIKE THAT?"

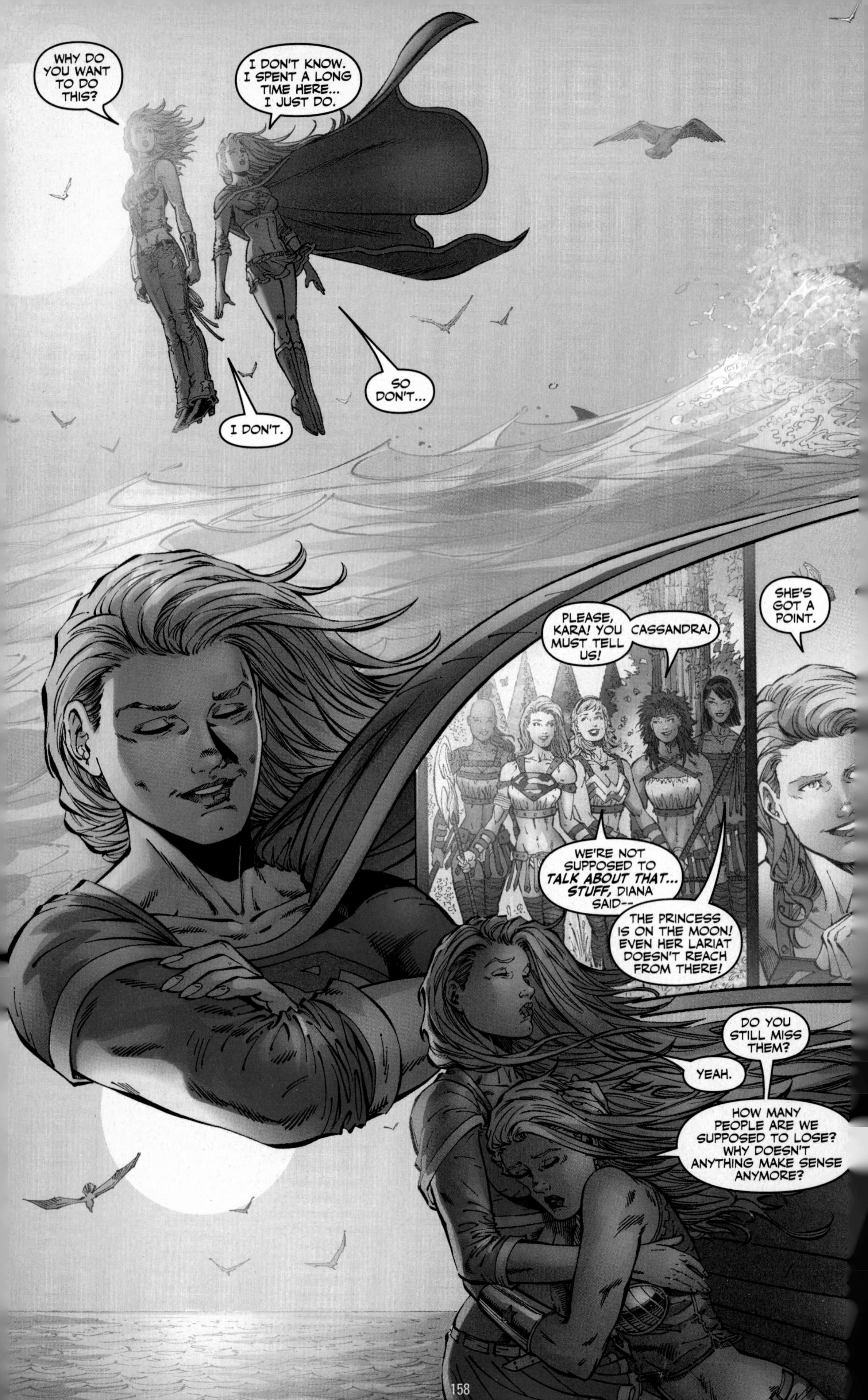
WHY DO YOU WANT TO DO THIS?
I DON'T KNOW. I SPENT A LONG TIME HERE... I JUST DO.
SO DON'T...
I DON'T.
PLEASE, KARA! YOU MUST TELL US!
CASSANDRA!
SHE'S GOT A POINT.
WE'RE NOT SUPPOSED TO TALK ABOUT THAT... STUFF, DIANA SAID--
THE PRINCESS IS ON THE MOON! EVEN HER LARIAT DOESN'T REACH FROM THERE!
DO YOU STILL MISS THEM?
YEAH.
HOW MANY PEOPLE ARE WE SUPPOSED TO LOSE? WHY DOESN'T ANYTHING MAKE SENSE ANYMORE?

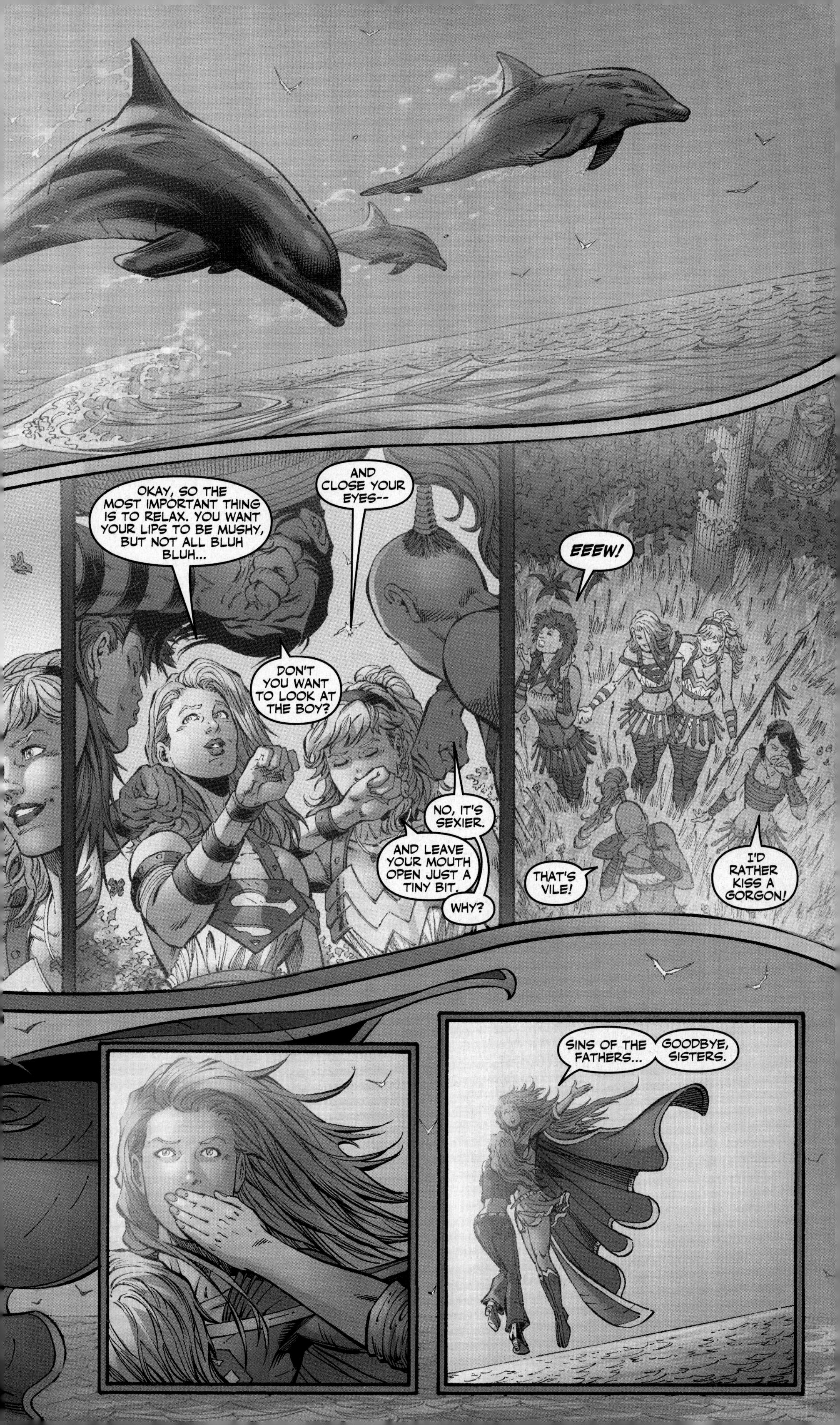
OKAY, SO THE MOST IMPORTANT THING IS TO RELAX. YOU WANT YOUR LIPS TO BE MUSHY, BUT NOT ALL BLUH BLUH...
AND CLOSE YOUR EYES--
DON'T YOU WANT TO LOOK AT THE BOY?
NO, IT'S SEXIER.
AND LEAVE YOUR MOUTH OPEN JUST A TINY BIT.
WHY?
EEEW!
THAT'S VILE!
I'D RATHER KISS A GORGON!
SINS OF THE FATHERS...
GOODBYE, SISTERS.

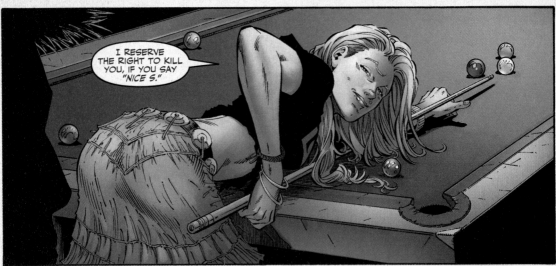

I RESERVE THE RIGHT TO KILL YOU, IF YOU SAY "NICE S."

YOU KNOW, YOU DON'T TALK LIKE A SIXTEEN-YEAR-OLD.

'CAUSE I'M NOT. I WAS IN SEMI-LUCID SUSPENDED ANIMATION FOR A LONG TIME.

"DANCE CRYSTALS"?

NO, SERIOUSLY... INTERSTELLAR SPACE SHIP, WARP DRIVES... IT'S ALL IN MY ORIGIN STORY. YOU SHOULD LOOK IT UP.

WHAT ABOUT YOU? HUH?

HEH, NOT HALF AS INTERESTING AS EXPLODING PLANETS AND SUCH.

BIT BY A RADIOACTIVE KANGAROO? SURVIVOR OF A FREAK SPORTING GOODS ACCIDENT?

MY FATHER WAS MURDERED.

OH.

THAT SUCKS.

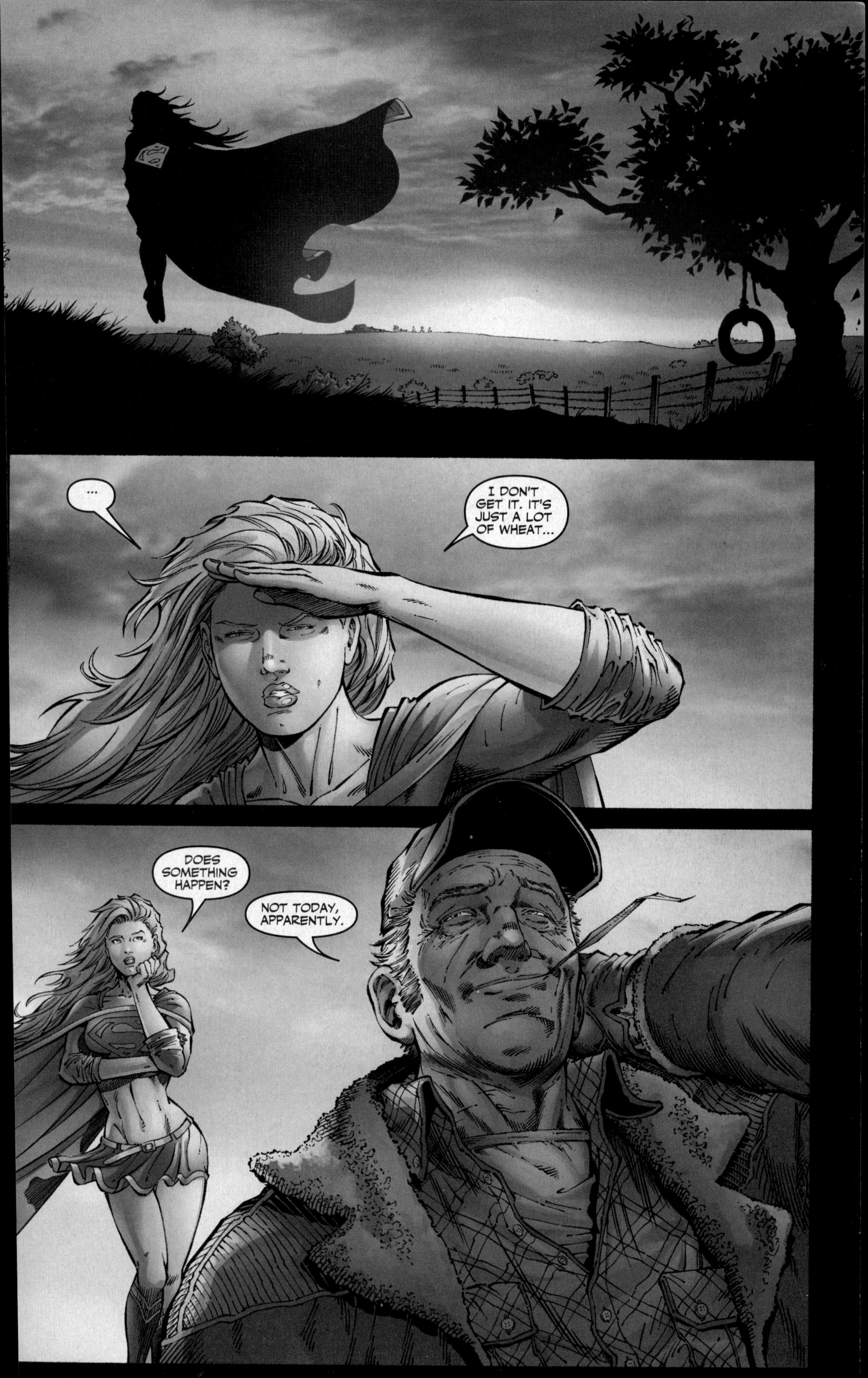
...
I DON'T GET IT. IT'S JUST A LOT OF WHEAT...
DOES SOMETHING HAPPEN?
NOT TODAY, APPARENTLY.

SOME DAYS, JONATHAN THINKS WE SHOULD CLEAR EVERYTHING OUT.

SOME DAYS I DO TOO.

NEVER THE SAME DAYS, THOUGH, SO I JUST MAKE SURE IT STAYS CLEAN.

CLEANER THAN IT EVER WAS WHEN HE WAS ALIVE, I BET.

THAT'S FOR DARN SURE.

NO ONE COMES BY, YOU KNOW...BESIDES LOIS AND CLARK, OF COURSE.

WHY ARE YOU HERE, KARA?

WHY DIDN'T KAL EVER INVITE ME TO LIVE HERE WITH YOU?

...

I DON'T KNOW, CHILD... I DON'T KNOW.

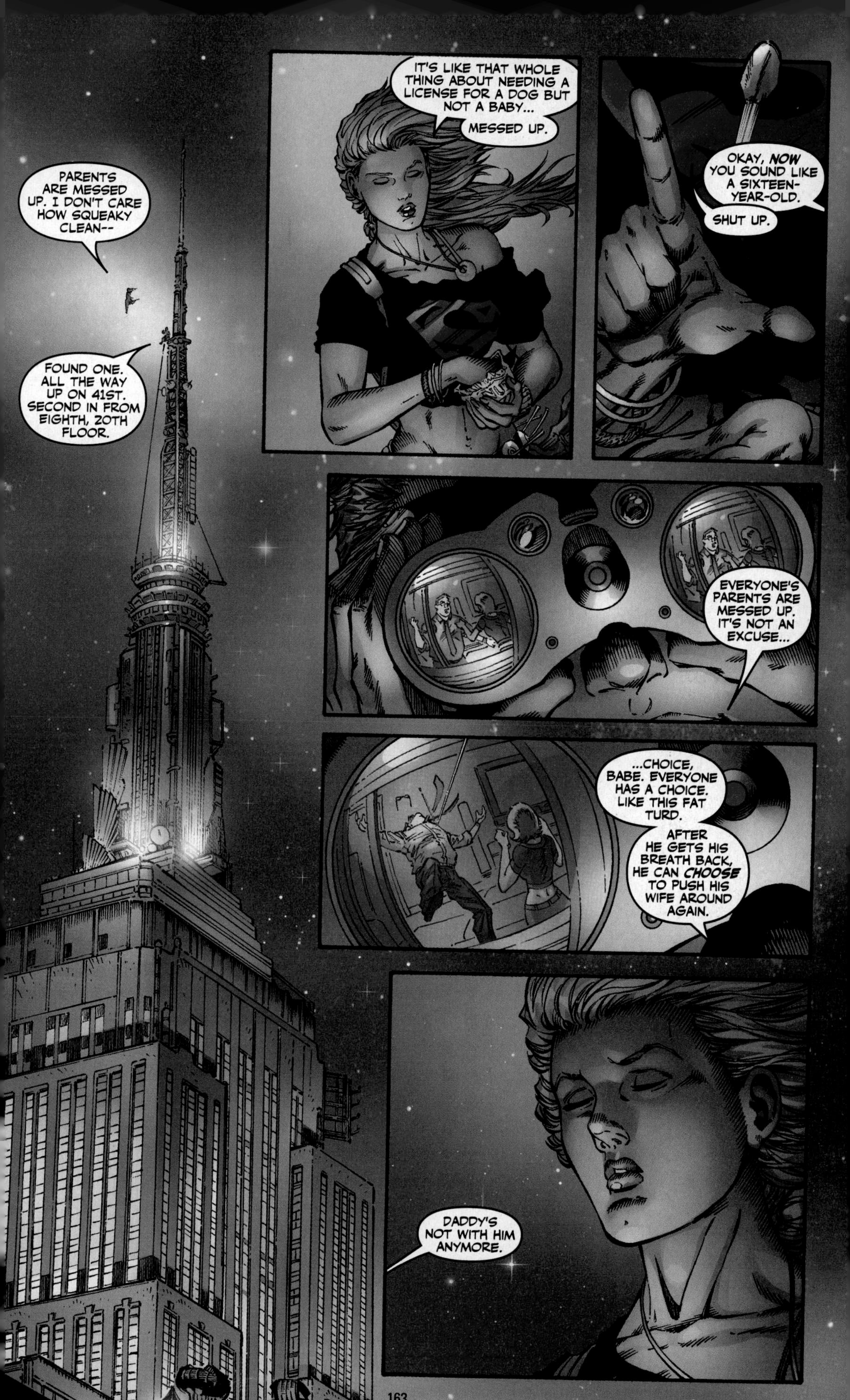
PARENTS ARE MESSED UP. I DON'T CARE HOW SQUEAKY CLEAN--
FOUND ONE. ALL THE WAY UP ON 41ST. SECOND IN FROM EIGHTH, 20TH FLOOR.
IT'S LIKE THAT WHOLE THING ABOUT NEEDING A LICENSE FOR A DOG BUT NOT A BABY...
MESSED UP.
OKAY, *NOW* YOU SOUND LIKE A SIXTEEN-YEAR-OLD.
SHUT UP.
EVERYONE'S PARENTS ARE MESSED UP. IT'S NOT AN EXCUSE...
...CHOICE, BABE. EVERYONE HAS A CHOICE. LIKE THIS FAT TURD.
AFTER HE GETS HIS BREATH BACK, HE CAN *CHOOSE* TO PUSH HIS WIFE AROUND AGAIN.
DADDY'S NOT WITH HIM ANYMORE.

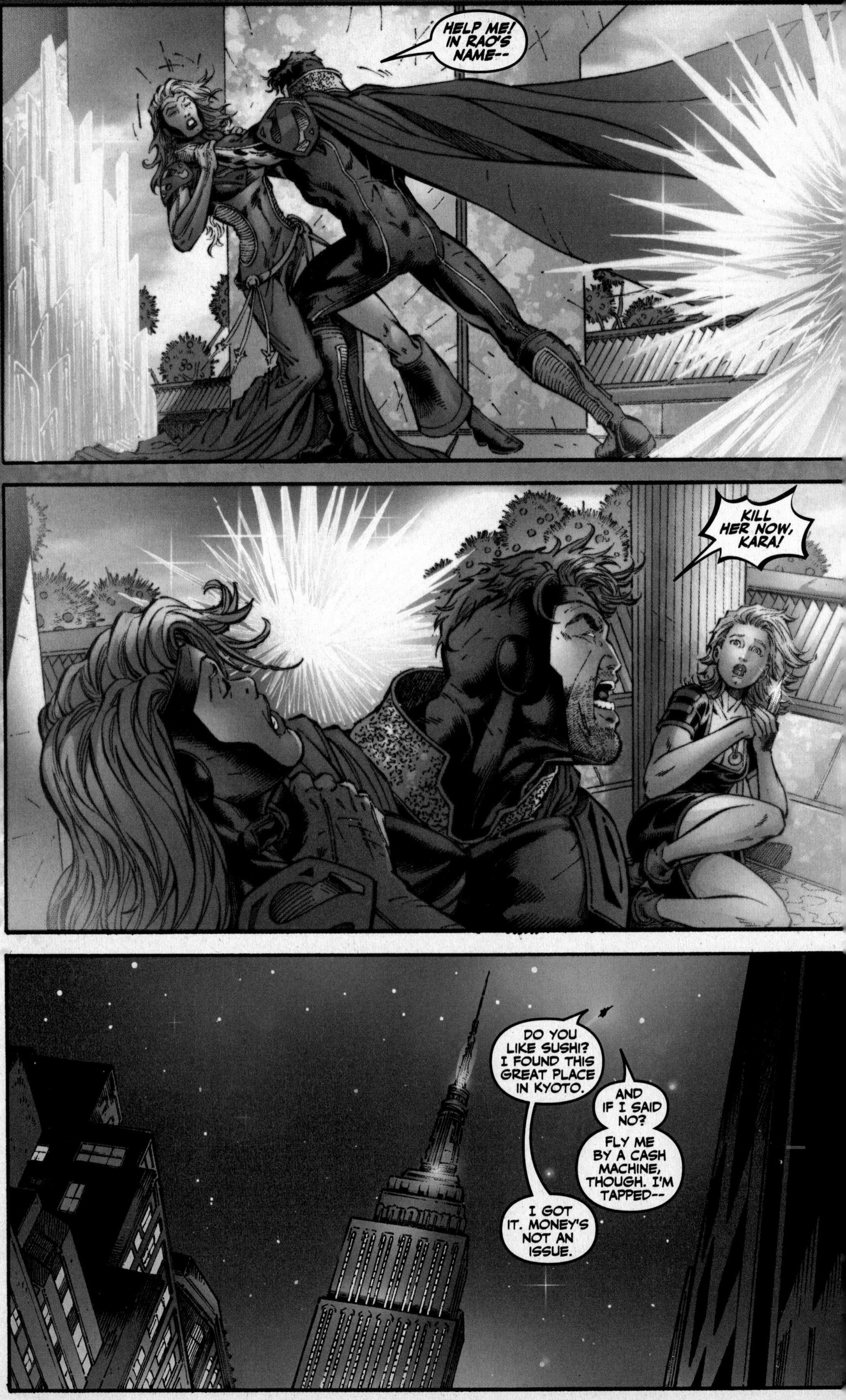
HELP ME! IN RAO'S NAME--
KILL HER NOW, KARA!
DO YOU LIKE SUSHI? I FOUND THIS GREAT PLACE IN KYOTO.
AND IF I SAID NO?
FLY ME BY A CASH MACHINE, THOUGH. I'M TAPPED--
I GOT IT. MONEY'S NOT AN ISSUE.

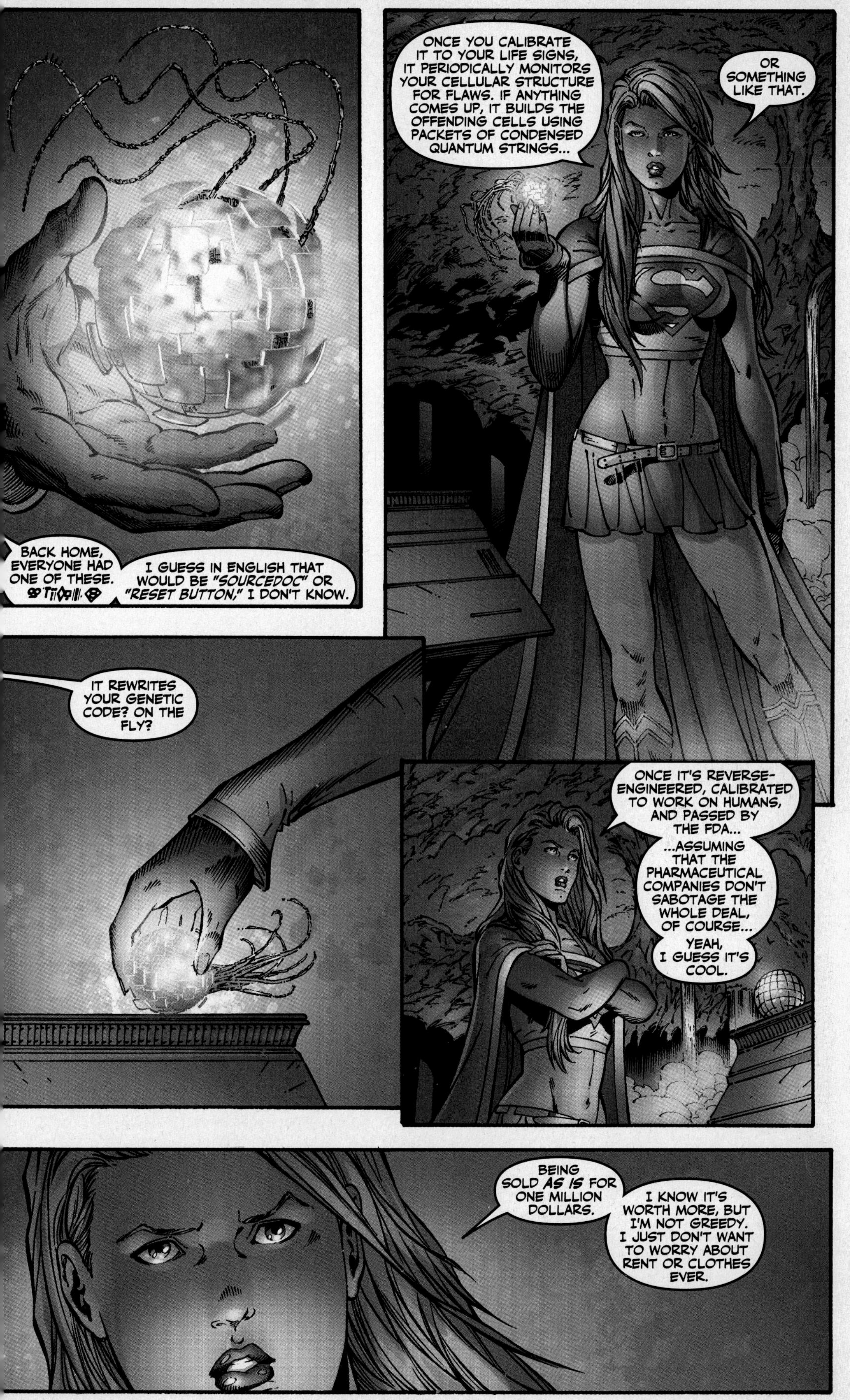
BACK HOME, EVERYONE HAD ONE OF THESE.
I GUESS IN ENGLISH THAT WOULD BE "SOURCEDOC" OR "RESET BUTTON," I DON'T KNOW.
ONCE YOU CALIBRATE IT TO YOUR LIFE SIGNS, IT PERIODICALLY MONITORS YOUR CELLULAR STRUCTURE FOR FLAWS. IF ANYTHING COMES UP, IT BUILDS THE OFFENDING CELLS USING PACKETS OF CONDENSED QUANTUM STRINGS...
OR SOMETHING LIKE THAT.
IT REWRITES YOUR GENETIC CODE? ON THE FLY?
ONCE IT'S REVERSE-ENGINEERED, CALIBRATED TO WORK ON HUMANS, AND PASSED BY THE FDA...
...ASSUMING THAT THE PHARMACEUTICAL COMPANIES DON'T SABOTAGE THE WHOLE DEAL, OF COURSE...
YEAH, I GUESS IT'S COOL.
BEING SOLD AS IS FOR ONE MILLION DOLLARS.
I KNOW IT'S WORTH MORE, BUT I'M NOT GREEDY. I JUST DON'T WANT TO WORRY ABOUT RENT OR CLOTHES EVER.

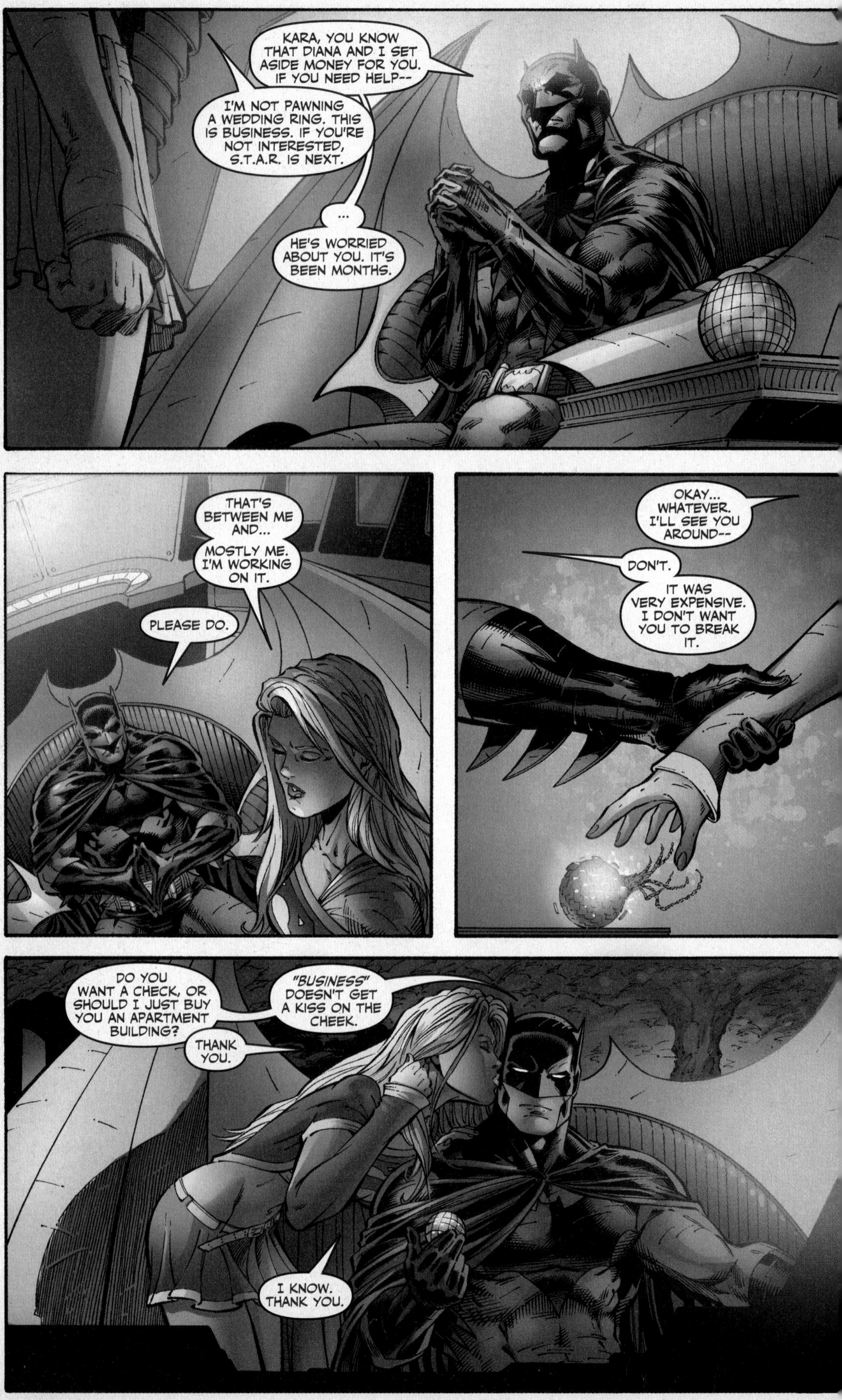
KARA, YOU KNOW THAT DIANA AND I SET ASIDE MONEY FOR YOU. IF YOU NEED HELP--
I'M NOT PAWNING A WEDDING RING. THIS IS BUSINESS. IF YOU'RE NOT INTERESTED, S.T.A.R. IS NEXT.
...
HE'S WORRIED ABOUT YOU. IT'S BEEN MONTHS.
THAT'S BETWEEN ME AND...
MOSTLY ME. I'M WORKING ON IT.
PLEASE DO.
OKAY... WHATEVER. I'LL SEE YOU AROUND--
DON'T.
IT WAS VERY EXPENSIVE. I DON'T WANT YOU TO BREAK IT.
DO YOU WANT A CHECK, OR SHOULD I JUST BUY YOU AN APARTMENT BUILDING?
"BUSINESS" DOESN'T GET A KISS ON THE CHEEK.
THANK YOU.
I KNOW. THANK YOU.

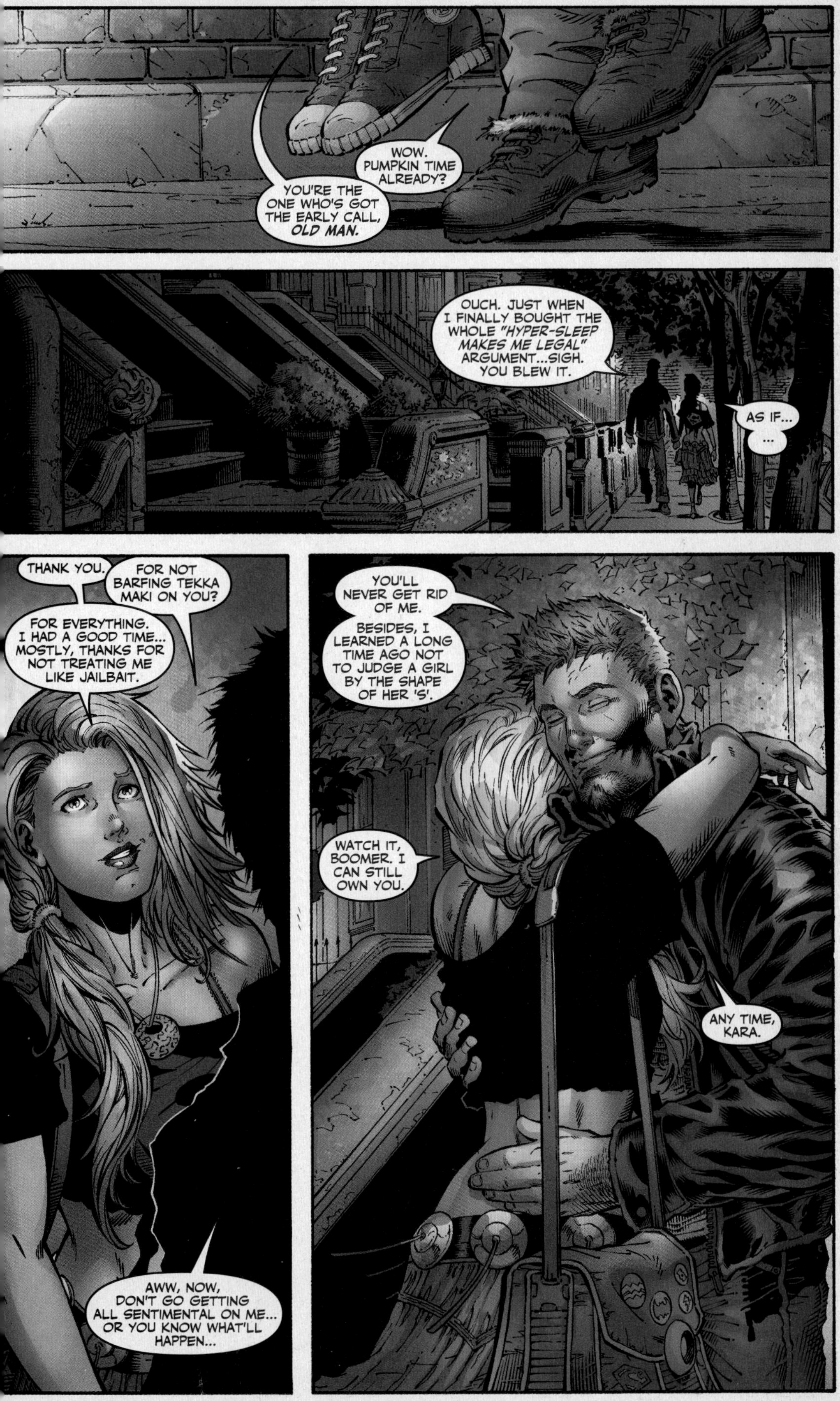

WOW. PUMPKIN TIME ALREADY?
YOU'RE THE ONE WHO'S GOT THE EARLY CALL, *OLD MAN.*
OUCH. JUST WHEN I FINALLY BOUGHT THE WHOLE *"HYPER-SLEEP MAKES ME LEGAL"* ARGUMENT...SIGH. YOU BLEW IT.
AS IF... ...
THANK YOU.
FOR NOT BARFING TEKKA MAKI ON YOU?
FOR EVERYTHING. I HAD A GOOD TIME... MOSTLY. THANKS FOR NOT TREATING ME LIKE JAILBAIT.
AWW, NOW, DON'T GO GETTING ALL SENTIMENTAL ON ME... OR YOU KNOW WHAT'LL HAPPEN...
YOU'LL NEVER GET RID OF ME.
BESIDES, I LEARNED A LONG TIME AGO NOT TO JUDGE A GIRL BY THE SHAPE OF HER 'S'.
WATCH IT, BOOMER. I CAN STILL OWN YOU.
ANY TIME, KARA.

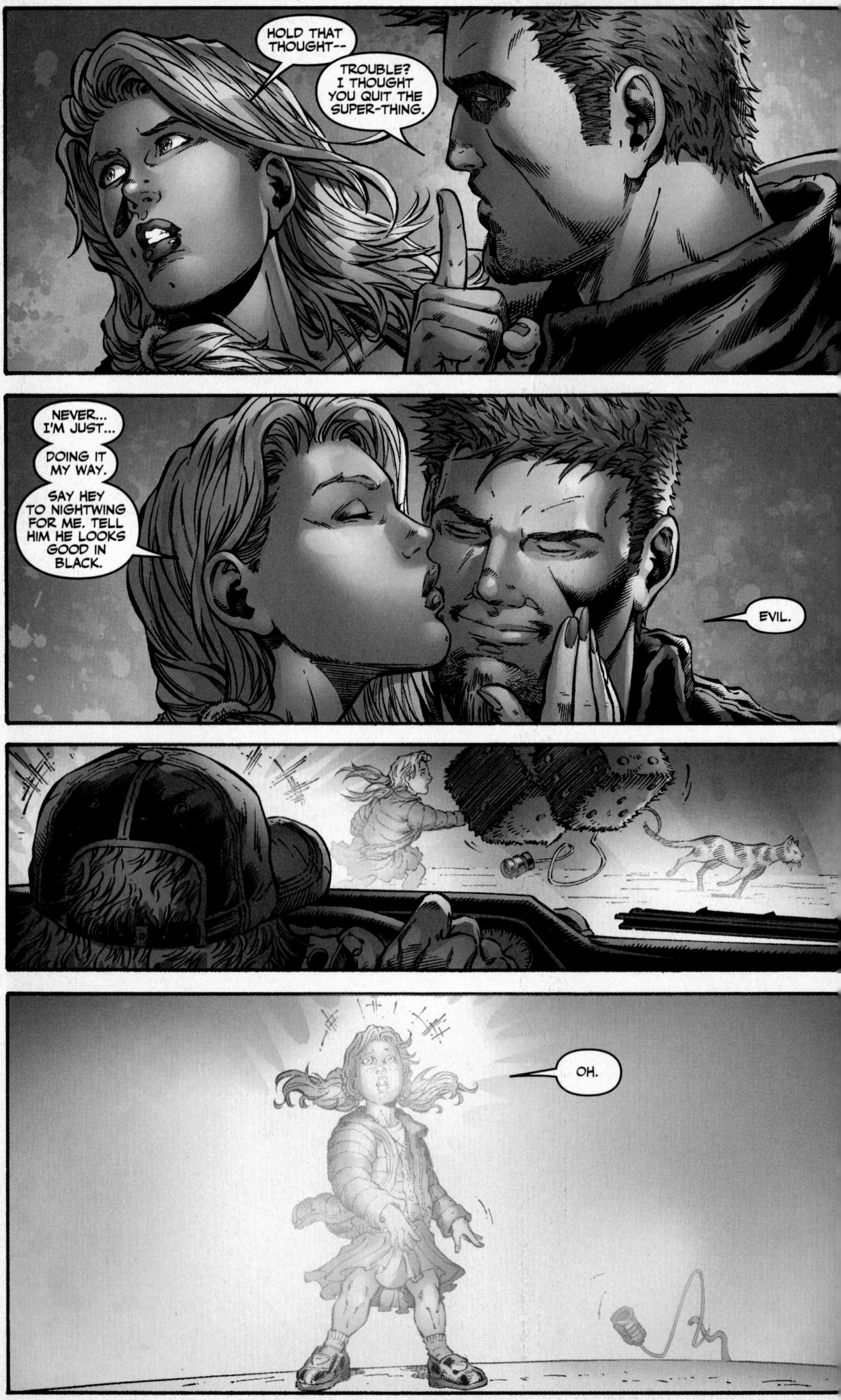
HOLD THAT THOUGHT--
TROUBLE? I THOUGHT YOU QUIT THE SUPER-THING.
NEVER... I'M JUST...
DOING IT MY WAY.
SAY HEY TO NIGHTWING FOR ME. TELL HIM HE LOOKS GOOD IN BLACK.
EVIL.
OH.

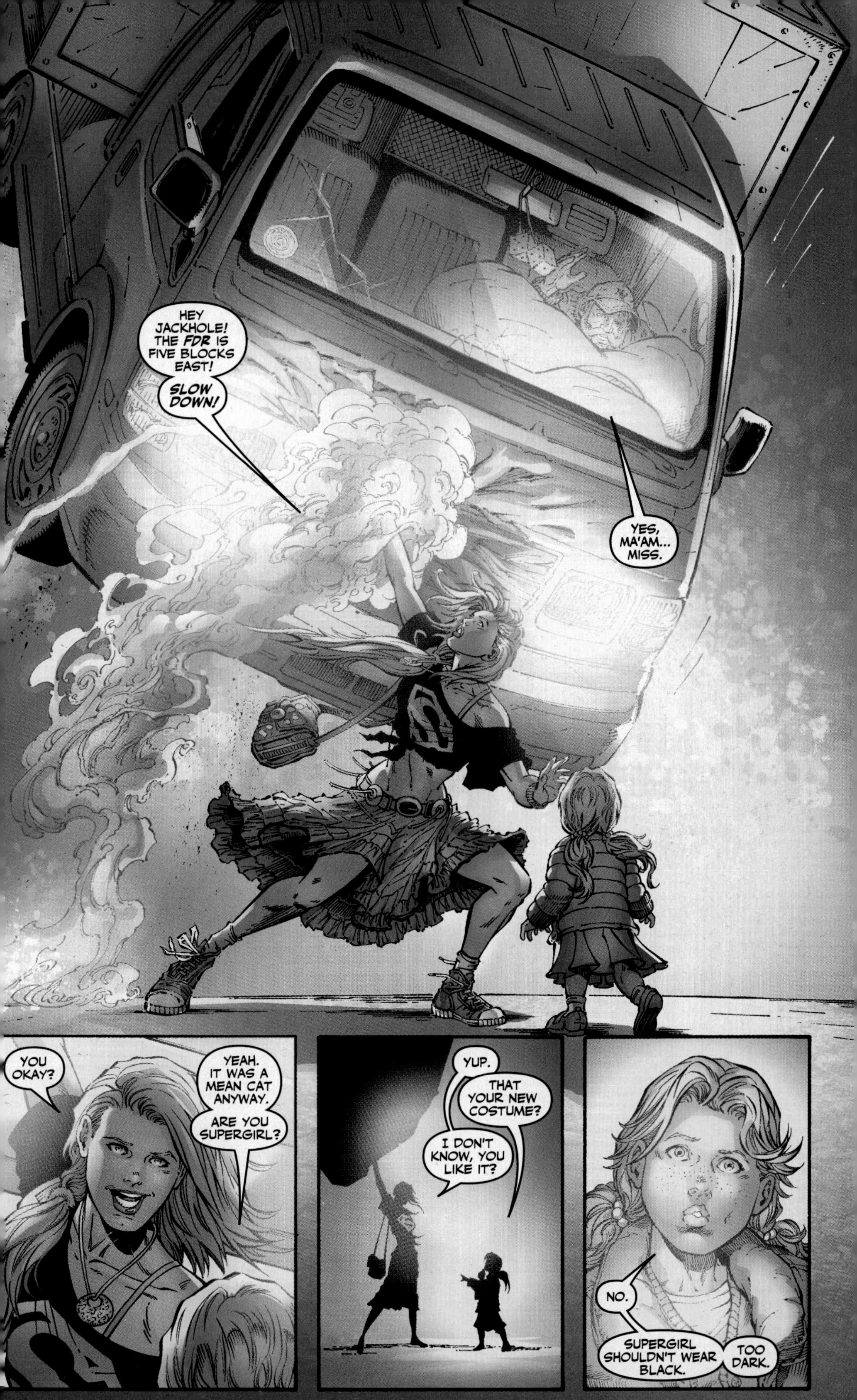

HEY JACKHOLE! THE FDR IS FIVE BLOCKS EAST!
SLOW DOWN!
YES, MA'AM... MISS.
YOU OKAY?
YEAH. IT WAS A MEAN CAT ANYWAY.
ARE YOU SUPERGIRL?
YUP.
THAT YOUR NEW COSTUME?
I DON'T KNOW, YOU LIKE IT?
NO.
SUPERGIRL SHOULDN'T WEAR BLACK.
TOO DARK.

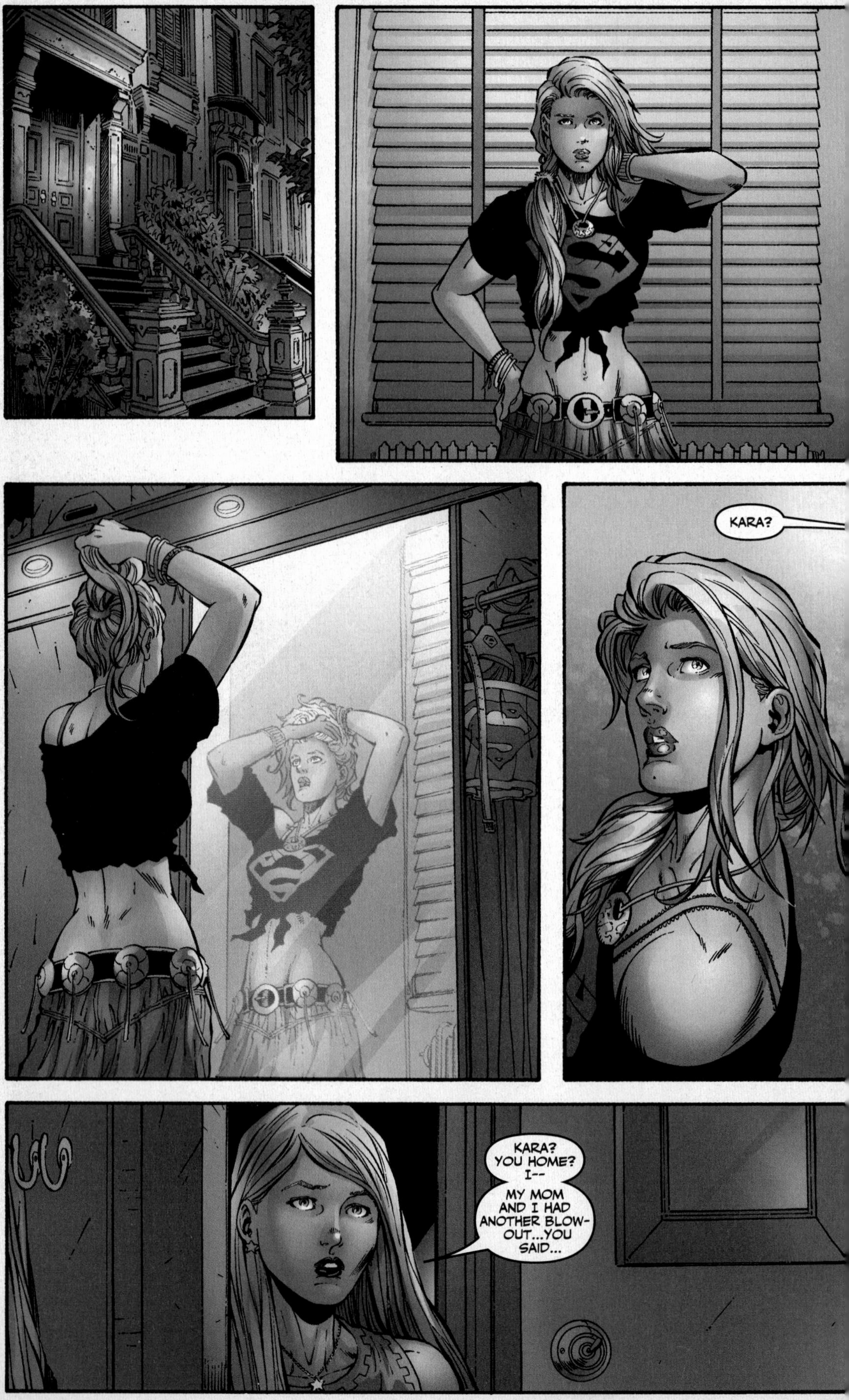
KARA?
KARA? YOU HOME? I--
MY MOM AND I HAD ANOTHER BLOW-OUT...YOU SAID...

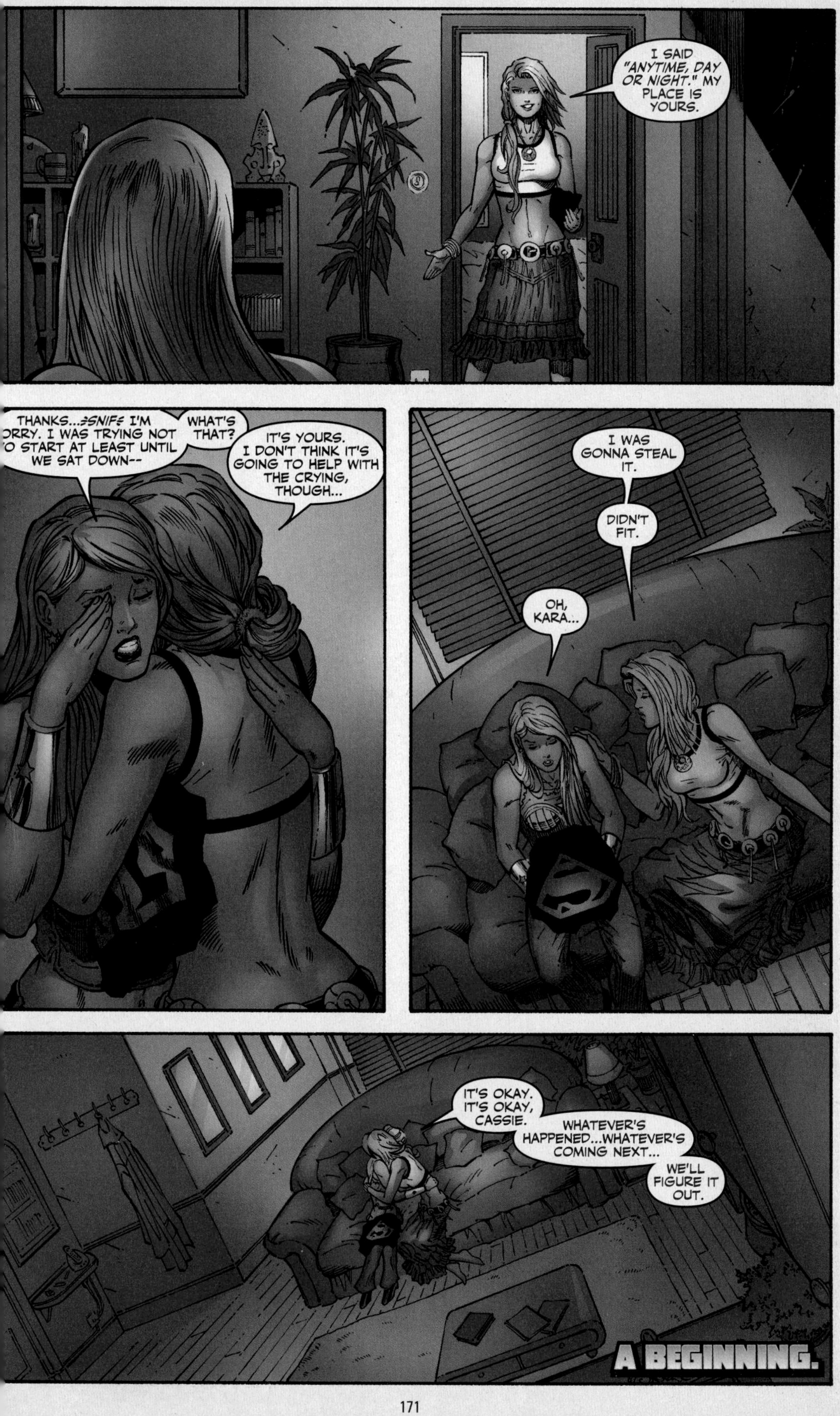
I SAID "ANYTIME, DAY OR NIGHT." MY PLACE IS YOURS.
THANKS... SNIF I'M ORRY. I WAS TRYING NOT O START AT LEAST UNTIL WE SAT DOWN--
WHAT'S THAT?
IT'S YOURS. I DON'T THINK IT'S GOING TO HELP WITH THE CRYING, THOUGH...
I WAS GONNA STEAL IT.
DIDN'T FIT.
OH, KARA...
IT'S OKAY. IT'S OKAY, CASSIE.
WHATEVER'S HAPPENED...WHATEVER'S COMING NEXT...
WE'LL FIGURE IT OUT.
A BEGINNING.

COVER GALLERY

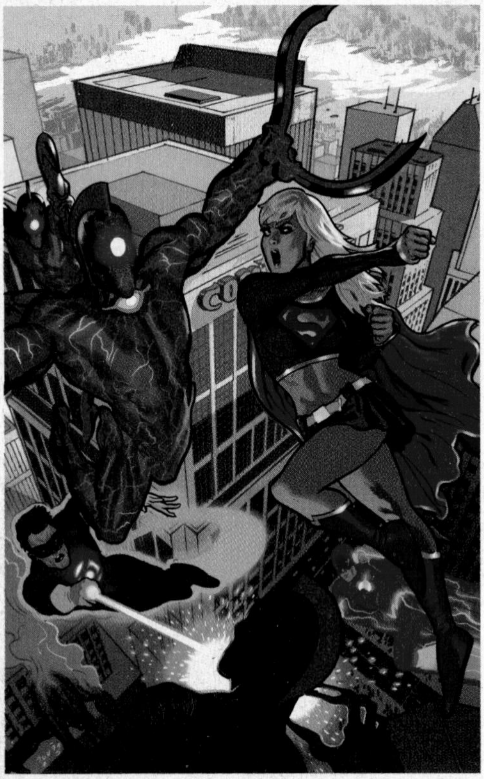

JLA #122 by Daniel Acuna

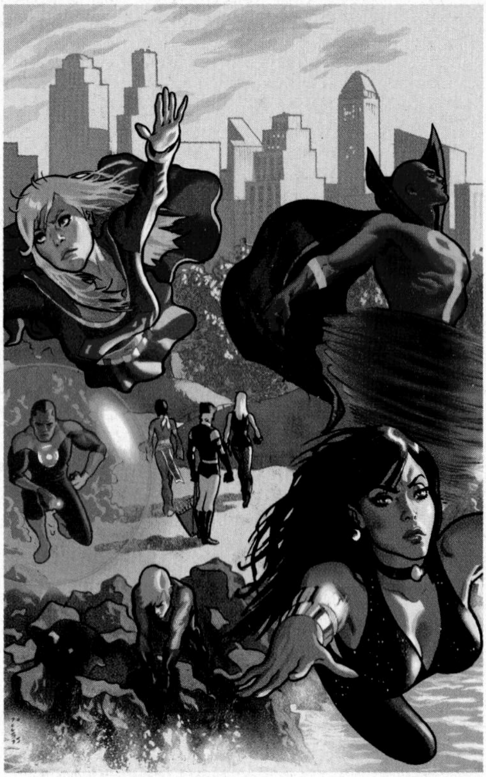

JLA #123 by Daniel Acuna

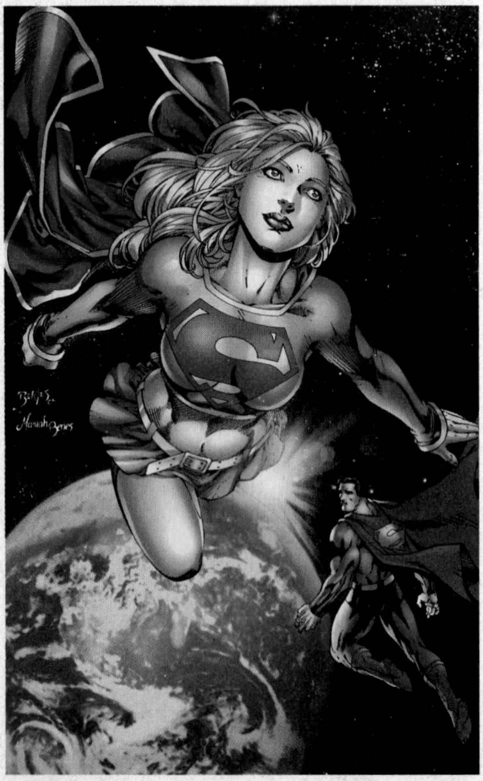

SUPERMAN #223 by Ed Benes, Mariah Benes

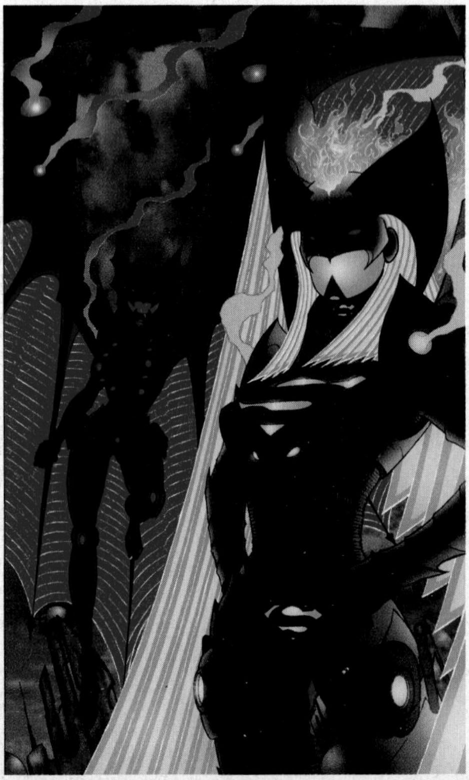

SUPERGIRL #6 Variant Cover by Ian Churchill